Advanced Macroeconomics

An Easy Guide

Filipe Campante, Federico Sturzenegger,
Andrés Velasco

Johns Hopkins University,
Universidad de San Andrés,
London School of Economics

2021

Published by
LSE Press
10 Portugal Street
London WC2A 2HD
press.lse.ac.uk

Text © The Authors 2021
First published 2021

Cover design by Diana Jarvis
Print and digital versions typeset by
diacriTech

ISBN (Paperback): 9781909890688
ISBN (PDF): 9781909890695
ISBN (EPUB): 9781909890701
ISBN (Mobi): 9781909890718

DOI: https://doi.org/10.31389/lsepress.ame

Supported by the LSE Knowledge Exchange and Impact Fund ■

The full text of this book has been peer-reviewed to ensure high academic standards. For our full
publishing ethics policies, see http://press.lse.ac.uk

Suggested citation:
Campante, F., Sturzenegger, F. and Velasco, A. 2021. *Advanced Macroeconomics: An Easy Guide*.
London: LSE Press. DOI: https://doi.org/10.31389/lsepress.ame. License: CC-BY-NC 4.0.

To read the free, open access version of this book online, visit https://doi.org/10.31389/lsepress.ame
or scan this QR code with your mobile device:

We dedicate this book to our families,

Renata, Sofia, Marina, Isabel
Josefina, Felipe, Agustín, Sofía
Consuelo, Rosa, Ema, Gaspar

because they mean everything to us.

We also dedicate this book to three dear mentors and friends whom we miss so very much. Let this be our token of appreciation for the wisdom they generously shared with us.

Alberto Alesina
Rudiger Dornbusch
Carlos Diaz Alejandro

Thanks to all of you.

Short Contents

Monetary and Fiscal Policy   **259**

Contents

Monetary and Fiscal Policy   259

List of Figures

List of Tables

Preface

Over many years, at different points in time, the three of us taught one of the core macroeconomics courses at the Harvard Kennedy School's Masters in Public Administration, in the International Development (MPA-ID) program. Initially, this was Andrés (the Chilean), who left to become Michelle Bachelet's Finance Minister during her first presidential term. Then came Federico (the Argentine), who left for public service in Argentina, eventually becoming the Governor of its Central Bank. Last was Filipe (the Brazilian), until he left and became Vice Dean at the School of Advanced International Studies (SAIS) at Johns Hopkins.

The MPA-ID is a program that teaches graduate-level economics, but for students with a (very) heavy policy bent. From the start, the macro course required tailor-made notes, trying to go over advanced macroeconomic theory with the requisite level of rigor, but translating it directly for an audience interested in the policy implications, and not in macro theory per se. Over the years, the three of us shared our class notes, each adding our specific view to the topics at hand. Throughout the process we received enthusiastic feedback from students who kept urging us to turn those notes into a book.

This is it. We like to think that the end result of this process is an agile text – an 'Easy Guide' – focused on what we believe are the main tools in macroeconomics, with a direct application to what we believe are the main policy topics in macroeconomics. For this reason, we do not pretend to offer an encyclopedic approach (for this you may consult other texts such as Ljungqvist and Sargent (2018), Acemoglu (2009), or the by now classic Blanchard and Fischer (1989)) but a more 'curated' one, where we have selected the main issues that we believe any policy-oriented macroeconomic student should grasp.

The book does not shy away from technical inputs, but nor does it focus on them or make them the objective. For instance, we talk about the overlapping generations model, one of the key tools in macroeconomic analysis, but we do so because we are interested in seeing the impact of different pension systems on capital accumulation. In other words, the objective is understanding real-world problems that policymakers in macroeconomics face all the time, and developing a way of thinking that helps students think through these (and many other) problems. Students need to learn the tools, because they allow them to think systematically about dynamic policy problems. As befits an easy/introductory guide, we have complemented each chapter with a selection of further readings for those that want to go deeper in any specific topic.

We are excited to share this material with our colleagues around the world. We believe it can be useful for an advanced course in macroeconomics at the graduate level, or for a core course in macroeconomics at a master level. We have tried to get to the point on every issue, though we have also shared different perspectives and opened the window to current debates in the different fields of macroeconomics. Students and teachers will also find additional material on a companion website (https://doi.org/10.31389/lsepress.ame) including teaching slides and additional appendices.

Enjoy,

Filipe Campante, Johns Hopkins University
Federico Sturzenegger, Universidad de San Andrés
Andrés Velasco, London School of Economics

Acknowledgments

We are indebted to a number of people who helped in the writing of this manuscript.

Santiago Mosquera helped by drafting the appendices for estimating the RBC and DSGE models. Can Soylu checked independently that the appendices were complete and provided useful inputs. Nicolas Der Meguerditchian took the task of doing all the graphs and tables of the paper, as well as helping with the references and proof editing. Delfina Imbrosciano went over all the text and math to help find typos and improve clarity. Francisco Guerrero and Hernán Lacunza were kind enough to point to us a few remaining typos. All of their work has been terrific and greatly improved the final product. Any and all remaining mistakes are certainly our fault.

Daron Acemoglu, Philippe Aghion, Richard Blundell, Rachel Griffith, Peter Howitt, Susanne Prantl, Philippe Jorion, William Goetzmann, and Paul Schmelzing all graciously accepted to have their graphs reproduced in this book. Sebastian Galiani, helped with useful references. Jeffrey Frankel and Gonzalo Huertas suggested additional material that we have incorporated into the companion website to the book. We are very grateful to all of them.

The team at LSE Press have also been superb. In particular, our gratitude to Lucy Lambe for her great partnership throughout the process, and to Patrick Dunleavy, who believed in this text from day one, and was supportive of the effort all along. Last, but not least, we are most grateful to Paige MacKay, and the team at Ubiquity Press, who worked tirelessly in the final stages of production.

We also owe special thanks to the generations of MPA-ID students at the Harvard Kennedy School who helped us develop, test, and hone the material in this book. They are an extraordinary group of brilliant individuals – many of whom have gone on to become high-level macroeconomic policymakers around the world. They kept us on our toes, pushed us forward, and made it all a very exciting endeavour.

Filipe Campante, Federico Sturzenegger, Andrés Velasco

About the Authors

Filipe Campante is Bloomberg Distinguished Associate Professor of International Economics at Johns Hopkins University and a Research Associate at the National Bureau of Economic Research (NBER). His work focuses on political economy and economic development, and has been published in leading academic journals such as the *American Economic Review* and the *Quarterly Journal of Economics*. He was previously Associate Professor of Public Policy at the Harvard Kennedy School, where he taught macroeconomics for many years. Born and raised in Rio de Janeiro, Brazil, he holds a Ph.D. in Economics from Harvard University.

Federico Sturzenegger is Full Professor at Universidad de San Andrés, Visiting Professor at Harvard's Kennedy School, and Honoris Causa Professor at HEC, Paris. His work focuses on macroeconomics and international finance and has been published in leading academic journals such as the *American Economic Review* and the *Journal of Economic Literature*. He was previously President of Banco Ciudad, a representative in Argentina's National Congress, and served as Governor of the Central Bank of Argentina. Born and raised in Argentina, he holds a Ph.D. in Economics from MIT.

Andrés Velasco is Professor of Public Policy and Dean of the School of Public Policy at the London School of Economics. He is also a Research Fellow of CEPR and an Associate Fellow at Chatham House, the Royal Institute of International Affairs. Earlier he held professorial roles at the Harvard Kennedy School, Columbia University and New York University. He served as the Minister of Finance of Chile between 2006 and 2010. In 2017-18 he was a member of the G20 Eminent Persons Group on Global Financial Governance. He holds a B.A. and an M.A. from Yale University and a Ph.D. in economics from Columbia University. ORCID: https://orcid.org/0000-0003-0441-5062.

CHAPTER 1

Introduction

Paul Samuelson once stated that "macroeconomics, even with all of our computers and with all of our information is not an exact science and is incapable of being an exact science". Perhaps this quote captures the view that the field of macroeconomics, the study of aggregate behaviour of the economy, is full of loose ends and inconsistent statements that make it difficult for economists to agree on anything.

While there is truth to the fact that there are plenty of disagreements among macroeconomists, we believe such a negative view is unwarranted. Since the birth of macroeconomics as a discipline in the 1930s, in spite of all the uncertainties, inconsistencies, and crises, macroeconomic performance around the world has been strong. More recently, dramatic shocks, such as the Great Financial Crisis or the Covid pandemic, have been managed – not without cost, but with effective damage control. There is much to celebrate in the field of macroeconomics.

Macroeconomics was born under the pain of both U.S. and UK's protracted recession of the 1930s. Until then, economics had dealt with markets, efficiency, trade, and incentives, but it was never thought that there was place for a large and systematic breakdown of markets. High and persistent unemployment in the U.S. required a different approach.

The main distinctive feature to be explained was the large disequilibrium in the labour market. How could it be that a massive number of people wanted to work, but could not find a job? This led to the idea of the possibility of aggregate demand shortfalls – and thus of the potential role for government to prop it up, and, in doing so, restore economic normalcy. "Have people dig a hole and fill them up if necessary" is the oft-quoted phrase by Keynes. In modern economic jargon, increase aggregate demand to move the equilibrium of the economy to a higher level of output.

Thus, an active approach to fiscal and monetary policy developed, entrusting policy makers with the role of moderating the business cycle. The relationship was enshrined in the so-called Phillips curve, a relationship that suggested a stable tradeoff between output and inflation. If so, governments simply had to choose their preferred spot on that tradeoff.

Then things changed. Higher inflation in the 60s and 70s, challenged the view of a stable tradeoff between output and inflation. In fact, inflation increased with no gain in output, the age of stagflation had arrived. What had changed?

The answer had to do with the role of expectations in macroeconomics.[1]

The stable relationship between output and inflation required static expectations. People did not expect inflation, then the government found it was in its interest to generate a bit of inflation – but

How to cite this book chapter:
Campante, F., Sturzenegger, F. and Velasco, A. 2021. *Advanced Macroeconomics: An Easy Guide.*
Ch. 1. 'Introduction', pp. 1–4. London: LSE Press. DOI: https://doi.org/10.31389/lsepress.ame.a
License: CC-BY-NC 4.0.

that meant people were always wrong! As they started anticipating the inflation, then its effect on employment faded away, and the effectiveness of macro policy had gone stale.

The rational expectations revolution in macroeconomics, initiated in the 1970s, imposed the constraint that a good macro model should allow agents in the model to understand it and act accordingly. This was not only a theoretical purism. It was needed to explain what was actually happening in the real world. The methodological change took hold very quickly and was embraced by the profession. As a working assumption, it is a ubiquitous feature of macroeconomics up to today.

Then an additional challenge to the world of active macroeconomic policy came about. In the early 1980s, some macroeconomists started the "real business cycles" approach: they studied the neoclassical growth model – that is, a model of optimal capital accumulation – but added to it occasional productivity shocks. The result was a simulated economy that, they argued, resembled on many dimensions the movements of the business cycle. This was a dramatic finding because it suggested that business cycles could actually be the result of optimal responses by rational economic agents, thereby eschewing the need for a stabilising policy response. What is more, active fiscal or monetary policy were not merely ineffective, as initially argued by the rational expectations view: they could actually be harmful.

This was the state of the discussion when a group of economists tackled the task of building a framework that recovered some of the features of the old Keynesian activism, but in a model with fully rational agents. They modelled price formation and introduced market structures that departed from a perfectly competitive allocation. They adhered strictly to the assumptions of rational expectations and optimisation, which had the added advantage of allowing for explicit welfare analyses. Thus, the New Keynesian approach was built. It also allowed for shocks, of course, and evolved into what is now known as dynamic stochastic general equilibrium (DSGE) models.

Macroeconomic policymaking evolved along those lines. Nowadays, DSGE models are used by any respectable central bank. Furthermore, because this type of model provides flexibility in the degree of price rigidities and market imperfections, it comprises a comprehensive framework nesting the different views about how individual markets operate, going all the way from the real business cycle approach to specifications with ample rigidities.

But the bottom line is that macroeconomics speaks with a common language. While differences in world views and policy preferences remain, having a common framework is a great achievement. It allows discussions to be framed around the parameters of a model (and whether they match the empirical evidence) – and such discussions can be more productive than those that swirl around the philosophical underpinnings of one's policy orientations.

This book, to a large extent, follows this script, covering the different views – and very importantly, the tools needed to speak the language of modern macroeconomic policymaking – in what we believe is an accessible manner. That language is that of dynamic policy problems.

We start with the Neoclassical Growth Model – a framework to think about capital accumulation through the lens of optimal consumption choices – which constitutes the basic grammar of that language of modern macroeconomics. It also allows us to spend the first half of the book studying economic growth – arguably the most important issue in macroeconomics, and one that, in recent decades, has taken up as much attention as the topic of business cycles. The study of growth will take us through the discussion of factor accumulation, productivity growth, the optimality of both the capital stock and the growth rate, and empirical work in trying to understand the proximate and fundamental causes of growth. In that process, we also develop a second canonical model in modern macroeconomics: the overlapping generations model. This lets us revisit some of the issues around capital accumulation and long-run growth, as well as study key policy issues, such as the design of pension systems.

We then move to discuss issues of consumption and investment. These are the key macroeconomic aggregates, of course, and their study allows us to explore the power of the dynamic tools we developed in the first part of the book. They also let us introduce the role of uncertainty and expectations, as well as the connections between macroeconomics and finance.

Then, in the second half of the book, we turn to the study of business cycle fluctuations, and what policy can and should do about it. We start with the real business cycle approach, as it is based on the neoclassical growth model. Then we turn to the Keynesian approach, starting from the basic IS-LM model, familiar to anyone with an undergraduate exposure to macroeconomics, but then showing how its modern version emerged: first, with the challenge of incorporating rational expectations, and then with the fundamentals of the New Keynesian approach. Only then, we present the canonical New Keynesian framework.

Once we've covered all this material, we discuss the scope and effectiveness of fiscal policy. We also go over what optimal fiscal policy would look like, as well as some of the reasons for why in practice it departs from those prescriptions. We then move to discuss monetary policy: the relationship between money and prices, the debate on rules vs discretion, and the consensus that arose prior to the 2008 financial crisis and the Great Recession. We then cover the post-crisis development of quantitative easing, as well as the constraints imposed by the zero lower bound on nominal interest rates. We finish off by discussing some current topics that have been influencing the thinking of policymakers on the fiscal and monetary dimensions: secular stagnation, the fiscal theory of the price level, and the role of asset-price bubbles and how policy should deal with them.

As you can see from this whirlwind tour, the book covers a lot of material. Yet, it has a clear methodological structure. We develop the basic tools in the first part of the book, making clear exactly what we need at each step. All you need is a basic knowledge of calculus, differential equations, and some linear algebra – and you can consult the mathematical appendix for the basics on the tools we introduce and use in the book. Throughout, we make sure to introduce the tools not for their own sake, but in the context of studying policy-relevant issues and helping develop a framework for thinking about dynamic policy problems. We then study a range of policy issues, using those tools to bring you to the forefront of macroeconomic policy discussions. At the very end, you will also find two appendices for those interested in tackling the challenge of running and simulating their own macroeconomic models.

All in all, Samuelson was right that macroeconomics cannot be an exact science. Still, there is a heck of a lot to learn, enjoy and discover – and this, we hope, will help you become an informed participant in exciting macroeconomic policy debates. Enjoy!

Note

[1] Surprisingly, the answer came from the most unexpected quarter: the study of agricultural markets. As early as 1960 John Muth was studying the cobweb model, a standard model in agricultural economics. In this model the farmers look at the harvest price to decide how much they plant, but then this provides a supply the following year which is inconsistent with this price. For example a bad harvest implies a high price, a high price implies lots of planting, a big harvest next year and thus a low price! The low price motivates less planting, but then the small harvest leads to a high price the following year! In this model, farmers were systematically wrong, and kept being wrong all the time. This is nonsense, argued Muth. Not only should they learn, they know the market and they should plant the equilibrium price, namely the price that induces the amount of planting that implies that next year that will be the price. There are no cycles, no mistakes, the market equilibrium holds from day one! Transferred to macroeconomic policy, something similar was happening.

Growth Theory

CHAPTER 2

Growth theory preliminaries

2.1 | Why do we care about growth?

It is hard to put it better than Nobel laureate Robert Lucas did as he mused on the importance of the study of economic growth for macroeconomists and for anyone interested in economic development.[1]

> 'The diversity across countries in measured per capita income levels is literally too great to be believed. (...) Rates of growth of real per capita GNP are also diverse, even over sustained periods. For 1960–80 we observe, for example: India, 1.4% per year; Egypt, 3.4%; South Korea, 7.0%; Japan, 7.1%; the United States, 2.3%; the industrial economies averaged 3.6%. (..) An Indian will, on average, be twice as well off as his grandfather; a Korean 32 times. (...) I do not see how one can look at figures like these without seeing them as representing possibilities. Is there some action a government of India could take that would lead the Indian economy to grow like Indonesia's or Egypt's? If so, what, exactly? If not, what is it about the 'nature of India' that makes it so? *The consequences for human welfare involved in questions like these are simply staggering: Once one starts to think about them, it is hard to think about anything else.*'

Lucas Jr. (1988) (emphasis added)

While it is common to think about growth today as being somehow natural, even expected – in fact, if world growth falls from 3.5 to 3.2%, it is perceived as a big crisis – it is worthwhile to acknowledge that this was not always the case. Pretty much until the end of the 18th century growth was quite low, if it happened at all. In fact, it was so low that people could not see it during their lifetimes. They lived in the same world as their parents and grandparents. For many years it seemed that growth was actually *behind* as people contemplated the feats of antiquity without understanding how they could have been accomplished. Then, towards the turn of the 18th century, as shown in Figure 2.1 something happened that created explosive economic growth as the world had never seen before. Understanding this transition will be the purpose of Chapter 10. Since then, growth has become the norm. This is the reason the first half of this book, in fact up to Chapter 10, will deal with understanding growth. As we proceed we will ask about the determinants of capital accumulation (Chapters 2 through 5, as well as 8 and 9), and discuss the process of technological progress (Chapter 6). Institutional factors will be addressed in Chapter 7. The growth process raises many interesting questions: should we expect this growth to continue? Should we expect it eventually to decelerate? Or, on the contrary, will it accelerate without bound?

How to cite this book chapter:

Campante, F., Sturzenegger, F. and Velasco, A. 2021. *Advanced Macroeconomics: An Easy Guide.*
Ch. 2. 'Growth theory preliminaries', pp. 7–22. London: LSE Press.
DOI: https://doi.org/10.31389/lsepress.ame.b License: CC-BY-NC 4.0.

Figure 2.1 The evolution of the world GDP per capita over the years 1–2008

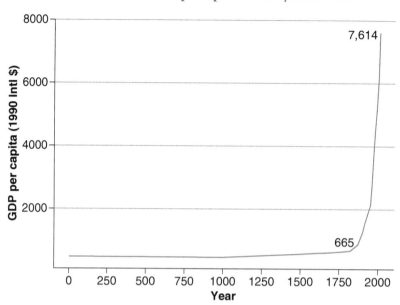

Figure 2.2 Log GDP per capita of selected countries (1820–2018)

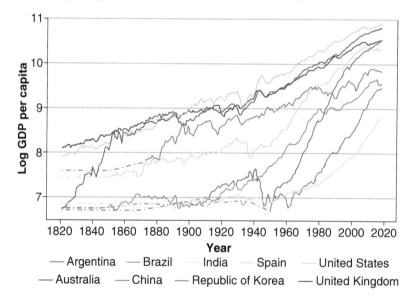

But the fundamental point of Lucas's quote is to realise that the mind-boggling differences in income per capita across countries are to a large extent due to differences in growth rates over time; and the power of exponential growth means that even relatively small differences in the latter will build into huge differences in the former. Figures 2.2 and 2.3 make this point. The richest countries

Figure 2.3 Log GDP per capita of selected countries (1960–2018)

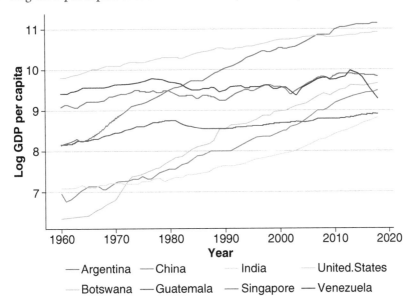

have been growing steadily over the last two centuries, and some countries have managed to converge to their income levels. Some of the performances are really stellar. Figure 2.2 shows how South Korea, with an income level that was 16% of that of the U.S. in 1940, managed to catch up in just a few decades. Today it's income is 68.5% compared to the U.S. Likewise, Spain's income in 1950 was 23% that of the U.S. Today it is 57%. At the same time other countries lagged. Argentina for example dropped from an income level that was 57% of U.S. income at the turn of the century to 33.5% today.

Figure 2.3 shows some diversity during recent times. The spectacular performances of Botswana, Singapore or, more recently, of China and India, contrast with the stagnation of Guatemala, Argentina or Venezuela. In 1960 the income of the average Motswana (as someone from Botswana is called) was only 6% as rich as the average Venezuelan. In 2018 he or she was 48% richer!

These are crucial reasons why we will spend about the initial half of this book in understanding growth. But those are not the only reasons! You may be aware that macroeconomists disagree on a lot of things; however, the issue of economic growth is one where there is much more of a consensus. It is thus helpful to start off on this relatively more solid footing. Even more importantly, the study of economic growth brings to the forefront two key ingredients of essentially all of macroeconomic analysis: general equilibrium and dynamics. First, understanding the behaviour of an entire economy requires thinking about how different markets interact and affect one another, which inevitably requires a general equilibrium approach. Second, to think seriously about how an economy evolves over time we must consider how today's choices affect tomorrow's – in other words, we must think dynamically! As such, economic growth is the perfect background upon which to develop the main methodological tools in macroeconomics: the model of intertemporal optimisation, known as the neoclassical growth model (NGM for short, also known as the Ramsey model), and the overlapping generations model (we'll call it the OLG model). A lot of what we will do later, as we explore different macroeconomic policy issues, will involve applications of these dynamic general-equilibrium tools that we will learn in the context of studying economic growth.

So, without further delay, to this we turn.

2.2 | The Kaldor facts

What are the key stylised facts about growth that our models should try to match? That there is growth in output and capital per worker with relatively stable income shares.

The modern study of economic growth starts in the post-war period and was mostly motivated by the experience of the developed world. In his classical article (Kaldor 1957), Nicolas Kaldor stated some basic facts that he observed economic growth seemed to satisfy, at least in those countries. These came to be known as the Kaldor facts, and the main challenge of growth theory as initially constituted was to account simultaneously for all these facts. But, what were these Kaldor facts? Here they are:[2]

1. *Output per worker shows continuous growth,* with no tendency to fall.
2. *The capital/output ratio is nearly constant.* (But what is capital?)
3. *Capital per worker shows continuous growth* (... follows from the other two).
4. *The rate of return on capital is nearly constant* (real interest rates are flat).
5. *Labour and capital receive constant shares of total income.*
6. *The growth rate of output per worker differs substantially across countries* (and over time, we can add, miracles and disasters).

Most of these facts have aged well. But not all of them. For example, we now know the constancy of the interest rate is not so when seen from a big historical sweep. In fact, interest rates have been on a secular downward trend that can be dated back to the 1300's (Schmelzing 2019). (Of course rates are way down now, so the question is how much lower can they go?) We will show you the data in a few pages.

In addition, in recent years, particularly since the early 1980s, the labour share has fallen significantly in most countries and industries. There is much argument in the literature as to the reasons why (see Karabarbounis and Neiman (2014) for a discussion on this) and the whole debate about income distribution trends recently spearheaded by Piketty (2014) has to do with this issue. We will come back to it shortly.

As it turns out Robert Solow established a simple model (Solow 1956) that became the first working model of economic growth.[3] Solow's contribution became the foundation of the NGM, and the backbone of modern growth theory, as it seemed to fit the Kaldor facts. Any study of growth must start with this model, reviewing what it explains – and, just as crucially, what it fails to explain.[4]

2.3 | The Solow model

We outline and solve the basic Solow model, introducing the key concepts of the neoclassical production function, the balanced growth path, transitional dynamics, dynamic inefficiency, and convergence.

Consider an economy with only two inputs: physical capital, K, and labour, L. The production function is

$$Y = F(K, L, t),$$
(2.1)

where Y is the flow of output produced. Assume output is a homogeneous good that can be consumed, C, or invested, I, to create new units of physical capital.

Let s be the fraction of output that is saved – that is, the *saving rate* – so that $1 - s$ is the fraction of output that is consumed. Note that $0 \leq s \leq 1$.

Assume that capital depreciates at the constant rate $\delta > 0$. The net increase in the stock of physical capital at a point in time equals gross investment less depreciation:

$$\dot{K} = I - \delta K = s \cdot F(K, L, t) - \delta K, \tag{2.2}$$

where a dot over a variable, such as $\dot{K}$, denotes differentiation with respect to time. Equation (2.2) determines the dynamics of K for a given technology and labour force.

Assume the population equals the labour force, L. It grows at a constant, exogenous rate, $\dot{L}/L = n \geq 0$.[5] If we normalise the number of people at time 0 to 1, then

$$L_t = e^{nt}. \tag{2.3}$$

where L_t is labour at time t.

If L_t is given from (2.3) and technological progress is absent, then (2.2) determines the time paths of capital, K, and output, Y. Such behaviour depends crucially on the properties of the production function, $F(\cdot)$. Apparently minor differences in assumptions about $F(\cdot)$ can generate radically different theories of economic growth.

2.3.1 | The (neoclassical) production function

For now, neglect technological progress. That is, assume that $F(\cdot)$ is independent of t. This assumption will be relaxed later. Then, the production function (2.1) takes the form

$$Y = F(K, L). \tag{2.4}$$

Assume also the following three properties are satisfied. First, for all $K > 0$ and $L > 0$, $F(\cdot)$ exhibits positive and diminishing marginal products with respect to each input:

$$\frac{\partial F}{\partial K} > 0, \qquad \frac{\partial^2 F}{\partial K^2} < 0$$

$$\frac{\partial F}{\partial L} > 0, \qquad \frac{\partial^2 F}{\partial L^2} < 0.$$

Second, $F(\cdot)$ exhibits constant returns to scale:

$$F(\lambda K, \lambda L) = \lambda \cdot F(K, L) \text{ for all } \lambda > 0.$$

Third, the marginal product of capital (or labour) approaches infinity as capital (or labour) goes to 0 and approaches 0 as capital (or labour) goes to infinity:

$$\lim_{K \to 0} \frac{\partial F}{\partial K} = \lim_{L \to 0} \frac{\partial F}{\partial L} = \infty,$$

$$\lim_{K \to \infty} \frac{\partial F}{\partial K} = \lim_{L \to \infty} \frac{\partial F}{\partial L} = 0.$$

These last properties are called *Inada conditions*.

We will refer to production functions satisfying those three sets of conditions as *neoclassical production functions*.

The condition of constant returns to scale has the convenient property that output can be written as

$$Y = F(K, L) = L \cdot F(K/L, 1) = L \cdot f(k),\tag{2.5}$$

where $k \equiv K/L$ is the capital-labour ratio, and the function $f(k)$ is defined to equal $F(k, 1)$. The production function can be written as

$$y = f(k),\tag{2.6}$$

where $y \equiv Y/L$ is per capita output.

One simple production function that satisfies all of the above and is often thought to provide a reasonable description of actual economies is the Cobb-Douglas function,

$$Y = AK^{\alpha}L^{1-\alpha},\tag{2.7}$$

where $A > 0$ is the level of the technology, and α is a constant with $0 < \alpha < 1$. The Cobb-Douglas function can be written as

$$y = Ak^{\alpha}.\tag{2.8}$$

Note that $f'(k) = A\alpha k^{\alpha-1} > 0$, $f''(k) = -A\alpha(1-\alpha)k^{\alpha-2} < 0$, $\lim_{k\to\infty} f'(k) = 0$, and $\lim_{k\to0} f'(k) = \infty$. In short, the Cobb-Douglas specification satisfies the properties of a neoclassical production function.

2.3.2 | The law of motion of capital

The change in the capital stock over time is given by (2.2). If we divide both sides of this equation by L, then we get

$$\dot{K}/L = s \cdot f(k) - \delta k.\tag{2.9}$$

The right-hand side contains per capita variables only, but the left-hand side does not. We can write $\dot{K}/L$ as a function of k by using the fact that

$$\dot{k} \equiv \frac{d(K/L)}{dt} = \dot{K}/L - nk,\tag{2.10}$$

where $n = \dot{L}/L$. If we substitute (2.10) into the expression for $\dot{K}/L$ then we can rearrange terms to get

$$\dot{k} = s \cdot f(k) - (n + \delta) \cdot k.\tag{2.11}$$

The term $n + \delta$ on the right-hand side of (2.11) can be thought of as the effective depreciation rate for the capital/labour ratio, $k \equiv K/L$. If the saving rate, s, were 0, then k would decline partly due to depreciation of K at the rate δ and partly due to the growth of L at the rate n.

Figure 2.4 shows the workings of (2.11). The upper curve is the production function, $f(k)$. The term $s \cdot f(k)$ looks like the production function except for the multiplication by the positive fraction s. The $s \cdot f(k)$ curve starts from the origin (because $f(0) = 0$), has a positive slope (because $f'(k) > 0$), and gets flatter as k rises (because $f''(k) < 0$). The Inada conditions imply that the $s \cdot f(k)$ curve is vertical at $k = 0$ and becomes perfectly flat as k approaches infinity. The other term in (2.11), $(n+\delta)\cdot k$, appears in Figure 2.1 as a straight line from the origin with the positive slope $n + \delta$.

Figure 2.4   **Dynamics in the Solow model**

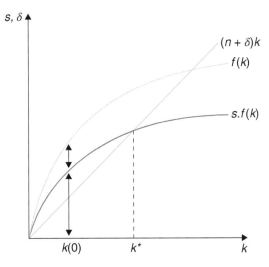

2.3.3 | Finding a balanced growth path

A *balanced growth path* (BGP) is a situation in which the various quantities grow at constant rates.[6] In the Solow model, the BGP corresponds to $\dot{k} = 0$ in (2.11).[7] We find it at the intersection of the $s \cdot f(k)$ curve with the $(n + \delta) \cdot k$ line in Figure 2.4. The corresponding value of k is denoted k^*. Algebraically, k^* satisfies the condition:

$$s \cdot f(k^*) = (n + \delta) \cdot k^*. \tag{2.12}$$

Since k is constant in the BGP, y and c are also constant at the values $y^* = f(k^*)$ and $c^* = (1 - s) \cdot f(k^*)$, respectively. Hence, in the Solow model, the per capita quantities k, y, and c do not grow in the BGP: it is a growth model without (long-term) growth!

Now, that's not quite right: the constancy of the per capita magnitudes means that the levels of variables – K, Y, and C – grow in the BGP at the rate of population growth, n. In addition, changes in the level of technology, represented by shifts of the production function, $f(\cdot)$; in the saving rate, s; in the rate of population growth, n; and in the depreciation rate, δ; all have effects on the per capita *levels* of the various quantities in the BGP.

We can illustrate the results for the case of a Cobb-Douglas production function. The capital/labour ratio on the BGP is determined from (2.12) as

$$k^* = \left(\frac{sA}{n + \delta}\right)^{\frac{1}{1-\alpha}}. \tag{2.13}$$

Note that, as we saw graphically for a more general production function $f(k)$, k^* rises with the saving rate, s, and the level of technology, A, and falls with the rate of population growth, n, and the depreciation rate, δ. Output per capita on the BGP is given by

$$y^* = A^{\frac{1}{1-\alpha}} \cdot \left(\frac{s}{n + \delta}\right)^{\frac{\alpha}{1-\alpha}}. \tag{2.14}$$

Thus, y^* is a positive function of s and A and a negative function of n and δ.

2.3.4 | Transitional dynamics

Moreover, the Solow model does generate growth in the transition to the BGP. To see the implications in this regard, note that dividing both sides of (2.11) by k implies that the growth rate of k is given by

$$\gamma_k \equiv \frac{\dot{k}}{k} = \frac{s \cdot f(k)}{k} - (n + \delta). \tag{2.15}$$

Equation (2.15) says that γ_k equals the difference between two terms, $s \cdot f(k)/k$ and $(n + \delta)$ which we plot against k in Figure 2.5. The first term is a downward-sloping curve, which asymptotes to infinity at $k = 0$ and approaches 0 as k tends to infinity. The second term is a horizontal line crossing the vertical axis at $n + \delta$. The vertical distance between the curve and the line equals the growth rate of capital per person, and the crossing point corresponds to the BGP. Since $n + \delta > 0$ and $s \cdot f(k)/k$ falls monotonically from infinity to 0, the curve and the line intersect once and only once. Hence (except for the trivial solution $k^* = 0$, where capital stays at zero forever), the BGP capital-labour ratio $k^* > 0$ exists and is unique.

Note also that output moves according to

$$\frac{\dot{y}}{y} = \alpha \frac{\dot{k}}{k} = \alpha \gamma_k. \tag{2.16}$$

A formal treatment of dynamics follows. From (2.11) one can calculate

$$\frac{d\dot{k}}{dk} = s \cdot f'(k) - (n + \delta). \tag{2.17}$$

We want to study dynamics in the neighbourhood of the BGP, so we evaluate this at k^*:

$$\left. \frac{d\dot{k}}{dk} \right|_{k=k^*} = s \cdot f'(k^*) - (n + \delta). \tag{2.18}$$

Figure 2.5   Dynamics in the Solow model again

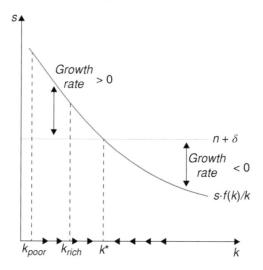

The capital stock will converge to its BGP if $\dot{k} > 0$ when $k < k^*$ and $\dot{k} < 0$ when $k > k^*$. Hence, this requires that $\left.\frac{d\dot{k}}{dk}\right|_{k=k^*} < 0$.

In the Cobb-Douglas case the condition is simple. Note that

$$\left.\frac{d\dot{k}}{dk}\right|_{k=k^*} = s \cdot A\alpha \left(\frac{sA}{n+\delta}\right)^{-1} - (n+\delta) = (n+\delta)(\alpha-1) \tag{2.19}$$

so that $\left.\frac{d\dot{k}}{dk}\right|_{k=k^*} < 0$ requires $\alpha < 1$. That is, reaching the BGP requires diminishing returns.

With diminishing returns, when k is relatively low, the marginal product of capital, $f'(k)$, is relatively high. By assumption, households save and invest a constant fraction, s, of this product. Hence, when k is relatively low, the marginal return to investment, $s \cdot f'(k)$, is relatively high. Capital per worker, k, effectively depreciates at the constant rate $n + \delta$. Consequently, the growth of capital, $\dot{k}$, is also relatively high. In fact, for $k < k^*$ it is positive. Conversely, for $k > k^*$ it is negative.

2.3.5 | Policy experiments

Suppose that the economy is initially on a BGP with capital per person k_1^*. Imagine that the government then introduces some policy that raises the saving rate permanently from s_1 to a higher value s_2. Figure 2.6 shows that the $s \cdot f(k)/k$ schedule shifts to the right. Hence, the intersection with the $n + \delta$ line also shifts to the right, and the new BGP capital stock, k_2^*, exceeds k_1^*. An increase in the saving rate generates temporarily positive per capita growth rates. In the long run, the levels of k and y are permanently higher, but the per capita growth rates return to 0.

A permanent improvement in the level of the technology has similar, temporary effects on the per capita growth rates. If the production function, $f(k)$, shifts upward in a proportional manner, then the

Figure 2.6 The effects of an increase in the savings rate

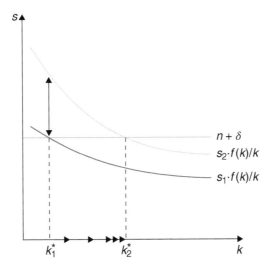

$s \cdot f(k) / k$ curve shifts upward, just as in Figure 2.6. Hence, γ_k again becomes positive temporarily. In the long run, the permanent improvement in technology generates higher levels of k and y, but no changes in the per capita growth rates.

2.3.6 | Dynamic inefficiency

For a given production function and given values of n and δ, there is a unique BGP value $k^* > 0$ for each value of the saving rate, s. Denote this relation by $k^* (s)$, with $dk^* (s) / ds > 0$. The level of per capita consumption on the BGP is $c^* = (1 - s) \cdot f\left[k^* (s)\right]$. We know from (2.12) that $s \cdot f(k^*) = (n + \delta) \cdot k^*$; hence we can write an expression for c^* as

$$c^* (s) = f\left[k^* (s)\right] - (n + \delta) \cdot k^*. \tag{2.20}$$

Figure 2.7 shows the relation between c^* and s that is implied by (2.20). The quantity c^* is increasing in s for low levels of s and decreasing in s for high values of s. The quantity c^* attains its maximum when the derivative vanishes, that is, when $\left[f' (k^*) - (n + \delta)\right] \cdot dk^*/ds = 0$. Since $dk^*/ds > 0$, the term in brackets must equal 0. If we denote the value of k^* by k_g that corresponds to the maximum of c^*, then the condition that determines k_g is

$$f' \left(k_g\right) = (n + \delta). \tag{2.21}$$

The corresponding savings rate can be denoted as s_g, and the associated level of per capita consumption on the BGP is given by $c_g = f\left(k_g\right) - (n + \delta) \cdot k_g$ and is is called the "golden rule" consumption rate.

If the savings rate is greater than that, then it is possible to increase consumption on the BGP, and also over the transition path. We refer to such a situation, where everyone could be made better off by an alternative allocation, as one of *dynamic inefficiency*. In this case, this dynamic inefficiency is brought about by oversaving: everyone could be made better off by choosing to save less and consume more. But this naturally begs the question: why would anyone pass up this opportunity? Shouldn't we

Figure 2.7 Feasible consumption

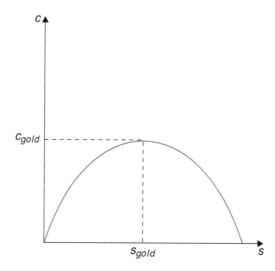

think of a better model of how people make their savings decisions? We will see about that in the next chapter.

2.3.7 | Absolute and conditional convergence

Equation (2.15) implies that the derivative of γ_k with respect to k is negative:

$$\partial \gamma_k / \partial k = \frac{s}{k} \left[f'(k) - \frac{f(k)}{k} \right] < 0. \tag{2.22}$$

Other things equal, smaller values of k are associated with larger values of γ_k. Does this result mean that economies with lower capital per person tend to grow faster in per capita terms? Is there *convergence* across economies?

We have seen above that economies that are structurally similar in the sense that they have the same values of the parameters s, n, and δ and also have the same production function, $F(\cdot)$, have the same BGP values k^* and y^*. Imagine that the only difference among the economies is the initial quantity of capital per person, $k(0)$. The model then implies that the less-advanced economies – with lower values of $k(0)$ and $y(0)$ – have higher growth rates of k. This hypothesis is known as *conditional convergence*: within a group of structurally similar economies (i.e. with similar values for s, n, and δ and production function, $F(\cdot)$), poorer economies will grow faster and catch up with the richer one. This hypothesis does seem to match the data – think about how poorer European countries have grown faster, or how the U.S. South has caught up with the North, over the second half of the 20th century.

An alternative, stronger hypothesis would posit simply that poorer countries would grow faster without conditioning on any other characteristics of the economies. This is referred to as *absolute convergence*, and does not seem to fit the data well.[8] Then again, the Solow model does *not* predict absolute convergence!

2.4 | Can the model account for income differentials?

We have seen that the Solow model does not have growth in per capita income in the long run. But can it help us understand income differentials?

We will tackle the empirical evidence on economic growth at a much greater level of detail later on. However, right now we can ask whether the simple Solow model can account for the differences in income levels that are observed in the world. According to the World Bank's calculations, the range of 2020 PPP income levels vary from $ 138,000 per capita in Qatar or $80,000 in Norway, all the way down to $ 700 in Burundi. Can the basic Solow model explain this difference in income per capita of a factor of more than 100 times or even close to 200 times?

In order to tackle this question we start by remembering what output is supposed to be on the BGP:

$$y^* = A^{\frac{1}{1-\alpha}} \left(\frac{s}{n+\delta} \right)^{\frac{\alpha}{1-\alpha}}. \tag{2.23}$$

Assuming $A = 1$ and $n = 0$ this simplifies to:

$$y^* = \left(\frac{s}{\delta} \right)^{\frac{\alpha}{1-\alpha}}. \tag{2.24}$$

The ability of the Solow model to explain these large differences in income (in the BGP), as can be seen from the expressions above, will depend critically on the value of α.

$$\text{If} \begin{cases} \alpha = \frac{1}{3} \text{ then } \frac{\alpha}{1-\alpha} = \frac{1/3}{2/3} = \frac{1}{2} \\ \alpha = \frac{1}{2} \text{ then } \frac{\alpha}{1-\alpha} = \frac{1/2}{1/2} = 1 \\ \alpha = \frac{2}{3} \text{ then } \frac{\alpha}{1-\alpha} = \frac{2/3}{1/3} = 2. \end{cases}$$

The standard (rough) estimate for the capital share is $\frac{1}{3}$. Parente and Prescott (2002), however, claim that the capital share in GDP is much larger than usually accounted for because there are large intangible capital assets. In fact, they argue that the share of investment in GDP is closer to two-thirds rather than the more traditional one-third. The reasons for the unaccounted investment are (their estimates of the relevance of each in parenthesis):

1. Repair and maintenance (5% of GDP)
2. R&D (3% of GDP) multiplied by three (i.e. 9% of GDP) to take into account perfecting the manufacturing process and launching new products (the times three is not well substantiated)
3. Investment in software (3% of GDP)
4. Firms investment in organisation capital. (They think 12% is a good number.)
5. Learning on the job and training (10% of GDP)
6. Schooling (5% of GDP)

They claim all this capital has a return and that it accounts for about 56% of total GDP!

At any rate, using the equation above:

$$\frac{y_1}{y_2} = \frac{\left(\frac{s_1}{\delta}\right)^{\frac{\alpha}{1-\alpha}}}{\left(\frac{s_2}{\delta}\right)^{\frac{\alpha}{1-\alpha}}} = \left(\frac{s_1}{s_2}\right)^{\frac{\alpha}{1-\alpha}}, \tag{2.25}$$

which we can use to estimate income level differences.

$\frac{s_1}{s_2}$	\multicolumn{3}{c}{$\left(\frac{y_1}{y_2} - 1\right) * 100$}
	$\alpha = \frac{1}{3}$	$\alpha = \frac{1}{2}$	$\alpha = \frac{2}{3}$
1	0%	0%	0%
1.5	22%	50%	125%
2	41%	100%	300%
3	73%	200%	800%

But even the 800% we get using the two-thirds estimate seems to be way too low relative to what we see in the data.

Alternatively, the differences in income may come from differences in total factor productivity (TFP), as captured by A. The question is: how large do these differences need to be to explain the output differentials? Recall from (2.23) that

$$y^* = A^{\frac{1}{1-\alpha}} \left(\frac{s}{n+\delta}\right)^{\frac{\alpha}{1-\alpha}}. \tag{2.26}$$

So if $\alpha = 2/3$, as suggested by Parente and Prescott (2002), then $A^{\frac{1}{1-\alpha}} = A^{\frac{1}{1/3}} = A^3$. Now, let's forget about s, δ, n (for example, by assuming they are the same for all countries), and just focus on differences in A. Notice that if TFP is 1/3, of the level in the other country, this indicates that the income level is then 1/27.

Parente and Prescott (2002) use this to estimate, for a group of countries, how much productivity would have to differ (relative to the United States) for us to replicate observed relative incomes over the period 1950–1988:

Country	Relative Income		Relative TFP
UK	60%	→	86%
Colombia	22%	→	64%
Paraguay	16%	→	59%
Pakistan	10%	→	51%

These numbers appear quite plausible, so the message is that the Solow model requires substantial cross-country differences in productivity to approximate existing cross-country differences in income. This begs the question of what makes productivity so different across countries, but we will come back to this later.

2.5 | The Solow model with exogenous technological change

We have seen that the Solow model does not have growth in per capita income in the long run. But that changes if we allow for technological change.

Allow now the productivity of factors to change over time. In the Cobb-Douglas case, this means that A increases over time. For simplicity, suppose that $\dot{A}/A = a > 0$. Out of the BGP, output then evolves according to

$$\frac{\dot{y}}{y} = \frac{\dot{A}}{A} + \alpha\frac{\dot{k}}{k} = a + \alpha\gamma_k. \tag{2.27}$$

On the BGP, where k is constant,

$$\frac{\dot{y}}{y} = a. \tag{2.28}$$

This is a strong prediction of the Solow model: in the long run, technological change is the only source of growth in per capita income.

Let's now embed this improvement in technology or efficiency in workers. We can define labour input as broader than just bodies, we could call it now human capital defined by

$$E_t = L_t \cdot e^{\lambda t} = L_0 \cdot e^{(\lambda+n)t}, \tag{2.29}$$

where E is the amount of labor in efficiency units. The production function is

$$Y = F\left(K_t, E_t\right). \tag{2.30}$$

To put it in per capita efficiency terms, we define

$$k = \frac{K}{E}. \tag{2.31}$$

So

$$\frac{\dot{k}}{k} = \frac{\dot{K}}{K} - \frac{\dot{E}}{E} = \frac{sy}{k} - \delta - n - \lambda, \tag{2.32}$$

$$\frac{\dot{k}}{k} = \frac{sf(k)}{k} - \delta - n - \lambda, \tag{2.33}$$

$$\dot{k} = sf(k) - (\delta + n + \lambda)\,k. \tag{2.34}$$

For $\dot{k} = 0$

$$\frac{sf(k)}{k} = (\delta + n + \lambda)\,. \tag{2.35}$$

On the BGP $\dot{k} = 0$, so

$$\frac{\dot{K}}{K} = \frac{\dot{E}}{E} = n + \lambda = \frac{\dot{Y}}{Y}. \tag{2.36}$$

But then

$$\frac{\left(\frac{Y}{L}\right)^{\cdot}}{\frac{Y}{L}} = \frac{\dot{Y}}{Y} - \frac{\dot{L}}{L} = \lambda \tag{2.37}$$

Notice that in this equilibrium income per person grows even on the BGP, and this accounts for all six Kaldor facts.

2.6 | What have we learned?

The Solow model shows that capital accumulation by itself cannot sustain growth in per capita income in the long run. This is because accumulation runs into diminishing marginal returns. At some point the capital stock becomes large enough – and its marginal product correspondingly small enough – that a given savings rate can only provide just enough new capital to replenish ongoing depreciation and increases in labour force. Alternatively, if we introduce exogenous technological change that increases productivity, we can generate long-run growth in income per capita, but we do not really explain it. In fact, any differences in long-term growth rates come from exogenous differences in the rate of technological change – we are not explaining those differences, we are just assuming them! As a result, nothing within the model tells you what policy can do about growth in the long run.

That said, we do learn a lot about growth in the transition to the long run, about differences in income levels, and how policy can affect those things. There are clear lessons about: (i) convergence – the model predicts conditional convergence; (ii) dynamic inefficiency – it is possible to save too much in this model; and (iii) long-run differences in income – they seem to have a lot to do with differences in productivity.

Very importantly, the model also points at the directions we can take to try and understand long-term growth. We can have a better model of savings behaviour: how do we know that individuals will save what the model says they will save? And, how does that relate to the issue of dynamic inefficiency?

We can look at different assumptions about technology: maybe we can escape the shackles of diminishing returns to accumulation? Or can we think more carefully about how technological progress comes about?

These are the issues that we will address over the next few chapters.

Notes

[1] Lucas's words hold up very well more than three decades later, in spite of some evidently dated examples.

[2] Once we are done with our study of economic growth, you can check the "new Kaldor facts" proposed by Jones and Romer (2010), which update the basic empirical regularities based on the progress over the subsequent half-century or so.

[3] For those of you who are into the history of economic thought, at the time the framework to study growth was the so-called Harrod-Domar model, due to the independent contributions of (you probably guessed it...) Harrod (1939) and Domar (1946). It assumed a production function with perfect complementarity between labour and capital ("Leontieff", as it is known to economists), and predicted that an economy would generate increasing unemployment of either labour or capital, depending on whether it saved a little or a lot. As it turns out, that was not a good description of the real world in the post-war period.

[4] Solow eventually got a Nobel prize for his trouble, in 1987 – also for his other contributions to the study of economic growth, to which we will return. An Australian economist, Trevor Swan, also published an independently developed paper with very similar ideas at about the same time, which is why sometimes the model is referred to as the Solow-Swan model. He did not get a Nobel prize.

[5] We will endogenise population growth in Chapter 10, when discussing unified growth theory.

[6] The BGP is often referred to as a "steady state", borrowing terminology from classical physics. We have noticed that talk of "steady state" tends to lead students to think of a situation where variables are not growing at all. The actual definition refers to constant growth rates, and it is only in certain cases and for certain variables, as we will see, that this constant rate happens to be zero.

[7] You should try to show mathematically from (2.11) that, with a neoclassical production function, the only way we can have a constant growth rate $\frac{\dot{k}}{k}$ is to have $\dot{k} = 0$.

[8] Or does it? More recently, Kremer et al. (2021) have argued that there has been a move towards absolute convergence in the data in the 21st century... Stay tuned!

References

Domar, E. D. (1946). Capital expansion, rate of growth, and employment. *Econometrica*, 137–147.

Harrod, R. F. (1939). An essay in dynamic theory. *The Economic Journal*, 49(193), 14–33.

Jones, C. I. & Romer, P. M. (2010). The new Kaldor facts: Ideas, institutions, population, and human capital. *American Economic Journal: Macroeconomics*, 2(1), 224–245.

Kaldor, N. (1957). A model of economic growth. *Economic Journal*, 67(268), 591–624.

Karabarbounis, L. & Neiman, B. (2014). The global decline of the labor share. *The Quarterly Journal of Economics*, 129(1), 61–103.

Kremer, M., Willis, J., & You, Y. (2021). Converging to convergence. *NBER Macro Annual 2021*. https://www.nber.org/system/files/chapters/c14560/c14560.pdf.

Lucas Jr., R. (1988). On the mechanics of economic development. *Journal of Monetary Economics, 22,* 3–42.

Parente, S. L. & Prescott, E. C. (2002). *Barriers to riches.* MIT Press.

Piketty, T. (2014). *Capital in the twenty-first century.* Harvard University Press.

Schmelzing, P. (2019). Eight centuries of global real rates, r-g, and the 'suprasecular' decline, 1311–2018, Available at SSRN: https://ssrn.com/abstract=3485734 or http://dx.doi.org/10.2139/ssrn.3485734.

Solow, R. M. (1956). A contribution to the theory of economic growth. *The Quarterly Journal of Economics, 70*(1), 65–94.

CHAPTER 3

The neoclassical growth model

3.1 | The Ramsey problem

We will solve the optimal savings problem underpinning the Neoclassical Growth Model, and in the process introduce the tools of dynamic optimisation we will use throughout the book. We will also encounter, for the first time, the most important equation in macroeconomics: the Euler equation.

$$\frac{\dot{c}_t}{c_t} = \sigma \left[f'\left(k_t\right) - \rho \right]$$

We have seen the lessons and shortcomings of the basic Solow model. One of its main assumptions, as you recall, was that the savings rate was constant. In fact, there was no optimisation involved in that model, and welfare statements are hard to make in that context. This is, however, a very rudimentary assumption for an able policy maker who is in possession of the tools of dynamic optimisation. Thus we tackle here the challenge of setting up an optimal program where savings is chosen to maximise intertemporal welfare.

As it turns out, British philosopher and mathematician Frank Ramsey, in one of the two seminal contributions he provided to economics before dying at the age of 26, solved this problem in 1928 (Ramsey (1928)).[1] The trouble is, he was so ahead of his time that economists would only catch up in the 1960s, when David Cass and Tjalling Koopmans independently revived Ramsey's contribution.[2] (That is why this model is often referred to either as the Ramsey model or the Ramsey-Cass-Koopmans model.) It has since become ubiquitous and, under the grand moniker of Neoclassical Growth Model (NGM), it is the foremost example of the type of *dynamic general equilibrium* model upon which the entire edifice of modern macroeconomics is built.

To make the problem manageable, we will assume that there is one representative household, all of whose members are both consumer and producer, living in a closed economy (we will lift this assumption in the next chapter). There is one good and no government. Each consumer in the representative household lives forever, and population growth is $n > 0$ as before. All quantities in small-case letters are per capita. Finally, we will look at the problem as solved by a benevolent central planner who maximises the welfare of that representative household, and evaluates the utility of future consumption at a discounted rate.

At this point, it is worth stopping and thinking about the model's assumptions. By now you are already used to outrageously unrealistic assumptions, but this may be a little too much. People

How to cite this book chapter:
Campante, F., Sturzenegger, F. and Velasco, A. 2021. *Advanced Macroeconomics: An Easy Guide.*
    Ch. 3. 'The neoclassical growth model', pp. 23–40. London: LSE Press.
    DOI: https://doi.org/10.31389/lsepress.ame.c License: CC-BY-NC 4.0.

obviously do not live forever, they are not identical, and what's this business of a benevolent central planner? Who are they? Why would they discount future consumption? Let us see why we use these shortcuts:

1. We will look at the central planner's problem, as opposed to the decentralised equilibrium, because it is easier and gets us directly to an efficient allocation. We will show that, under certain conditions, it provides the same results as the decentralised equilibrium. This is due to the so-called welfare theorems, which you have seen when studying microeconomics, but which we should perhaps briefly restate here:
   a. A competitive equilibrium is Pareto Optimal.
   b. All Pareto Optimal allocations can be decentralised as a competitive equilibrium under some convexity assumptions. Convexity of production sets means that we cannot have increasing returns to scale. (If we do, we need to depart from competitive markets.)
2. There's only one household? Certainly this is not very realistic, but it is okay if we think that typically people react similarly (not necessarily identically) to the parameters of the model. Specifically, do people respond similarly to an increase in the interest rate? If you think they do, then the assumption is okay.
3. Do all the people have the same utility function? Are they equal in all senses? Again, as above, not really. But, we believe they roughly respond similarly to basic tradeoffs. In addition, as shown by Caselli and Ventura (2000), one can incorporate a lot of sources of heterogeneity (namely, individuals can have different tastes, skills, initial wealth) and still end up with a representative household representation, as long as that heterogeneity has a certain structure. The assumption also means that we are, for the most part, ignoring distributional concerns, but that paper also shows that a wide range of distributional dynamics are compatible with that representation. (We will also raise some points about inequality as we go along.)
4. Do they live infinitely? Certainly not, but it does look like we have some intergenerational links. Barro (1974) suggests an individual who cares about the utility of their child: $u\left(c_t\right) + \beta V\left[u\left(c_{child}\right)\right]$. If that is the case, substituting recursively gives an intertemporal utility of the sort we have posited. And people do think about the future.
5. Why do we discount future utility? To some extent it is a revealed preference argument: interest rates are positive and this only makes sense if people value more today's consumption than tomorrow's, which is what we refer to when we speak of discounting the future. On this you may also want to check Caplin and Leahy (2004), who argue that a utility such as that in (3.1) imposes a sort of tyranny of the present: past utility carries no weight, whereas future utility is discounted. But does this make sense from a planner's point of view? Would this make sense from the perspective of tomorrow? In fact, Ramsey argued that it was unethical for a central planner to discount future utility.[3]

Having said that, let's go solve the problem.

3.1.1 | The consumer's problem

The utility function is[4]

$$\int_0^\infty u(c_t)e^{nt}e^{-\rho t}dt, \tag{3.1}$$

where c_t denotes consumption per capita and $\rho\,(>n)$ is the rate of time preference.[5] Assume $u'(c_t) > 0$, $u''(c_t) \leq 0$, and Inada conditions are satisfied.

3.1.2 | The resource constraint

The resource constraint of the economy is

$$\dot{K}_t = Y_t - C_t = F\left(K_t, L_t\right) - C_t, \tag{3.2}$$

with all variables as defined in the previous chapter. (Notice that for simplicity we assume there is no depreciation.) In particular, $F\left(K_t, L_t\right)$ is a neoclassical production function – hence neoclassical growth model. You can think of household production: household members own the capital and they work for themselves in producing output. Each member of the household inelastically supplies one unit of labour per unit of time.

This resource constraint is what makes the problem truly dynamic. The capital stock in the future depends on the choices that are made in the present. As such, the capital stock constitutes what we call the *state variable* in our problem: it describes the state of our dynamic system at any given point in time. The resource constraint is what we call the *equation of motion*: it characterises the evolution of the state variable over time. The other key variable, consumption, is what we call the *control variable*: it is the one variable that we can directly choose. Note that the control variable is jumpy: we can choose whatever (feasible) value for it at any given moment, so it can vary discontinuously. However, the state variable is sticky: we cannot change it discontinuously, but only in ways that are consistent with the equation of motion.

Given the assumption of constant returns to scale, we can express this constraint in per capita terms, which is more convenient. Dividing (3.2) through by L we get

$$\frac{\dot{K}_t}{L_t} = F\left(k_t, 1\right) - c_t = f\left(k_t\right) - c_t, \tag{3.3}$$

where $f(.)$ has the usual properties. Recall

$$\frac{\dot{K}_t}{L_t} = \dot{k}_t + nk_t. \tag{3.4}$$

Combining the last two equations yields

$$\dot{k}_t = f\left(k_t\right) - nk_t - c_t, \tag{3.5}$$

which we can think of as the relevant budget constraint. This is the final shape of the equation of motion of our dynamic problem, describing how the variable responsible for the dynamic nature of the problem – in this case the per capita capital stock k_t – evolves over time.

3.1.3 | Solution to consumer's problem

The household's problem is to maximise (3.1) subject to (3.5) for given k_0. If you look at our mathematical appendix, you will learn how to solve this, but it is instructive to walk through the steps here, as they have intuitive interpretations. You will need to set up the (current value) Hamiltonian for the problem, as follows:

$$H = u(c_t)e^{nt} + \lambda_t \left[f\left(k_t\right) - nk_t - c_t\right]. \tag{3.6}$$

Recall that c is the control variable (jumpy), and k is the state variable (sticky), but the Hamiltonian brings to the forefront another variable: λ, the *co-state variable*. It is the multiplier associated with the intertemporal budget constraint, analogously to the Lagrange multipliers of static optimisation.

Just like its Lagrange cousin, the co-state variable has an intuitive economic interpretation: it is the marginal value as of time t (i.e. the current value) of an additional unit of the state variable (capital, in this case). It is a (shadow) price, which is also jumpy.

First-order conditions (FOCs) are

$$\frac{\partial H}{\partial c_t} = 0 \Rightarrow u'(c_t)e^{nt} - \lambda_t = 0, \tag{3.7}$$

$$\dot{\lambda}_t = -\frac{\partial H}{\partial k_t} + \rho\lambda_t \Rightarrow \dot{\lambda}_t = -\lambda_t \left[f'(k_t) - n \right] + \rho\lambda_t, \tag{3.8}$$

$$\lim_{t\to\infty} \left(k_t \lambda_t e^{-\rho t} \right) = 0. \tag{3.9}$$

What do these optimality conditions mean? First, (3.7) should be familiar from static optimisation: differentiate with respect to the control variable, and set that equal to zero. It makes sure that, at any given point in time, the consumer is making the optimal decision – otherwise, she could obviously do better... The other two are the ones that bring the dynamic aspects of the problem to the forefront. Equation (3.9) is known as the transversality condition (TVC). It means, intuitively, that the consumer wants to set the optimal path for consumption such that, in the "end of times" (at infinity, in this case), they are left with no capital. (As long as capital has a positive value as given by λ, otherwise they don't really care...) If that weren't the case, I would be "dying" with valuable capital, which I could have used to consume a little more over my lifetime.

Equation (3.8) is the FOC with respect to the state variable, which essentially makes sure that at any given point in time the consumer is leaving the optimal amount of capital for the future. But how so? As it stands, it has been obtained mechanically. However, it is much nicer when we derive it purely from economic intuition. Note that we can rewrite it as follows:

$$\frac{\dot{\lambda}_t}{\lambda_t} = \rho - \left(f'(k_t) - n \right) \Rightarrow \rho + n = \frac{\dot{\lambda}_t}{\lambda_t} + f'(k_t). \tag{3.10}$$

This is nothing but an arbitrage equation for a typical asset price, where in this case the asset is the capital stock of the economy. Such arbitrage equations state that the opportunity cost of holding the asset (ρ in this case), equals its rate of return, which comprises the dividend yield ($f'(k_t) - n$) plus whatever capital gain you may get from holding the asset ($\frac{\dot{\lambda}_t}{\lambda_t}$). If the opportunity cost were higher (resp. lower), you would not be in an optimal position: you should hold less (resp. more) of the asset. We will come back to this intuition over and over again.

3.1.4 | The balanced growth path and the Euler equation

We are ultimately interested in the dynamic behaviour of our control and state variables, c_t and k_t. How can we turn our FOCs into a description of that behaviour (preferably one that we can represent graphically)? We start by taking (3.7) and differentiating both sides with respect to time:

$$u''(c_t)\dot{c}_t e^{nt} + nu'(c_t)e^{nt} = \dot{\lambda}_t. \tag{3.11}$$

Divide this by (3.7) and rearrange:

$$\frac{u''(c_t)c_t}{u'(c_t)} \frac{\dot{c}_t}{c_t} = \frac{\dot{\lambda}_t}{\lambda_t} - n. \tag{3.12}$$

Next, define

$$\sigma \equiv -\frac{u'(c_t)}{u''(c_t)c_t} > 0 \qquad (3.13)$$

as the elasticity of intertemporal substitution in consumption.[6] Then, (3.12) becomes

$$\frac{\dot{c}_t}{c_t} = -\sigma \left(\frac{\dot{\lambda}_t}{\lambda_t} - n \right). \qquad (3.14)$$

Finally, using (3.10) in (3.14) we obtain

$$\frac{\dot{c}_t}{c_t} = \sigma \left[f'(k_t) - \rho \right]. \qquad (3.15)$$

This dynamic optimality condition is known as the Ramsey rule (or Keynes-Ramsey rule), and in a more general context it is referred to as the *Euler equation*. It may well be the most important equation in all of macroeconomics: it encapsulates the essence of the solution to any problem that trades off today versus tomorrow.[7]

But what does it mean intuitively? Think about it in these terms: if the consumer postpones the enjoyment of one unit of consumption to the next instant, it will be incorporated into the capital stock, and thus yield an extra $f'(\cdot)$. However, this will be worth less, by a factor of ρ. They will only consume more in the next instant (i.e. $\frac{\dot{c}_t}{c_t} > 0$) if the former compensates for the latter, as mediated by their proclivity to switch consumption over time, which is captured by the elasticity of intertemporal substitution, σ. Any dynamic problem we will see from now on involves some variation upon this general theme: the optimal growth rate trades off the rate of return of postponing consumption (i.e. investment) against the discount rate.

Mathematically speaking, equations (3.5) and (3.15) constitute a system of two differential equations in two unknowns. These plus the initial condition for capital and the TVC fully characterise the dynamics of the economy: once we have c_t and k_t, we can easily solve for any remaining variables of interest.

To make further progress, let us characterise the BGP of this economy. Setting (3.5) equal to zero yields

$$c^* = f(k^*) - nk^*, \qquad (3.16)$$

which obviously is a hump-shaped function in c, k space. The dynamics of capital can be understood with reference to this function (Figure 3.1): for any given level of capital, if consumption is higher (resp. lower) than the BGP level, this means that the capital stock will decrease (resp. increase).

By contrast, setting (3.15) equal to zero yields

$$f'(k^*) = \rho. \qquad (3.17)$$

This equation pins down the level of the capital stock on the BGP, and the dynamics of consumption can be seen in Figure 3.2: for any given level of consumption, if the capital stock is below (resp. above) its BGP level, then consumption is increasing (resp. decreasing). This is because the marginal product of capital will be relatively high (resp. low).

Expressions (3.16) and (3.17) together yield the values of consumption and the capital stock (both per-capita) in the BGP, as shown in Figure 3.3. This already lets us say something important about the behaviour of this economy. Let's recall the concept of the *golden rule*, from our discussion of the

Figure 3.1 Dynamics of capital

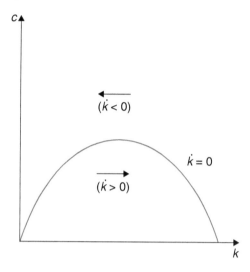

Figure 3.2 Dynamics of consumption

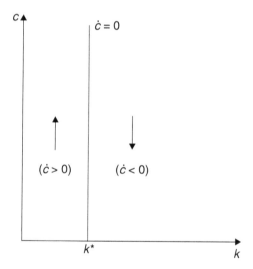

Solow model: the maximisation of per-capita consumption on the BGP. From (3.16) we see that this is tantamount to setting

$$\frac{\partial c^*}{\partial k^*} = f'\left(k_G^*\right) - n = 0 \Rightarrow f'\left(k_G^*\right) = n. \tag{3.18}$$

(Recall here we have assumed the depreciation rate is zero ($\delta = 0$).) If we compare this to (3.17), we see that the the optimal BGP level of capital per capita is *lower* than in the golden rule from the Solow model. (Recall the properties of the neoclassical production function, and that we assume $\rho > n$.)

Because of this comparison, (3.17) is sometimes known as the *modified golden rule*. Why does optimality require that consumption be lower on the BGP than what would be prescribed by the Solow

Figure 3.3 Steady state

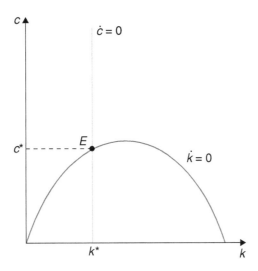

golden rule? Because future consumption is discounted, it is not optimal to save so much that BGP consumption is maximised – it is best to consume more along the transition to the BGP. Keep in mind that it is (3.17), not (3.18), that describes the optimal allocation. The kind of oversaving that is possible in the Solow model disappears once we consider optimal savings decisions.

Now, you may ask: is it the case then that this type of oversaving is not an issue in practice (or even just in theory)? Well, we will return to this issue in Chapter 8. For now, we can see how the question of dynamic efficiency relates to issues of inequality.

3.1.5 | A digression on inequality: Is Piketty right?

It turns out that we can say something about inequality in the context of the NGM, even though the representative agent framework does not address it directly. Let's start by noticing that, as in the Solow model, on the BGP output grows at the rate n of population growth (since capital and output per worker are constant). In addition, once we solve for the decentralised equilibrium, which we sketch in Section 2 below, we will see that in that equilibrium we have $f'(k) = r$, where r is the interest rate, or equivalently, the rate of return on capital.

This means that the condition for dynamic efficiency, which holds in the NGM, can be interpreted as the $r > g$ condition made famous by Piketty (2014) in his influential *Capital in the 21st Century*. The condition $r > g$ is what Piketty calls the "Fundamental Force for Divergence": an interest rate that exceeds the growth rate of the economy. In short, he argues that, if $r > g$ holds, then there will be a tendency for inequality to explode as the returns to capital accumulate faster than overall income grows. In Piketty's words:

> 'This fundamental inequality (...) will play a crucial role in this book. In a sense, it sums up the overall logic of my conclusions. When the rate of return on capital significantly exceeds the growth rate of the economy (...), then it logically follows that inherited wealth grows faster than output and income.' (pp. 25–26)

Does that mean that, were we to explicitly consider inequality in a context akin to the NGM we would predict it to explode along the BGP? Not so fast. First of all, when taking the model to the data, we could ask what k is. In particular, k can have a lot of human capital i.e. be the return to labour mostly, and this may help undo the result. In fact, it could even turn it upside down if human capital is most of the capital and is evenly distributed in the population. You may also want to see Acemoglu and Robinson (2015), who have a thorough discussion of this prediction. In particular, they argue that, in a model with workers and capitalists, modest amounts of social mobility – understood as a probability that some capitalists may become workers, and vice-versa – will counteract that force for divergence.

Yet the issue has been such a hot topic in the policy debate that two more comments on this issue are due.

First, let's understand better the determinants of labour and income shares. Consider a typical Cobb-Douglas production function:

$$Y = AL^{\alpha}K^{1-\alpha}. \tag{3.19}$$

With competitive factor markets, the FOC for profit maximisation would give:

$$w = \alpha AL^{\alpha-1}K^{1-\alpha}. \tag{3.20}$$

Computing the labour share using the equilibrium wage gives:

$$\frac{wL}{Y} = \frac{\alpha AL^{\alpha-1}K^{1-\alpha}L}{AL^{\alpha}K^{1-\alpha}} = \alpha, \tag{3.21}$$

which implies that for a Cobb-Douglas specification, labour and capital shares are constant. More generally, if the production function is

$$Y = \left(\beta K^{\frac{\epsilon-1}{\epsilon}} + \alpha (AL)^{\frac{\epsilon-1}{\epsilon}}\right)^{\frac{\epsilon}{\epsilon-1}} \quad \text{with } \epsilon \in [0, \infty), \tag{3.22}$$

then ϵ is the (constant) elasticity of substitution between physical capital and labour. Note that when $\epsilon \to \infty$, the production function is linear (K and L are perfect substitutes), and one can show that when $\epsilon \to 0$ the production function approaches the Leontief technology of fixed proportions, in which one factor cannot be substituted by the other at all.

From the FOC of profit maximisation we obtain:

$$w = \left(\beta K^{\frac{\epsilon-1}{\epsilon}} + \alpha (AL)^{\frac{\epsilon-1}{\epsilon}}\right)^{\frac{1}{\epsilon-1}} \alpha A (AL)^{-\frac{1}{\epsilon}}, \tag{3.23}$$

the labour share is now:

$$\frac{wL}{Y} = \frac{\alpha \left(\beta K^{\frac{\epsilon-1}{\epsilon}} + \alpha (AL)^{\frac{\epsilon-1}{\epsilon}}\right)^{\frac{1}{\epsilon-1}} A^{\frac{\epsilon-1}{\epsilon}} L^{-\frac{1}{\epsilon}} L}{\left(\beta K^{\frac{\epsilon-1}{\epsilon}} + \alpha (AL)^{\frac{\epsilon-1}{\epsilon}}\right)^{\frac{\epsilon}{\epsilon-1}}} = \alpha \left(\frac{AL}{Y}\right)^{\frac{\epsilon-1}{\epsilon}}. \tag{3.24}$$

Notice that as $\frac{L}{Y} \longrightarrow 0$, several things can happen to the labour share, and what happens depends on A and ϵ:

$$\text{If } \epsilon > 1 \Longrightarrow \alpha \left(\frac{AL}{Y}\right)^{\frac{\epsilon-1}{\epsilon}} \longrightarrow 0 \tag{3.25}$$

$$\text{If } \epsilon < 1 \Longrightarrow \alpha \left(\frac{AL}{Y}\right)^{\frac{\epsilon-1}{\epsilon}} \text{ increases.} \tag{3.26}$$

These two equations show that the elasticity of substitution is related to the concept of how essential a factor of production is. If the elasticity of substitution is less than one, the factor becomes more and more important with economic growth. If this factor is labour this may undo the Piketty result. This may be (and this is our last comment on the issue!) the reason why over the last centuries, while interest rates have been way above growth rates, inequality does not seem to have worsened. If anything, it seems to have moved in the opposite direction.

In Figure 3.4, Schmelzing (2019) looks at interest rates since the 1300s and shows that, while declining, they have consistently been above the growth rates of the economy at least until very recently. If those rates would have led to plutocracy, as Piketty fears, we would have seen it a long while ago. Yet the world seems to have moved in the opposite direction towards more democratic regimes.[8]

Figure 3.4   Real rates 1317–2018, from Schmelzing (2019)

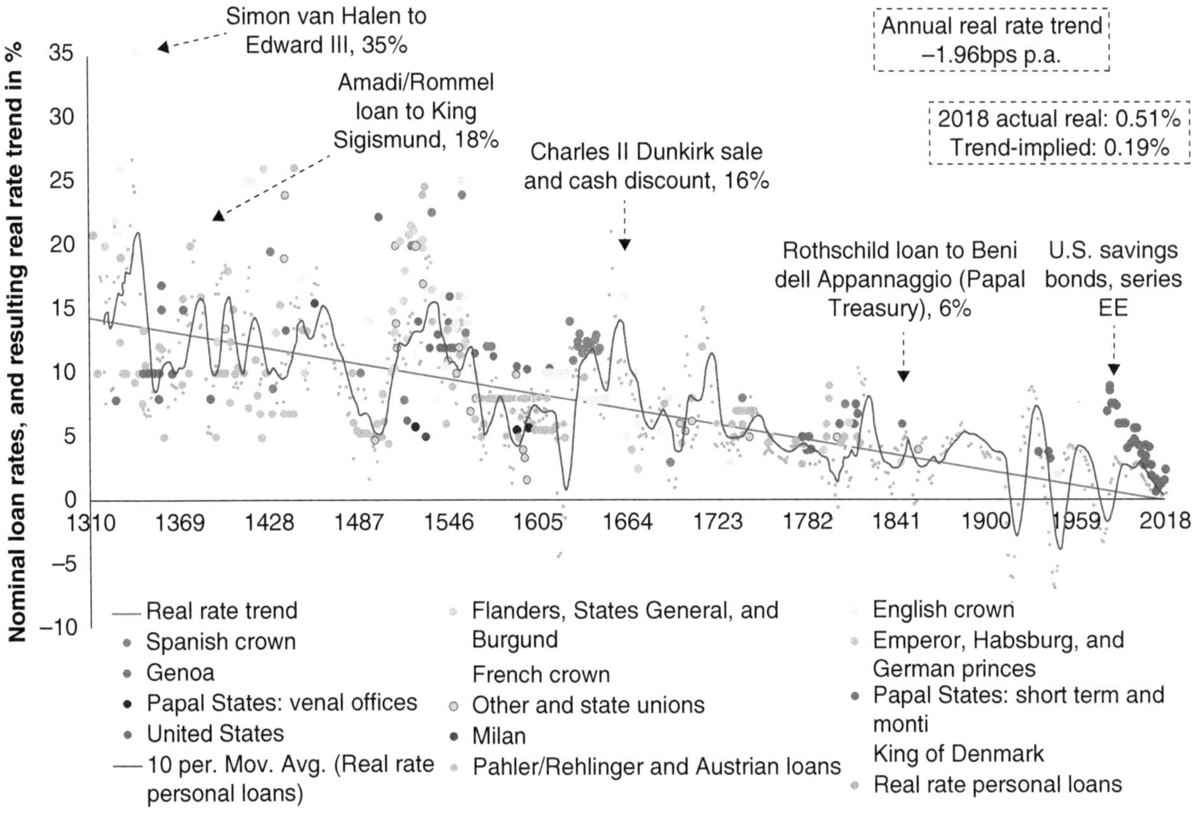

3.1.6 | Transitional dynamics

How do we study the dynamics of this system? We will do so below graphically. But there are some shortcuts that allow you to understand the nature of the dynamic system, and particularly the relevant question of whether there is one, none, or multiple equilibria.

A dynamic system is a bunch of differential equations (difference equations if using discrete time). In the mathematical appendix, that you may want to refer to now, we argue that one way to approach this issue is to linearise the system around the steady state. For example, in our example here, Equations (3.5) and (3.15) are a system of two differential equations in two unknowns: c and k. To linearise the system around the BGP or steady state we compute the derivatives relative to each variable as shown below:

$$\begin{bmatrix} \dot{k}_t \\ \dot{c}_t \end{bmatrix} = \Omega \begin{bmatrix} k_t - k^* \\ c_t - c^* \end{bmatrix}, \tag{3.27}$$

where

$$\Omega = \begin{bmatrix} \frac{\partial \dot{k}}{\partial k}\Big|_{SS} & \frac{\partial \dot{k}}{\partial c}\Big|_{SS} \\ \frac{\partial \dot{c}}{\partial k}\Big|_{SS} & \frac{\partial \dot{c}}{\partial c}\Big|_{SS} \end{bmatrix} \tag{3.28}$$

and

$$\frac{\partial \dot{k}}{\partial k}\Big|_{SS} = f'(k^*) - n = \rho - n \tag{3.29}$$

$$\frac{\partial \dot{k}}{\partial c}\Big|_{SS} = -1 \tag{3.30}$$

$$\frac{\partial \dot{c}}{\partial k}\Big|_{SS} = \sigma c^* f''(k^*) \tag{3.31}$$

$$\frac{\partial \dot{c}}{\partial c}\Big|_{SS} = 0. \tag{3.32}$$

These computations allow us to define a matrix with the coefficients of the response of each variable to those in the system, at the steady state. In this case, this matrix is

$$\Omega = \begin{bmatrix} \rho - n & -1 \\ \sigma c^* f''(k^*) & 0 \end{bmatrix}. \tag{3.33}$$

In the mathematical appendix we provide some tools to understand the importance of this matrix of coefficients. In particular, this matrix has two associated eigenvalues, call them λ_1 and λ_2 (not to be confused with the marginal utility of consumption). The important thing to remember from the appendix is that the dynamic equations for the variables will be of the form $Ae^{\lambda_1} + Be^{\lambda_2}$. Thus, the nature of these eigenvalues turns out to be critical for understanding the dynamic properties of the system. If they are negative their effect dilutes over time (this configuration is called a sink, as variables converge to their steady state). If positive, the variable blows up (we call these systems a source, where variables drift away from the steady state). If one is positive and the other is negative the system typically blows up, except if the coefficient of the positive eigenvalue is zero (we call these saddle-path systems).

You may think that what you want is a sink, a system that converges to an equilibrium. While this may be the natural approach in sciences such as physics, this reasoning would not be correct in the realm of economics. Imagine you have one state variable (not jumpy) and a control variable (jumpy), as in this system. In the system we are analysing here k is a state variable that moves slowly over time and c

is the control variable that can jump. So, if you have a sink, you would find that *any c* would take you to the equilibrium. So rather than having a unique stable equilibrium you would have infinite alternative equilibria! Only if the two variables are state variables do you want a sink. In this case the equilibrium is unique because the state variables are uniquely determined at the start of the program.

In our case, to pin down a unique equilibria we would need a saddle-path configuration. Why? Because for this configuration there is only one value of the control variable that makes the coefficient of the explosive eigenvalue equal to zero. This feature is what allows to pin the unique converging equilibria. In the figures below this will become very clear.

What happens if all variables are control variables? Then you need the system to be a source, so that the control variables have only one possible value that attains sustainability. We will find many systems like this throughout the book.

In short, there is a rule that you may want to keep in mind. You need as many positive eigenvalues as jumpy or forward-looking variables you have in your system. If these two numbers match you have uniqueness![9]

Before proceeding, one last rule you may want to remember. The determinant of the matrix is the product of the eigenvalues, and the trace is equal to the sum. This is useful, because, for example, in our two-equation model, if the determinant is negative, this means that the eigenvalues have different sign, indicating a saddle path. In fact, in our specific case,

- $\text{Det}(\Omega) = \sigma c^* f''(k^*) < 0.$

If $\text{Det}(\Omega)$ is the product of the eigenvalues of the matrix Ω and their product is negative, then we know that the eigenvalues must have the opposite sign. Hence, we conclude one eigenvalue is positive, while the other is negative.

Recall that k is a slow-moving, or sticky, variable, while c can jump. Hence, since we have the same number of negative eigenvalues as of sticky variables, we conclude the system is saddle-path stable, and the convergence to the equilibrium unique. You can see this in a much less abstract way in the the phase diagram in Figure 3.5.

Figure 3.5 The phase diagram

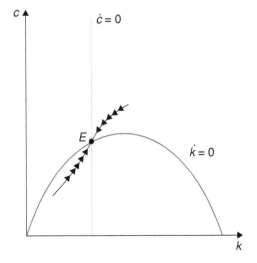

Notice that since c can jump, from any initial condition for $k(0)$, the system moves vertically (c moves up or down) to hit the saddle path and converge to the BGP along the saddle path. Any other trajectory is divergent. Alternative trajectories appear in Figure 3.6.

Figure 3.6 Divergent trajectories

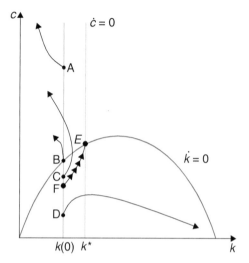

The problem is that these alternative trajectories either eventually imply a jump in the price of capital, which is inconsistent with rationality, or imply above-optimal levels of the capital stock. In either case this violates the transversality condition. In short, the first two dynamic equations provide the dynamics at any point in the (c,k) space, but only the TVC allows us to choose a single path that we will use to describe our equilibrium dynamics.[10]

3.1.7 | The effects of shocks

Consider the effects of the following shock. At time 0 and unexpectedly, the discount rate falls forever (people become less impatient). From the relevant $\dot{k} = 0$ and $\dot{c} = 0$ schedules, we see that the former does not move (ρ does not enter) but the latter does. Hence, the new BGP will have a higher capital stock. It will also have higher consumption, since capital and output are higher. Figure 3.7 shows the old BGP, the new BGP, and the path to get from one to the other. On impact, consumption falls (from point E to point A). Thereafter, both c and k rise together until reaching point E'.

Similar exercises can be carried out for other permanent and unanticipated shocks.

Consider, for example, an increase in the discount rate (Figure 3.8). (The increase is transitory, and that is anticipated by the planner.) The point we want to make is that there can be no anticipated jump in the control variables throughout the optimal path as this would allow for infinite capital gains. This is why the trajectory has to put you on the new saddle path when the discount rate goes back to normal.

Figure 3.7 A permanent increase in the discount rate

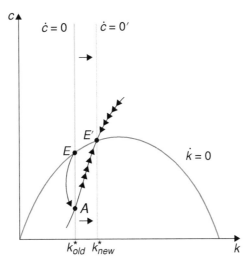

Figure 3.8 A transitory increase in the discount rate

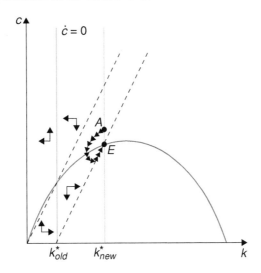

3.2 | The equivalence with the decentralised equilibrium

We will show that the solution to the central planner's problem is exactly the same as the solution to a decentralised equilibrium.

Now we will sketch the solution to the problem of finding the equilibrium in an economy that is identical to the one we have been studying, but without a central planner. We now have households and firms (owned by households) who independently make their decisions in a perfectly competitive environment. We will only sketch this solution.

The utility function to be maximised by each household is

$$\int_0^\infty u(c_t)e^{nt}e^{-\rho t}dt, \qquad (3.34)$$

where c_t is consumption and $\rho\ (> n)$ is the rate of time preference.

The consumer's budget constraint can be written as

$$c_t L_t + \dot{A} = w_t L_t + rA_t, \qquad (3.35)$$

where L_t is population, A_t is the stock of assets, $\dot{A}$ is the increase in assets, w_t is the wage per unit of labour (in this case per worker), and r is the return on assets. What are these assets? The households own the capital stock that they then rent out to firms in exchange for a payment of r; they can also borrow and lend money to each other, and we denote their total debt by B_t. In other words, we can define

$$A_t = K_t - B_t. \qquad (3.36)$$

You should be able to go from (3.35) to the budget constraint in per worker terms:

$$c_t + \frac{da_t}{dt} + na_t = w_t + ra_t. \qquad (3.37)$$

Households supply factors of production, and firms maximise profits. Thus, at each moment, you should be able to show that equilibrium in factor markets involves

$$r_t = f'\left(k_t\right), \qquad (3.38)$$

$$w_t = f\left(k_t\right) - f'\left(k_t\right)k_t. \qquad (3.39)$$

In this model, we must impose what we call a no-Ponzi-game (NPG) condition.[11] What does that mean? That means that households cannot pursue the easy path of getting arbitrarily rich by borrowing money and borrowing even more to pay for the interest owed on previously contracted debt. If possible that would be the optimal solution, and a rather trivial one at that. The idea is that the market will not allow these Ponzi schemes, so we impose this as a constraint on household behaviour.

$$\lim_{t\to\infty} a_t e^{-(r-n)t} \ge 0. \qquad (3.40)$$

You will have noticed that this NPG looks a bit similar to the TVC we have seen in the context of the planner's problem, so it is easy to mix them up. Yet, they are different! The NPG is a *constraint* on optimisation – it wasn't needed in the planner's problem because there was no one in that closed economy from whom to borrow. In contrast, the TVC is an optimality condition – that is to say, something that is chosen in order to achieve optimality. They are related, in that both pertain to what happens in the limit, as $t \to \infty$. We will see how they help connect the decentralised equilibrium with the planner's problem.

3.2.1 | Integrating the budget constraint

The budget constraint in (3.37) holds at every instant t. It is interesting to figure out what it implies for the entire path to be chosen by households. To do this, we need to integrate that budget constraint. In future chapters we will assume that you know how to do this integration, and you can consult the mathematical appendix for that. But the first time we will go over all the steps.

So let's start again with the budget constraint for an individual family:

$$\dot{a}_t - (r - n) a_t = w_t - c_t. \tag{3.41}$$

This is a first-order differential equation which (as you can see in the Mathematical Appendix) can be solved using integrating factors. To see how that works, multiply both sides of this equation by $e^{-(r-n)t}$:

$$\dot{a}_t e^{-(r-n)t} + (n - r) a_t e^{-(r-n)t} = (w_t - c_t)e^{-(r-n)t}. \tag{3.42}$$

The left-hand side is clearly the derivative of $a_t e^{(n-r)t}$ with respect to time, so we can integrate both sides between 0 and t:

$$a_t e^{-(r-n)t} - a_0 = \int_0^t (w_s - c_s)e^{-(r-n)s} ds. \tag{3.43}$$

Taking the $\lim t \longrightarrow \infty$ (and using the no-Ponzi condition) yields:

$$0 = \int_0^\infty \left(w_s - c_s \right) e^{-(r-n)s} ds + a_0, \tag{3.44}$$

which can be written as a standard intertemporal budget constraint:

$$\int_0^\infty w_s e^{-(r-n)s} ds + a_0 = \int_0^\infty c_s e^{-(r-n)s} ds. \tag{3.45}$$

This is quite natural and intuitive: all of what is consumed must be financed out of initial assets or wages (since we assume that Ponzi schemes are not possible).

3.2.2 | Back to our problem

Now we can go back to solve the consumer's problem

$$Max \int_0^\infty u(c_t)e^{nt}e^{-\rho t} dt \tag{3.46}$$

s.t.

$$c_t + \dot{a} + (n - r) a_t = w_t. \tag{3.47}$$

The Hamiltonian now looks like this

$$H = u\left(c_t \right) e^{nt} + \lambda_t \left[w_t - c_t - (n - r) a_t \right]. \tag{3.48}$$

From this you can obtain the FOCs and, following the same procedure from the previous case, you should be able to get to

$$-c_t \frac{u''\left(c_t \right) \dot{c}_t}{u'\left(c_t \right) c_t} = (r - \rho). \tag{3.49}$$

How does that compare to (3.15), the Euler equation, which is one of our dynamic equations in the central planner's solution? We leave that to you.

You will also notice that, from the equivalent FOCs (3.7) and (3.8), we have

$$\frac{\dot{u}'}{u'} = (\rho - r), \tag{3.50}$$

or

$$u'\left(c_t\right) = e^{(\rho - r)t}. \tag{3.51}$$

Using this in the equivalent of (3.7) yields:

$$e^{(n-r)t} = \lambda_t e^{-\rho t}. \tag{3.52}$$

This means that the NPG becomes:

$$\lim_{t \to \infty} a_t \lambda_t e^{-\rho t} = \lim_{t \to \infty} a_t e^{-(r-n)t}. \tag{3.53}$$

You can show that this is exactly the same as the TVC for the central planner's problem. (Think about it: since all individuals are identical, what is the equilibrium level of b_t? If an individual wants to borrow, would anyone else want to lend?)

Finally, with the same reasoning on the equilibrium level of b_t, you can show that the resource constraint also matches the dynamic equation for capital, (3.5), which was the relevant resource constraint for the central planner's problem.

3.3 | Do we have growth after all?

Not really.

Having seen the workings of the Ramsey model, we can see that on the BGP, just as in the Solow model, there is no growth in per capita variables: k is constant at k^* such that $f'(k^*) = \rho$, and y is constant at $f(k^*)$. (It is easy to show that once again we can obtain growth if we introduce exogenous technological progress.)

3.4 | What have we learned?

We are still left with a growth model without long-run growth: it was not the exogeneity of the savings rate that generated the unsatisfactory features of the Solow model when it comes to explaining long-run growth. We will have to keep looking by moving away from diminishing returns or by modelling technological progress.

On the other hand, our exploration of the Ramsey model has left us with a microfounded framework that is the foundation of a lot of modern macroeconomics. This is true not only of our further explorations that will lead us into endogenous growth, but eventually also when we move to the realm of short term fluctuations. At any rate, the NGM is a dynamic general equilibrium framework that we will use over and over again.

Even in this basic application some key results have emerged. First, we have the Euler equation that encapsulates how consumers make optimal choices between today and tomorrow. If the marginal benefit of reducing consumption – namely, the rate of return on the extra capital you accumulate –

is greater than the consumer's impatience – the discount rate – then it makes sense to postpone consumption. This crucial piece of intuition will appear again and again as we go along in the book, and is perhaps the key result in modern macroeconomics. Second, in this context there is no dynamic inefficiency, as forward-looking consumers would never choose to oversave in an inefficient way.

Most importantly, now we are in possession of a powerful toolkit for dynamic analysis, and we will make sure to put it to use from now on.

Notes

[1] The other one was to the theory of optimal taxation (Ramsey 1927).

[2] See Cass (1965) and Koopmans et al. (1963).

[3] Another interesting set of questions refer to population policies: say you impose a policy to reduce population growth. How does that play into the utility function? How do you count people that have not been and will not be born? Should a central planner count those people?

[4] We are departing from standard mathematical convention, by using subscripts instead of parentheses to denote time, even though we are modelling time as continuous and not discrete. We think it pays off to be unconventional, in terms of making notation look less cluttered, but we apologise to the purists in the audience nonetheless!

[5] Note that we must assume that $\rho > n$, or the problem will not be well-defined. Why? Because if $\rho < n$, the representative household gets more total utility out of a given level of consumption per capita in the future as there will be more "capitas" then. If the discount factor does not compensate for that, it would make sense to always postpone consumption! And why do we have e^{nt} in the utility function in the first place? Because we are incorporating the utility of all the individuals who are alive at time t – the more, the merrier!

[6] Recall that the elasticity of a variable x with respect to another variable y is defined as $\frac{\frac{dx}{dy}}{\frac{x}{y}}$.

As such, $\frac{1}{\sigma}$ is the elasticity of the marginal utility of consumption with respect to consumption – it measures how sensitive the marginal utility is to increases in consumption. Now, think about it: the more sensitive it is, the more I will want to smooth consumption over time, and this means I will be less likely to substitute consumption over time. That is why the inverse of that captures the intertemporal elasticity of substitution: the greater σ is, the more I am willing to substitute consumption over time.

[7] This is the continuous-time analogue of the standard optimality condition that you may have encountered in microeconomics: the marginal rate of substitution (between consumption at two adjacent points in time) must be equal to the marginal rate of transformation.

[8] At any rate, it may also be argued that maybe we haven't seen plutocracies because Piketty was right. After all, the French and U.S. revolutions may be explained by previous increases in inequality.

[9] It works the same for a system of difference equation in discrete time, except that the cutoff is with eigenvalues being larger or smaller than one.

[10] To rule out the path that leads to the capital stock of when the $\dot{k} = 0$ locus crosses the horizontal axis to the right of the golden rule, notice that λ from (3.8) grows at the rate $\rho + n - f'(k)$ so that $\lambda e^{-\rho t}$ grows at rate $n - f'(k)$, but to the right of the golden rule $n > f'(k)$, so that the term increases. Given that the capital stock is eventually fixed we conclude that the transversality condition cannot hold. The paths that lead to high consumption and a zero capital stock imply a collapse of consumption to zero when the path reaches the vertical axis. This trajectory is not feasible because at some point

it cannot continue. When that happens the price of capital increases, and consumers would have arbitraged that jump away, so that that path would have not occurred in the first place.

[11] Or should it now be the no-Madoff-game condition?

References

Acemoglu, D. & Robinson, J. A. (2015). The rise and decline of general laws of capitalism. *Journal of Economic Perspectives, 29*(1), 3–28.

Barro, R. J. (1974). Are government bonds net wealth? *Journal of Political Economy, 82*(6), 1095–1117.

Caplin, A. & Leahy, J. (2004). The social discount rate. *Journal of Political Economy, 112*(6), 1257–1268.

Caselli, F. & Ventura, J. (2000). A representative consumer theory of distribution. *American Economic Review, 90*(4), 909–926.

Cass, D. (1965). Optimum growth in an aggregative model of capital accumulation. *The Review of Economic Studies, 32*(3), 233–240.

Koopmans, T. C. et al. (1963). *On the concept of optimal economic growth* (tech. rep.) Cowles Foundation for Research in Economics, Yale University.

Piketty, T. (2014). *Capital in the twenty-first century*. Harvard University Press.

Ramsey, F. P. (1927). A contribution to the theory of taxation. *The Economic Journal, 37*(145), 47–61.

Ramsey, F. P. (1928). A mathematical theory of saving. *The Economic Journal, 38*(152), 543–559.

Schmelzing, P. (2019). Eight centuries of global real rates, r-g, and the 'suprasecular' decline, 1311–2018, Available at SSRN: https://ssrn.com/abstract=3485734 or http://dx.doi.org/10.2139/ssrn.3485734.

CHAPTER 4

An application: The small open economy

The Neoclassical Growth Model (NGM) is more than just a growth model. It provides us with a powerful tool to think about a number of questions in macroeconomics, which require us to think dynamically. So let's now put it to work!

We will do so in a simple but important application: understanding the capital accumulation dynamics for a small open economy. As we will see shortly, in an open economy the capital accumulation process is modified by the possibility of using foreign savings. This really allows countries to move much faster in the process of capital accumulation (if in doubt ask the Norwegians!), and is one of the main reasons why integrating into world capital markets is often seen as a big positive for any economy.

The use of foreign savings (or the accumulation of assets abroad) is summarised in the economy's current account, so the NGM applied to a small open economy can be thought of as yielding a model of the behaviour of the current account. The current account provides a measure of how fast the country is building foreign assets (or foreign debt), and as such it is a key piece to assess the sustainability of macroeconomic policies. We will also see that the adjustment of the current account to different shocks can lead to surprising and unexpected results. Finally, the framework can be used to analyse, for example, the role of stabilisation funds in small open economies.

4.1 | Some basic macroeconomic identities

A quick refresher that introduces the concept of the current account.

A good starting point is to start with the basic macroeconomic identities, which you have seen before in your introductory and intermediate macro courses. Recall the relationship between GNP (Gross National Product, the amount that is paid to a country's residents) and GDP (Gross Domestic Product, the amount of final goods produced in a particular country):

$$GDP + rB = GNP, \qquad (4.1)$$

How to cite this book chapter:
Campante, F., Sturzenegger, F. and Velasco, A. 2021. *Advanced Macroeconomics: An Easy Guide.*
    Ch. 4. 'An application: The small open economy', pp. 41–50. London: LSE Press.
    DOI: https://doi.org/10.31389/lsepress.ame.d License: CC-BY-NC 4.0.

where B is the position held by residents in foreign assets (net of domestic assets held by foreigners), and r is the rate of return paid on those assets. In other words, rB is the total (net) interest payments made by foreigners to residents. Notice that countries with foreign assets will have a GNP which is larger than GDP, whereas countries with debt will have a GNP which is smaller than their GDP.

Starting from the output equation we have that

$$GNP = C + I + G + X - M + rB, \qquad (4.2)$$

where C, I, G, X and M, stand, as usual, for consumption, investment, government expenditures, exports and imports. This can be rewritten as:

$$\underbrace{GNP - C - G - I} = X - M + rB = CA, \qquad (4.3)$$

$$S - I = X - M + rB = CA. \qquad (4.4)$$

The right-hand side (RHS) is roughly the current account CA (the trade balance plus the net income on net foreign assets, which is typically called primary income, add up to the current account).[1] The equation says that the current account is equal to the difference between what the economy saves (S) and what it invests (I).[2]

Another alternative is to write this as:

$$GNP - \underbrace{C - G - I} = X - M + rb = CA,$$

$$Y - Absorption = X - M + rb = CA,$$

which clearly shows that a current account is the difference between income and absorption. In common parlance: if a country spends more than it earns, it runs a current account deficit. Importantly, and as we will see over and over again, this does not mean that current account deficits are bad! They simply mean that a country is using debt and, as always, whether that is a good or a bad thing hinges on whether that is done in a sustainable way. To figure that out, we need to embed these accounting identities into an optimising intertemporal model of how consumption and investment are chosen given current and future output.

As luck would have it, this is exactly what the NGM is!

4.2 | The Ramsey problem for a small open economy

We will solve the (benevolent central planner) Ramsey problem for a small open economy. The key conclusions are: (i) $c = c^*$: consumption can be perfectly smoothed; (ii) $f'(k^*) = r$: the capital stock can adjust immediately via foreign borrowing, and thus becomes independent of domestic savings. This is because the current account allows the economy to adjust to shocks while maintaining optimal levels of consumption and capital stock.

Here is where we will start using, right away, what we learnt in the previous chapter. As before, there is one infinitely-lived representative household whose members consume and produce. Population growth is now assumed to be $n = 0$ for simplicity; initial population L_0 is normalised to 1, so that all quantities are in per capita terms (in small-case letters). There is one good, and no government.

The key difference is that now the economy is open, in the sense that foreigners can buy domestic output, and domestic residents can buy foreign output. Whenever domestic income exceeds domestic expenditure, locals accumulate claims on the rest of the world, and vice versa. These claims take the form of an internationally-traded bond, denominated in units of the only good. The economy is also small, in the sense that it does not affect world prices (namely the interest rate), and thus takes them as given.

We will assume also that the country faces a constant interest rate. The constancy of r is a key defining feature of the small country model. However, this is a strong assumption – if a country borrows a lot, probably its country risk would increase and so would the interest rate it would have to pay – but we will keep this assumption for now. (We will return to issues of risk when we talk about consumption and investment, in (Chapters 13 and 14.)

The utility function is exactly as before (with $n = 0$):

$$\int_0^\infty u(c_t)e^{-\rho t}dt. \tag{4.5}$$

The resource constraint of the economy is

$$\dot{k}_t + \dot{b}_t = f(k_t) + rb_t - c_t. \tag{4.6}$$

The novelty is that now domestic residents own a stock b_t of the bond, whose rate of return is r, which is a constant from the standpoint of the small open economy. What is the current account in this representation? It is income (GNP), which is $f(k_t) + rb_t$, minus consumption c_t, minus investment $\dot{k}_t$. In other words, it is equal to $\dot{b}_t$. A current-account surplus is equivalent to an increase in foreign bond holdings.

In the open economy, we also have to impose a no-Ponzi game (NPG) condition (or solvency condition):

$$\lim_{T\to\infty} \left(B_T e^{-rT}\right) = \lim_{T\to\infty} \left(b_T e^{-rT}\right) \geq 0. \tag{4.7}$$

This condition – again, not to be confused with the transversality condition (TVC) we met in the previous chapter – did not apply to the benevolent central planner (BCP) in the last chapter because they could not borrow in the context of a closed economy. It did apply to the consumers in the decentralised equilibrium though, and here it must apply to the economy as a whole. It means that the economy cannot run a Ponzi scheme with the rest of the world by borrowing money indefinitely to pay interest on its outstanding debt. In other words, this rules out explosive trajectories of debt accumulation under the assumption that foreigners would eventually stop lending money to this pyramid scheme.

4.2.1 | A useful transformation

Define total domestic assets per capita as

$$a_t = k_t + b_t. \tag{4.8}$$

Then, (4.6) becomes

$$\dot{a}_t = ra_t + f(k_t) - rk_t - c_t, \tag{4.9}$$

and (4.7) becomes

$$\lim_{T\to\infty} \left[\left(a_T - k_T\right)e^{-rT}\right] \geq 0. \tag{4.10}$$

4.2.2 | Solution to consumer's problem

The consumer maximises (4.5) subject to (4.9) and (4.10) for given k_0 and b_0. The Hamiltonian for the problem can be written as

$$H = u(c_t) + \lambda_t \left[ra_t + f(k_t) - rk_t - c_t \right].$$ (4.11)

Note c is one control variable (jumpy), and k now is another control variable (also jumpy). It is now a that is the state variable (sticky), the one that has to follow the equation of motion. λ is the costate variable (the multiplier associated with the intertemporal budget constraint, also jumpy). The costate has the same intuitive interpretation as before: the marginal value as of time t of an additional unit of the state (assets a, in this case). (Here is a question for you to think about: why is capital a jumpy variable now, while it used to be sticky in the closed economy?)

The first order conditions are then:

$$u'(c_t) = \lambda_t,$$ (4.12)

$$f'(k_t) = r,$$ (4.13)

$$\dot{\lambda} = -r\lambda_t + \rho\lambda_t,$$ (4.14)

and

$$\lim_{t \to \infty} a_t \lambda_t e^{-\rho t} = 0.$$ (4.15)

Using (4.12) in (4.14), we obtain

$$u''(c_t) \, \dot{c}_t = (-r + \rho)u'(c_t).$$ (4.16)

Dividing both sides by $u'(c_t)$ and using the definition of the elasticity of intertemporal substitution, σ, gets us to our Euler equation for the dynamic behaviour of consumption:

$$\frac{\dot{c}_t}{c_t} = \sigma(r - \rho).$$ (4.17)

This equation says that per-capita consumption is constant only if $r = \rho$, which we assume from now on. Notice that we can do this because r and ρ are exogenous. This assumption eliminates any inessential dynamics (including endogenous growth) and ensures a well-behaved BGP.[3] It follows then that consumption is constant:

$$c_t = c^*.$$ (4.18)

4.2.3 | Solving for the stock of domestic capital

FOC (4.13) says that the marginal product of (per-capita) capital is constant and equal to the interest rate on bonds. Intuitively, the marginal return on both assets is equalised. This means that capital is always at its steady state level k^*, which is defined by

$$f'(k^*) = r.$$ (4.19)

This means, in turn, that domestic per capita income is constant, and given by

$$y^* = f(k^*). \tag{4.20}$$

Note that the capital stock is completely independent of savings and consumption decisions, which is a crucial result of the small open economy model. One should invest in capital according to its rate of return (which is benchmarked by the return on bonds), and raise the necessary resources not out of savings, but out of debt.

4.2.4 | The steady state consumption and current account

Now that you have the level of income you should be able to compute the level of consumption. How do we do that? By solving the differential equation that is the budget constraint (4.9), which we can rewrite as

$$\dot{a}_t - ra_t = f(k^*) - rk^* - c^*, \tag{4.21}$$

using the solutions for optimal consumption and capital stock. Using our strategy of integrating factors, we can multiply both sides by e^{-rt}, and integrate the resulting equation between 0 and t:

$$a_t e^{-rt} - a_0 = \frac{c^* + rk^* - f(k^*)}{r}(e^{-rt} - 1). \tag{4.22}$$

Now evaluate this equation as $t \to \infty$. Considering the NPC and the TVC, it follows that:

$$c^* = ra_0 + f(k^*) - rk^*. \tag{4.23}$$

We can also find the optimal level of debt at each time period. It is easy to see that a_t is kept constant at a_0, from which it follows that $b_t = b_0 + k_0 - k^*$. The current account is zero. In other words, the NGM delivers a growth model with no growth, as we saw in the last chapter, and a model of the current account dynamics without current account surpluses or deficits.

Not so fast, though! We saw that the NGM did have predictions for growth outside of the BGP. Let's look at the transitional dynamics here as well, and see what we can learn.

4.2.5 | The inexistence of transitional dynamics

There are no transitional dynamics in this model: output per capita converges instantaneously to that of the rest of the world!

Suppose that initial conditions are $k_0 < k^*$ and $b_0 > 0$. But, condition (4.19) says that capital must always be equal to k^*. Hence, in the first instant, capital must jump up from k_0 to k^*. How is this accomplished? Domestic residents purchase the necessary quantity of capital (the single good) abroad and instantaneously install it. Put differently, the speed of adjustment is infinite.

How do the domestic residents pay for this new capital? By drawing down their holdings of the bond. If $\Delta k_0 = k^* - k_0$, then $\Delta b_0 = -\Delta k_0 = -(k^* - k_0)$. Note that this transaction does not affect initial net national assets, since

$$\Delta a_0 = \Delta k_0 + \Delta b_0 = \Delta k_0 - \Delta k_0 = 0. \tag{4.24}$$

An example

Suppose now that the production function is given by

$$f(k_t) = Ak_t^\alpha, A > 0, 0 \leq \alpha \leq 1. \tag{4.25}$$

This means that condition (4.19) is

$$\alpha A (k^*)^{\alpha-1} = r \tag{4.26}$$

so that the level of capital on the BGP is

$$k^* = \left(\frac{\alpha A}{r}\right)^{\frac{1}{1-\alpha}}, \tag{4.27}$$

which is increasing in A and decreasing in r.

Using this solution for the capital stock we can write y^* as

$$y^* = Ak^{*\alpha} = A\left(\frac{\alpha A}{r}\right)^{\frac{\alpha}{1-\alpha}} = A^{\frac{1}{1-\alpha}}\left(\frac{\alpha}{r}\right)^{\frac{\alpha}{1-\alpha}} \equiv z(A), \tag{4.28}$$

with $z(A)$ increasing in A.

It follows that consumption can be written as

$$c^* = ra_0 - rk^* + z(A) = ra_0 + (1-\alpha)z(A), \tag{4.29}$$

with $z'(A) > 0$.

4.2.6 | Productivity shocks and the current account

Suppose the economy initially has total factor productivity A^H, with corresponding optimal stock of capital $(k^*)^H$ and consumption level $(c^*)^H$. At time 0 there is an unanticipated and permanent fall in productivity from A^H to A^L, where $A^L < A^H$ (maybe because this economy produced oil, guano, or diamonds and its price has come down). This means, from (4.28), that $z(A)$ falls from $z(A^H)$ to $z(A^L)$. Capital holdings are reduced: residents sell capital in exchange for bonds, so after the shock they have $(k^*)^L < (k^*)^H$, where $(k^*)^H$ was the optimal stock of capital before the shock. Assets a_0 are unchanged on impact.

From (4.29) it follows that consumption adjusts instantaneously to its new (and lower) value:

$$(c^*)^L = ra_0 - (1-\alpha)z(A^L) < ra_0 - (1-\alpha)z(A^H) = (c^*)^H, \text{ for all } t \geq 0. \tag{4.30}$$

What happens to the current account? After the instantaneous shock, assets remain unchanged, and $\dot{b}_t$ is zero. The economy immediately converges to the new BGP, where the current account is in balance.

At this point, you must be really disappointed: don't we ever get any interesting current account dynamics from this model? Actually, we do! Consider a *transitory* fall in productivity at time 0, from A^H to A^L, with productivity eventually returning to A^H after some time T. Well, it should be clear that consumption will fall, but not as much as in the permanent case. You want to smooth consumption, and you understand that things will get back to normal in the future, so you don't have to bring it down so much now. At the same time, the capital stock does adjust down fully, otherwise its return would be below what the domestic household could get from bonds. If current output falls just as in the permanent case, but consumption falls by less, where is the difference? A simple inspection of (4.9) reveals that $\dot{b}$ has to fall below zero: it's a current-account deficit! Quite simply, residents can smooth consumption, in spite of the negative shock, by borrowing resources from abroad. Once the shock reverts, the current account returns to zero, while consumption remains unchanged. In the new BGP, consumption will remain lower relative to its initial level, and the difference will pay for the interest incurred on the debt accumulated over the duration of the shock – or more generally, the reduction in net foreign asset income.

This example underscores the role of the current account as a mechanism through which an economy can adjust to shocks. It also highlights one feature that we will see over and over again: the optimal response and resulting dynamics can be very different depending on whether a shock is permanent or transitory.

4.2.7 | Sovereign wealth funds

This stylised model actually allows us to think of other simple policy responses. Imagine a country that has a finite stock of resources, like copper.[4] Furthermore let's imagine that this stock of copper is being extracted in a way that it will disappear in a finite amount of time. The optimal program is to consume the net present value of the copper over the infinite future. So, as the stock of copper declines the economy should use those resources to accumulate other assets. This is the fiscal surplus rule implemented by Chile to compensate for the depletion of their resources. In fact, Chile also has a rule to identify transitory from permanent shocks, with the implication that all transitory increases (decreases) in the price level have to be saved (spent).

Does this provide a rationale for some other sovereign wealth funds? The discussion above suggests that a country should consume:

$$r \int_{-\infty}^{\infty} R_t e^{-rt} dt, \tag{4.31}$$

where R is the value of the resources extracted in period t. This equation says that a country should value its intertemporal resources (which are the equivalent of the a_0 above, an initial stock of assets), and consume the real return on it.

Is that how actual sovereign funds work? Well, the Norwegian sovereign fund rule, for instance, does not do this. Their rule is to spend at time t the real return of the assets accumulated until then:

$$r \int_{-\infty}^{t} R_t e^{-r(s-t)} ds. \tag{4.32}$$

This rule can only be rationalised if you expect no further discoveries and treat each new discovery as a surprise. Alternatively, one could assume that the future is very uncertain, so one does not want to commit debt ahead of time. (We will come back to this precautionary savings idea in our study of consumption in Chapter 11.) In any event, the key lesson is that studying our stylised models can help clarify the logic of existing policies, and where and why they depart from our basic assumptions.

4.3 | What have we learned?

The NGM provides the starting point for a lot of dynamic macroeconomic analysis, which is why it is one of the workhorse models of modern macroeconomics. In this chapter, we have seen how it provides us, in the context of a small open economy, with a theory of the current account. When an economy has access to international capital markets, it can use them to adjust to shocks, while smoothing consumption and maintaining the optimal capital stock. Put simply, by borrowing and lending (as reflected by the current account), the domestic economy need not rely on its own savings in order to make adjustments.

This brings to the forefront a couple of important messages. First, current account deficits (contrary to much popular perception) are not inherently bad. They simply mean that the economy is making use of resources in excess of its existing production capacity. That can make a lot of sense, if the economy has accumulated assets or otherwise expects to be more productive in the future.

Second, access to capital markets can be a very positive force. It allows economies to adjust to shocks, thereby reducing volatility in consumption. It is important to note that this conclusion is coming from a model without risk or uncertainty, without frictions in capital markets, and where decisions are being taken optimally by a benevolent central planner. We will lift some of those assumptions later in the book, but, while we will not spend much more time talking about open economies, it is important to keep in mind those caveats here as well.

Third, we have seen how the adjustment to permanent versus transitory shocks can be very different. We will return to this theme over and over again over the course of this book.

Last but not least, we have illustrated how our stylised models can nevertheless illuminate actual policy discussions. This will, again, be a recurrent theme in this book.

4.4 | What next?

The analysis of the current account has a long pedigree in economics. As the counterpart of current accounts are either capital flows or changes in Central Bank reserves it has been the subject of much controversy. Should capital accounts be liberalised? Is there a sequence of liberalisation? Can frictions in capital markets or incentive distortions make these markets not operate as smoothly and beneficially as we have portrayed here? The literature on moral hazard, the policy discussion on bailouts, and, as a result, all the discussion on sovereign debt, which is one key mechanism countries, smooth consumption over time. The presentation here follows Blanchard and Fischer (1989), but if you want to start easy you can check the textbook by Caves et al. (2007), which covers all the policy issues. Obstfeld and Rogoff (1996) is the canonical textbook in international finance. More recently, you can dwell in these discussions by checking out Vegh (2013) and Uribe and Schmitt-Grohé (2017). Last, but not least, the celebrated paper by Aguiar and Gopinath (2007) distinguishes between shocks to output and shocks to trends in output growth, showing that the latter are relevant empirically and help understand the current account dynamics in emerging economies.

Notes

[1] We should add secondary income, but we will disregard for the analysis.

[2] The fact that current accounts seem to be typically quite small relative to the size of the economy, so that savings is roughly similar to investment, is called the Feldstein-Horioka puzzle.

[3] Think about what happens, for instance, if $r > \rho$. We would have consumption increasing at a constant rate. This patient economy, with relatively low ρ, would start accumulating assets indefinitely. But in this case, should we expect that the assumption that it is a small economy would keep being appropriate? What if $r < \rho$? This impatient economy would borrow heavily to enjoy a high level of

consumption early on, and consumption would asymptotically approach zero as all income would be devoted to debt payments – not a very interesting case.

[4] Is this example mere coincidence, or related to the fact that one of us is from Chile, which is a major exporter of copper? We will let you guess.

References

Aguiar, M. & Gopinath, G. (2007). Emerging market business cycles: The cycle is the trend. *Journal of Political Economy, 115*(1), 69–102.

Blanchard, O. & Fischer, S. (1989). *Lectures on macroeconomics*. MIT Press.

Caves, R. E., Frankel, J., & Jones, R. (2007). *World trade and payments: An introduction*. Pearson.

Obstfeld, M. & Rogoff, K. (1996). *Foundations of international macroeconomics*. MIT Press.

Uribe, M. & Schmitt-Grohé, S. (2017). *Open economy macroeconomics*. Princeton University Press.

Vegh, C. (2013). *Open economy macroeconomics in developing countries*. MIT Press.

CHAPTER 5

Endogenous growth models I: Escaping diminishing returns

We are still searching for the Holy Grail of endogenous growth. How can we generate growth within the model, and not as an exogenous assumption, as in the Neoclassical Growth Model with exogenous technological progress? Without that, we are left unable to really say much about policies that could affect long-run growth. We have mentioned two possible approaches to try and do this. First, we can assume different properties for the production function. Perhaps, in reality, there are features that allow economies to escape the limitations imposed by diminishing returns to accumulation. Second, we can endogenise the process of technological change so we can understand its economic incentives. The former is the subject of this chapter, and we will discuss the latter in the next one.

5.1 | The curse of diminishing returns

You will recall that a crucial lesson from the Neoclassical Growth Model was that capital accumulation, in and of itself, cannot sustain long-run growth in per capita income. This is because of *diminishing returns* to the use of capital, which is a feature of the neoclassical production function. In fact, not only are there diminishing returns to capital (i.e. $\frac{\partial^2 F}{\partial K^2} < 0$) but these diminishing returns are strong enough that we have the Inada condition that $\lim_{K \to \infty} \frac{\partial F}{\partial K} = 0$. Because of this, as you accumulate capital, the incentive to save and invest further will become smaller, and the amount of capital per worker will eventually cease to grow. The crucial question is: Are there any features of real-world technologies that would make us think that we can get away from diminishing returns?

5.2 | Introducing human capital

We show, in the context of the Solow model, how expanding the concept of capital accumulation can generate endogenous growth. This, however, depends on total returns to accumulation being non-diminishing.

One possibility is that the returns to accumulation are greater than we might think at first. This is because there is more to accumulation than machines and plants and bridges. For instance, we can also invest in and accumulate human capital!

How to cite this book chapter:

Campante, F., Sturzenegger, F. and Velasco, A. 2021. *Advanced Macroeconomics: An Easy Guide.*
    Ch. 5. 'Endogenous growth models I: Escaping diminishing returns', pp. 51–68. London: LSE Press.
    DOI: https://doi.org/10.31389/lsepress.ame.e   License: CC-BY-NC 4.0.

Could that allow us to escape the curse, and achieve sustainable growth? Here is where a formal model is once again required. We will do that in the simplest possible context, that of the Solow model, but now introducing a new assumption on the production function: the presence of human capital as an additional factor. To fix ideas, let's go to the Cobb-Douglas case:

$$Y = K^\alpha H^\beta (AL)^\gamma . \tag{5.1}$$

Note that we are assuming the technological parameter A to be of the labour-augmenting kind. It enters into the production function by making labour more effective.[1] Dividing through by L we obtain

$$\frac{Y}{L} = A^\gamma \left(\frac{K}{L}\right)^\alpha \left(\frac{H}{L}\right)^\beta L^{(\alpha+\beta+\gamma)-1}, \tag{5.2}$$

where $\alpha + \beta + \gamma$ is the scale economies parameter. If $\alpha + \beta + \gamma = 1$, we have constant returns to scale (CRS). If $\alpha + \beta + \gamma > 1$, we have increasing returns to scale; doubling all inputs more than doubles output.

Assume CRS for starters. We can then write the production function as

$$y = A^\gamma k^\alpha h^\beta, \tag{5.3}$$

where, as before, small-case letters denote per-capita variables.

5.2.1 | Laws of motion

Let us start way back in the Solow world. As in the simple Solow model, assume constant propensities to save out of current income for physical and human capital, $s_k, s_h \in (0, 1)$. Let δ be the common depreciation rate. We then have

$$\dot{K} = s_k Y - \delta K, \tag{5.4}$$

$$\dot{H} = s_h Y - \delta H, \tag{5.5}$$

and, therefore,

$$\frac{\dot{K}}{L} = s_k y - \delta k, \tag{5.6}$$

$$\frac{\dot{H}}{L} = s_h y - \delta h. \tag{5.7}$$

Recall next that

$$\frac{\dot{K}}{L} = \dot{k} + nk, \tag{5.8}$$

$$\frac{\dot{H}}{L} = \dot{h} + nh. \tag{5.9}$$

Using these expressions we have

$$\dot{k} = s_k A^\gamma k^\alpha h^\beta - (\delta + n) k, \tag{5.10}$$

$$\dot{h} = s_h A^\gamma k^\alpha h^\beta - (\delta + n) h, \tag{5.11}$$

which yield:

$$\gamma_k = \frac{\dot{k}}{k} = s_k A^\gamma k^{\alpha-1} h^\beta - (\delta + n),$$
(5.12)

$$\gamma_h = \frac{\dot{h}}{h} = s_h A^\gamma k^\alpha h^{\beta-1} - (\delta + n).$$
(5.13)

5.2.2 | Balanced growth path

You will recall that a BGP is a situation where all variables grow at a constant rate. From (5.12) and (5.13) (and in the absence of technological progress), we see that constant γ_k and γ_h require, respectively[2],

$$(\alpha - 1)\gamma_k + \beta\gamma_h = 0,$$
(5.14)
$$\alpha\gamma_k + (\beta - 1)\gamma_h = 0.$$
(5.15)

Substituting the second equation into the first equation yields

$$\frac{1 - \alpha - \beta}{1 - \beta}\gamma_k = 0.$$
(5.16)

But given CRS, we have assumed that $\alpha + \beta < 1$, so we must have $\gamma_k = \gamma_h = 0$. In other words, just as before, without technical progress (A constant), this model features constant per-capita capital k and constant per-capita human capital h. No growth again! Of course, we can obtain long-run growth again by assuming exogenous (labour-augmenting) technological progress, $\frac{\dot{A}}{A} = g$. Consider a BGP in which $\frac{\dot{k}}{k}$ and $\frac{\dot{h}}{h}$ are constant over time. From (5.12) and (5.13), this requires that $\frac{k}{y}$ and $\frac{h}{y}$ be constant over time. Consequently, if a BGP exists, y, k, and h, must all be increasing at the same rate. When the production function exhibits CRS, this BGP can be achieved by setting $\frac{\dot{y}}{y} = \frac{\dot{k}}{k} = \frac{\dot{h}}{h} = g$.[3] The long-run growth rate is thus independent of s_k, s_h, n or anything that policy affects, unless g is endogenised somehow. (But again, long-run levels of income do depend on these behavioural parameters.)

5.2.3 | Still looking for endogenous growth

Why is the long-run growth rate still pinned down by the exogenous rate of technological growth as in the Solow Model? CRS implies that the marginal products of K and H decline as these factors accumulate, tending to bring growth rates down. Moreover, Cobb-Douglas production functions satisfy the Inada conditions so that, in the limit, these marginal products asymptotically go to 0. In other words, CRS still keeps us in the domain of diminishing returns to capital accumulation, regardless of the fact that we have introduced human capital!

How can we change the model to make long-run growth rates endogenous (i.e., potentially responsive to policy)? You should see immediately from (5.16) that there is a possibility for a BGP, with γ_k and γ_h different from zero: if $\alpha + \beta = 1$. That is to say, if we have constant returns to capital and human capital, the reproducible factors, taken together.

It is easy to see, from (5.12) and (5.13), that in a BGP we must have

$$\frac{\dot{k}}{k} = \frac{\dot{h}}{h} \longrightarrow \frac{k^*}{h^*} = \frac{s_k}{s_h}.$$
(5.17)

In other words, in a BGP k and h must grow at the same rate. This is possible since diminishing returns does not set in to either factor ($\alpha + \beta = 1$). What rate of growth is this? Using (5.17) in (5.12) and (5.13) we obtain (normalizing $A = 1$ for simplicity)

$$\frac{\dot{k}}{k} = \frac{\dot{h}}{h} = s_h \left(\frac{s_k}{s_h} \right)^\alpha - (\delta + n) = s_k^\alpha s_h^{1-\alpha} - (\delta + n). \tag{5.18}$$

The long-run (BGP) growth rate of output is

$$\frac{\dot{y}}{y} = \alpha \frac{\dot{k}}{k} + (1 - \alpha) \frac{\dot{h}}{h} = s_k^\alpha s_h^{1-\alpha} - (\delta + n). \tag{5.19}$$

Now s_k, s_h do affect long-run growth. If policy affects these, then policy affects growth. For instance, increasing the savings rates leads to higher growth in the long run. In other words, when we have human capital *and constant returns to reproducible factors of production*, it is possible to explain long-run growth (see Figure 5.1).

Figure 5.1   Endogenous growth

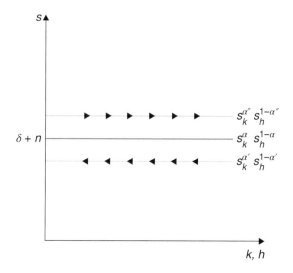

A couple of observations are in order. First, with permanent differences in growth rates across countries, the cross-national variation of per-capita incomes will blow up over time. In other words, there is no convergence in such a model. Also, if there is technical progress, growth rates will be higher.

5.3 | The AK model

We embed the notion of non-diminishing returns to accumulation into the setting of the Ramsey problem: $f(k) = Ak$. The resulting Euler equation, $\frac{\dot{c}_t}{c_t} = \sigma(A - \rho)$, displays endogenous growth. This is a very different world from the NGM: there are no transitional dynamics, policies affect long-run growth, there is no convergence, and temporary shocks have permanent effects.

The model in the previous section, just like the Solow model, was not micro-founded in terms of individual decisions. Let us now consider whether its lessons still hold in a framework with optimising individuals.

We have seen that the key aspect to obtaining long-run growth in the previous model is to have constant returns to reproducible factors when taken together. Including human capital as one such factor is but one way of generating that. To keep things as general as possible, though, we can think of all reproducible factors as capital, and we can subsume all of these models into the so-called AK model.

Consider once again a model with one representative household living in a closed economy, members of which consume and produce. There is one good, and no government. Population growth is 0, and the population is normalised to 1. All quantities (in small-case letters) are per-capita. Each consumer in the representative household lives forever.

The utility function is

$$\int_0^\infty \left(\frac{\sigma}{\sigma-1}\right) c_t^{\frac{\sigma-1}{\sigma}} e^{-\rho t} dt, \ \rho > 0, \tag{5.20}$$

where c_t denotes consumption, ρ is the rate of time preference and σ is the elasticity of intertemporal substitution in consumption.

We have the linear production function from which the model derives its nickname:

$$Y_t = Ak_t, \ A > 0. \tag{5.21}$$

Again, think of household production: the household owns the capital and uses it to produce output.

The resource constraint of the economy is

$$\dot{k}_t = Ak_t - c_t. \tag{5.22}$$

5.3.1 | Solution to household's problem

The household's problem is to maximise (5.20) subject to (5.22) for given k_0. The Hamiltonian for the problem can be written as

$$H = \left(\frac{\sigma}{\sigma-1}\right) c_t^{\frac{\sigma-1}{\sigma}} + \lambda_t \left(Ak_t - c_t\right). \tag{5.23}$$

Note c is the control variable (jumpy), k is the state variable (sticky), and λ is the costate.

First order conditions are

$$\frac{\partial H}{\partial c_t} = c_t^{-\frac{1}{\sigma}} - \lambda_t = 0, \tag{5.24}$$

$$\dot{\lambda}_t = -\frac{\partial H}{\partial k_t} + \rho\lambda_t = -A\lambda_t + \rho\lambda_t, \tag{5.25}$$

$$\lim_{t\to\infty}\left(k_t\lambda_t e^{-\rho t}\right) = 0. \tag{5.26}$$

This last expression is, again, the transversality condition (TVC).

5.3.2 | At long last, a balanced growth path with growth

Take (5.24) and differentiate both sides with respect to time, and divide the result by (5.24) to obtain

$$-\frac{1}{\sigma}\frac{\dot{c}_t}{c_t} = \frac{\dot{\lambda}_t}{\lambda_t}. \tag{5.27}$$

Multiplying through by $-\sigma$, (5.27) becomes

$$\frac{\dot{c}_t}{c_t} = -\sigma\left(\frac{\dot{\lambda}_t}{\lambda_t}\right). \tag{5.28}$$

Finally, using (5.25) in (5.28) we obtain

$$\frac{\dot{c}_t}{c_t} = \sigma(A - \rho), \tag{5.29}$$

which is the Euler equation. Note that here we have $f'(k) = A$, so this result is actually the same as in the standard Ramsey model. The difference is in the nature of the technology, as now we have constant returns to capital.

Define a BGP once again as one in which all variables grow at a constant speed. From (5.22) we get

$$\frac{\dot{k}_t}{k_t} = A - \frac{c_t}{k_t}. \tag{5.30}$$

This implies that capital and consumption must grow at the same rate – otherwise we wouldn't have $\frac{\dot{k}_t}{k_t}$ constant. And since $y_t = Ak_t$, output grows at the same rate as well. From (5.29) we know that this rate is $\sigma(A - \rho)$. Hence,

$$\frac{\dot{c}_t}{c_t} = \frac{\dot{k}_t}{k_t} = \frac{\dot{y}_t}{y_t} = \sigma(A - \rho). \tag{5.31}$$

Note, there will be positive growth only if $A > \rho$ that is, only if capital is sufficiently productive so that it is desirable to accumulate it.

Second, from (5.30) we see that along a BGP we must have

$$y_t - c_t = \sigma(A - \rho)k_t \Rightarrow c_t = [(1 - \sigma)A + \sigma\rho]\,k_t = \left[\frac{(1 - \sigma)A + \sigma\rho}{A}\right]y_t. \tag{5.32}$$

In words, consumption is proportional to capital. Or, put differently, the agent consumes a fixed share of output every period. Notice that this is much like the assumption made in Solow. If s is the savings rate, here $1 - s = \frac{(1-\sigma)A+\sigma\rho}{A}$, or $s = \sigma\left(\frac{A-\rho}{A}\right)$. The difference is that this is now optimal, not arbitrary.

There are no transitional dynamics: the economy is always on the BGP.

5.3.3 | Closing the model: The TVC and the consumption function

We must now ask the following question. Are we sure the BGP is optimal? If $A > \rho$, the BGP implies that the capital stock will be growing forever. How can this be optimal? Would it not be better to deplete the capital stock? More technically, is the BGP compatible with the TVC? Since we did not use it in constructing the BGP, we cannot be sure. So, next we check the BGP is indeed optimal in that, under some conditions, it does satisfy the TVC.

Using (5.24) the TVC can be written as

$$\lim_{t \to \infty} \left(k_t c_t^{-\frac{1}{\sigma}} e^{-\rho t} \right) = 0. \tag{5.33}$$

Note next that equation (5.29) is a differential equation which has the solution

$$c_t = c_0 e^{\sigma(A-\rho)t}. \tag{5.34}$$

Combining the last two equations the TVC becomes

$$\lim_{t \to \infty} \left(k_t c_0^{-\frac{1}{\sigma}} e^{-At} \right) = 0. \tag{5.35}$$

From the solution to expression (5.31) we have

$$k_t = k_0 e^{\sigma(A-\rho)t}. \tag{5.36}$$

Using this to eliminate k_T, the TVC becomes

$$\lim_{t \to \infty} \left(k_0 c_0^{-\frac{1}{\sigma}} e^{\sigma(A-\rho)t} e^{-At} \right) = \lim_{t \to \infty} \left(k_0 c_0^{-\frac{1}{\sigma}} e^{-\theta t} \right) = 0, \tag{5.37}$$

where

$$\theta \equiv (1 - \sigma) A + \sigma \rho. \tag{5.38}$$

Hence, for the TVC we need $\theta > 0$, which we henceforth assume. Note that with logarithmic utility ($\sigma = 1$), $\theta = \rho$.

5.3.4 | The permanent effect of transitory shocks

In the AK model, as we have seen, growth rates of all pertinent variables are given by $\sigma(A - \rho)$. So, if policy can affect preferences (σ, ρ) or technology (A), it can affect growth.

If it can do that, it can also affect levels. From the production function, in addition to (5.31) and (5.32), we have

$$k_t = k_0 e^{\sigma(A-\rho)t}, \tag{5.39}$$

$$y_t = A k_0 e^{\sigma(A-\rho)t}, \tag{5.40}$$

$$c_t = [(1 - \sigma) A + \sigma \rho] k_0 e^{\sigma(A-\rho)t}. \tag{5.41}$$

Clearly, changes in σ, ρ and A matter for the levels of variables.

Notice here that there is no convergence in per capita incomes whatsoever. Countries with the same σ, ρ, and A retain their income gaps forever.[4]

Consider the effects of a sudden increase in the marginal product of capital A, which suddenly and unexpectedly rises (at time $t = 0$), from A to $A' > A$. Then, by (5.31), the growth rate of all variables immediately rises to $\sigma\left(A' - \rho\right)$.

What happens to the levels of the variables? The capital stock cannot jump at time 0, but consumption can. The instant after the shock ($t = 0^+$), it is given by

$$c_{0^+} = \left[(1 - \sigma)A' + \sigma\rho\right]k_{0^+} > c_0 = \left[(1 - \sigma)A + \sigma\rho\right]k_{0^+}, \tag{5.42}$$

where $k_{0^+} = k_0$ by virtue of the sticky nature of capital.

So, consumption rises by $(1 - \sigma)\left(A' - A\right)k_0$. But, output rises by $\left(A' - A\right)k_0$. Since output rises more than consumption, growth picks up right away.

It turns out that the AK model has very different implications from the Neoclassical Growth Model when it comes to the effects of transitory shocks. To see that, consider a transitory increase in the discount factor, i.e. suppose ρ increases for a fixed interval of time; for simplicity, assume that the new ρ is equal to A.

Figure 5.2 shows the evolution of the economy: the transitory increase in the discount rate jolts consumption, bringing growth down to zero while the discount factor remains high. When the discount factor reverts, consumption decreases, and growth restarts. But there is a permanent fall in the level of output relative to the original path. In other words, there is full persistence of shocks, even if the shock itself is temporary. You may want to compare this with the Neoclassical Growth Model trajectories (Figure 5.3), where there is catch-up to the original path and there are no long-run effects.

Figure 5.2 Transitory increase in discount rate

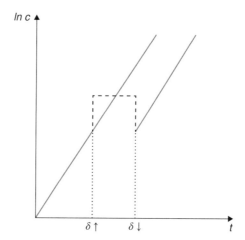

5.3.5 │ In sum

In AK models of endogenous growth:

1. There is no transitional dynamics;
2. Policies that affect the marginal product of capital (e.g. taxes) do affect growth;
3. There is no convergence;
4. Even temporary policies have permanent effects.

Figure 5.3   Comparison with Solow model

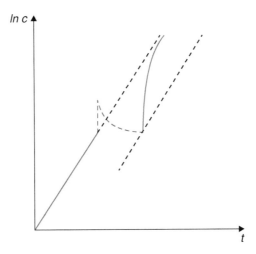

These results are surprising and were initially presented by Romer (1987), as part of the contributions that eventually won him the Nobel Prize in Economics in 2018. You have to admit that this is very different from the world of diminishing returns depicted by the NGM. Now look at the graph from the U.S. recovery after the Great Recession of 2008/2009 and notice the similarities with the dynamics of the AK model: no return to the previous growth trend. The graph even suggests that it is not the first time a pattern like this plays out. Maybe this model is onto something, after all.

Figure 5.4   U.S. real GDP and extrapolated trends

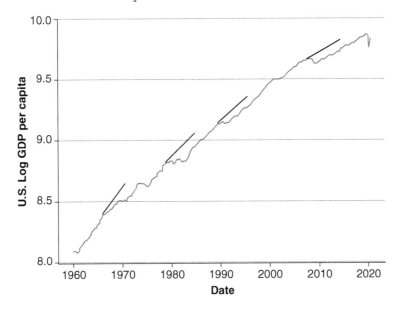

5.4 | Knowledge as a factor of production

We argue that knowledge explains why accumulation may not face diminishing returns. We develop different models of how this may happen (learning-by-doing, specialisation). In the process, we show that in a world with non-diminishing returns to accumulation (and hence increasing returns to scale), the decentralised equilibrium need not be efficient: growth will be lower than than the social optimum as private incentives to accumulate knowledge are below the social returns.

We have seen that the key to obtaining long-run growth in our models is to get constant returns in the reproducible factors. But this begs the question: why do we think that this would actually be the case in reality?

As we have seen, a world of constant returns to reproducible factors is, actually, a world with *increasing returns to scale* (IRS) – after all, there is at least labour and technology in the production functions as well. But, this is a problem because IRS implies that our simple model with perfect competition doesn't really work anymore.

To see why, note that with perfect competition, each factor of production gets paid its marginal product – you know that from Econ 101. However, if the production function is

$$F(A, X), \tag{5.43}$$

where X has constant returns, then we have

$$F(A, X) < A\frac{\partial F}{\partial A} + X\frac{\partial F}{\partial X}. \tag{5.44}$$

There is not enough output to pay each factor their marginal productivity!

We had sidestepped this discussion up to this point, assuming that technology was there and was left unpaid. But now the time has come to deal with this issue head-on.

In doing so, we will build a bridge between what we have learned about accumulation and what we have talked about when referring to productivity. The crucial insight again is associated with Paul Romer, and can be summarised in one short sentence: economies can grow by accumulating "knowledge".

But what drives the accumulation of knowledge? Knowledge is a tricky thing because it is difficult to appropriate, i.e. it has many of the properties of a public good. As you may remember, the two distinguishing characteristics of any good are

- Rivalry $\longrightarrow$ if I use it you can't.
- Excludability $\longrightarrow$ I can prevent you from using it.

Private goods are rival and excludable, pure public goods are neither. Technology/knowledge is peculiar because it is non-rival, although excludable to some extent (with a patent, for example).

The non-rivalry of knowledge immediately gives rise to increasing returns. If you think about it, knowledge is a fixed cost: in order to produce one flying car, I need one blueprint for a flying car, but I don't need a second blueprint to build a second unit of that flying car. In other words, one doesn't need to double all inputs in order to double output.

This complicates our picture. If factors of production cannot be paid their marginal returns, and there is not enough output to pay them all, then how is the accumulation of knowledge paid for? Here are the options:

1. *A* is public and provided by the government;
2. Learning by doing (i.e. externalities, again);
3. Competitive behaviour is not preserved.

We will not deal much with #1 (though it is clear that in the areas where research has more externalities and is less excludable, as in basic research, there is a larger participation of the public sector), but we will address some relevant issues related to #2 (here) and #3 (next chapter).

5.4.1 | Learning by doing

This was first suggested by Romer (1987). The idea is that you become better at making stuff as you make it: knowledge is a by-product of production itself. This means that production generates an externality. If each firm does not internalise the returns to the knowledge they generate and that can be used by others, firms still face convex technologies even though there are increasing returns at the level of the economy. It follows that competitive behaviour can be preserved.

Let us model this with the following production function,

$$y = A k^{\alpha} \bar{k}^{\eta}, \tag{5.45}$$

where $\bar{k}$ is the stock of knowledge (past investment). Given this we compute the (private) marginal product of capital and the growth rate:

$$f'(k) = A \alpha k^{\alpha-1} \bar{k}^{\eta} = A \alpha k^{\alpha+\eta-1}, \tag{5.46}$$

$$\gamma_c = \sigma \left(A \alpha k^{\alpha+\eta-1} - \rho \right). \tag{5.47}$$

We have endogenous growth if $\alpha + \eta \geq 1$. Notice that we need CRS in the reproducible factors, and, hence, sufficiently strong IRS. It is not enough to have IRS; we need that $\eta \geq 1 - \alpha$.

For a central planner who sees through the learning-by-doing exercise:

$$f(k) = A k^{\alpha+\eta}, \tag{5.48}$$

$$f'(k) = (\alpha + \eta) A k^{\alpha+\eta-1}, \tag{5.49}$$

$$\gamma_p > \gamma_c. \tag{5.50}$$

It follows that the economy does not deliver the right amount of growth. Why? Because of the externality: private agents do not capture the full social benefit of their investment since part of it spills over to everyone else. This is a crucial lesson of the endogenous growth literature. Once we introduce IRS, there will typically be a wedge between the decentralised equilibrium and the optimal growth rate.

5.4.2 | Adam Smith's benefits to specialisation

The second story, (from Romer 1990), suggests that economies can escape diminishing returns by increasing the range of things they produce, an idea akin to Adam Smith's suggestion that specialisation increases productivity. Suppose the production function could use a continuum of potential inputs.

$$Y(X, L) = L^{1-\alpha} \int_0^\infty X(i)^\alpha \, di. \tag{5.51}$$

But not all varieties are produced. Let's say only the fraction $[0, M]$ are currently available. Say the average cost of production of each intermediate unit is 1, this implies that of each unit I will use

$$X(i) = \bar{X} = \frac{Z}{M}, \tag{5.52}$$

where Z are total resources devoted to intermediate inputs. So, this yields

$$Y = L^{1-\alpha} M \left(\frac{Z}{M} \right)^\alpha = L^{1-\alpha} Z^\alpha M^{1-\alpha}. \tag{5.53}$$

Note that we can write $Z = M\bar{X}$, so an expansion in Z can be accomplished by increasing M, the number of varieties, or increasing $\bar{X}$, the amount of each variety that is used. In other words, you can either pour more resources into what you already do, or into doing different things. We can thus write

$$Y = L^{1-\alpha} (M\bar{X})^\alpha M^{1-\alpha} = L^{1-\alpha} \bar{X}^\alpha M. \tag{5.54}$$

Lo and behold: increasing $\bar{X}$ encounters diminishing returns ($\alpha < 1$), but that is *not* the case when one increases M. In other words, specialisation prevents diminishing returns. Choosing units appropriately, we can have

$$M = Z. \tag{5.55}$$

But this then yields

$$Y = L^{1-\alpha} Z. \tag{5.56}$$

If $\dot{Z} = Y - C$ we are done: we are back to the AK model!

A nice example of the power of diversification in the production function is obtained in Gopinath and Neiman (2014), where they use Argentina's crisis of 2001/2002, which restricted access of firms to intermediate inputs, to estimate a large impact on productivity.

We should model next how the private sector will come up with new varieties (R&D). This will typically involve non-competitive behaviour: one will only invest in R&D if there is a way of recouping that investment (e.g. patents, monopoly power). This will also lead to a wedge between the optimal growth rate and the one that is delivered by the decentralised equilibrium: monopolies will undersupply varieties. But, careful: this will not always be so. In fact, we will develop a model where monopolies will oversupply varieties as well! At any rate, we will look at this in a bit more detail in the next chapter.

In the meantime, note in particular that these wedges introduce a potential role for public policy. For instance, if there is undersupply of varieties, one could introduce a subsidy to the purchase of intermediate inputs so that producers wouldn't face monopoly prices.

5.5 | Increasing returns and poverty traps

We digress into how a specific kind of increasing returns can be associated with the existence of poverty traps: situations where economies are stuck in a stagnating equilibrium when a better one would be available with an injection of resources. We discuss whether poverty traps are an important feature in the data and policy options to overcome them.

We have just argued that the presence of IRS (associated with non-diminishing returns to accumulation) is a key to understanding long-run growth. It turns out that the presence of (certain kinds of) IRS can also explain the condition of countries that seem to be mired in poverty and stagnation – as captured by the idea of poverty traps.

The concept of a poverty trap describes a situation in which some countries are stuck with stagnant growth and/or low levels of income per capita, while other (presumably similar) countries race ahead. The key for the emergence of this pattern is the presence of IRS, at least for a range of capital-labour ratios. The idea is as old as Adam Smith, but Rosenstein-Rodan (1943), Rosenstein-Rodan (1961), Singer (1949), Nurkse (1952), Myrdal and Sitohang (1957) and Rostow (1959) appropriated it for development theory. They argued that increasing returns only set in after a nation has achieved a particular threshold level of output per capita. Poor countries, they argued, were caught in a poverty trap because they had been hitherto unable to push themselves above that threshold. The implication is that nations that do not manage to achieve increasing returns are left behind. Those that do take off into a process of growth that leads to a steady state with higher standards of living (or maybe even to never-ending growth). You should keep in mind that, while the idea of poverty traps, and the calls for "big push" interventions to lift countries above the threshold that is needed to escape them, have been around for quite a while, they are still very much in the agenda. See for instance, Sachs (2005). Of course this view has plenty of critics as well – on that you may want to check Easterly (2001)'s book, which provides a particularly merciless critique.

Let's develop one version for a story generating poverty traps based on a simple modification of the Solow model highlighting the role of increasing returns in the production function. This makes the argument in the simplest possible fashion. You can refer to the paper by Kraay and McKenzie (2014) for a discussion of what could generate this sort of increasing returns. For instance, there could be fixed costs (lumpy investments) required to access a better technology (coupled with borrowing constraints). They also tell stories based on savings behaviour, or nutritional traps, among others.

5.5.1 | Poverty trap in the Solow model

Recall that, in per capita terms, the change in the capital stock over time is given by

$$\dot{k} = s \cdot f(k) - (n + \delta) \cdot k. \tag{5.57}$$

The key to generating growth traps in the Solow model is assuming a particular shape to the production function. In particular, we assume a (twice-continuously differentiable) function such that

$$f''(k) = \begin{cases} < 0 \text{ if } 0 < k < k_a \\ > 0 \text{ if } k_a < k < k_b \\ < 0 \text{ if } k > k_b. \end{cases} \tag{5.58}$$

The key is that the production function $f(k)$ has a middle portion where it exhibits increasing returns to scale.

Notice that the term $\frac{sf(k)}{k}$, crucial for the dynamics of the Solow model, has a derivative equal to

$$\frac{\partial \frac{sf(k)}{k}}{\partial k} = \frac{skf'(k) - sf(k)}{k^2} = \frac{sf'(k)}{k}\left(1 - \frac{f(k)}{kf'(k)}\right). \tag{5.59}$$

This derivative can only be zero whenever $f''(k) = 0$, which by (5.58) happens when $k = k_a$ and $k = k_b$.[5] It can also be shown that

$$\frac{\partial^2 \frac{sf(k)}{k}}{\partial k^2} = \begin{cases} > 0 \ \ if \ k = k_a \\ < 0 \ \ if \ k = k_b. \end{cases} \tag{5.60}$$

It follows that the function $\frac{sf(k)}{k}$ has the shape depicted in Figure 5.5.

Figure 5.5 Multiple equilibria in the Solow model

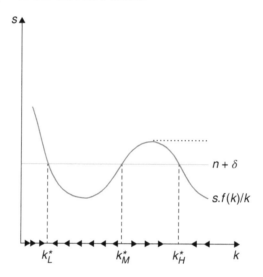

The dynamic features of this system, including the possibility of a poverty trap, can be read from the diagram directly. We have three steady states, at k_L^*, k_M^* and k_H^*. Of these, k_L^* and k_H^* are stable, while k_M^* is unstable. The implication is that if a country begins with a capital-labor ratio that is below k_M^*, then it will inexorably approach the steady state ratio k_L^*. If its initial capital-labour ratio is above k_M^*, then it will approach the much better steady state at k_H^*. The capital-labour ratio k_M^*, then, is the threshold capital stock (per capita) that a nation has to reach to take off and achieve the higher steady state.

Notice that in the end different countries may be at different steady state ratios, but they still exhibit identical growth rates (equal to zero). In Figure 5.5, a poor economy at steady state k_L^* and a rich economy at steady state k_H^* experience the same growth rates of aggregate variables and no growth in per capita variables. Notice, however, that the poor economy has per-capita income of $f\left(k_L^*\right)$ and the rich economy has per capita income of $f\left(k_H^*\right)$, which means that residents of the poor economy only get to enjoy consumption of magnitude $(1 - s)f\left(k_L^*\right)$, while residents of the rich economy enjoy the higher level $(1 - s) f(k_H^*)$. Hence, differences in initial conditions imply lasting differences in consumption and welfare among economies that are fundamentally identical. (Note that the production function $f(k)$, the savings rate s, the population growth rate n, and the depreciation rate δ are the same across these economies.)

5.5.2 | Policy options to overcome poverty traps

There are a few alternative policy options for nations caught in a poverty trap. The first is to temporarily increase the savings rate. Consider Figure 5.5 and suppose that we have a country with savings rate s_1 stuck at the stagnant steady state ratio k_L^*. A rise in the savings rate will result in a situation where there is only one stable steady state ratio at a high level of k^*. Maintaining the higher savings rate for a while, the nation will enjoy a rapid rise in the capital-labour ratio towards the new steady state. However, it need not maintain this savings rate forever. Once the capital-labour ratio has gone past k_M^*, it can lower the savings rate back down to s_1. Then the country is within the orbit of the high capital-labour ratio k_H^*, and will move inexorably towards it by the standard properties of Solow adjustment. Thus, a temporary rise in the savings rate is one way for a nation to pull itself out of the poverty trap.

Similarly, another way of escaping this poverty trap is to temporarily lower the population growth rate. A nation stuck at k_L^* could move the horizontal schedule down by decreasing population growth temporarily, thereby leaving a very high k^* as the only steady-state capital-labour ratio. The old population growth can be safely restored once the Solovian dynamics naturally push the economy above k_M^*.

There is an obvious third possibility, beyond the scope of the country and into the realm of the international community, to provide a country that is mired in a poverty trap with an injection of capital, through aid, that increases its capital stock past the threshold level. This is the big push in aid advocated by some economists, as well as many politicians, multilateral organisations, and pop stars.

In all of these cases, you should note the *permanent* effects of *temporary* policy. You will recall that this is a general feature of growth models with increasing returns, and this illustrates the importance of this aspect for designing policy.

5.5.3 | Do poverty traps exist in practice?

While many people believe poverty traps are an important phenomenon in practice – thereby providing justification for existing aid efforts – the issue is very controversial. Kraay and McKenzie (2014) consider the evidence, and come down on the skeptical side.

First, they argue that the kind of income stagnation predicted by poverty trap models are unusual in the data. The vast majority of countries have experienced positive growth over recent decades, and low-income countries show no particular propensity for slower growth. Since standard models predict a threshold above which a country would break free from the trap, that indicates that most countries would have been able to do so.

Second, they argue that the evidence behind most specific mechanisms that have been posited to generate poverty traps is limited. For instance, when it comes to the fixed cost story we have mentioned, it seems that for the most part individuals don"t need a lot of capital to start a business, and the amount of capital needed to start a business appears relatively continuous.

This doesn't mean, however, as they recognise, that poverty traps cannot explain the predicament of *some* countries, regions, or individuals. Being stuck in a landlocked country in an arid region is actually terrible! Also, we shouldn't conclude from the relatively sparse evidence that aid, for instance, is bad or useless. Poverty may be due to poor fundamentals, and aid-financed investments can help improve these fundamentals. But, it should temper our view on what we should expect from these policy interventions.

5.6 | What have we learned?

We have seen that long-term growth is possible when accumulation is not subject to diminishing returns, and that this entails a world where there are increasing returns to scale. We have also argued that one key source of these increasing returns to scale, in practice, is the accumulation of knowledge: you do not have to double knowledge in order to double output. This in turn requires us to think about what drives knowledge accumulation, and we have seen a couple of alternative stories (learning-by-doing, specialisation) that help us think that through.

Very importantly, we have seen that a world of increasing returns is one that is very different from the standpoint of policy. There is no convergence – we shouldn't expect poor countries to catch up with rich countries, even when they have the same fundamental parameters. By the same token, temporary shocks have permanent consequences. This has disheartening implications, as we shouldn't expect countries to return to a pre-existing growth trend after being hit by temporary negative shocks. But it also has more cheerful ones as temporary policy interventions can have permanent results.

We have also seen how these lessons can be applied to a specific case of increasing returns, which can generate poverty traps. Whether such traps are widespread or not remains a source of debate, but the concept nevertheless illustrates the powerful policy implications of increasing returns.

5.7 | What next?

To learn more about the endogenous growth models that we have started to discuss here, the book by Jones and Vollrath (2013) provides an excellent and accessible overview. Barro and Sala-i-Martin (2003) also covers a lot of the ground at a higher technical level that should still be accessible to you if you are using this book – it's all about the dynamic optimisation techniques we have introduced here.

For a policy-oriented and non-technical discussion on growth, an excellent resource is Easterly (2001). As we have mentioned, he is particularly skeptical when it comes to big push aid-based approaches. On poverty traps, it is worth noting that there are many other stories for sources of increasing returns of the sort we discussed. A particularly interesting one is studied by Murphy et al. (1989), which formalises a long-standing argument based on demand externalities (e.g. Rosenstein-Rodan (1943)) and investigates the conditions for their validity. This is a remarkable illustration of how helpful it is to formally model arguments. Another powerful story for increasing returns (and possible traps) comes from Diamond (1982), which studies how they can come about when market participants need to search for one another, generating the possibility of coordination failures. We will return to related concepts later in the book, when discussing unemployment (Chapter 16).

Notes

[1] Again, you should be able to see quite easily that in a Cobb-Douglas production function it doesn't really matter if we write $Y = A_1 K^\alpha H^\beta (L)^\gamma$ or $Y = K^\alpha H^\beta (A_2 L)^\gamma$; it is just a matter of setting

$A_1 \equiv A_2^\gamma$, which we can always do. It is important for the existence of a BGP that technology be labour-augmenting – though this is a technical point that you shouldn't worry about for our purposes here. You can take a look at Barro and Sala-i-Martin (2003) for more on that.

[2] Take logs and derive with respect to time.

[3] Check the math! Hint: log-differentiate (5.1).

[4] Here, for simplicity, we have set population growth n and depreciation δ to zero. They would also matter for levels and rates of growth of variables. In fact, introducing depreciation is exactly equivalent to reducing A – you should try and check that out!

[5] Recall that the function is twice-continuously differentiable, such that f'' has to be zero at those points. To see why $f''(k) = 0$ implies that (5.59) is equal to zero, recall from Econ 101 that "marginal product is less (more) than the average product whenever the second derivative is negative (positive)". It's all tied to Euler's homogenous function theorem, which is also behind why factors cannot be paid their marginal products when there are increasing returns to scale. As usual in math, it's all in Euler (or almost).

References

Barro, R. J. & Sala-i-Martin, X. (2003). *Economic growth* (2nd ed.). MIT press.

Diamond, P. A. (1982). Aggregate demand management in search equilibrium. *Journal of Political Economy*, 90(5), 881–894.

Easterly, W. (2001). *The elusive quest for growth: Economists' adventures and misadventures in the tropics*. MIT press.

Gopinath, G. & Neiman, B. (2014). Trade adjustment and productivity in large crises. *American Economic Review*, 104(3), 793–831.

Jones, C. I. & Vollrath, D. (2013). *Introduction to economic growth*. WW Norton & Company, Inc. New York, NY.

Kraay, A. & McKenzie, D. (2014). Do poverty traps exist? Assessing the evidence. *Journal of Economic Perspectives*, 28(3), 127–48.

Murphy, K. M., Shleifer, A., & Vishny, R. W. (1989). Industrialization and the big push. *Journal of Political Economy*, 97(5), 1003–1026.

Myrdal, G. & Sitohang, P. (1957). *Economic theory and under-developed regions*. London: Duckworth.

Nurkse, R. (1952). Some international aspects of the problem of economic development. *The American Economic Review*, 42(2), 571–583.

Romer, P. M. (1987). Growth based on increasing returns due to specialization. *The American Economic Review*, 77(2), 56–62.

Romer, P. M. (1990). Endogenous technological change. *Journal of Political Economy*, 98(5, Part 2), S71–S102.

Rosenstein-Rodan, P. N. (1943). Problems of industrialisation of eastern and south-eastern Europe. *The Economic Journal*, 53(210/211), 202–211.

Rosenstein-Rodan, P. N. (1961). Notes on the theory of the 'big push'. *Economic development for Latin America* (pp. 57–81). Springer.

Rostow, W. W. (1959). The stages of economic growth. *The Economic History Review*, 12(1), 1–16.

Sachs, J. (2005). *The end of poverty: How we can make it happen in our lifetime*. Penguin UK.

Singer, H. W. (1949). Economic progress in underdeveloped countries. *Social Research*, 1–11.

CHAPTER 6

Endogenous growth models II: Technological change

As we've seen, the challenge of the endogenous growth literature is how to generate growth within the model, and not simply as an assumption as in the Neoclassical Growth Model (NGM) with exogenous technological progress. The basic problem with the NGM (without exogenous technological progress) was that the incentives to capital accumulation decreased with the marginal product of capital. So, if we are to have perpetual growth we need a model that somehow gets around this issue. To do so, the literature has gone two ways. One is to change features of the production function or introduce additional factors that are complementary to the factors that are being accumulated in a way that keep the incentives to accumulation strong. The other alternative is to endogenise technological change. The first approach was the subject of the previous chapter, this chapter will focus on the second one.

Our final discussion in the previous chapter already hinted at the issues that arise when endogenising technological change. Most crucially, knowledge or ideas have many of the properties of a public good. In particular, ideas might be (or be made) *excludable* (e.g. using patents or secrecy), but they are distinctly *non-rival*. Because of that, there is a big incentive to free-ride on other people's ideas – which is a major reason why governments intervene very strongly in the support of scientific activities. We have already looked at stories based on externalities (from learning-by-doing) and specialisation. We have also seen how they give rise to a wedge between the decentralised equilibrium and the optimal rate of growth.

In this chapter, we will take this discussion further by properly studying models where technological change emerges endogenously, through firms purposefully pursuing innovation. This is not only for the pure pleasure of solving models – though that can also be true, if you are so inclined! In fact, we will be able to see how the incentives to innovate interplay with market structure. This in turn opens a window into how the links between policy domains such as market competition, intellectual property rights, or openness to trade are fundamentally related to economic growth. We will also see that it may be the case (perhaps surprisingly) that technological innovation – and, hence economic growth – may be too fast from a social welfare perspective.

There are two ways of modelling innovation: one where innovation creates additional varieties, and another where new products sweep away previous versions in a so-called quality ladder. In the product variety model, innovation introduces a new variety but it does not (fully) displace older alternatives, like introducing a new car model or a new type of breakfast cereal. This is very much along the lines of

How to cite this book chapter:
Campante, F., Sturzenegger, F. and Velasco, A. 2021. *Advanced Macroeconomics: An Easy Guide.*
    Ch. 6. 'Endogenous growth models II: Technological change', pp. 69–86. London: LSE Press.
    DOI: https://doi.org/10.31389/lsepress.ame.f License: CC-BY-NC 4.0.

the model of specialisation that we have already seen (and to which we will return later in the chapter). In the quality ladder approach (also known as the Schumpeterian model), a new variety is simply better than old versions of the same thing and displaces it fully. (Schumpeter famously talked about firms engaging in "creative destruction" – this is what gives this approach its name.) Examples we face everyday: typewriters wiped out by word-processing computer software; the USB keys phasing out the older 5.4-inch diskette, and in turn later being displaced by cloud storage; VCRs displaced by DVD players, and eventually by online streaming; lots of different gadgets being killed by smartphones, and so on. We will develop two standard models of innovation, one for each version, and discuss some of the most important among their many implications for policy.

6.1 | Modelling innovation as product specialisation

Following up on the previous chapter, we develop a full-fledged model of innovation through the development of new product varieties. It highlights a few important points: the role of monopoly profits in spurring the pursuit of innovation by firms, and the presence of scale effects (larger economies grow faster).

We start with this version because it will be familiar from the previous chapter. It is the model of innovation through specialisation, from Romer (1990). While we then left unspecified the process through which innovation takes place – where did the new varieties come from, after all? – we will now take a direct look at that.

Let's consider a slightly different version of the production function we posited then

$$Y(X) = \left[\int_0^M X(i)^\alpha \, di \right]^{\frac{1}{\alpha}},$$ (6.1)

where again $X(i)$ stands for the amount of intermediate input of variety i, and M is the range of varieties that are currently available. Recall that we treat each sector i as infinitesimally small within a continuum of sectors. We are leaving aside the role of labour in producing final output for simplicity. Instead, we will assume that labour is used in the production of intermediate inputs on a one-for-one basis so that $X(i)$ also stands for the amount of labour used to produce that amount of intermediate input.[1]

How are new varieties developed? First of all, we must devote resources to producing new varieties – think about this as the resources used in the R&D sector. To be more concrete, let's say we need workers in the R&D sector, which we will denote as Z_M, and workers to produce intermediate inputs, which we will label Z to follow the notation from the previous chapter, where we had (somewhat vaguely) used that designation for the total resources devoted to intermediate inputs. It follows from this that $Z \equiv \int_0^M X(i)di$. To pin down the equilibrium, we will posit a labour market-clearing condition: $Z_M + Z = L$, the total labour force in the economy, which we will assume constant. We will also take Z_M (and, hence, Z) to be constant.[2] We will assume that the production of new varieties is linear in R&D labour, and proportional to the existing stock of varieties, according to

$$\dot{M}_t = BZ_M M_t.$$ (6.2)

Note also that we can use in (6.1) the fact that each symmetric intermediate sector in equilibrium will use $X(i) = \bar{X} = \frac{Z}{M}$, given the definition of Z, just as in the previous chapter. This means we can write

$Y_t = M^{\frac{1-\alpha}{\alpha}} Z$. Given that Z is constant, it follows that Y grows at $\frac{1-\alpha}{\alpha}$ times the growth rate of M, and, hence (using (6.2)) the growth rate of Y is $\frac{1-\alpha}{\alpha} BZ_M$. It follows that, to figure out the growth rate of the economy, we need to figure out the amount of resources devoted to producing new varieties, Z_M. In short, just as in the previous chapter, economic growth comes from the amount of resources devoted to the R&D sector, which is what drives innovation.

So we need to figure out what determines Z_M. For that, we need to start by positing the market structure in this economy, in terms of the intermediate inputs, final output, and the production of varieties. On the first, we assume that each variety is produced by a monopolist that holds exclusive rights to it. The final output is then produced by competitive firms that take the price of inputs as given as well. What would one of these competitive firms do? They would try to minimise the cost of producing each unit of output at any given point in time. If $p(i)$ is the price of variety i of the intermediate input, this means choosing $X(i)$ to minimise:

$$\int_0^M p(i)X(i)\, di, \tag{6.3}$$

subject to $\left[\int_0^M X(i)^\alpha\, di \right]^{\frac{1}{\alpha}} = 1$, that is, the unit of final output. The FOC for each $X(i)$ is[3]

$$p(i) = \lambda X(i)^{\alpha-1}, \tag{6.4}$$

where λ is the corresponding Lagrange multiplier. This yields a downward-sloping demand curve for the monopolist producing intermediate input i:

$$X(i) = \left[\frac{\lambda}{p(i)} \right]^{\frac{1}{1-\alpha}}. \tag{6.5}$$

You will know from basic microeconomics – but can also easily check! – that this is a demand function with a constant elasticity equal to $\varepsilon \equiv \frac{1}{1-\alpha}$.

As for the R&D sector: there is free entry into the development of new varieties such that anyone can hire R&D workers, and take advantage of (6.2), without needing to compensate the creators of previous varieties. Free entry implies that firms will enter into the sector as long as it is possible to obtain positive profits. To determine the varieties that will emerge, we thus need to figure out what those profits are. It will take a few steps, but it will all make sense!

First, consider that if you create a new variety of the intermediate input, you get perpetual monopoly rights to its production. A profit-maximising monopolist facing a demand curve with constant elasticity ε will choose to charge a price equal to $\frac{\varepsilon}{\varepsilon-1}$ times the marginal cost, which in our case translates into the marginal cost divided by α. Since you have to use one worker to produce one unit of the intermediate input, the marginal cost is equal to the wage, and the profit per unit will be given by $\left[\frac{w_t}{\alpha} - w_t \right] = \frac{1-\alpha}{\alpha} w_t$.

But how many units will the monopolist sell or, in other words, what is $X(i)$? As we have indicated above, given the symmetry of the model, where all varieties face the same demand, we can forget about the i label and write $X(i) = \bar{X} = \frac{Z}{M}$. We can thus write the monopolist's profit at any given point in time:

$$\pi_t = \frac{1-\alpha}{\alpha} \frac{L - Z_M}{M_t} w_t. \tag{6.6}$$

So we now see that profits will be a function of Z_M, but we need to find the present discounted value of the flow of profits, and for that we need the interest rate.

That's where we use the NGM, for which the solution is given by (you guessed it) the Euler equation. We can write the interest rate as a function of the growth rate of consumption, namely (with logarithmic utility),

$$r_t = \frac{\dot{c}_t}{c_t} + \rho. \tag{6.7}$$

But consumption must grow at the same rate of output, since all output is consumed in this model. Hence,

$$r_t = \frac{1-\alpha}{\alpha} B Z_M + \rho, \tag{6.8}$$

which is constant. The present value of profits is thus given by[4]

$$\Pi_t = \frac{\frac{1-\alpha}{\alpha} \frac{L-Z_M}{M_t} w_t}{B Z_M + \rho}. \tag{6.9}$$

The free-entry (zero profit) condition requires that the present discounted value of the flow of profits be equal to the cost of creating an additional variety, which (using (6.2)) is given by $\frac{w_t}{BM_t}$. In sum:

$$\frac{\frac{1-\alpha}{\alpha} \frac{L-Z_M}{M_t} w_t}{B Z_M + \rho} = \frac{w_t}{BM_t}. \tag{6.10}$$

Solving this for Z_M allows us to pin down

$$Z_M = (1-\alpha)L - \frac{\alpha\rho}{B}. \tag{6.11}$$

This gives us, at long last, the endogenous growth rate of output:

$$\frac{\dot{Y}_t}{Y_t} = \frac{(1-\alpha)^2}{\alpha} BL - (1-\alpha)\rho, \tag{6.12}$$

again using the fact that the growth rate of Y is $\frac{1-\alpha}{\alpha} B Z_M$.

An increase in the productivity of innovation (B) would lead to a higher growth rate, and, as before, the same would be true for a decrease in the discount rate. So far, so predictable. More importantly, the model shows *scale effects*, as a higher L leads to higher innovation. The intuition is that scale plays a two-fold role, on the supply and on the demand side for ideas. On the one hand, L affects the number of workers in the R&D sector and, as described in (6.2), this increases the production of new varieties. In short, more people means more ideas, which leads to more growth. But L also affects the demand for final output and, hence, for new varieties. This is why profits also depend on the scale of the economy, as can be seen by substituting (6.11) into (6.9). In short, a larger market size allows for bigger profits, and bigger profits make innovation more attractive. This is fundamentally related to the presence of increasing returns. As per the last chapter: developing ideas (new varieties) is a fixed cost in production, and a larger market allows that fixed cost to be further diluted, thereby increasing profits.

The model also brings to the forefront the role of competition, or lack thereof. Innovation is fueled by monopoly profits obtained by the firms that develop new varieties. There is competition in the entry to innovation, of course, which ultimately brings profits to zero once you account for innovation costs. Still, in the absence of monopoly profits in the production of intermediate inputs, there is no incentive to innovate. This immediately highlights the role of policies related to competition and property rights.

We will return to these central insights of endogenous growth models later in the chapter. (Spoiler alert: things are a bit more subtle than in the basic model...)

6.2 | Modelling innovation in quality ladders

We develop a model of innovation through quality ladders, capturing the creative destruction feature of innovation. Besides a similar role as before for scale and monopoly profits as drivers of technological progress and growth, there is now the possibility of excessive growth. Innovation effort may driven by the possibility of replacing existing monopolies and reaping their profits, even when the social payoff of the innovation is small.

The Schumpeterian approach to modelling innovation is associated with Aghion and Howitt (1990) and Grossman and Helpman (1991). We will follow the latter in our discussion.

The model has a continuum of industries $j \in [0, 1]$. Unlike in the previous model, the number of sectors is now fixed, but each of them produces a good with infinite potential varieties. We will think of these varieties as representing different qualities of the product, ordered in a quality ladder. Let's call $q_m(j)$ the quality m of variety j. The (discrete) jumps in quality have size $\lambda > 1$, which we assume exogenous and common to all products so that $q_m(j) = \lambda q_{m-1}(j)$.

The representative consumer has the following expected utility:

$$u_t = \int_0^\infty e^{-\rho t} \left(\int_0^1 \log(\sum_m q_m(j) \, x_m(j, t)) dj \right) dt,$$

where ρ is the discount factor, and $x_m(j, t)$ is the quantity of variety j (with quality m) consumed in period t. The consumer derives (log) utility from each of the goods and, within each good, preferences are linear. This means that any two varieties are perfect substitutes, which in turn means that the consumer will allocate all their spending on this good to the variety that provides the lowest quality-adjusted cost. As cost of production will be the same in equilibrium, this entails that only the highest-quality variety will be used. Yet, the consumer has the same preferences across varieties, often referred to as Dixit-Stiglitz preferences. They imply that the consumer will allocate their spending equally across varieties, which will come in handy below when solving the model. We call the term $D = \int_0^1 \log \sum_m q_m(j) \, x_m(j, t) dj$ the period demand for goods.

All of this can be summarised as follows: If we denote by $E(t)$ the total amount spent in period t, in all goods put together, the solution to the consumer problem implies

$$x_{mt}(j) = \begin{cases} \frac{E(t)}{p_m(j,t)} & \text{if } \frac{q_m(j)}{p_m(j,t)} = \max\{\frac{q_n(j)}{p_n(j,t)}\} \; \forall n\} \\ 0 & \text{if } \frac{q_m(j)}{p_m(j,t)} \neq \max\{\frac{q_n(j)}{p_n(j,t)}\} \; \forall n\}. \end{cases}$$

In words, you spend the same amount on each good, and within each good, only on the highest-quality variety. We can set $E(t)$ equal to one (namely, we choose aggregate consumption to be the numeraire) for simplicity of notation.

The structure of demand provides a fairly straightforward framework for competition. On the one hand, there is monopolistic competition across industries. Within industry, however, competition is fierce because products are perfect substitutes, and firms engage in Bertrand competition with the lowest (quality-adjusted) price taking the whole market. A useful way to think about this is to assume firms have monopoly rights (say, because of patent protection) over their varieties. Thus, only they can produce their variety, but innovators do know the technology so that if they innovate they do so relative to the state-of-the-art producer. This splits the market between state-of-the-art (leading) firms and follower firms, all trying to develop a new highest-quality variety that allows them to dominate the market.

We assume the production function of quality m in industry j to be such that one unit of labour is required to produce one unit of the good. The cost function is trivially

$$c_m(j) = w x_m(j),$$

with w being the wage rate. It follows that the minimum price required to produce is w, and, at this price, profits are driven to zero. If followers' price their product at w, the best response for the leading firm is to charge ever-so-slightly below λw, as consumers would still be willing to pay up to that amount given the quality adjustment. For practical purposes, we assume that price to be equal to λw, and this will be common to all industries. Using $E(t) = 1$, profits are trivially given by

$$\pi(t) = x_m(j, t)p_m(j, t) - c_m(j, t) = 1 - \frac{w}{\lambda w} = 1 - \frac{1}{\lambda} = 1 - \delta.$$

where $\delta = 1/\lambda$.

The innovation process is modelled as follows. Firms invest resources, with intensity i for a period dt, to obtain a probability $i\,dt$ of discovering a new quality for the product, and become the state-of-the-art firm. To produce intensity i we assume the firm needs α units of labour with cost $w\alpha$.

Let us think about the incentives to innovate, for the different types of firms. First, note that the state-of-the-art firm has no incentive to innovate. Why so? Intuitively, by investing in R&D the firm has a probability of a quality jump that allows it to set its price at $\lambda^2 w$. This corresponds to an increase in profit of $\frac{\lambda-1}{\lambda^2}$. However, this is smaller than the increase in benefits for followers, for whom profits move from zero to $(1-1/\lambda)$. In equilibrium, the cost of resources is such that only followers will be able to finance the cost of investment, as they outcompete the state-of-the-art firm for resources, and thus make the cost of capital too high for the latter to turn an expected profit. (Do we really think that leading firms do not invest in innovation? We will return to that later on.)

How about followers? If a follower is successful in developing a better variety, it will obtain a flow of profits in the future. We will denote the present discounted value for the firm as V, which of course will need to consider the fact that the firm will eventually lose its edge because of future innovations. So the firm will invest in R&D if the expected value of innovation is bigger than the cost, that is if $Vidt \geq w\alpha idt$ or $V \geq w\alpha$. In an equilibrium with free entry, we must have $V = w\alpha$.

But what is V, that is, the value of this equity? In equilibrium, it is easy to see that

$$V = \frac{(1 - \delta)}{i + \rho}. \tag{6.13}$$

The value of the firm is the discounted value of profits, as usual. But here the discounting has two components: the familiar discount rate, capturing time preferences, and the rate at which innovation may displace this producer.[5]

The final equation that closes the model is the labour market condition. Similar to the model in the previous section, equilibrium in the labour market requires

$$\alpha i + \frac{\delta}{w} = L, \tag{6.14}$$

which means that the labour demand in R&D (αi) plus in production ($\frac{\delta}{w}$) equals the supply of labour.[6]

Equations (6.13) and (6.14), plus the condition that $V = w\alpha$, allow us to solve for the rate of innovation

$$i = (1 - \delta)\frac{L}{\alpha} - \delta\rho. \tag{6.15}$$

Note that innovation is larger the more patient people are, since innovation is something that pays off in the future. It also increases in how efficient the innovation process is – both in terms of the jump it produces and of the cost it takes to obtain the breakthrough. Finally, we once again see scale effects: larger L means larger incentives to innovation. In other words, larger markets foster innovation for the same reasons as in the product-variety model from the previous section . Even though the process of innovation is discrete, by the law of large numbers the process smooths out in the aggregate. This means that the growth rate of consumption is $g = i \log \lambda$, which is the growth rate delivered by the model.

What are the implications for welfare? We know from our previous discussion that, in this world with increasing returns and monopolistic behaviour, there can be a wedge between social optimum and market outcomes. But how does that play out here? To answer this question, we can distinguish three effects. First, there is the effect of innovation on consumption, which we can call the *consumer surplus* effect: more innovation produces more quality, which makes consumption cheaper. Second, there is an effect on future innovators, which we can call the *intertemporal spillover* effect: future innovations will occur relative to existing technology, so, by moving the technological frontier, innovation generates additional future benefits. There is, however, a third effect that is negative on current producers that become obsolete, and whose profits evaporate as a result. We call this the *business stealing* effect.

When we put all of this together, a surprising result emerges: the model can deliver a rate of innovation (and growth) that is higher than the social optimum. To see this, imagine that λ is very close to 1, but still larger, such that $\delta = 1 - v$ for a small but positive v. In other words, there is very little social benefit to innovation. However, followers still benefit from innovation because displacing the incumbent (even by a tiny sliver of a margin) gives them monopoly profits. From (6.15) it is clear that, for any given v, L (and hence profits) can be large enough that we will have innovation although the social value is essentially not there. The divergence between the social and private value, because of the business stealing effect, is what delivers this result.

6.3 | Policy implications

We show how endogenous growth models allow us to think about many policy issues, such as imitation, competition, and market size.

As it turns out, these models of technological change enable us to study a whole host of policy issues as they affect economic growth. Let us consider issues related to distance to the technological frontier, competition policy, and scale effects.

6.3.1 | Distance to the technological frontier and innovation

Put yourself in the role of a policy-maker trying to think about how to foster technological progress and growth. Our models have focused on (cutting-edge) innovation, but there is another way of improving technology: just copy what others have developed elsewhere. What are the implications of that possibility for policy?

To organise our ideas, let us consider a reduced-form, discrete-time setting that captures the flavour of a Schumpeterian model, following Aghion and Howitt (2006). We have an economy with many sectors, indexed by i, each of which has a technology described by

$$Y_{it} = A_{it}^{1-\alpha} K_{it}^{\alpha}, \qquad (6.16)$$

where A_{it} is the productivity attained by the most recent technology in industry i at time t, and K_{it} is the amount of capital invested in that sector. If we assume that all sectors are identical *ex ante*, aggregate output (which is the sum of Y_{it}'s) will be given by

$$Y_t = A_t^{1-\alpha} K_t^{\alpha}, \qquad (6.17)$$

where A_t is the unweighted sum of A_{it}'s.[7] The Solow model tells us that the long-run growth rate of this economy will be given by the growth rate of A_t. But how is it determined? Following the ideas in the previous section, we assume that, in each sector, only the producer with the most productive technology will be able to stay in business. Now assume that a successful innovator in sector i improves the parameter A_{it}; they will thus be able to displace the previous innovator and become a monopolist in that sector, until another innovator comes along to displace them. This is the creative destruction we have examined.

Now consider a given sector in a given country. A technological improvement in this context can be a new cutting-edge technology that improves on the existing knowledge available in the global economy. Or, more humbly, it can be the adoption of a best practice that is already available some-where else in the globe. We will distinguish between these two cases by calling them leading-edge and implementation innovation, respectively. As before, leading-edge innovation implies that the innova-tor obtains a new productivity parameter that is a multiple λ of the previous technology in use in that sector. Implementation, in contrast, implies catching up to a global technology frontier, described by $\bar{A}_t$. We denote μ_n and μ_m the frequency with which leading-edge and implementation innovations take place in that country, as a reduced-form approach of capturing the mechanics from the previous section.

It follows that the change in aggregate productivity will be given by

$$A_{t+1} - A_t = \mu_n \lambda A_t + \mu_m \bar{A}_t + (1 - \mu_n - \mu_m)A_t - A_t = \mu_n(\lambda - 1)A_t + \mu_m(\bar{A}_t - A_t). \qquad (6.18)$$

The growth rate will be

$$g = \frac{A_{t+1} - A_t}{A_t} = \mu_n(\lambda - 1) + \mu_m(a_t - 1), \qquad (6.19)$$

where $a_t \equiv \frac{\bar{A}_t}{A_t}$ measures the country's average distance to the global technological frontier.

Here's the crucial insight from this simple framework: growth depends on how close the country is to the technological frontier. Given a certain frequency of innovations, being far from the frontier will lead to faster growth since there is room for greater jumps in productivity – the "advantages of backwardness", so to speak, benefit the imitators. The distance to the frontier also affects the mix of innovation that is more growth-enhancing. A country that is far from the frontier will be better off investing more in implementation than another country that is closer to the frontier. This has far-reaching consequences in terms of growth policy. The policies and institutions that foster leading-edge innovation need not be the same as those that foster implementation (see Acemoglu et al. 2006). For instance, think about investment in primary education versus investment in tertiary education, or the role of intellectual property rights protection.[8]

6.3.2 | Competition and innovation

We have seen in the previous sections that the incentive to innovate depends on firms' ability to keep the profits generated by innovation, as captured by the monopoly power innovators acquire. As we pointed out, this formalises an important message regarding the role of monopolies. While monopolies are inefficient in a static context, they are crucial for economic growth.[9] This tradeoff is precisely what lies behind intellectual property rights and the patent system, as had already been noted by Thomas Jefferson in the late 1700s.[10] But is competition always inimical to growth?

The modern Schumpeterian view is more subtle than that. Aghion and coauthors have shown that the relationship between innovation and competition is more complex. The key is that, in addition to this *appropriability* effect, there is also an *escape competition* effect. Increased competition may lead to a greater incentive to innovate as firms will try to move ahead and reap some monopoly profits. In other words, while competition decreases the monopoly rents enjoyed by an innovator, it may decrease the profits of a non-innovator by even more. The overall effect of competition on innovation will critically depend on the nature of where the firms are relative to the frontier. In sectors where competition is neck-and-neck, the escape competition effect is strong. However, if firms are far behind, competition discourages innovation because there is little profit to be made from catching up with the leaders. (Note that this escape competition effect can justify innovation by the leading firms, unlike in the most basic model. In other words, innovation is not simply done by outsiders!)

A similar effect emerges as a result of competition by firms that did not exist previously, namely entrants. We can see that in a simple extension of the reduced-form model above, now focusing on leading-edge innovation. Assume the incumbent monopolist in sector i earns profits equal to

$$\pi_{it} = \gamma A_{it}.$$

In every sector the probability of a potential entrant appearing is p, which is also our measure of entry threat. We focus on technologically advanced entry. Accordingly, each potential entrant arrives with the leading-edge technology parameter $\bar{A}_t$, which grows by the factor λ with certainty each period. If the incumbent is also on the leading edge, with $A_{it} = \bar{A}_t$, then we assume he can use a first-mover advantage to block entry and retain his monopoly. But if he is behind the leading edge, with $A_{it} < \bar{A}_t$, then entry will occur, Bertrand competition will ensue, and the technologically-dominated incumbent will be eliminated and replaced by the entrant.

The effect of entry threat on incumbent innovation will depend on the marginal benefit v_{it}, which the incumbent expects to receive from an innovation. Consider first an incumbent who was on the frontier last period. If they innovate then they will remain on the frontier, and hence will be immune to entry. Their profit will then be $\gamma \bar{A}_t$. If they fail to innovate then with probability p they will be eliminated by entry and earn zero profit, while, with probability $1 - p$, they will survive as the incumbent earning a profit of $\gamma \bar{A}_{t-1}$. The expected marginal benefit of an innovation to this firm is the difference between the profit they will earn with certainty if they innovate and the expected profit they will earn if not:

$$v_{it} = [\lambda - (1-p)]\gamma \bar{A}_{t-1}.$$

Since v_{it} depends positively on the entry threat p, an increase in entry threat will induce this incumbent to spend more on innovating and, hence, to innovate with a larger probability. Intuitively, a firm close to the frontier responds to increased entry threat by innovating more in order to escape the threat.

Next consider an incumbent who was behind the frontier last period, and who will therefore remain behind the frontier even if they manage to innovate, since the frontier will also advance by the factor λ. For this firm, profits will be zero if entry occurs, whether they innovate or not, because they cannot catch up with the frontier. Thus their expected marginal benefit of an innovation will be

$$v_{it} = (1-p)(\lambda - 1)\gamma A_{i,t-1}.$$

The expected benefit is thus a profit gain that will be realised with probability $(1-p)$, the probability that no potential entrant shows up. Since in this case v_{it} depends negatively on the entry threat p, therefore an increase in entry threat will induce the firm to spend less on innovating. Intuitively, the firm that starts far behind the frontier is discouraged from innovating by an increased entry threat because they are unable to prevent the entrant from destroying the value of their innovation if one happens to show up.

The theory generates the following predictions:

1. Entry and entry threat enhance innovation and productivity growth among incumbents in sectors or countries that are initially close to the technological frontier, as the escape entry effect dominates in that case.
2. Entry and entry threat reduce innovation and productivity growth among incumbents in sectors or countries that are far below the frontier, as the discouragement effect dominates in that case.
3. Entry and entry threat enhance average productivity growth among incumbent firms when the threat has exceeded some threshold, but reduce average productivity growth among incumbents below that threshold. This is because as the probability p measuring the threat approaches unity, then almost all incumbents will be on the frontier, having either innovated or entered last period, and firms near the frontier respond to a further increase in p by innovating more frequently.
4. Entry (and therefore, turnover) is growth-enhancing overall in the short run, because even in those sectors where incumbent innovation is discouraged by the threat of entry, the entrants themselves will raise productivity by implementing a frontier technology.

Figure 6.1, taken from Aghion et al. (2009), provides empirical support for the claim. The graph shows data for UK industries at the four-digit level. Firms are split as those close to the frontier and those away from the frontier (below the sample median for that industry). The level of competition is measured by the rate of foreign firm entry which is measured in the horizontal axis. The vertical axis shows subsequent productivity growth for domestic incumbents. As can be seen, close to the frontier entry accelerates growth. Further away it tends to slow it down.

Figure 6.1   Entry effects, from Aghion et al. (2009)

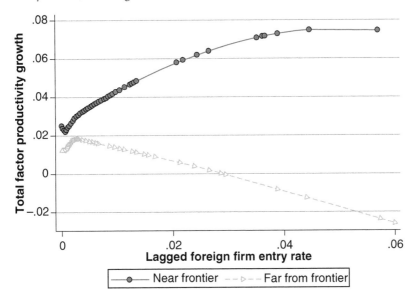

Interest groups as barriers to innovation

There's another way in which monopolies can affect innovation. Imagine that monopolists use some of their profits to actually block the entry of new firms with better technologies – say, by paying off regulators to bar such entry. In fact, it may be a better deal than trying to come up with innovations! If that's the case, then monopoly profits may actually facilitate the imposition of these barriers, by giving these monopolists more resources to invest in erecting barriers.

Monopolies are particularly dangerous in this regard, because they tend to be better able to act on behalf of their interests. Mancur Olson's *The Logic of Collective Action* Olson (2009) argues that policy is a recurrent conflict between the objectives of concentrated interest groups and those of the general public, for which benefits and costs are typically diffused. According to Olson, the general public has less ability to organise collective action because each actor has less at stake, at least relative to concentrated interest groups, which thus have the upper hand when designing policy. In short, monopolies have an advantage in organising and influencing policy. One implication of this logic is that the seeds of the decline of an economy are contained in its early rise: innovation generates rents that help the development of special-interest lobbies that can then block innovation. This is the argument raised by Mancur Olson, again, in his 1983 book *The Rise and Decline of Nations* Olson (1983).

More recently, the theme of incumbents blocking innovation and development has been taken up by other authors. Parente and Prescott (1999) develop a model capturing this idea, and argue that the effects can be quantitatively large. Restricting the model so that it is consistent with a number of observations between rich and poor countries, they find that eliminating monopoly rights would increase GDP by roughly a factor of 3! Similarly, in their the popular book *Why Nations Fail*,

Acemoglu and Robinson (2012) argue, with evidence from a tour de force through history and across every continent, that the typical outcome is that countries fail to develop because incumbents block innovation and disruption.

6.3.3 | Scale effects

The models of the previous section delivered a specific but fundamental result: *scale effects*. In other words, they predict that the growth rates will increase with the size of the population or markets. Intuitively, as we discussed, there are two sides to this coin. On the supply side, if growth depends on ideas, and ideas are produced by people, having more people means having more ideas. On the demand side, ideas are a fixed cost – once you produce a blueprint for a flying car, you can produce an arbitrary amount of flying cars using the same blueprint – and having a larger market enables one to further dilute that fixed cost.

The big question is: do the data support that prediction? Kremer (1993) argues that over the (very) long run of history the predictions of a model with scale effects are verified. He does so by considering what scale effects imply for population growth, which is determined endogenously in his model: population growth is increasing in population. He goes on to test this by checking that, using data from 1,000,000 B.C. to 1990, it does seem to be the case that population growth increases with population size. He also shows that, comparing regions that are isolated from each other (e.g. the continents over pre-modern history), those with greater population displayed faster technological progress.

This suggests that scale effects are present on a global scale, but that remains controversial. For instance, Jones (1995) argues that the data does not support the function in (6.2). For example, the number of scientists involved in R&D grew manifold in the post-World War II period without an increase in the rate of productivity growth. Instead, he argues that the evidence backs a modified version of the innovation production function, in which we would adapt (6.2) to look like this:

$$\frac{\dot{M}}{M} = B Z_M M^{-\beta}, \tag{6.20}$$

with $\beta > 0$. This means that ideas have a diminishing return as you need more people to generate the same rate of innovation. In a world like this, research may deliver a constant rate of innovation (such as the so-called Moore's law on the evolution of the processing capability of computers), but only due to substantially more resources devoted to the activity. This model leads to growth without scale effects, which Jones (1995) refers to as semi-endogenous growth.

It is also worth thinking about what scale effects mean for individual countries. Even if there are scale effects for the global economy, it seems quite obvious that they aren't really there for individual countries: it's not as if Denmark has grown that much slower than the U.S., relative to the enormous difference in size of the two economies. This can be for two reasons. First, countries are not fully isolated from each other, so the benefits of scale leak across borders. Put simply, Danish firms can have access to the U.S. market (and beyond) via trade. This immediately generates a potential connection between trade policy and growth, operating via scale effects. A second reason, on the flip-side, is that countries are not fully integrated domestically, i.e. there are internal barriers to trade that prevent countries from benefiting from their size. A paper by Ramondo et al. (2016) investigates the two possibilities, calibrating a model where countries are divided into regions, and find that the second point is a lot more important in explaining why the Denmarks of the world aren't a lot poorer than the Indias and Chinas and U.S.

6.4 | The future of growth

Are we headed to unprecedented growth? Or to stagnation?

The forces highlighted in these models of innovation, and their policy implications, have huge consequences for what we think will happen in the future when it comes to economic growth. There is a case for optimism, but also for its opposite.

Consider the first. If scale effects are present on a global scale, then as the world gets bigger growth will be faster, not the other way around. To see this, it is worth looking at the Kremer (1993) model in more detail, in a slightly simplified version. Consider the production function in

$$Y = Ap^{\alpha} T^{1-\alpha} = Ap^{\alpha}, \tag{6.21}$$

where p is population and T is land which is available in fixed supply which, for simplicity, we will assume is equal to 1. We can rewrite it as

$$y = Ap^{\alpha-1}. \tag{6.22}$$

The population dynamics have a Malthusian feature in the sense that they revert to a steady state that is sustainable given the technology. In other words, population adjusts to technology so that output per capita remains at subsistence level; as in the Malthusian framework, all productivity gains translate into a larger population, not into higher standards of living. (This is usually thought of as a good description of the pre-industrial era, as we will discuss in detail in Chapter 10.)

$$p = \left(\frac{\bar{y}}{A}\right)^{\frac{1}{\alpha-1}}. \tag{6.23}$$

Critically, the scale effects come into the picture via the assumption that

$$\frac{\dot{A}}{A} = pg. \tag{6.24}$$

i.e. the rate of technological progress is a function of world population, along the lines of the endogenous growth models we have seen. We can now solve for the dynamics of population, using (6.23) and then (6.24):

$$\ln p = \left(\frac{1}{\alpha-1}\right) [\ln \bar{y} - \ln A], \tag{6.25}$$

$$\frac{\dot{p}}{p} = -\left(\frac{1}{\alpha-1}\right) \frac{\dot{A}}{A} = \frac{1}{1-\alpha} \frac{\dot{A}}{A} = \frac{1}{1-\alpha} pg, \tag{6.26}$$

$$\frac{\dot{p}}{p} = \left(\frac{g}{1-\alpha}\right) p. \tag{6.27}$$

In other words, population growth is increasing in population – which means that growth is explosive!

If true, this has enormous consequences for what we would expect growth to be in the future. For instance, if we think that both China and India have recently become much more deeply integrated into the world economy, can you imagine how many ideas these billions of people can come up with?

Can you fathom how much money there is to be made in developing new ideas and selling the resulting output to these billions of people? China and India's integration into the world economy is an added boost to growth prospects on a global scale. In fact, as growth accelerates we may reach a point where machines take over in the accumulation of knowledge, making growth explode without bounds. (You may have heard of this being described as the singularity point.[11])

Yet others have argued that, to the contrary, we are looking at a future of stagnation. Gordon (2018) argues that technological progress has so far relied on three main waves of innovation: the first industrial revolution (steam engine, cotton spinning, and railroads), the second industrial revolution (electricity, internal combustion engine, and running water), and the third industrial revolution (computers and the internet). He argues that the fruit of those waves has been reaped, and mentions a number of factors that may lead to lower future growth:

- The end of the demographic dividend. The process of absorption of women in the labour forces has ended, and the decline in birth rates further pushes down the growth of the labour force.
- Growth in education achievements also has been steadily declining as all the population achieves a minimum standard.
- The scope for growth via imitation falls as previous imitators reach the technological frontier.
- Climate change will require a reduction in future growth.

Some of these factors apply to a greater or lesser degree to other countries. China, for example, also faces a population challenge as its population ages at an unheard-of rate, and education levels have universally improved. At the same time, one might argue that the scope for imitation remains huge. Only assuming that all countries below average world income attain average world income in the next 100 years will deliver an extra 2% growth in world GDP for the next 100 years. Time will tell, we suppose.

6.5 | What have we learned?

In this chapter we presented models of technological innovation, but including technology as a factor of production implies increasing returns to scale, meaning that innovation has to be paid for in some way that cannot be simply via its marginal product. We tackled the issue in three steps. First, we modelled innovation as an increase in the complexity of the production function through a larger number of varieties. Second, as a process of improved quality in varieties which displace previous versions, we developed a framework more akin to Schumpeter's idea of creative destruction. We saw that these two versions both highlight the importance of non-competitive behaviour, with monopoly profits driving the incentive to innovation. They also showcase scale effects: bigger market size implies faster innovation and growth because of the supply and demand for new ideas. In addition, the Schumpeterian version highlighted that there can be too much innovation and growth from a social perspective, as some of the incentive to innovate for private firms is simply to steal monopoly rents from incumbents without a counterpart in social welfare.

We then went over a number of policy issues, through the lens of the models of endogenous growth based on innovation. We saw that distance to the technological frontier can affect the incentives to innovate or imitate. We also saw that the relationship between competition and growth is more subtle than the basic model may indicate. Competition stimulates innovation for firms close to the frontier, but discourages innovation for firms farther away from the frontier. We then went over the debate on the extent to which scale effects matter in practice, presenting a number of arguments on both directions. Finally, we briefly discussed an ongoing debate between those who believe growth will falter and those who think that growth will accelerate.

6.6 | What next?

Acemoglu's (2009) textbook on economic growth provides further details and nuances on the issues discussed here. You can also follow Acemoglu's more recent work on automation. How would the world look if growth accelerates and, for example, robots become ubiquitous? Will this lead to pervasive unemployment? Will this lead to increased income inequality? This has been explored in Acemoglu and Restrepo (2017) and Acemoglu and Restrepo (2020).

In terms of innovation models, an excellent source is the classic Grossman and Helpman (1991) book. In our description of their models we have focused on the steady states, whereas there you will find a full description of the dynamics of the models discussed here. They also go into a lot more detail on the links between trade and economic growth, well beyond our discussion on market size and protection. Similarly, the book by Aghion and Howitt (2008) is a great starting point for further exploration of the Schumpeterian approach that the authors pioneered, and especially on the subtle interplay between competition and innovation. A more recent book by Aghion et al. (2021) also covers and develops these ideas in highly accessible fashion.

If you want more on the debate on the future of growth, the book by Gordon (2017) is a good starting point. That discussion is also the bread-and-butter of futurologists, among which Harari (2018) is a good example. It is interesting to read these books through the lenses of the endogenous growth models we have seen here.

Notes

[1] You may also notice the new exponent $\frac{1}{\alpha}$, which will afford notational simplicity as we pursue the algebra.

[2] This happens to be a property of the equilibrium of this model, and not an assumption, but we will simply impose it here for simplicity.

[3] To see this, note that differentiating the term $\left[\int_0^M X(i)^\alpha \, di\right]^{\frac{1}{\alpha}}$ with respect to $X(i)$ yields $X(i)^{\alpha-1}$ $\left[\int_0^M X(i)^\alpha \, di\right]^{\frac{1-\alpha}{\alpha}}$, and $\left[\int_0^M X(i)^\alpha \, di\right]^{\frac{1-\alpha}{\alpha}} = 1$ because of our normalisation to unit output.

[4] Why is the denominator $BZ_M + \rho$ the appropriate discount rate by which to divide π_t? If π_t were constant, obtaining the present value of profits would require simply dividing it by the (constant) interest rate. But π_t is not constant: it grows at the rate at which $\frac{w_t}{M_t}$ grows. Since wages must in equilibrium grow at the rate of output, it follows that $\frac{w_t}{M_t}$ grows at the growth rate of output minus the growth rate of M_t: $\frac{1-2\alpha}{\alpha}BZ_M$. Subtracting this from the interest rate gives us the appropriate discount rate: $BZ_M + \rho$.

[5] We can use the consumer discount rate ρ because we assume firms are held in a diversified portfolio and there is no idiosyncratic risk.

[6] Labour demand in production follows from this: each sector uses one unit of labor per unit of the good being produced. With total expenditure normalized to one, it follows that they sell $x = \frac{1}{p} = \frac{1}{lambdaw} = \frac{\delta}{w}$ units each, which integrated between 0 and 1, for all sectors, yields the result.

[7] Not quite the sum, but close enough. For those of you who are more mathematically inclined: define $x_{it} \equiv \log X_{it}$ for any X, then from (6.16) you can write $y_{it} = (1 - \alpha)a_{it} + \alpha k_{it}$. Now assume the many sectors in the economy fall in the interval $[0, 1]$, and integrate y_{it} over that interval: $\int_0^1 y_{it}di = (1 - \alpha)\int_0^1 a_{it} + \alpha \int_0^1 k_{it} \Rightarrow y_t = (1 - \alpha)a_t + \alpha k_t$. Define $Y_t \equiv \exp(y_t)$, and (6.17) follows. In sum, (6.17) essentially defines $X_t = \exp\left(\left(\int_0^1 \log X_{it}di\right)\right)$ for any variable X. These are all monotonic transformations, so we are fine.

[8] Williams (2013) shows an interesting piece of evidence: gene sequences subject to IP protection by private firm Celera witnessed less subsequent scientific research and product development, relative to those sequenced by the public Human Genome Project.

[9] This is an insight that Schumpeter himself had pioneered in his book *Capitalism, Socialism and Democracy*, back in 1942. See Schumpeter (1942).

[10] See https://www.monticello.org/site/research-and-collections/patents.

[11] As in $\frac{1}{x}$ when it approaches 0.

References

Acemoglu, D. (2009). *Introduction to modern economic growth*. Princeton University Press.

Acemoglu, D., Aghion, P., & Zilibotti, F. (2006). Distance to frontier, selection, and economic growth. *Journal of the European Economic Association, 4*(1), 37–74.

Acemoglu, D. & Restrepo, P. (2017). Secular stagnation? The effect of aging on economic growth in the age of automation. *American Economic Review, 107*(5), 174–79.

Acemoglu, D. & Restrepo, P. (2020). Robots and jobs: Evidence from U.S. labor markets. *Journal of Political Economy, 128*(6), 2188–2244.

Acemoglu, D. & Robinson, J. A. (2012). *Why nations fail: The origins of power, prosperity, and poverty*. Currency.

Aghion, P., Blundell, R., Griffith, R., Howitt, P., & Prantl, S. (2009). The effects of entry on incumbent innovation and productivity. *The Review of Economics and Statistics, 91*(1), 20–32.

Aghion, P. & Howitt, P. (1990). *A model of growth through creative destruction*. National Bureau of Economic Research.

Aghion, P. & Howitt, P. (2006). Appropriate growth policy: A unifying framework. *Journal of the European Economic Association, 4*(2-3), 269–314.

Aghion, P. & Howitt, P. W. (2008). *The economics of growth*. MIT Press.

Gordon, R. J. (2017). *The rise and fall of American growth: The U.S. standard of living since the Civil War*. Princeton University Press.

Gordon, R. J. (2018). *Why has economic growth slowed when innovation appears to be accelerating?* National Bureau of Economic Research.

Grossman, G. M. & Helpman, E. (1991). *Innovation and growth in the global economy*. MIT Press.

Harari, Y. N. (2018). *21 lessons for the 21st century*. Random House.

Jones, C. I. (1995). R & d-based models of economic growth. *Journal of Political Economy, 103*(4), 759–784.

Kremer, M. (1993). Population growth and technological change: One million B.C. to 1990. *The Quarterly Journal of Economics, 108*(3), 681–716.

Olson, M. (1983). *The rise and decline of nations: Economic growth, stagflation, and social rigidities*. Yale University Press.

Olson, M. (2009). *The logic of collective action: Public goods and the theory of groups, second printing with a new preface and appendix.* Harvard University Press.

Parente, S. L. & Prescott, E. C. (1999). Monopoly rights: A barrier to riches. *American Economic Review, 89*(5), 1216–1233.

Ramondo, N., Rodríguez-Clare, A., & Saborío-Rodríguez, M. (2016). Trade, domestic frictions, and scale effects. *American Economic Review, 106*(10), 3159–84.

Romer, P. M. (1990). Endogenous technological change. *Journal of Political Economy, 98*(5, Part 2), S71–S102.

Schumpeter, J. A. (1942). Capitalism. *Socialism and democracy, 3,* 167.

Williams, H. L. (2013). Intellectual property rights and innovation: Evidence from the human genome. *Journal of Political Economy, 121*(1), 1–27.

CHAPTER 7

Proximate and fundamental causes of growth

Now let's talk a little bit about what the data say regarding economic growth. There is a very long line of research trying to empirically assess the determinants of growth – an area that is still very vibrant. In order to organise what this literature has to say, it is useful to start by distinguishing between what Acemoglu (2009) calls *proximate* and *fundamental* causes of economic growth. If we think of any generic production function $Y = F(\mathbf{X}, A)$, where $\mathbf{X}$ is a vector of inputs (capital, labour, human capital) and A captures productivity, we can attribute any increase in output to an increase in $\mathbf{X}$ or A. In that sense, the accumulation of physical capital, human capital, or technological progress generates growth, but we still want to learn why different societies choose different accumulation paths. We can thus think of these as *proximate* causes, but we want to be able to say something about the *fundamental* causes that determine those choices. Our survey of the empirical literature will address what economists have been able to say about each of those sets of causes.

7.1 | The proximate causes of economic growth

There are three basic empirical tools to assess the importance of proximate causes of growth (factor accumulation, productivity): growth accounting, regression-based approaches, and calibration. We briefly go over the advantages and pitfalls, and the message they deliver. Factor accumulation has significant explanatory power, but in the end productivity matters a lot.

The natural starting point for this investigation is our workhorse, the Neoclassical Growth Model (NGM). The basic question, to which we have already alluded, is: how well does the NGM do in explaining differences in income levels and in growth rates?[1]

Several methods have been devised and used to assess this question, and they can be broadly grouped into three classes: *growth accounting, growth regressions, and calibration.* Let us address each of these.

How to cite this book chapter:
Campante, F., Sturzenegger, F. and Velasco, A. 2021. *Advanced Macroeconomics: An Easy Guide.*
   Ch. 7. 'Proximate and fundamental causes of growth', pp. 87–112. London: LSE Press.
   DOI: https://doi.org/10.31389/lsepress.ame.g   License: CC-BY-NC 4.0.

7.1.1 | Growth accounting

This is another founding contribution of Robert Solow to the study of economic growth. Right after publishing his "Contribution to the Theory of Economic Growth" in 1956, he published another article in 1957 (Solow 1957) noting that an aggregate production function such as

$$Y(t) = A(t) F\left(K_t, L_t\right),$$ (7.1)

when combined with competitive factor markets, immediately yields a framework that lets us account for the (proximate) sources of economic growth. Take the derivative of the log of the production function with respect to time,

$$\frac{\dot{Y}}{Y} = \frac{\dot{A}}{A} + \frac{AF_K}{Y}\dot{K} + \frac{AF_L}{Y}\dot{L} \Rightarrow$$

$$\frac{\dot{Y}}{Y} = \frac{\dot{A}}{A} + \frac{AF_K K}{Y}\frac{\dot{K}}{K} + \frac{AF_L L}{Y}\frac{\dot{L}}{L} \Rightarrow$$

$$g_Y = g_A + \alpha_K g_K + \alpha_L g_L,$$ (7.2)

where g_X is the growth rate of variable X, and $\alpha_X \equiv \frac{AF_X X}{Y}$ is the elasticity of output with respect to factor X. This is an identity, but adding the assumption of competitive factor markets (i.e. factors are paid their marginal productivity) means that α_X is also the share of output that factor X obtains as payment for its services. Equation (7.2) then enables us to estimate the contributions of factor accumulation and technological progress (often referred to as total factor productivity (TFP)) to economic growth.

This is how it works in practice: from national accounts and other data sources, one can estimate the values of g_Y, g_K, g_L, α_K, and α_L; from (7.2) one can then back out the estimate for g_A.[2] (For this reason, g_A is widely referred to as the Solow residual.) Solow actually computed this for the U.S. economy, and reached the conclusion that the bulk of economic growth, about 2/3, could be attributed to the residual. Technological progress, and not factor accumulation, seems to be the key to economic growth.

Now, here is where a caveat is needed: g_A is calculated as a residual, not directly from measures of technological progress. It is the measure of our ignorance![3] More precisely, any underestimate of the increase in K or L (say, because it is hard to adjust for the increased quality of labour input), will result in an overestimate of g_A. As a result, a lot of effort has been devoted to better measure the contribution of the different factors of production.

In any event, this approach has been used over and over again. A particularly famous example was Alwyn Young's research in the early 1990s (1995), where he tried to understand the sources of the fantastic growth performance of the East Asian "tigers", Hong Kong, Singapore, South Korea, and Taiwan.[4] Most observers thought that this meant they must have achieved amazing rates of technological progress, but Young showed that their pace of factor accumulation had been astonishing. Rising rates of labour force participation (increasing L), skyrocketing rises in investment rates (from 10% of GDP in 1960 to 47% of GDP in 1984, in Singapore, for instance!) (increasing K), and increasing educational achievement (increasing H). Once all of this is accounted for, their Solow residuals were not particularly outliers compared to the rest of the world. (This was particularly the case for Singapore, and not so much for Hong Kong.) Why is this important? Well, we know from the NGM that factor accumulation cannot sustain growth in the long run! This seemed to predict that the tigers' performance would soon hit the snag of decreasing returns. Paul Krugman started to become famous beyond the circles of economics by explicitly predicting as much in a famous article in 1994 (Krugman 1994), which was interpreted by many as having predicted the 1997 East Asian crisis.

Of course, the tigers resumed growing fast soon after that crisis – have they since then picked up with productivity growth?

7.1.2 | Using calibration to explain income differences

We have seen in Chapter 2 that a major issue in growth empirics is to assess the relative importance of factor accumulation and productivity in explaining differences in growth rates and income levels. A different empirical approach to this question is *calibration*, in which differences in productivity are calculated using imputed parameter values that come from microeconomic evidence. As it is closely related to the methodology of growth accounting, we discuss it here. (We will see later, when discussing business cycle fluctuations, that calibration is one of the main tools of macroeconomics, when it comes to evaluating models empirically.)

One of the main contributions in this line of work is a paper by Hall and Jones (1999). In their approach, they consider a Cobb-Douglas production function for country i,

$$Y_i = K_i^\alpha \left(A_i H_i\right)^{1-\alpha}, \tag{7.3}$$

where K_i is the stock of physical capital, H_i is the amount of human capital-augmented labour and A_i is a labour-augmenting measure of productivity. If we know α, K_i and H_i, and given that we can observe Y, we can back out productivity A_i:

$$A_i = \frac{Y_i^{\frac{1}{1-\alpha}}}{K_i^{\frac{\alpha}{1-\alpha}} H_i}. \tag{7.4}$$

But how are we to know those?

For human capital-augmented labour, we start by assuming that labour L_i is homogeneous within a country, and each unit of it has been trained with E_i years of schooling. Human capital-augmented labour is given by

$$H_i = e^{\phi(E_i)} L_i. \tag{7.5}$$

The function $\phi(E)$ reflects the efficiency of a unit of labour with E years of schooling relative to one with no schooling ($\phi(0) = 0$). $\phi'(E)$ is the return to schooling estimated in a Mincerian wage regression (i.e. a regression of log wages on schooling and demographic controls, at the individual level). As such, we can run a Mincerian regression to obtain H_i. (Hall and Jones do so assuming that different types of schooling affect productivity differently.)

How about physical capital? We can compute it from data on past investment, using what is called the perpetual inventory method. If we have a depreciation rate δ, it follows that

$$K_{i,t} = (1-\delta)K_{i,t-1} + I_{i,t-1}. \tag{7.6}$$

It also follows that

$$K_{i,t} = (1-\delta)^t K_{i,0} + \sum_{s=0}^{t} I_{i,s}(1-\delta)^{t-s-1}. \tag{7.7}$$

If we have a complete series of investment, we can calculate this for any point in time. (We assume $\delta = 0.06$ for all countries). Since we don't, we assume that, before the start of our data series, investment had been growing at the same rate that we observe in the sample. By doing that, we can compute the $K_{i,0}$ and obtain our value for the capital stock.

How about α? Well, we go for our usual assumption of $\alpha = 1/3$, which is thought of as a reasonable value given the share of capital returns in output as measured by national accounts. This is subject to the caveats we have already discussed, but it is a good starting point.

Since we are interested in cross-country comparisons, we benchmark the data with comparisons to the U.S. series. This comparison can be seen in Figure 7.1, from Acemoglu (2009).

Figure 7.1   Productivity differences, from Acemoglu (2012)

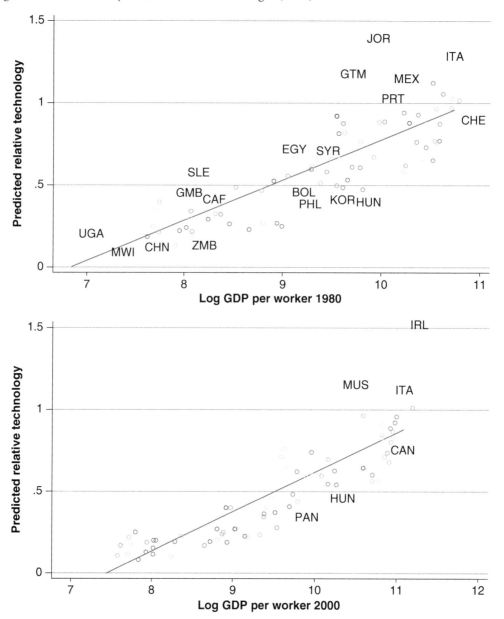

If all countries had the same productivity, and all differences in income were due to differences in factor accumulation, we would see all countries bunched around a value of 1 in the y-axis. This is clearly not the case! Note also that the pattern seems to become stronger over time: we were farther from that benchmark in 2000 than in 1980.

To summarise the message quantitatively, we can do the following exercise. Output per worker in the five countries with the highest levels of output per worker was 31.7 times higher than output per worker in the five lowest countries. Relatively little of this difference was due to physical and human capital:

- Capital intensity per worker contributed a factor of 1.8
- Human capital per worker contributed a factor of 2.2
- Productivity contributed a factor of 8.3!

Hall and Jones associate this big impact of productivity to the role of social capital: the ability of societies to organise their economic activity with more or less costs. For example, a society where theft is prevalent will imply the need to spend resources to protect property; a society full of red tape would require lots of energy in counteracting it, and so on. In short, productivity seems a much bigger concept than just technological efficiency.

However, just as in the regression approaches, calibration also relies on important assumptions. Now, functional forms make a huge difference, both in the production function and in the human capital equation. If we lift the Cobb-Douglas production function or change the technological assumptions in the production of human capital (e.g. assuming externalities), things can change a lot.

7.1.3 | Growth regressions

Another approach to the empirics of economic growth is that of growth regressions – namely, estimating regressions with growth rates as dependent variables. The original contribution was an extremely influential paper by Robert Barro (1991), that established a canonical specification. Generally speaking, the equation to be estimated looks like this:

$$g_{i,t} = \mathbf{X}'_{i,t}\beta + \alpha \log(y_{i,t-1}) + \epsilon_{i,t}, \tag{7.8}$$

where $g_{i,t}$ is the growth rate of country i from period $t-1$ to period t, $\mathbf{X}'_{i,t}$ is a vector of variables that one thinks can affect a country's growth rate, both in steady state (i.e. productivity) and along the transition path, β is a vector of coefficients, $y_{i,t-1}$ is country i's output in the previous period $t-1$, α is a coefficient capturing convergence, and $\epsilon_{i,t}$ is a random term that captures all other factors omitted from the specification.

Following this seminal contribution, innumerable papers were written over the subsequent few years, with a wide range of results. In some one variable was significant; in others, it was not. Eventually, the results were challenged on the basis of their robustness. Levine and Renelt (1991), for example, published a paper in which they argued *no* results were robust. The counterattack was done by a former student and colleague of Barro, Sala-i-Martin (1997), that applied a similar robustness check to all variables used by any author in growth regressions, in his amusingly titled paper, "I Just Ran Two Million Regressions". He concluded that, out of the 59 variables that had shown up as significant somewhere in his survey of the literature, some 22 seem to be robust according to his more lax, or less extreme, criteria (compared to Levine and Renelt's). These include region and religion dummies, political variables (e.g. rule of law), market distortions (e.g. black market premium), investment, and openness.

Leaving aside the issues of robustness, the approach, at least in its basic form, faces other severe challenges, which are of two types, roughly speaking.

1. Causality (aka Identification; aka Endogeneity): The variables in $\mathbf{X}_{i,t}$ are typically endogenous, i.e. jointly determined with the growth rate. As you have seen in your courses on econometrics, this introduces bias in our estimates of β, which in turn makes it unlikely that we identify the causal effect of any of those variables (at the end of this chapter, when discussing institutions, we will discuss the solution of this problem suggested by Acemoglu et al. (2001), one of the most creative and influential proposed solutions to this endogeneity problem).
2. Interpretation: The economic interpretation of the results might be quite difficult. Suppose that openness truly affects economic growth, but it does so (at least partly) by increasing investment rates; if our specification includes both variables in $\mathbf{X}_{i,t}$, the coefficient on openness will not capture the full extent of its true effect.

Both of these are particularly problematic if we want to investigate the relationship between policies and growth, a point that is illustrated by Dani Rodrik's (2012) critique. Rodrik's point is that if policies are endogenous (and who could argue they are not?) we definitely have a problem. The intuition is as follows. Imagine you want to test whether public banks are associated with higher or lower growth. If you run a regression of growth on, say, share of the financial sector that is run by public banks, you may find a negative coefficient. But is that because public banks are bad for growth? Or is it because politicians resort to public banks when the economy faces a lot of constraints (and thus its growth is bound to be relatively low)?

To see the issue more clearly, consider a setup, from a modified AK model, in which

$$g = (1 - \theta) A - \rho, \tag{7.9}$$

where θ is a distortion. Now consider a policy intervention s, which reduces the distortion, but that has a cost of its own. Then,

$$g(s, \theta, \phi) = (1 - \theta (1 - s)) A - \phi\alpha(s) - \rho. \tag{7.10}$$

The optimal intervention delivers growth as defined by the implicit equation

$$g_s(s^{**}, \theta, \phi) = 0. \tag{7.11}$$

In addition, there is a diversion function of the policy maker $\pi(s)$, with $\pi'(s) > 0$, $\pi''(s) < 0$, and $\pi'(s^P) = 0$ with $s^P > s^{**}$. This means that the politicians will use the intervention more than is actually desirable from a social perspective. The politician will want to maximise growth and their own benefit, placing a weight λ on growth. This means solving

$$\max_{s} u(s, \theta, \phi) = \lambda g(s, \theta, \phi) + \pi(s), \tag{7.12}$$

which from simple optimisation yields the FOC

$$\lambda g_s(s^*, \theta, \phi) + \pi'(s^*) = 0. \tag{7.13}$$

Because we have assumed that $\pi'(s) > 0$, it follows from (7.13) that $g_s(s^*, \theta, \phi) < 0$, and this implies that a reduction in s will increase growth. Does this imply that we should reduce s? Marginally, yes, but not to zero, which is the conclusion that people typically read from growth regressions.

Now, what if we were to run a regression to study the links between policy s and growth? We need to take into account the changes in s that happen when the parameters vary across countries. Consider the effect of changes in the level of distortions θ. Recall that, from (7.10):

$$g_s(s, \theta, \phi) = \theta A - \phi \alpha'(s). \tag{7.14}$$

Replacing in (7.13) and totally differentiating yields

$$d\theta \lambda A + \left[-\lambda \phi \alpha''(s) + \pi''(s^*)\right] ds^* = 0 \tag{7.15}$$

$$\frac{ds^*}{d\theta} = \underbrace{\frac{\overset{(+)}{\lambda A}}{\lambda \phi \alpha''(s) - \pi''(s^*)}}_{(+)} > 0. \tag{7.16}$$

This implies that in an economy with greater inefficiencies we will see a higher level of the policy intervention, as long as politicians care about growth. But growth will suffer with the greater inefficiencies: differentiating (7.10) with respect to θ we have

$$\frac{dg}{d\theta} = -A(1 - s^*) + g_s(s^*, \theta, \phi)\frac{ds^*}{d\theta} < 0 \Rightarrow \frac{\frac{dg}{d\theta}}{\frac{ds^*}{d\theta}} < 0. \tag{7.17}$$

The fact that this coefficient is negative means nothing, at least from a policy perspective (remember that it is optimal to increase the policy intervention if the distortion increases).

Because of challenges like these, people later moved to analyse panel growth regressions, which rearrange (7.8) as

$$g_{i,t} = \mathbf{X}'_{i,t}\beta + \alpha \log(y_{i,t-1}) + \delta_i + \mu_t + \epsilon_{i,t}, \tag{7.18}$$

where δ_i and μ_t are country and time fixed effects, respectively. By including country fixed effects, this removes fixed country characteristics that might affect both growth and other independent variables of interest, and thus identifies the effects of such variables out of within-country variation. However, in so doing they might be getting rid of most of the interesting variation, which is across countries, while also increasing the potential bias due to measurement error. Finally, these regressions do not account for time-varying country-specific factors. In sum, they are no panacea.

Convergence

Another vast empirical debate that has taken place within the framework of growth regressions is one to which we have already alluded when discussing the Solow model: convergence. We have talked, very briefly, about what the evidence looks like; let us now get into more detail.

Absolute convergence

As you recall, this is the idea that poorer countries grow faster than richer countries, unconditionally. Convergence is a stark prediction of the NGM, and economists started off by taking this (on second thought, naive) version of it to the data. Baumol (1986) took Maddison's core sample of 16 rich countries over the long run and found

$$\text{growth} = 5.251 - 0.749 \text{ initial income}$$
$$(0.075)$$

with $R^2 = 0.87$. He thus concluded that there was strong convergence!

However, De Long (1988) suggested a reason why this result was spurious: only successful countries took the effort to construct long historical data series. So the result may be a simple fluke of sample selection bias (another problem is measurement error in initial income that also biases the results in favour of the convergence hypothesis). In fact, broadening the sample of countries beyond Madison's sixteen leads us immediately to reject the hypothesis of convergence. By the way, there has been extensive work on convergence, within countries and there is fairly consistent evidence of absolute convergence for different regions of a country.[5]

Conditional convergence

The literature then moved to discuss the possibility of conditional convergence. This means including in a regression a term for the initial level of GDP, and checking whether the coefficient is negative when controlling for the other factors that determine the steady state of each economy. In other words, we want to look at the coefficient α in (7.8), which we obtain by including the control variables in $\mathbf{X}$. By including those factors in the regression, we partial out the steady state from initial income and measure deviations from this steady state. This, of course, is the convergence that is actually predicted by the NGM.

Barro (1991) and Barro and Sala-i-Martin (1992) found evidence of a negative α coefficient, and we can say that in general the evidence is favourable to conditional convergence. Nevertheless, the same issues that apply to growth regressions in general will be present here as well.

7.1.4 | Explaining cross-country income differences, again

Another regression-based approach to investigate how the NGM fares in explaining the data was pioneered by Mankiw et al. (1992) (MWR hence). Their starting point is playfully announced in the very first sentence: "This paper takes Robert Solow seriously" (p. 407).[6] This means that they focus simply on the factor accumulation determinants that are directly identified by the Solow model as the key proximate factors to explain cross-country income differences, leaving aside the productivity differences. They claim that the NGM (augmented with human capital) does a good job of explaining the existing cross-country differences.

Basic Solow model

There are two inputs, capital and labour, which are paid their marginal products. A Cobb-Douglas production function is assumed

$$Y_t = K_t^\alpha \left(A_t L_t\right)^{1-\alpha} \qquad 0 < \alpha < 1. \tag{7.19}$$

L and A are assumed to grow exogenously at rates n and g:

$$\frac{\dot{L}}{L} = n \tag{7.20}$$

$$\frac{\dot{A}}{A} = g. \tag{7.21}$$

The number of effective units of labour $A(t)L(t)$ grows at rate $n + g$.

As usual, we define k as the stock of capital per effective unit of labour $k = \frac{K}{AL}$ and $y = \frac{Y}{AL}$ as the level of output per effective unit of labour.

The model assumes that a constant fraction of output s is invested. The evolution of k is

$$\dot{k}_t = sy_t - \left(n + g + \delta\right) k_t \tag{7.22}$$

or

$$\dot{k}_t = sk_t^{\alpha} - \left(n + g + \delta\right) k_t, \tag{7.23}$$

where δ is the rate of depreciation. The steady state value k^* is

$$k^* = \left[\frac{s}{\left(n + g + \delta\right)} \right]^{\frac{1}{1-\alpha}}. \tag{7.24}$$

Output per capita is

$$\left(\frac{Y_t}{L_t}\right) = K_t^{\alpha} A_t^{1-\alpha} L_t^{-\alpha} = k_t^{\alpha} A_t. \tag{7.25}$$

Substituting (7.24) into (7.25)

$$\left(\frac{Y_t}{L_t}\right) = \left[\frac{s}{\left(n + g + \delta\right)} \right]^{\frac{\alpha}{1-\alpha}} A_t \tag{7.26}$$

and taking logs

$$\log\left(\frac{Y_t}{L_t}\right) = \frac{\alpha}{1-\alpha} \log(s) - \frac{\alpha}{1-\alpha} \log\left(n + g + \delta\right) + \log A(0) + gt. \tag{7.27}$$

MRW assume that g (representing advancement of knowledge) and δ do not vary across countries, but A reflects not only technology but also resource endowments. It thus differs across countries as in

$$\log A(0) = a + \epsilon, \tag{7.28}$$

where a is a constant and ϵ is a country-specific shock. So we have

$$\log\left(\frac{Y}{L}\right) = a + \frac{\alpha}{1-\alpha} \log(s) - \frac{\alpha}{1-\alpha} \log\left(n + g + \delta\right) + \epsilon \tag{7.29}$$

We assume s and n are not correlated with ϵ. (What do you think of this assumption?) Since it is usually assumed that the capital share is $\alpha \cong \frac{1}{3}$, the model predicts an elasticity of income per capita with respect to the saving rate $\frac{\alpha}{1-\alpha} \cong \frac{1}{2}$ and an elasticity with respect to $n+g+\delta$ of approximately -0.5.

Table 7.1 Estimates of the basic Solow model

| | Update | | |
| | Log GDP per Capita | | |
	MRW 1985	Acemoglu 2000	Update 2017
$\log(s_k)$	1.42***	1.22***	.96*
	(.14)	(.13)	(.48)
$\log(n+g+\delta)$	−1.97***	−1.59***	−1.48***
	(.56)	(.36)	(.21)
Implied α	.59	.55	.49
Adjusted R^2	.59	.49	.49

Note: *p<0.1; **p<0.05; ***p<0.01

What do the data say?

With data from the real national accounts constructed by Summers and Heston (1988) for the period 1960-1985, they run (7.29), using ordinary least squares (OLS) for all countries for which data are available minus countries where oil production is the dominant industry.

We reproduce their results in Table 7.1, to which we add an update by Acemoglu (2009), and one of our own more than 30 years after the original contribution. In all three cases, aspects of the results support the Solow model:

1. Signs of the coefficients on saving and population growth are OK.
2. Equality of the coefficients for $\log(s)$ and $-\log(n+g+\delta)$ is not rejected.
3. A high percentage of the variance is explained (see R^2 in the table).

But the estimate for α contradicts the prediction that $\alpha = 1/3$. While the implicit value of α seems to be falling, in each update it is still around or above .5. Some would have said it is OK (remember our discussion in Chapter 2), but for MRW it was not.

Introducing human capital

MRW go on to consider the implications of considering the role of human capital. Let us now recall the augmented Solow model that we saw in Chapter 5. The production function is now

$$Y_t = K_t^\alpha H_t^\beta \left(A_t L_t\right)^{1-\alpha-\beta},$$ (7.30)

where H is the stock of human capital. If s_k is the fraction of income invested in physical capital and s_h the fraction invested in human capital, the evolution of k and h are determined by

$$\dot{k}_t = s_k y_t - \left(n+g+\delta\right) k_t$$ (7.31)

$$\dot{h}_t = s_h y_t - \left(n+g+\delta\right) h_t,$$ (7.32)

where k, h and y are quantities per effective unit of labour.

It is assumed that $\alpha + \beta < 1$, so that there are decreasing returns to all capital and we have a steady state for the model. The steady-state level for k and h are

$$k^* = \left[\frac{s_k^{1-\beta} s_h^{\beta}}{(n+g+\delta)} \right]^{\frac{1}{1-\alpha-\beta}} \tag{7.33}$$

$$h^* = \left[\frac{s_k^{\alpha} s_h^{1-\alpha}}{(n+g+\delta)} \right]^{\frac{1}{1-\alpha-\beta}}. \tag{7.34}$$

Substituting (7.33) and (7.34) into the production function and taking logs, income per capita is

$$\log\left(\frac{Y_t}{L_t}\right) = \frac{\alpha}{1-\alpha-\beta} \log(s_k) + \frac{\beta}{1-\alpha-\beta} \log(s_h)$$

$$- \frac{\alpha+\beta}{1-\alpha-\beta} \log(n+g+\delta) + \log A(0) + gt. \tag{7.35}$$

To implement the model, investment in human capital is restricted to education. They construct a SCHOOL variable that measures the percentage of the working age population that is in secondary school, and use it as a proxy for human capital accumulation s_h.

The results are shown in Table 7.2. It turns out that now 78% of the variation is explained, and the numbers seem to match: $\hat{\alpha} \cong 0.3$, $\hat{\beta} \cong 0.3$. (For the updated data we have a slightly lower R^2 and a higher $\hat{\beta}$ indicating an increasing role of human capital, in line with what we found in the previous section.)

Table 7.2   Estimates of the augmented Solow model

| | Update | | |
| | Log GDP per Capita | | |
	MRW 1985	Acemoglu 2000	Update 2017
$\log(s_k)$	.69***	.96***	.71
	(.13)	(.13)	(.44)
$\log(n+g+\delta)$	−1.73***	−1.06***	−1.43***
	(.41)	(.33)	(.19)
$\log(s_h)$	.66***	.70***	1.69***
	(.07)	(.13)	(.43)
Implied α	.30	.36	.28
Implied β	.28	.26	.33
Adjusted R^2	.78	.60	.59

Note: *p<0.1; **p<0.05; ***p<0.01

Challenges

The first difficulty with this approach is: is it really OK to use OLS? Consistency of OLS estimates requires that the error term be orthogonal to the other variables. But that error term includes technology differences, and are these really uncorrelated with the accumulation of physical and human capital? If not, the omitted variable bias (and reverse causality) would mean that the estimates for the effects of physical and human capital accumulation (and for the R^2) are biased upwards, and the NGM doesn't do as good a job as MRW think, when it comes to explaining cross-country income differences. This is the very same difficulty that arises from the growth regressions approach – not surprising, since the econometric underpinnings are very much similar.

A second difficulty has to do with the measure of human capital: is it really a good one? The microeconometric evidence suggests that the variation in average years of schooling across countries that we see in the data is not compatible with the estimate $\hat{\beta}$ obtained by MRW.

7.1.5 | Summing up

We have seen many different empirical approaches, and their limitations. Both in terms of explaining differences in growth and in income levels at the cross-country level, there is a lot of debate on the extent to which the NGM can do the job.

It does seem that the consensus in the literature today is that productivity differences are crucial for understanding cross-country differences in economic performance. (A paper by Acemoglu and Dell (2010) makes the point that productivity differences are crucial for *within*-country differences as well.) This means that the endogenous growth models that try to understand technological progress are a central part of understanding those differences.

In the previous chapter we talked about some of the questions surrounding those models, such as the effects of competition and scale, but these models focused on productive technology, that is, how to build a new blueprint or a better variety for a good. The empirical research, as we mentioned above, suggests that productivity differences don't necessarily mean technology in a narrow sense. A country can be less productive because of market or organisational failures, even for a given technology. The reasons for this lower productivity may be manifold, but they lead us into the next set of questions: what explains them? What explains differences in factor accumulation? In other words, what are the *fundamental* causes of economic performance? We turn to this question now.

7.2 | The fundamental causes of economic growth

We go over four types of fundamental explanations for differences in economic performance: luck (multiple equilibria), geography, culture, and institutions.

As North (1990) point out, things like technological progress and factor accumulation "are not causes of growth; *they are growth*" (p.2). The big question is, what in turn causes them? Following Acemoglu (2009), we can classify the main hypotheses into four major groups:

1. *Luck*: Countries that are identical in principle may diverge because small factors lead them to select different equilibria, assuming that multiple equilibria exist.

2. *Geography*: Productivity can be affected by things that are determined by the physical, geographical, and ecological environment: soil quality, presence of natural resources, disease environment, inhospitable climate, etc.
3. *Culture*: Beliefs, values, and preferences affect economic behaviour, and may lead to different patterns of factor accumulation and productivity: work ethic, thrift, attitudes towards profit, trust, etc.
4. *Institutions*: Rules, regulations, laws, and policies that affect economic incentives to invest in technology, physical, and human capital. The crucial aspect is that institutions are *choices* made by society.

Let us discuss each one of them.

7.2.1 | Luck

This is essentially a catchier way of talking about multiple equilibria. If we go back to our models of poverty traps, we will recall that, in many cases, the same set of parameters is consistent with more than one equilibrium. Moreover, these equilibria can be ranked in welfare terms. As a result, it is possible (at least theoretically) that identical countries will end up in very different places.

But is the theoretical possibility that important empirically? Do we really believe that Switzerland is rich and Malawi is poor essentially because of luck? It seems a little hard to believe. Even if we go back in time, it seems that initial conditions were very different in very relevant dimensions. In other words, multiple equilibria might explain relatively small and short-lived divergence, but not the bulk of the mind-boggling cross-country differences we see – at least not in isolation.

In addition, from a conceptual standpoint, a drawback is that we need to explain the coordination failures and how people fail to coordinate even when they are trapped in a demonstrably bad equilibrium. This pushes back the explanatory challenge by another degree.

In sum, it seems that multiple equilibria and luck might be relevant, but in conjunction with other explanations. For instance, it may be that a country happened to be ruled by a growth-friendly dictator, while another was stuck with a growth-destroying one. Jones and Olken (2005) use random deaths of country leaders to show that there does seem to be an impact on subsequent performance. The question then becomes why the effects of these different rulers would matter over the long run, and for this we would have to consider some of the other classes of explanations.[7]

7.2.2 | Geography

This is somewhat related to the luck hypothesis, but certainly distinctive: perhaps the deepest source of heterogeneity between countries is the natural environment they happened to be endowed with. From a very big picture perspective, geographical happenstance of this sort is a very plausible candidate for a determinant of broad development paths, as argued for instance by Jarred Diamond in his 1999 Pulitzer-Prize-winning book *Guns, Germs and Steel*[8]. As an example, Diamond suggests that one key reason Europe conquered America, and not the other way around, was that Europe had an endowment of big animal species that were relatively easy to domesticate, which in turn led to improved immunisation by humans exposed to animal-borne diseases, and more technological advances. But can geography also explain differences in economic performance at the scale on which we usually think about them, say between different countries over decades or even a couple of centuries?

On some level, it is hard to think that the natural environment would not affect economic performance, on any time frame. Whether a country is in the middle of the Sahara desert, the Amazon rain forest, or some temperate climate zone must make some difference for the set of economic opportunities that it faces. This idea becomes more compelling when we look at the correlation between certain geographical variables and economic performance, as illustrated by the Figure (7.2), again taken from Acemoglu (2009). It is clear from that picture that countries that are closer to the equator are poorer on average. At the very least, any explanation for economic performance would have to be consistent with this stylised fact. The question, once again, is to assess to what extent these geographical differences underlie the ultimate performance, and this is not an easy empirical question.

Let us start by considering the possible conceptual arguments. The earliest version of the geography hypothesis has to do with the effect of the climate on the effort – the old idea that hot climates are not conducive to hard work. While this seems very naive (and not too politically correct) to our 21st century ears, the idea that climate (and geography more broadly) affects technological productivity, especially in agriculture, still sounds very plausible. If these initial differences in turn condition subsequent technological progress (as argued by Jared Diamond, as we have seen, and as we will see, in different forms, by Jeffrey Sachs), it just might be that geography is the ultimate determinant of the divergence between societies over the very long run.

A big issue with this modern version of the geography hypothesis is that it is much more appealing to think of geography affecting agricultural productivity, but modern growth seems to have a lot more to do with industrialisation. While productivity in agriculture might have conditioned the development of industry to begin with, once industrial technologies are developed we would have to explain why they are not adopted by some countries. Geography is probably not enough to account for that, at least in this version of the story.

Figure 7.2 Distance from the equator and income, from Acemoglu (2012)

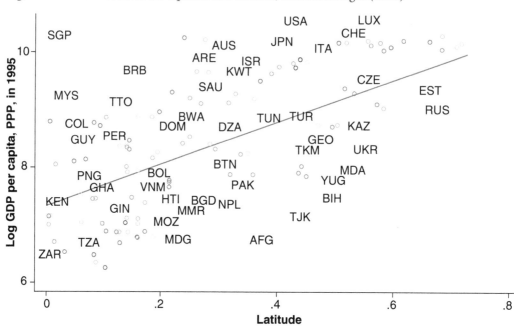

Another version has to do with the effect of geography on the disease environment, and the effect of the latter on productivity. This is a version strongly associated with Jeffrey Sachs (2002), who argues that the disease burden in the tropics (malaria in particular) can explain a lot of why Africa is so poor. The basic idea is very simple: unhealthy people are less productive. However, many of these diseases have been (or could potentially be) tamed by technological progress, so the question becomes one of why some countries have failed to benefit from that progress. In other words, the disease environment that prevails in a given country is also a consequence of its economic performance. While this doesn't mean that there cannot be causality running in the other direction, at the very least it makes the empirical assessment substantially harder.

What does the evidence say, broadly speaking? Acemoglu et al. (2002) (henceforth AJR) make the argument of the *reversal of fortune* to suggest that geography cannot explain that much. Consider the set of countries that were colonised by the Europeans, starting in the 15th century. The point is that countries that were richer before colonisation eventually became poorer – think about Peru or Mexico versus Canada, Australia, or the U.S. (see Figures 7.3 and 7.4). But geography, if the concept is to mean anything, is largely constant over time! (At least over the time periods we talk about.)

But how about the version that operates through the disease environment? This might operate on a smaller scale than the one that is belied by the reversal of fortunes argument. To assess this argument, we want to have some exogenous variation in the disease environment, that enables us to disentangle the two avenues of causality. Acemoglu and Johnson (2007) use the worldwide technological shocks that greatly improved control over many of the world's worst diseases. They measure this exogenous impact, at the country level, by considering the date at which a technological breakthrough

Figure 7.3   Reversal of fortunes - urbanization, from Acemoglu (2012)

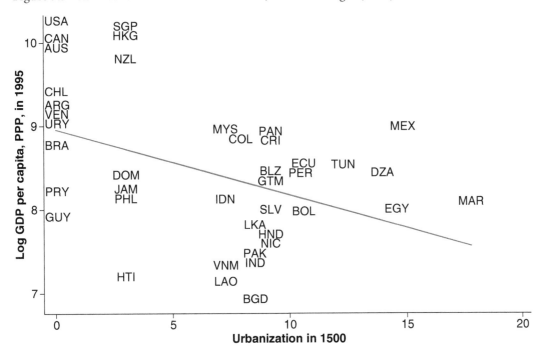

Figure 7.4 **Reversal of fortunes -pop. density, from Acemoglu (2012)**

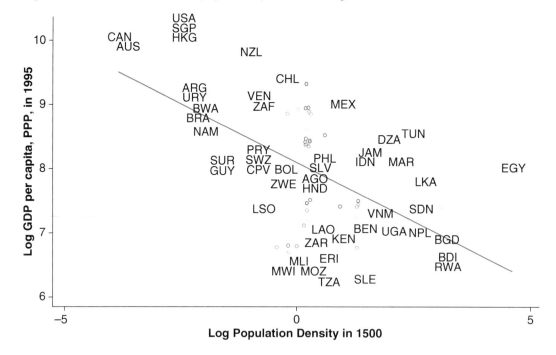

was obtained against a given disease, such as tuberculosis or malaria, and the country's initial exposure to that disease. What they show is that, quite beyond not having a quantitatively important effect
on output per capita, these health interventions actually seem not to have had any significant effect
at all.[9]

Finally, another version of the geography argument relates to the role of natural resources and
growth. Sachs and Warner (2001) tackle this issue and find a surprising result: countries endowed with
natural resources seem to grow slower than countries that do not (think of Congo, Zambia or Iran,
vs Japan and Hong Kong). How could this be so? Shouldn't having more resources be good? Sachs
associates the poorer performance to the fact that societies that are rich in resources become societies
of rent-seekers, societies where appropriating the wealth of natural resources is more important than
creating new wealth. Another explanation has to do with relative prices. Commodity booms lead to
a sustained real exchange rate appreciation that fosters the growth of non-tradable activities, where
productivity growth seems a bit slower. Finally, commodity economies suffer large volatility in their
real exchange rates, making economic activity more risky both in the tradable and non-tradable sectors. This decreases the incentives to invest, as we will see later in the book, and also hurts growth
prospects. Obviously, this is not a foregone conclusion. Some countries like Norway or Chile have
learnt to deal with the challenge of natural resources by setting sovereign wealth funds or investment
strategies that try to diminish these negative effects. But then this, once again, pushes the question of
this dimension of geography to that of institutions, to which we will shortly turn below.

7.2.3 | Culture

What do we mean by culture? The standard definition used by economists, as spelled out by Guiso et al. (2006), refers to "those customary beliefs and values that ethnic, religious, and social groups transmit fairly unchanged from generation to generation" (p. 23). In other words, culture is something that lives inside people's heads – as opposed to being external to them – but it is not something idiosyncratic to individuals; it is built and, importantly, transmitted at the level of groups.

It is hard to argue against the assertion that people's beliefs, values, and attitudes affect their economic decisions. It is just as clear that those beliefs, values and attitudes vary across countries (and over time). From this it is easy to conclude that culture matters for economic performance, an argument that goes back at least to Max Weber's thesis that Protestant beliefs and values, emphasising hard work and thrift, and with a positive view of wealth accumulation as a signal of God's grace, were an important factor behind the development of capitalism and the modern industrial development. In his words, the "Protestant ethic" lies behind the "spirit of capitalism".

Other arguments in the same vein have suggested that certain cultural traits are more conducive to economic growth than others (David Landes is a particularly prominent proponent of this view, as in Landes (1998)), and the distribution of those traits across countries is the key variable to ultimately understand growth. "Anglo-Saxon" values are growth-promoting, compared to "Latin" or "Asian" values, and so on. More recently, Joel Mokyr (2018) has argued that Enlightenment culture was the key driving force behind the emergence of the Industrial Revolution in Europe, and hence of the so-called "Great Divergence" between that continent and the rest of the world.

A number of issues arise with such explanations. First, culture is hard to measure, and as such may lead us into the realm of tautology. A country is rich because of its favourable culture, and a favourable culture is defined as that which is held by rich countries. This doesn't get us very far in understanding the causes of good economic performance. This circularity is particularly disturbing when the same set of values (say, Confucianism) is considered inimical to growth when Asian countries perform poorly, and suddenly becomes growth-enhancing when the same countries perform well. Second, even if culture is indeed an important causal determinant of growth, we still need to figure out where it comes from if we are to consider implications for policy and predictions for future outcomes.

These empirical and conceptual challenges have now been addressed more systematically, as better data on cultural attitudes have emerged. With such data, a vibrant literature has emerged, with economists developing theories and testing their predictions on the role that specific types of values (as opposed to a generic "culture" umbrella) play in determining economic performance. Many different types of cultural attitudes have been investigated: trust, collectivism, gender roles, beliefs about fairness, etc. This literature has often exploited historical episodes – the slave trade, the formation of medieval self-governing cities, colonisation, immigration, recessions – and specific cultural practices – religious rites, civic festivities, family arrangements – to shed light on the evolution of cultural attitudes and their impact on economic outcomes. Our assessment is that this avenue of research has already borne a lot of fruit, and remains very promising for the future. (For an overview of this literature, see the surveys by Guiso et al. (2006), Alesina and Giuliano (2015), and Nunn (2020).

As an example of this research, Campante and Yanagizawa-Drott (2015) address the question of whether one specific aspect of culture, namely religious practices, affects economic growth. They do so by focusing on the specific example of Ramadan fasting (one of the pillars of Islam). To identify a causal effect of the practice, they use variation induced by the (lunar) Islamic calendar: do (exogenously) longer Ramadan fasting hours affect economic growth? The answer they find is yes, and negatively (in Muslim countries only, reassuringly). They find a substantial effect, beyond the month of Ramadan itself, which cannot be fully explained by toll exacted by the fasting, but that they attribute to changes in labour supply decisions. People also become happier, showing that there is more to life than GDP growth. These results are consistent with existing theory on the emergence of costly religious practices. They work as screening devices to prevent free riding, and the evidence shows that more religious people become more intensely engaged, while the less committed drop out. In addition, there is an effect on individual attitudes. There is a decline in levels of general trust, suggesting that religious groups may be particularly effective in generating trust. (Given that trust is associated with good economic outcomes, we may speculate about the possible long-term impact of these changes.) In short, this illustrates how we can try to find a causal effect of cultural practices on growth, as well as trying to elucidate some of the relevant mechanisms.

7.2.4 | Institutions

Last but not least, there is the view that institutions are a fundamental source of economic growth. This idea also has an old pedigree in economics, but in modern times it has been mostly associated, in its beginnings, with the work of Douglass North (who won the Nobel Prize for his work), and more recently with scholars such as Daron Acemoglu and James Robinson. From the very beginning, here is the million-dollar question: what do we mean by institutions?

North's famous characterisation is that institutions are "the rules of the game" in a society, "the humanly devised constraints that shape human interaction" (North (1990), p. 3). Here are the key elements of his argument:

- Humanly devised: Unlike geography, institutions are chosen by groups of human beings.
- Constraints: Institutions are about placing constraints on human behaviour. Once a rule is imposed, there is a cost to breaking it.
- Shape interactions: Institutions affect incentives.

OK, fair enough. But here is the *real* question: What *exactly* do we mean by institutions? A first stab at this question is to follow the Acemoglu et al. (2005) distinctions between economic and political institutions, and between *de facto* and *de jure* institutions.

The first distinction is as follows. Economic institutions are those that directly affect the economic incentives: property rights, the presence and shape of market interactions, and regulations. They are obviously important for economic growth, as they constitute the set of incentives for accumulation and technological progress. Political institutions are those that configure the process by which society makes choices: electoral systems, constitutions, the nature of political regimes, the allocation of political power etc. There is clearly an intimate connection between those two types, as political power affects the economic rules that will prevail.

The second distinction is just as important, having to do with formal vs informal rules. For instance, the law may state that all citizens have the right to vote, but in practice it might be that certain groups can have enough resources (military or otherwise) to intimidate or influence others, thereby constraining their right in practice. Formal rules, the de jure institutions, are never enough to fully characterise the rules of the game; the informal, de facto rules must be taken into consideration.

These distinctions help us structure the concepts, but we also hit the same issue that plagues the cultural explanations: since institutions are made by people, we need to understand where they come from, and how they come about. Acemoglu et al. (2005) is a great starting point to survey this literature, and (Acemoglu and Robinson 2012) provides an extremely readable overview of the ideas.

How do we assess empirically the role of institutions as a fundamental determinant of growth? At a very basic level, we can start by focusing on one thing that generates discontinuous change in institutions, but not so much in culture, and arguably not at all in geography: borders. Consider the following two examples. Figure 7.5 shows a Google Earth image of the border between Bolivia (on the left) and Brazil. We can see how the Brazilian side is fully planted with (mostly) soybeans, unlike the Bolivian side. A better-known version showing the same idea, in even starker form, is the satellite image of the Korean Peninsula at night (Figure 7.6).

How can we do this more systematically? Here the main challenge is similar to the one facing the investigation on the effects of disease environment: is a country rich because it has good institutions, or does it have good institutions because it's rich? The seminal study here is Acemoglu et al. (2001), and it is worth going through that example in some detail – not so much for the specific answers they find, which have been vigorously debated for a couple of decades, at this point – but for how it illustrates the challenges involved, how to try and circumvent them, and the many questions that come from that process.

The paper explores the effects of a measure of institutional development given by an index of protection from expropriation. (What kind of institution is that? What are the problems with a measure like this?) The key challenge is to obtain credible exogenous variation in that measure – something that affects institutions, but not the outcome of interest (income per capita), other than through its effect on the former.

Their candidate solution for this identification problem comes again from the natural experiment of European colonisation. The argument is that current institutions are affected by the institutions that Europeans chose to implement in their colonies (persistence of institutions), and those in turn were affected by the geographical conditions they faced – in particular, the disease environment. In more inhospitable climates (from their perspective), Europeans chose not to settle, and instead set up extractive institutions. In more favourable climates they chose to settle and, as a result, ended up choosing institutions that protected the rights of the colonists. (Note that this brings in geography as a variable that affects outcomes, but *through its effect on institutions*. In particular, this helps explain the correlations with geographical variables that we observe in the data.) The key assumption is that the disease environment at the time of colonisation doesn't really affect economic outcomes today except

Figure 7.5   **Border between Bolivia (left) and Brazil**

Figure 7.6 The Korean Peninsula at night

through their effect on institutional development. If so, we can use variation in that environment to identify the causal effect of institutions.

Under these assumptions, they use historical measures of mortality of European settlers as an instrument for the measure of contemporaneous institutions (property rights protection), which allows them to estimate the impact of the former on contemporaneous income per capita. The resulting estimate of the impact of institutions on income per capita is 0.94. This implies that the 2.24 difference in expropriation risk between Nigeria and Chile should translate into a difference of 206 log points (approximately 8 times, since $e^{2.06} = 7.84$). So their result is that institutional factors can explain a lot of observed cross-country differences. Also, the results suggest that, once the institutional element is controlled for, there is no additional effect of the usual geographical variables, such as distance to the equator.

Their paper was extremely influential, and spawned a great deal of debate. What are some of the immediate problems with it? The most obvious is that the disease environment may have a direct impact on output (see geography hypothesis), and the disease environment back in the days of colonisation is related to that of today. They tackle this objection, and argue that the mortality of European settlers is to a large extent unrelated to the disease environment for natives, who had developed immunity to a lot of the diseases that killed those settlers. An objection that is not as obvious is whether the impact of the European settlers was through institutions, or something else. Was it culture that they brought? They argue that accounting for institutions wipes out the effect of things such as the identity of the coloniser. Was it human capital? Glaeser et al. (2004) argue that what they brought was not good institutions, but themselves: the key was their higher levels of human capital, which in turn are what is behind good institutions. This is a much harder claim to settle empirically, so the question remains open.

Broadly speaking, there is wide acceptance in the profession, these days, that institutions play an important role in economic outcomes. However, there is a lot of room for debate as to which are the relevant institutions, and where they come from. How do societies choose different sets of institutions? Particularly if some institutions are better for economic performance than others, why do some countries choose bad institutions? Could it be because some groups benefit from inefficient institutions? If so, how do they manage to impose them on the rest of society? In other words, we need to understand the political economy of institutional development. This is a very open and exciting area of research, both theoretically and empirically.

As an example of the themes in the literature, Acemoglu and Robinson (2019) asks not only why certain countries develop a highly capable state and others don't, but also why, among those that do, some have that same state guarantee the protection of individual rights and liberties, while others have a state that tramples on those rights and liberties. Their argument is that institutional development proceeds as a race between the power of the state and the power of society, as people both demand the presence of the Leviathan enforcing rules and order, and resent its power. If the state gets too powerful relative to society, the result is a despotic situation; if the state is too weak, the result is a state incapable of providing the needed underpinnings for development. In the middle, there is the "narrow corridor" along which increasing state capacity pushes for more societal control, and the increased power of society pushes for a more capable (and inclusive) state. The dynamics are illustrated by Figure 7.7, and one crucial aspect is worth mentioning: small differences in initial conditions – say, two economies just on opposite sides of the border between two regions in the figure – can evolve into vastly different institutional and development paths.

7.3 | What have we learned?

When it comes to the proximate causes of growth, in spite of the limitations of each specific empirical approach – growth accounting, regression methods, and calibration – the message from the data is reasonably clear, yet nuanced: factor accumulation can arguably explain a substantial amount of income differences, and specific growth episodes, but ultimately differences in productivity are very important. This is a bit daunting, since the fact is that we don't really understand what productivity *is*, in a deeper sense. Still, it underscores the importance of the process of technological progress – and the policy issues raised in Chapter 6 – as a primary locus for growth policies.

How about the fundamental causes? There is certainly a role for geography and luck (multiple equilibria), but our reading of the literature is that culture and institutions play a key part. There remains a lot to be learned about how these things evolve, and how they affect outcomes, and these are bound to be active areas of research for the foreseeable future.

Figure 7.7 Weak, despotic and inclusive states, from Acemoglu and Robinson (2017)

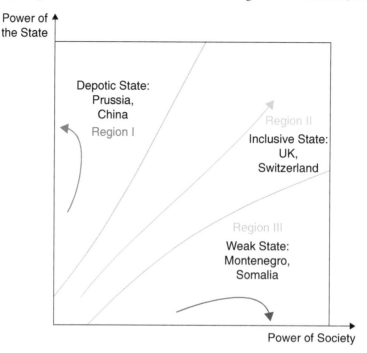

7.4 | What next?

Once again, the growth textbook by Acemoglu (2009) is a superb resource, and it contains a more in-depth discussion of the empirical literature on the proximate causes of growth. It also has a very interesting discussion on the fundamental causes, but it's useful to keep in mind that, its author being one of the leading proponents of the view that institutions matter most, it certainly comes at that debate from that specific point of view.

Specifically on culture, the best places to go next are the survey articles we mentioned in our discussion. The survey by Guiso et al. (2006) is a bit outdated, of course, but still a great starting point. The more recent surveys by Alesina and Giuliano (2015), focusing particularly on the links between culture and institutions, and by Nunn (2020), focusing on the work using historical data, are very good guides to where the literature is and is going.

On institutions, there is no better place to go next than the books by Acemoglu and Robinson (2012) and Acemoglu and Robinson (2019). They are very ambitious intellectual exercises, encompassing theory, history, and empirical evidence, and meant for a broad audience – which makes them a fun and engaging read.

These being very active research fields, there are a lot of questions that remain open. Anyone interested in the social sciences, as the readers of this book most likely are, will find a lot of food for thought in these sources.

Notes

[1] We know, of course, that the NGM does not generate long-run growth, except through exogenous technical progress. However, keep in mind that we also live in the transition path!

[2] Measuring each of these variables is an art by itself, and hundreds of papers have tried to refine these measures. Capital stocks are usually computed from accumulating past net investment and human capital from accumulating population adjusted by their productivity, assessed through Mincer equations relating years of schooling and income.

[3] This memorable phrase is attributed to Moses Abramovitz.

[4] Check out the priceless first paragraph of his 1995 paper summarising his findings: "This is a fairly boring and tedious paper, and is intentionally so. This paper provides no new interpretations of the East Asian experience to interest the historian, derives no new theoretical implications of the forces behind the East Asian growth process to motivate the theorist, and draws no new policy implications from the subtleties of East Asian government intervention to excite the policy activist. Instead, this paper concentrates its energies on providing a careful analysis of the historical patterns of output growth, factor accumulation, and productivity growth in the newly industrializing countries (NICs) of East Asia, i.e., Hong Kong, Singapore, South Korea, and Taiwan" (p. 640).

[5] As we mentioned, Kremer et al. (2021) have argued that the data has moved in the direction of absolute convergence across countries in the 21st century.

[6] This allegiance is also behind their just as playful title, "A Contribution to the Empirics of Economic Growth", which substitutes empirics for the theory from Solow's original article.

[7] For instance, the aforementioned work by Jones and Olken (2005) shows that the effect of leaders is present in non-democracies, but not in democracies, suggesting that luck of this sort may matter insofar as it interacts with (in this case) institutional features.

[8] Diamond (2013).

[9] How can that be? Think about what happens, in the context of the Solow model, when population increases.

References

Acemoglu, D. (2009). *Introduction to modern economic growth*. Princeton University Press.

Acemoglu, D. & Dell, M. (2010). Productivity differences between and within countries. *American Economic Journal: Macroeconomics*, *2*(1), 169–88.

Acemoglu, D. & Johnson, S. (2007). Disease and development: The effect of life expectancy on economic growth. *Journal of Political Economy*, *115*(6), 925–985.

Acemoglu, D., Johnson, S., & Robinson, J. A. (2001). The colonial origins of comparative development: An empirical investigation. *American Economic Review*, *91*(5), 1369–1401.

Acemoglu, D., Johnson, S., & Robinson, J. A. (2002). Reversal of fortune: Geography and institutions in the making of the modern world income distribution. *The Quarterly Journal of Economics*, *117*(4), 1231–1294.

Acemoglu, D., Johnson, S., & Robinson, J. A. (2005). Institutions as a fundamental cause of long-run growth. *Handbook of Economic Growth*, *1*, 385–472.

Acemoglu, D. & Robinson, J. A. (2012). *Why nations fail: The origins of power, prosperity, and poverty*. Currency.

Acemoglu, D. & Robinson, J. A. (2017). *The emergence of weak, despotic and inclusive states*. National Bureau of Economic Research.

Acemoglu, D. & Robinson, J. A. (2019). *The narrow corridor: How nations struggle for liberty*. Penguin UK.

Alesina, A. & Giuliano, P. (2015). Culture and institutions. *Journal of Economic Literature*, *53*(4), 898–944.

Barro, R. J. (1991). Economic growth in a cross section of countries. *The Quarterly Journal of Economics*, *106*(2), 407–443.

Barro, R. J. & Sala-i-Martin, X. (1992). Convergence. *Journal of Political Economy*, *100*(2), 223–251.

Baumol, W. J. (1986). Productivity growth, convergence, and welfare: What the long-run data show. *The American Economic Review*, 1072–1085.

Campante, F. & Yanagizawa-Drott, D. (2015). Does religion affect economic growth and happiness? Evidence from Ramadan. *The Quarterly Journal of Economics*, *130*(2), 615–658.

De Long, J. B. (1988). Productivity growth, convergence, and welfare: Comment. *The American Economic Review*, *78*(5), 1138–1154.

Diamond, J. (2013). *Guns, germs and steel: A short history of everybody for the last 13,000 years*. Random House.

Glaeser, E. L., La Porta, R., Lopez-de-Silanes, F., & Shleifer, A. (2004). Do institutions cause growth? *Journal of Economic Growth*, *9*(3), 271–303.

Guiso, L., Sapienza, P., & Zingales, L. (2006). Does culture affect economic outcomes? *Journal of Economic Perspectives*, *20*(2), 23–48.

Hall, R. E. & Jones, C. I. (1999). Why do some countries produce so much more output per worker than others? *The Quarterly Journal of Economics*, *114*(1), 83–116.

Jones, B. F. & Olken, B. A. (2005). Do leaders matter? National leadership and growth since World War II. *The Quarterly Journal of Economics*, *120*(3), 835–864.

Kremer, M., Willis, J., & You, Y. (2021). Converging to convergence. *NBER Macro Annual 2021*. https://www.nber.org/system/files/chapters/c14560/c14560.pdf.

Krugman, P. (1994). The myth of Asia's miracle. *Foreign Affairs*, *73*(6), 62–78.

Landes, D. S. (1998). Culture counts. *Challenge*, *41*(4), 14–30.

Levine, R. & Renelt, D. (1991). *Cross-country studies of growth and policy: Methodological, conceptual, and statistical problems* (Vol. 608). World Bank Publications.

Mankiw, N. G., Romer, D., & Weil, D. N. (1992). A contribution to the empirics of economic growth. *The Quarterly Journal of Economics*, *107*(2), 407–437.

Mokyr, J. (2018). *The British industrial revolution: An economic perspective*. Routledge.

North, D. (1990). Institutions, institutional change and economic performance. Cambridge University Press: New York.

Nunn, N. (2020). The historical roots of economic development. *Science*, *367*(6485).

Rodrik, D. (2012). Why we learn nothing from regressing economic growth on policies. *Seoul Journal of Economics*, *25*.

Sachs, J. & Malaney, P. (2002). The economic and social burden of malaria. *Nature*, *415*(6872), 680–685.

Sachs, J. D. & Warner, A. M. (2001). The curse of natural resources. *European Economic Review*, *45*(4-6), 827–838.

Sala-i-Martin, X. X. (1997). *I just ran four million regressions* (tech. rep.) National Bureau of Economic Research.

Solow, R. M. (1957). Technical change and the aggregate production function. *The Review of Economics and Statistics*, 312–320.

Summers, R. & Heston, A. (1988). A new set of international comparisons of real product and price levels estimates for 130 countries, 1950–1985. *Review of Income and Wealth, 34*(1), 1–25.

Young, A. (1995). The tyranny of numbers: Confronting the statistical realities of the east asian growth experience. *The Quarterly Journal of Economics, 110*(3), 641–680.

Overlapping Generations Models

CHAPTER 8

Overlapping generations models

The neoclassical growth model (NGM), with its infinitely-lived and identical individuals, is very useful for analysing a large number of topics in macroeconomics, as we have seen, and will continue to see, for the remainder of the book. However, there are some issues that require a departure from those assumptions. An obvious example involves those issues related to the understanding of the interaction of individuals who are at different stages in their life cycles. If lives are finite and not infinite, as in the NGM, individuals are *not* the same (or at a minimum are not at the same moment in their lives). This diversity opens a whole new set of issues, such as that of optimal consumption and investment over the life cycle, and the role of bequests. It also requires a redefinition of optimality. Not only because we need to address the issue of how to evaluate welfare when agents have different utility functions, but also because we will need to check if the optimality properties of the NGM prevail. For example, if there are poor instruments to save, yet people need to save for retirement, can it be possible that people accumulate too much capital?

This richer framework will provide new perspectives for evaluating policy decisions such as pensions, taxation, and discussing the impact of demographic changes. Of course, the analysis becomes more nuanced, but the added difficulty is not an excuse for not tackling the issue, particularly because in many instances the fact that individuals are different is the key aspect that requires attention.

To study these very important issues, in the next three chapters we develop the *overlapping generations* (OLG) model, the second workhorse framework of modern macroeconomics. We will see that, when bringing in some of these nuances, the implications of the model turn out to be very different from those of the NGM. This framework will also allow us to address many of the most relevant current policy debates in macroeconomics, including low interest rates, secular stagnation, and topics in fiscal and monetary policy.

8.1 | The Samuelson-Diamond model

The Samuelson-Diamond model simplifies by assuming two generations: young and old. The young save for retirement, and this is the capital stock next period. The dynamics of capital will be summarised by a savings equation of the form $s(w, r)$. This savings equation will allow us to trace the evolution of capital over time.

How to cite this book chapter:
Campante, F., Sturzenegger, F. and Velasco, A. 2021. *Advanced Macroeconomics: An Easy Guide.*
    Ch. 8. 'Overlapping generations models', pp. 115–134. London: LSE Press.
    DOI: https://doi.org/10.31389/lsepress.ame.h License: CC-BY-NC 4.0.

Here we present a discrete time model initially developed by Diamond (1965), building on earlier work by Samuelson (1958), in which individuals live for two periods (young and old). The economy lasts forever as new young people enter in every period. We first characterise the decentralised competitive equilibrium of the model. We then ask whether the market solution is the same as the allocation that would be chosen by a central planner, focusing on the significance of the golden rule, which will allow us to discuss the possibility of dynamic inefficiency (i.e. excessive capital accumulation).

8.1.1 | The decentralized equilibrium

The market economy is composed of individuals and firms. Individuals live for two periods. They work for firms, receiving a wage. They also lend their savings to firms, receiving a rental rate.

An individual born at time t consumes c_{1t} in period t and c_{2t+1} in period $t+1$, and derives utility

$$\left(\frac{\sigma}{\sigma-1}\right) c_{1t}^{\frac{\sigma-1}{\sigma}} + (1+\rho)^{-1} \left(\frac{\sigma}{\sigma-1}\right) c_{2t+1}^{\frac{\sigma-1}{\sigma}}, \quad \rho \geq 0, \ \sigma \geq 0. \tag{8.1}$$

Note that the subscript "1" refers to consumption when young, and "2" labels consumption when old. Individuals work only in the first period of life, inelastically supplying one unit of labour and earning a real wage of w_t. They consume part of their first-period income and save the rest to finance their second-period retirement consumption. The saving of the young in period t generates the capital stock that is used to produce output in period $t+1$ in combination with the labour supplied by the young generation of period $t+1$.

The time structure of the model appears in Figure 8.1.

The number of individuals born at time t and working in period t is L_t. Population grows at rate n so that $L_t = L_0 (1+n)^t$.

Figure 8.1 Time structure of overlapping generations model

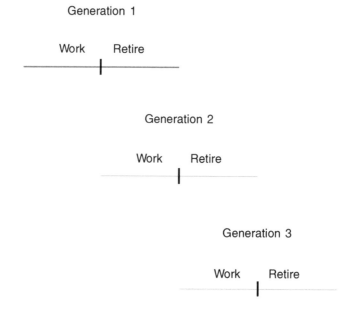

Firms act competitively and use the constant returns technology $Y = F(K, L)$. For simplicity, assume that capital fully depreciates after use, which is akin to assuming that $F(\cdot, \cdot)$ is a net production function, with depreciation already accounted for. As before, output per worker, Y/L, is given by the production function $y = f(k)$, where k is the capital-labour ratio. This production function is assumed to satisfy the Inada conditions. Each firm maximises profits, taking the wage rate, w_t, and the rental rate on capital, r_t, as given.

We now examine the optimisation problem of individuals and firms and derive the market equilibrium.

Individuals

Consider an individual born at time t. His maximisation problem is

$$\max \left\{ \left(\frac{\sigma}{\sigma - 1} \right) c_{1t}^{\frac{\sigma-1}{\sigma}} + (1 + \rho)^{-1} \left(\frac{\sigma}{\sigma - 1} \right) c_{2t+1}^{\frac{\sigma-1}{\sigma}} \right\} \tag{8.2}$$

subject to

$$c_{1t} + s_t = w_t, \tag{8.3}$$

$$c_{2t+1} = \left(1 + r_{t+1} \right) s_t, \tag{8.4}$$

where w_t is the wage received in period t and r_{t+1} is the interest rate paid on savings held from period t to period $t+1$. In the second period the individual consumes all his wealth, both interest and principal. (Note that this assumes that there is no altruism across generations, in that people do not care about leaving bequests to the coming generations. This is crucial.)

The first-order condition for a maximum is

$$c_{1t}^{-\frac{1}{\sigma}} - \left(\frac{1 + r_{t+1}}{1 + \rho} \right) c_{2t+1}^{-\frac{1}{\sigma}} = 0, \tag{8.5}$$

which can be rewritten as

$$\frac{c_{2t+1}}{c_{1t}} = \left(\frac{1 + r_{t+1}}{1 + \rho} \right)^{\sigma}. \tag{8.6}$$

This is the Euler equation for the generation born at time t. Note that this has the very same intuition, in discrete time, as the Euler equation (Ramsey rule) we derived in the context of the NGM.

Next, using (8.3) and (8.4) to substitute out for c_{1t} and c_{2t+1} and rearranging we get

$$s_t = \left(\frac{1}{\left(1 + r_{t+1} \right)^{1-\sigma} (1 + \rho)^{\sigma} + 1} \right) w_t. \tag{8.7}$$

We can think of this as a saving function:

$$s_t = s \left(w_t, r_{t+1} \right), \qquad 0 < s_w \equiv \frac{\partial s_t}{\partial w_t} < 1, \ s_r \equiv \frac{\partial s_t}{\partial r_{t+1}} \geq 0 \text{ or } \leq 0. \tag{8.8}$$

Saving is an increasing function of wage income since the assumption of separability and concavity of the utility function ensures that both goods (i.e. consumption in both periods) are normal. The effect of an increase in the interest rate is ambiguous, however, because of the standard income and substitution effects with which you are familiar from micro theory. An increase in the interest rate decreases the relative price of second-period consumption, leading individuals to shift consumption from the first to the second period, that is, to substitute second- for first-period consumption. But it also increases the feasible consumption set, making it possible to increase consumption in both periods; this is the income effect. The net effect of these substitution and income effects is ambiguous. If the elasticity of substitution between consumption in both periods is greater than one, then in this two-period model the substitution effect dominates and an increase in interest rates leads to an increase in saving.

Firms

Firms act competitively, renting capital to the point where the marginal product of capital is equal to its rental rate, and hiring labour to the point where the marginal product of labour is equal to the wage

$$f'\left(k_t\right) = r_t \tag{8.9}$$

$$f\left(k_t\right) - k_t f'\left(k_t\right) = w_t, \tag{8.10}$$

where k_t is the firm's capital-labour ratio. Note that $f\left(k_t\right) - k_t f'\left(k_t\right)$ is the marginal product of labour, because of constant returns to scale.

8.1.2 | Goods and factor market equilibrium

The goods market equilibrium requires that the demand for goods in each period be equal to supply, or equivalently that investment be equal to saving:

$$K_{t+1} - K_t = L_t s\left(w_t, r_{t+1}\right) - K_t. \tag{8.11}$$

The left-hand side is net investment: the change in the capital stock between t and $t+1$. The right-hand side is net saving: the first term is the saving of the young; the second is the dissaving of the old.

Eliminating K_t from both sides tells us that capital at time $t+1$ is equal to the saving of the young at time t. Dividing both sides by L_t gives us the equation of motion of capital in per capita terms:

$$(1 + n)\, k_{t+1} = s\left(w_t, r_{t+1}\right). \tag{8.12}$$

The services of labour are supplied inelastically; the supply of services of capital in period t is determined by the savings decision of the young made in period $t-1$. Equilibrium in the factor markets obtains when the wage and the rental rate on capital are such that firms wish to use the available amounts of labour and capital services. The factor market equilibrium conditions are therefore given by equations (8.9) and (8.10).

8.1.3 | The dynamics of the capital stock

The capital accumulation equation (8.12), together with the factor market equilibrium conditions (8.9) and (8.10), implies the dynamic behaviour of the capital stock:

$$k_{t+1} = \frac{s\left[w\left(k_t\right), r\left(k_{t+1}\right)\right]}{1 + n}, \tag{8.13}$$

or

$$k_{t+1} = \frac{s\left[f(k_t) - k_t f'(k_t), f'(k_{t+1})\right]}{1+n}. \tag{8.14}$$

This last equation implies a relationship between k_{t+1} and k_t. We will describe this as the savings locus. The properties of the savings locus depend on the derivative:

$$\frac{dk_{t+1}}{dk_t} = \frac{-s_w(k_t)\, k_t f''(k_t)}{1+n - s_r(k_{t+1}) f''(k_{t+1})}. \tag{8.15}$$

The numerator of this expression is positive, reflecting the fact that an increase in the capital stock in period t increases the wage, which increases savings. The denominator is of ambiguous sign because the effects of increases in the interest rate on savings are ambiguous. If $s_r \geq 0$, then the denominator in (8.15) is positive, and then so is dk_{t+1}/dk_t.

The savings locus in Figure 8.2 summarises both the dynamic and the steady-state behaviour of the economy. The 45-degree line in Figure 8.2 is the line along which steady states, at which $k_{t+1} = k_t$, must lie. Any point at which the savings locus s crosses that line is a steady state. We have drawn a locus that crosses the 45-degree line only once, and hence guarantees that the steady state capital stock both exists and is unique. But this is not the only possible configuration. The model does not, without further restrictions on the utility and/or production functions, guarantee either existence or uniqueness of a steady-state equilibrium with positive capital stock.

If there exists a unique equilibrium with positive capital stock, will it be stable? To answer this, evaluate the derivative around the steady state:

$$\left.\frac{dk_{t+1}}{dk_t}\right|_{SS} = \frac{-s_w k^* f''(k^*)}{1+n - s_r f''(k^*)}. \tag{8.16}$$

Figure 8.2 The steady-state capital stock

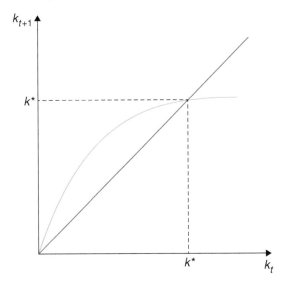

(Local) stability requires that $\left.\frac{dk_{t+1}}{dk_t}\right|_{SS}$ be less than one in absolute value:

$$\left| \frac{-s_w k^* f''(k^*)}{1 + n - s_r f''(k^*)} \right| < 1.$$

Again, without further restrictions on the model, the stability condition may or may not be satisfied. To obtain definite results on the comparative dynamic and steady-state properties of the model, it is necessary either to specify functional forms for the underlying utility and production functions, or to impose conditions sufficient for uniqueness of a positive steady-state capital stock.[1]

8.1.4 | A workable example

In this sub-section, we analyse the properties of the OLG model under a fairly simple set of assumptions: log utility (i.e. the limit case where $\sigma = 1$) and Cobb-Douglas production. (This is sometimes referred to as the canonical OLG model.) This permits a simple characterisation of both dynamics and the steady state.

With this assumption on preferences, the saving function is

$$s_t = \left(\frac{1}{2 + \rho} \right) w_t, \tag{8.17}$$

so that savings is proportional to wage income. Notice that the interest rate cancels out in the case of log utility, but not otherwise. This is a case in which the savings rate will be constant over time (as in the Solow model), though, once again, here this is the result of an optimal choice (as in the version of the AK model that we studied in Chapter 5).

With Cobb-Douglas technology, the firm's rules for optimal behaviour (8.9) and (8.10) become

$$r_t = \alpha k_t^{\alpha - 1} \tag{8.18}$$

and

$$w_t = (1 - \alpha) k_t^{\alpha} = (1 - \alpha) y_t. \tag{8.19}$$

Using (8.17) and (8.19) in (8.12) yields

$$k_{t+1} = \left(\frac{1 - \alpha}{2 + \rho} \right) \left(\frac{1}{1 + n} \right) k_t^{\alpha}, \tag{8.20}$$

which is the new law of motion for capital.

Define as usual the steady state as the situation in which $k_{t+1} = k_t = k^*$. Equation (8.20) implies that the steady state is given by

$$k^* = \left(\frac{1 - \alpha}{2 + \rho} \frac{1}{1 + n} \right)^{\frac{1}{1 - \alpha}}, \tag{8.21}$$

so that we have a unique and positive steady-state per-capita capital stock. This stock is decreasing in ρ (the rate of discount) and n (the rate of population growth). Note the similarities with the NGM and the Solow model.

Similarly, we can write steady-state income per-capita as $y^* = (k^*)^\alpha$, or

$$y^* = \left(\frac{1-\alpha}{2+\rho}\frac{1}{1+n}\right)^{\frac{\alpha}{1-\alpha}}. \qquad (8.22)$$

Again, this steady-state level is decreasing in ρ and n.

Will the system ever get to the steady state? Local stability requires that $\frac{dk_{t+1}}{dk_t}\Big|_{SS}$ be less than one in absolute value, which in this case implies

$$\alpha\left(\frac{1-\alpha}{2+\rho}\right)\left(\frac{1}{1+n}\right)(k^*)^{\alpha-1} = \alpha < 1, \qquad (8.23)$$

which is always satisfied. Hence, if the initial capital stock is larger than zero it will gradually converge to k^*. Convergence is depicted in Figure 8.3. The economy starts out at k_0 and gradually moves toward the steady-state capital stock.

The effects of a shock

Suppose next that the economy is at the steady state and at some time 0 the discount rate falls from ρ to ρ', where $\rho' < \rho$. This shock is unexpected, and will last forever.

From (8.21) we see that the new steady-state per capita capital stock will clearly rise, with $k^*_{new} > k^*_{old}$. In Figure 8.4 we show the dynamic adjustment toward the new stationary position. The economy starts out at k^*_{old} and gradually moves toward k^*_{new}. Income per capita rises in the transition and in the new steady state.

Figure 8.3   Convergence to the steady state

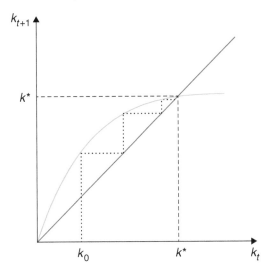

Figure 8.4   Fall in the discount rate

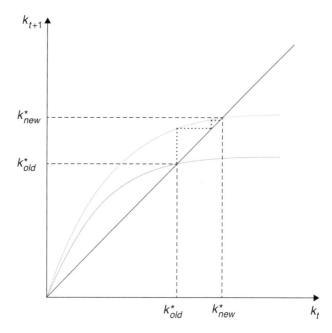

8.2 | Optimality

The distinctive characteristic of the OLG model is that the interest rate may be smaller than the growth rate. In this case, there is a potential gain of reducing the stock of capital. The OLG model can lead to dynamic inefficiency.

We now ask how the market allocation compares to that which would be chosen by a central planner who maximises an intertemporal social welfare function. This raises a basic question, that of the relevant social welfare function. When individuals have infinite horizons and are all alike, it is logical to take the social welfare function to be their own utility function. But here the generations that are alive change as time passes, so it is not obvious what the central planner should maximise.

8.2.1 | The steady-state marginal product of capital

In any event, as in the Solow model, there is something we can say about efficiency here. Notice that, at the steady state, the marginal product of capital is

$$f'(k^*) = \alpha(k^*)^{\alpha-1} = r^* = \left(\frac{\alpha}{1-\alpha}\right)(2+\rho)(1+n). \tag{8.24}$$

Notice that this interest rate depends on more parameters than in the NGM. The relationship between the discount factor and the interest rate is still there. A higher discount factor implies less savings today and a higher interest rate in equilibrium. But notice that now that the population growth affects the interest rate. Why is this the case? The intuition is simple. A higher growth rate of population decreases the steady-state stock of capital thus increasing the marginal product of capital. How does this compare with the golden rule of $f'\left(k_G\right) = n$? From the above it is clear that $k^* > k_G$ if

$$r^* < n, \tag{8.25}$$

which in turn implies

$$\alpha < \frac{n}{n + (1 + n)(2 + \rho)}. \tag{8.26}$$

That is, if α is sufficiently low (or, alternatively, if n is sufficiently high), the steady-state capital stock in the decentralised equilibrium can exceed that of the golden rule.

Dynamic inefficiency

Suppose a benevolent planner found that the economy was at the steady state with k^* and y^*. Suppose further that $k^* > k_G$. Is there anything the planner could do to redistribute consumption across generations that would make at least one generation better off without making any generation worse off? Put differently, is this steady state Pareto efficient?

Let resources available for per-capita consumption (of the young and old), in any period t, be given by x_t. Note next that in any steady state,

$$x_{SS} = k_{SS}^{\alpha} - nk_{SS}. \tag{8.27}$$

Note that, by construction, k_G is the k_{SS} that maximises x_{SS}, since $\frac{\partial x_{SS}}{\partial k_{SS}} = 0$.

The initial situation is one $k_{SS} = k^*$, so that $x_{SS} = c^*$. Suppose next that, at some point $t = 0$, the planner decides to allocate more to consumption and less to savings in that period, so that next period the capital stock is $k_G < k^*$.

Then, in period 0, resources available for consumption will be

$$x_0 = (k^*)^{\alpha} - nk_G + \left(k^* - k_G\right). \tag{8.28}$$

In every subsequent period $t > 0$, resources available for consumption will be

$$x_t = k_G^{\alpha} - nk_G, t > 0. \tag{8.29}$$

Clearly, in $t > 0$ available resources for consumption will be higher than in the status quo, since k_G maximises x_{SS}. Note next that $x_0 > x_t$ (this should be obvious, since at time 0 those alive can consume the difference between k^* and k_G). Therefore, in $t = 0$ resources available will also be higher than in the status quo. We conclude that the change increases available resources at all times. The planner can then split them between the two generations alive at any point in time, ensuring that everyone is at least as well off as in the original status quo, with at least one generation being better off. Put differently, the conclusion is that the decentralised solution leading to a steady state with a capital stock of k^* is not Pareto efficient. Generally, an economy with $k^* > k_G$ (alternatively, one with $r^* < n$) is known as a dynamically inefficient economy.

8.2.2 | Why is there dynamic inefficiency?

If there is perfect competition with no externalities or other market failures, why is the competitive solution inefficient? Shouldn't the First Welfare Theorem apply here as well? The reason why this isn't the case is the infinity of agents involved, while the welfare theorems assume a finite number of agents.[2]

An alternative way to build this intuition is that when the interest rate is below the growth rate of the economy, budget constraints are infinite and not well-defined, making our economic restrictions meaningless. This infinity gives the planner a way of redistributing income and consumption across generations that is not available to the market. In a market economy, individuals wanting to consume in old age must hold capital, even if the marginal return on capital is low. The planner, by contrast, can allocate resources between the current old and young in any manner they desire. They can take part of the fruit of the labour income of the young, for instance, and transfer it to the old without forcing them to carry so much capital. They can make sure that no generation is worse off by requiring each succeeding generation to do the same (and remember, there are infinitely many of them).[3] And, if the marginal product of capital is sufficiently low (lower than n, so the capital stock is above the golden rule), this way of transferring resources between young and old is more efficient than saving, so the planner can do better than the decentralized allocation.

8.2.3 | Are actual economies dynamically inefficient?

Recall that in the decentralised equilibrium we had

$$r_{SS} = f'\left(k_{SS}\right), \tag{8.30}$$

so the rental rate is equal to the marginal product of capital. Notice also that the rate of growth of the economy is n (income per-capita is constant, and the number of people is growing at the rate n). Therefore, the condition for dynamic inefficiency is simply that r_{SS} be lower than the rate of growth of the economy, or, taking depreciation into account (which we have ignored here), that the rate of interest minus depreciation be lower than the rate of growth of the economy.

Abel et al. (1989) extend the model to a context with uncertainty (meaning that there is more than one observed interest rate, since you have to adjust for risk), and show that in this case a sufficient condition for dynamic efficiency is that net capital income exceeds investment. To understand why, notice that the condition for dynamic efficiency is that the marginal product of capital (r) exceeds the growth rate of population (n), which happens to be the growth rate of the economy g. So, rK is the total return to capital and nK is total investment, so the condition $r > g$ can be tested by comparing the return on capital vs new investment: the net flow out of firms. Their evidence from seven industrialised countries suggests that this condition seems to be comfortably satisfied in practice.

However, a more recent appraisal, by Geerolf (2013), suggests that this picture may have actually changed or never been quite as sanguine. He updates the Abel et al. data, and provides a different treatment to mixed income and land rents.[4] With these adjustments, he finds that, in general, countries are in dynamically efficient positions, though some countries such as Japan and South Korea are definitely in a dynamically *inefficient* state! (And Australia joins the pack more recently...) In other words, it seems at the very least that we cannot so promptly dismiss dynamic inefficiency as a theoretical curiosity.

8.2.4 | Why is this important?

At this point you may be scratching your head asking why we seem to be spending so much time with the question of dynamic efficiency. The reason is that it is actually very relevant for a number of issues. For example, a dynamically inefficient economy is one in which fiscal policy has more leeway. Any debt level will eventually be wiped out by growth. Blanchard (2019) (p. 1197) takes this point seriously and argues

... the current U.S. situation, in which safe interest rates are expected to remain below growth rates for a long time, is more the historical norm than the exception. If the future is like the past, this implies that debt rollovers, that is the issuance of debt without a later increase in taxes, may well be feasible. Put bluntly, public debt may have no fiscal cost.

Not surprisingly, during 2020/2021, in response to the Covid-19 pandemic, many countries behaved as if they could tap unlimited resources through debt issuing. Dynamic inefficiency, if present and expected to remain in the future, would say that was feasible. If, on the contrary, economies are dynamically efficient, the increases in debt will required more taxes down the road.

The second issue has to do with the possibility of bubbles, that is, assets with no intrinsic value. By arbitrage, the asset price of a bubble will need to follow a typical pricing equation

$$(1 + r)P_t = P_{t+1}, \tag{8.31}$$

assuming for simplification a constant interest rate. The solution to this equation is

$$P_t = P_0(1 + r)^t, \tag{8.32}$$

(simply replace to check it is a solution). The price of the asset needs to grow at the rate of interest rate (you may hold a dividend-less asset, but you need to get your return!). In an NGM where $r > g$, this asset cannot exist, because it will eventually grow to become larger than the economy. But if $r < g$ this is not the case, and the bubble can exist. We will come back to this later. What are examples of such assets? Well, you may have heard about Bitcoins and cryptocurrency. In fact, money itself is really a bubble!

Finally, notice that the OLG model can deliver very low interest rates. So, it is an appropriate setup to explain the current world of low interest rates. We will come back to this in our chapters on fiscal and monetary policy.

Before this, however, we need to provide a continuous-time version of the OLG model, to provide continuity with the framework we have been using so far, and because it will be useful later on.

8.3 | Overlapping generations in continuous time

The OLG model can be modelled in continuous time through an ingenious mechanism: a constant probability of death and the possibility of pre-selling your assets upon death in exchange for a payment while you live. This provides cohorts and steady-state behaviour that make the model tractable. Even so, the details get a bit eerie. This section is only for the brave-hearted.

The trick to model the OLG model in a continuous-time framework is to include an age-independent probability of dying p. By the law of large numbers this will also be the death rate in the population. Assume a birth rate $n > p$. Together these two assumptions imply that population grows at the rate $n - p$.[5] This assumption is tractable but captures the spirit of the OLG model: not everybody is the same at the same time.

As in Blanchard (1985), we assume there exist companies that allow agents to insure against the risk of death (and, therefore, of leaving behind unwanted bequests). This means that at the time of death all of an individual's assets are turned over to the insurance company, which in turn pays a return of p on savings to all agents who remain alive. If r_t is the interest rate, then from the point of view of an individual agent, the return on savings is $r_t + p$.

We will also assume logarithmic utility which will make the algebra easier. As of time t the representative agent of the generation born at time τ maximises

$$\int_t^\infty \log c_{s,\tau} e^{-(\rho+p)(s-t)} ds, \tag{8.33}$$

subject to the flow budget constraint

$$\dot{a}_{t,\tau} = \left(r_t + p\right) a_{t,\tau} + y_{t,\tau} - c_{t,\tau}, \tag{8.34}$$

where $a_{t,\tau}$ is the stock of assets held by the individual and $y_{t,\tau}$ is labour income. The other constraint is the no-Ponzi game condition requiring that if the agent is still alive at time s, then

$$\lim_{s\to\infty} a_{s,\tau} e^{-\int_t^s (r_v+p)dv} \geq 0. \tag{8.35}$$

If we integrate the first constraint forward (look at our Mathematical Appedix!) and use the second constraint, we obtain

$$\int_t^\infty c_{s,\tau} e^{-\int_t^s (r_v+p)dv} ds \leq a_{t,\tau} + h_{t,\tau}, \tag{8.36}$$

where

$$h_{t,\tau} = \int_t^\infty y_{s,\tau} e^{-\int_t^s (r_v+p)dv} ds, \tag{8.37}$$

can be thought of as human capital. So the present value of consumption cannot exceed available assets, a constraint that will always hold with equality.

With log utility the individual Euler equation is our familiar

$$\dot{c}_{s,\tau} = \left(r_s - \rho\right) c_{s,\tau}, \tag{8.38}$$

which can be integrated forward to yield

$$c_{s,\tau} = c_{t,\tau} e^{\int_t^s (r_v-\rho)dv}. \tag{8.39}$$

Using this in the present-value budget constraint gives us the individual consumption function

$$\int_t^\infty c_{t,\tau} e^{\int_t^s (r_v-\rho)dv} e^{-\int_t^s (r_v+p)dv} ds = a_{t,\tau} + h_{t,\tau},$$

$$c_{t,\tau} \int_t^\infty e^{-(\rho+p)(s-t)} ds = a_{t,\tau} + h_{t,\tau}, \tag{8.40}$$

$$c_{t,\tau} = (\rho + p)(a_{t,\tau} + h_{t,\tau}),$$

so that the individual consumes a fixed share of available assets, as is standard under log utility. That completes the description of the behaviour of the representative agent in each generation.

The next task is to aggregate across generations or cohorts. Let $N_{t,\tau}$ be the size at time t of the cohort born at τ. Denoting the total size of the population alive at time τ as N_τ, we can write the initial size of the cohort born at τ (that is, the newcomers to the world at τ) as nN_τ. In addition, the probability that someone born at τ is still alive at $t \geq \tau$ is $e^{-p(t-\tau)}$. It follows that

$$N_{t,\tau} = nN_\tau e^{-p(t-\tau)}. \tag{8.41}$$

Now taking into account deaths and births, we can write the size of the total population alive at time t as a function of the size of the population that was alive at some time τ in the past: $N_t = N_\tau e^{(n-p)(t-\tau)}$. It follows that

$$\frac{N_{t,\tau}}{N_t} = ne^{-p(t-\tau)}e^{-(n-p)(t-\tau)} = ne^{-n(t-\tau)}. \qquad (8.42)$$

We conclude that the relative size at time t of the cohort born at τ is simply $ne^{-n(t-\tau)}$. For any variable $x_{t,\tau}$ define the per capita (or average) x_t as

$$x_t = \int_{-\infty}^t x_{t,\tau} \left(\frac{N_{t,\tau}}{N_t}\right) d\tau$$

$$x_t = \int_{-\infty}^t x_{t,\tau} ne^{-n(t-\tau)} d\tau. \qquad (8.43)$$

Applying this definition to individual consumption from (8.40) we have

$$c_t = (\rho + p)\left(a_t + h_t\right), \qquad (8.44)$$

so that per capita consumption is proportional to per capita assets, where

$$a_t = \int_{-\infty}^t a_{t,\tau} ne^{-n(t-\tau)} d\tau, \qquad (8.45)$$

and

$$h_t = \int_{-\infty}^t h_{t,\tau} ne^{-n(t-\tau)} d\tau, \qquad (8.46)$$

are non-human and human wealth, respectively. Focus on each, beginning with human wealth, which using the expression for $h_{t,\tau}$ in (8.37) can be written as

$$h_t = \int_{-\infty}^t \left\{\int_t^\infty y_{s,\tau} e^{-\int_t^s (r_v + p)dv} ds\right\} ne^{-n(t-\tau)} d\tau. \qquad (8.47)$$

Now, if labour income is the same for all agents who are alive at some time s, we have

$$h_t = \int_{-\infty}^t \left\{\int_t^\infty y_s e^{-\int_t^s (r_v + p)dv} ds\right\} ne^{-n(t-\tau)} d\tau, \qquad (8.48)$$

where the expression in curly brackets is the same for all agents. It follows that

$$h_t = \int_t^\infty y_s e^{-\int_t^s (r_v + p)dv} ds. \qquad (8.49)$$

Finally, differentiating with respect to time t (with the help of Leibniz's rule) we arrive at[6]

$$\dot{h}_t = \left(r_t + p\right) h_t - y_t, \qquad (8.50)$$

which is the equation of motion for human capital. It can also we written as

$$r_t + p = \frac{\dot{h}_t + y_t}{h_t}. \qquad (8.51)$$

This has our familiar, intuitive asset pricing interpretation. If we think of human capital as an asset, then the RHS is the return on this asset, including the capital gain $\dot{h}_t$ and the dividend y_t, both expressed in proportion to the value h_t of the asset. That has to be equal to the individual discount rate $r_t + p$, which appears on the LHS.

Turn next to the evolution of non-human wealth. Differentiating a_t, from (8.45), with respect to t (again using Leibniz's rule!) we have

$$\dot{a}_t = na_t + n \int_{-\infty}^{t} \left\{ -a_{t,\tau} n e^{-n(t-\tau)} + e^{-n(t-\tau)} \dot{a}_{t,\tau} \right\} d\tau,$$

$$\dot{a}_t = na_{t,0} - na_t + n \int_{-\infty}^{t} \dot{a}_{t,\tau} e^{-n(t-\tau)} d\tau,$$

(8.52)

since $a_{t,0}$ is non-human wealth at birth, which is zero for all cohorts, we have

$$\dot{a}_t = -na_t - n \int_{-\infty}^{t} \dot{a}_{t,\tau} e^{-n(t-\tau)} d\tau,$$

$$\dot{a}_t = -na_t + \int_{-\infty}^{t} \left\{ (r_t + p) a_{t,\tau} + y_t - c_{t,\tau} \right\} n e^{-n(t-\tau)} d\tau,$$

$$\dot{a}_t = -na_t + (r_t + p) \int_{-\infty}^{t} a_{t,\tau} n e^{-n(t-\tau)} d\tau + y_t \int_{-\infty}^{t} n e^{-n(t-\tau)} d\tau - \int_{-\infty}^{t} c_{t,\tau} n e^{-n(t-\tau)} d\tau,$$

(8.53)

$$\dot{a}_t = \left[r_t - (n - p) \right] a_t + y_t - c_t.$$

Notice that while the individual the rate of return is $r_t + p$, for the economy as a whole the rate of return is only r_t, since the p is a transfer from people who die to those who remain alive, and washes out once we aggregate. Recall, however, that a_t is assets per capita, so naturally $(n - p)$, the rate of growth of population, must be subtracted from r_t.

The consumption function (8.40) and the laws of motion for per capita human and non-human wealth, (8.50) and (8.53), completely characterise the dynamic evolution of this economy. It can be expressed as a two-dimensional system in the following way. Differentiate the consumption function with respect to time in order to obtain

$$\dot{c}_t = (\rho + p) \left(\dot{a}_t + \dot{h}_t \right).$$

(8.54)

Next use the laws of motion for both forms of wealth to obtain

$$\dot{c}_t = (\rho + p) \left[(r_t - n + p) a_t - c_t + (r_t + p) h_t \right].$$

(8.55)

Write the consumption function in the following way

$$h_t = \frac{c_t}{\rho + p} - a_t,$$

(8.56)

and use it to substitute out h_t from the $\dot{c}_t$ equation (8.55):

$$\dot{c}_t = (\rho + p) \left[(r_t - n + p) a_t - c_t - (r_t + p) a_t + \frac{r_t + p}{\rho + p} c_t \right],$$

$$\dot{c}_t = (\rho + p) \left[-na_t + \frac{r_t - \rho}{\rho + p} c_t \right],$$

(8.57)

$$\dot{c}_t = (r_t - \rho) c_t - n(p + \rho) a_t.$$

This is a kind of modified Euler equation. The first term is standard, of course, but the second term is not. That second term comes from the fact that, at any instant, there are n newcomers for each person alive, and they dilute assets per capita by na_t since at birth they have no assets. This slows down the average rate of consumption growth.

This modified Euler equation plus the law of motion for non-human wealth (8.53) are a two-dimensional system of differential equations in c_t and a_t. That system, plus an initial condition and a transversality condition for a_t, fully describes the behaviour of the economy.

8.3.1 | The closed economy

We have not taken a stance on what kind of asset a_t is. We now do so. In the closed economy we assume that $a_t = k_t$, and k_t is per-capita productive capital that yields output according to the function $y_t = k_t^\alpha$, where $0 < \alpha < 1$. In this context profit maximisation dictates that $r_t = \alpha k_t^{\alpha-1}$, so that our two differential equations become

$$\dot{c}_t = \left(\alpha k_t^{\alpha-1} - \rho \right) c_t - n(p + \rho)k_t,$$

$$\dot{k}_t = (1 + \alpha)k_t^\alpha - (n - p)k_t - c_t. \tag{8.58}$$

In steady state we have

$$\frac{c^*}{k^*} = \frac{n(p+\rho)}{\alpha k^{*\alpha-1}-\rho},$$

$$(1 + \alpha)k^{*\alpha-1} - (n - p) = \frac{c^*}{k^*}. \tag{8.59}$$

Combining the two yields

$$(1 + \alpha)k^{*\alpha-1} = (n - p) + \frac{n(p + \rho)}{\alpha k^{*\alpha-1-\rho}}, \tag{8.60}$$

which pins down the capital stock. For given k^*, the first SS equation yields consumption. Rewrite the last equation as

$$\alpha k^{*\alpha-1} - \rho = \frac{n(p + \rho)}{(1 + \alpha)k^{*\alpha-1} - (n - p)} > 0. \tag{8.61}$$

So the steady-state level of the (per capita) capital stock is smaller than the modified golden rule level that solves $\alpha k^{\alpha-1} = \rho$, implying under-accumulation of capital.[7] This is in contrast to the NGM, in which the modified golden rule applies, and the discrete-time OLG model with two-period lives, in which over-accumulation may occur. Before examining that issue, consider dynamics, described in Figure 8.5.

Along the saddle-path c_t and k_t move together. If the initial condition is at $k > k^*$, then consumption will start above its SS level and both c_t and k_t will gradually fall until reaching the steady-state level. If, by contrast, the initial condition is at $k < k^*$, then consumption will start below its steady-state level and both c_t and k_t will rise gradually until reaching the steady state.

8.3.2 | A simple extension

But how come we have no dynamic inefficiency in this model? Just switching to continuous time does away with this crucial result? Not really. The actual reason is that the model so far is not quite like what we had before, in another aspect: there is no retirement! In contrast to the standard OLG model, individuals have a smooth stream of labour income throughout their lives, and hence do not need to save a great deal in order to provide for consumption later in life.

Figure 8.5   Capital accumulation in the continuous time OLG model

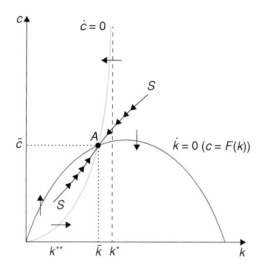

Introducing retirement (i.e. a stretch of time with no income, late in life) is analytically cumbersome, but as Blanchard (1985) demonstrates, there is an alternative that is easily modelled, has the same flavour, and delivers the same effects: assuming labour income declines gradually as long as an individual is alive.

Let's take a look. Blanchard (1985) assumes that each individual starts out with one unit of effective labour and thereafter his available labour declines at the rate $\gamma > 0$. At time t, the labour earnings of a person in the cohort born at τ is given by $w_t e^{-\gamma(t-\tau)}$, where w_t is the market wage per unit of effective labour at time t. It follows that individual human wealth for a member of the τ generation is

$$h_{t,\tau} = \int_t^\infty w_s e^{-\gamma(s-\tau)} e^{-\int_t^s (r_v + p)dv} ds. \tag{8.62}$$

Using the same derivation as in the baseline model, we arrive at a modified Euler equation

$$\dot{c}_t = \left(\alpha k_t^{\alpha-1} + \gamma - \rho\right) c_t - (n + \gamma)(p + \rho)k_t, \tag{8.63}$$

which now includes the parameter γ.

The steady state per-capita capital stock is now again pinned down by the expression

$$k^{*\alpha-1} = (n - p) + \frac{(n + \gamma)(p + \rho)}{\alpha + \gamma - \rho}, \tag{8.64}$$

which can be rewritten as

$$\alpha k^{*\alpha-1} - \rho = \frac{(n + \gamma)(p + \rho)}{k^{*\alpha-1} - (n - p)} - \gamma. \tag{8.65}$$

So if γ is sufficiently large, then the steady-state per capita capital stock can be larger than the golden rule level, which is the one that solves the equation $\alpha k^{\alpha-1} = \rho$. This would imply over-accumulation of capital. The intuition is that the declining path of labour income forces people to save more, too

Figure 8.6 Capital accumulation with retirement

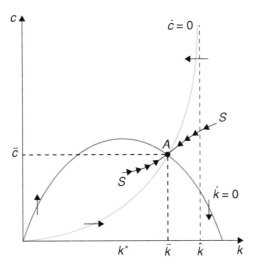

much in fact. Again, intergenerational transfers would have been a more efficient way to pay for retirement, but they cannot happen in the decentralized equilibrium, in the absence of intergenerational altruism.

In this case, dynamics are given by Figure 8.6, with the steady state to the right of the modified golden-rule level of capital:

8.3.3 | Revisiting the current account in the open economy

We can also revisit the small open economy as a special case of interest. For that, let's go back to the case in which $\gamma = 0$, and consider what happens when the economy is open, and instead of being capital, the asset is a foreign bond f_t that pays the fixed world interest rate r. In turn, labour income is now, for simplicity, an exogenous endowment $y_{t,\tau} = y$ for all moments t and for all cohorts τ.

The two key differential equations now become

$$\dot{c}_t = (r - \rho)c_t - n(p + \rho)f_t,$$

$$\dot{f}_t = [r - (n - p)]f_t + y - c_t,$$

(8.66)

with steady-state values

$$[r - (n - p)]f^* + y = c^*,$$

(8.67)

$$(r - \rho)c^* = n(p + \rho)f^*,$$

(8.68)

which together pin down the levels of consumption and foreign assets. The first equation reveals that in steady state the current account must be balanced, with consumption equal to endowment income plus interest earnings from foreign assets. As the second equation reveals, the steady-state stock of foreign assets can be positive or negative, depending on whether r is larger or smaller than ρ.

If $r > \rho$, individual consumption is always increasing, agents are accumulating over their lifetimes, and the steady-state level of foreign assets is positive. If $r = \rho$, individual consumption is flat and they neither save nor dissave; steady-state foreign assets are zero. Finally, if $r < \rho$, individual consumption is always falling, agents are decumulating over their lifetimes, and in the steady state the economy is a net debtor.

Equilibrium dynamics are given by Figure 8.7, drawn for the case $r > \rho$. It is easy to show that the system is saddle-path stable if $r < \rho + p$. So the diagram below corresponds to the case $\rho < r < \rho + p$. Along the saddle-path, the variables c_t and f_t move together until reaching the steady state.

In this model the economy does not jump to the steady state (as the open-economy model in Chapter 4 did). The difference is that new generations are constantly being born without any foreign assets and they need to accumulate them. The steady state is reached when the accumulation of the young offsets the decumulation of the older generation.

Figure 8.7 The current account in the continuous time OLG model

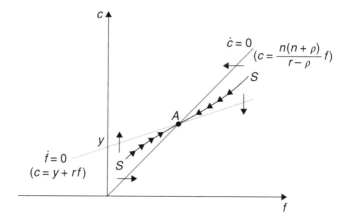

8.4 | What have we learned?

In this chapter we developed the second workhorse model of modern macroeconomics: the OLG model. This framework allows us to look at questions in which assuming a single representative agent is not a useful shortcut. We will see how this will enable us to tackle some key policy issues, starting in the next chapter.

Moreover, we have already shown how this model yields new insights about capital accumulation, relative to the NGM. For instance, the possibility of dynamic inefficiency – that is to say, of over-accumulation of capital – emerges. This is a result of the absence of intergenerational links, which entail that individuals may need to save too much, as it is the only way to meet their consumption needs as their labor income declines over their life cycle.

Notes

[1] If the production function makes the function hit the 45-degree line with a negative slope the model can give origin to cyclical behaviour around the steady-state. This cycle can be stable or unstable depending on the slope of the curve.

[2] The First Welfare Theorem can be extended to deal with an infinite number of agents, but this requires a condition that the total value of resources available to all agents taken together be finite (at equilibrium prices). This is not satisfied in the OLG economy, which lasts forever.

[3] For those of you who are mathematically inclined, the argument is similar to Hilbert's Grand Hotel paradox. If the argument sounds counter-intuitive and esoteric, it's because it is – so much so that some people apparently think the paradox can be used to prove the existence of God! (see http://en.wikipedia.org/wiki/Hilbert's_paradox_of_the_Grand_Hotel).

[4] Mixed income is that which is registered as accruing to capital, because it comes from the residual income of businesses, but that Geerolf argues should be better understood, at least partly as, returns to entrepreneurial labour. Land rents, which Abel et al. only had for the U.S., should not be understood as capital in their sense, as land cannot be accumulated.

[5] Suppose, in addition, that the economy starts with a population $N_0 = 1$.

[6] Leibniz's rule? Why, of course, you recall it from calculus: that's how you differentiate an integral. If you need a refresher, here it is: take a function $g(x) = \int_{a(x)}^{b(x)} f(x, s)ds$, the derivative of g with respect to x is: $\frac{dg}{dx} = f(x, b(x))\frac{db}{dx} - f(x, a(x))\frac{da}{dx} + \int_{a(x)}^{b(x)} \frac{df(x,s)}{dx}ds$. Intuitively, there are three components of the marginal impact of changing x on g: those of increasing the upper and lower limits of the integral (which are given by f evaluated at those limits), and that of changing the function f at every point between those limits (which is given by $\int_{a(x)}^{b(x)} \frac{df(x,s)}{dx}ds$). All the other stuff is what you get from your run-of-the-mill chain rule.

[7] Because individuals discount the future ($\rho > 0$), this is not the same as the golden rule in the Solow model, which maximises consumption on the steady state. In the modified golden rule, the capital stock is smaller than that which maximises consumption, precisely because earlier consumption is preferred to later consumption.

References

Abel, A. B., Mankiw, N. G., Summers, L. H., & Zeckhauser, R. J. (1989). Assessing dynamic efficiency: Theory and evidence. *The Review of Economic Studies, 56*(1), 1–19.

Blanchard, O. (2019). Public debt and low interest rates. *American Economic Review, 109*(4), 1197–1229.

Blanchard, O. J. (1985). Debt, deficits, and finite horizons. *Journal of Political Economy, 93*(2), 223–247.

Diamond, P. A. (1965). National debt in a neoclassical growth model. *The American Economic Review, 55*(5), 1126–1150.

Geerolf, F. (2013). Reassessing dynamic efficiency. *Manuscript, Toulouse School of Economics.*

Samuelson, P. A. (1958). An exact consumption-loan model of interest with or without the social contrivance of money. *Journal of Political Economy, 66*(6), 467–482.

CHAPTER 9

An application: Pension systems and transitions

Let us put our OLG framework to work in analysing the topic of pensions, a particularly suitable topic to be discussed using this framework. This is a pressing policy issue both in developed and developing countries, particularly in light of the ongoing demographic transition by which fewer working-age individuals will be around to provide for the obligations to retired individuals.

It is also a controversial policy issue because the question always looms as to whether people save enough for retirement on their own. Also, even though the models of the previous chapter suggested there may be instances in which it may be socially beneficial to implement intergenerational transfers such as pensions, this hinged on a context of dynamic inefficiency that was far from established. And then, if the economies are not dynamically inefficient, should the government interfere with the savings decisions of individuals? These are interesting but difficult policy questions. Particularly because it confronts us head-on with the difficulties of assessing welfare when there is no representative agent. Also, because, as we will see, once general equilibrium considerations are taken into account, sometimes things turn out exactly opposite to the way you may have thought they would!

So, let's tackle the basics of how pension systems affect individual savings behaviour and, eventually, capital accumulation. As in the previous chapter, the market economy is composed of individuals and firms. Individuals live for two periods (this assumption can easily be extended to allow many generations). They work for firms, receiving a wage, and also lend their savings to firms, receiving a rental rate. If there is a pension system, they make contributions and receive benefits as well.

9.1 | Fully funded and pay-as-you-go systems

There are two types of pension systems. In pay-as-you-go, the young are taxed to pay for retirement benefits. In the fully funded regimes, each generation saves for its own sake. The implications for capital accumulation are radically different.

Let d_t be the contribution of a young person at time t, and let b_t be the benefit received by an old person at time t. There are two alternative ways of organising and paying for pensions: *fully funded* and *pay-as-you-go*. We consider each in turn.

How to cite this book chapter:
Campante, F., Sturzenegger, F. and Velasco, A. 2021. *Advanced Macroeconomics: An Easy Guide.*
 Ch. 9. 'An application: Pension systems and transitions', pp. 135–146. London: LSE Press.
 DOI: https://doi.org/10.31389/lsepress.ame.i License: CC-BY-NC 4.0.

Fully funded system Under a fully funded system, the contributions made when young are returned with interest when old:

$$b_{t+1} = (1 + r_{t+1})d_t. \tag{9.1}$$

This is because the contribution is invested in real assets at the ongoing interest rate.

Pay-as-you-go system Under a pay-as-you-go system, the contributions made by the current young go directly to the current old:

$$b_t = (1 + n)d_t. \tag{9.2}$$

The reason why population growth pops in is because if there is population growth there is a larger cohort contributing than receiving. Notice the subtle but critical change of subscript on the benefit on the left-hand side.

There are many questions that can be asked about the effects of such pension programs on the economy. Here we focus on only one: Do they affect savings, capital accumulation, and growth?[1]

With pensions, the problem of an individual born at time t becomes

$$\max \log\left(c_{1t}\right) + (1 + \rho)^{-1} \log\left(c_{2t+1}\right), \tag{9.3}$$

subject to

$$c_{1t} + s_t + d_t = w_t, \tag{9.4}$$

$$c_{2t+1} = (1 + r_{t+1})s_t + b_{t+1}. \tag{9.5}$$

The first-order condition for a maximum is still the Euler equation

$$c_{2t+1} = \left(\frac{1 + r_{t+1}}{1 + \rho}\right) c_{1t}. \tag{9.6}$$

Substituting for c_{1t} and c_{2t+1} in terms of s, w, and r implies a saving function

$$s_t = \left(\frac{1}{2 + \rho}\right) w_t - \frac{\left(1 + r_{t+1}\right) d_t + (1 + \rho) b_{t+1}}{(2 + \rho)\left(1 + r_{t+1}\right)}. \tag{9.7}$$

Again, savings is an increasing function of wage income, and is a decreasing function of contributions and benefits – leaving aside the link between those, and the general equilibrium effects through factor prices. These will mean, however, that savings will be affected by the pension variables in a complicated way.

With Cobb-Douglas technology, the firm's rules for optimal behaviour are

$$r_t = \alpha k_t^{\alpha-1}, \tag{9.8}$$

and

$$w_t = (1 - \alpha) k_t^{\alpha} = (1 - \alpha) y_t. \tag{9.9}$$

9.1.1 | Fully funded pension system

Fully funded systems do not affect capital accumulation. What people save through the pension system they dissave in their private savings choice.

Let us start by looking at the effect of this kind of program on individual savings. (The distinction between individual and aggregate savings will become critical later on.) We can simply insert (9.1) into (9.7) to get

$$s_t = \left(\frac{1}{2+\rho}\right) w_t - d_t. \tag{9.10}$$

Therefore,

$$\frac{\partial s_t}{\partial d_t} = -1. \tag{9.11}$$

In words, holding the wage constant, pension contributions decrease private savings exactly one for one. The intuition is that the pension system provides a rate of return equal to that of private savings, so it is as if the system were taking part of that individual's income and investing that amount itself. The individual is indifferent about who does the saving, caring only about the rate of return.

Hence, including the pension savings in total savings, a change in contributions d leaves overall, or aggregate savings (and, therefore, capital accumulation and growth) unchanged. To make this clear, let's define aggregate savings as the saving that is done privately plus through the pension system. In a fully funded system the aggregate savings equals

$$s_t^{agg} = s_t + d_t = \left(\frac{1}{2+\rho}\right) w_t. \tag{9.12}$$

This is exactly the same as in Chapter 7, without pensions.

9.1.2 | Pay-as-you-go pension system

Pay-as-you-go pension schemes reduce the capital stock of the economy.

To see the effect of this program on savings, insert (9.2) into (9.7) (paying attention to the appropriate time subscripts) to get

$$s_t = \left(\frac{1}{2+\rho}\right) w_t - \frac{\left(1+r_{t+1}\right) d_t + (1+\rho)(1+n) d_{t+1}}{(2+\rho)\left(1+r_{t+1}\right)}. \tag{9.13}$$

This is a rather complicated expression that depends on d_t and d_{t+1} – that is, on the size of the contributions made by each generation. But there is one case that lends itself to a simple interpretation. Assume $d_t = d_{t+1} = d$, so that contributions are the same per generation. Then equation (9.13) becomes

$$s_t = \left(\frac{1}{2+\rho}\right) w_t - d \left[\frac{\left(1+r_{t+1}\right) + (1+\rho)(1+n)}{(2+\rho)\left(1+r_{t+1}\right)}\right]. \tag{9.14}$$

Note that, from an individual's perspective, the return on her contributions is given by n, and not r. This return depends on there being more individuals to make contributions to the pension system in each period – you can see how demographic dynamics play a crucial role here!

From (9.14) we have

$$\frac{\partial s_t}{\partial d_t} = -\frac{\left(1 + r_{t+1}\right) + \left(1 + \rho\right)\left(1 + n\right)}{\left(2 + \rho\right)\left(1 + r_{t+1}\right)} < 0. \tag{9.15}$$

We can see contributions decrease individual savings – and, in principle, aggregate savings, as here they coincide (see the caveat below). Why do private and aggregate savings coincide? Because the pension system here is a transfer scheme from young to old, and not an alternative savings scheme. The only source of capital is private savings s_t.

9.1.3 | How do pensions affect the capital stock?

So far we have asked what happens to savings holding interest and wages constant – that is to say, the partial equilibrium effect of pensions. In the case of a fully funded system, that is of no consequence, since changes in contributions leave savings – and hence, capital accumulation, wages, and interest rates – unchanged. But it matters in the case of a pay-as-you-go system.

To examine the general equilibrium effects of changes in contributions within the latter system, recall that capital accumulation is given by

$$k_{t+1} = \frac{s_t}{1 + n}. \tag{9.16}$$

Substituting (9.14) into this equation we have

$$k_{t+1} = \left(\frac{1}{2 + \rho}\right)\frac{w_t}{1 + n} - h\left(k_{t+1}\right)d, \tag{9.17}$$

where

$$h\left(k_{t+1}\right) = \frac{1 + \left(1 + \rho\right)\left(1 + n\right)\left(1 + r_{t+1}\right)^{-1}}{\left(1 + n\right)\left(2 + \rho\right)}, \tag{9.18}$$

$$= \frac{1 + \left(1 + \rho\right)\left(1 + n\right)\left(1 + \alpha k_{t+1}^{\alpha-1}\right)^{-1}}{\left(1 + n\right)\left(2 + \rho\right)}, \tag{9.19}$$

and where $h'\left(k_{t+1}\right) > 0$. (Note the use of (9.8) above.)

Next, totally differentiating (9.17), holding k_t constant, and rearranging, we have

$$\frac{dk_{t+1}}{dd_t} = -\frac{h\left(k_{t+1}\right)}{1 + h'\left(k_{t+1}\right)d} < 0. \tag{9.20}$$

Therefore, the effect of an increase in contributions in a pay-as-you-go system is to shift down the savings locus. The consequences appear in Figure 9.1. The new steady-state capital stock is lower. If the capital stock at the time of the policy shock is to the left of the new steady state, the economy continues to accumulate capital, but at a rate slower than before the change.

Figure 9.1   Introduction of pay-as-you-go social security

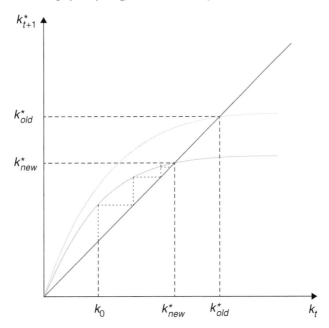

9.1.4 | Pensions and welfare

Is this a desirable outcome? Does it raise or lower welfare? Suppose before the change $d_t = 0$, so the change amounts to introducing pensions in a pay-as-you-go manner. Who is better off as a result?

The old at time t, who now receive total benefits equal to $(1+n)d_t$ and contribute nothing, are clearly better off. What about other generations? If r was less than n before the introduction of pensions, then the policy change reduces (perhaps totally eliminates) dynamic inefficiency, and all other generations benefit as well. In that case, introducing pensions is Pareto improving. The recent work that we saw in the last chapter suggests that this possibility is not as remote as one may have previously thought. In fact, this idea has coloured some recent policy thinking about reform in places like China.[2]

But if r is equal to or larger than n before the introduction of the pension system, then the policy change creates a conflict. The old at time t still benefit, but other generations are worse off. In this case, introducing pensions is not Pareto improving. Even if that is the case, this by no means implies that it is always a bad idea politically, or even that is always socially undesirable. The point is that there will be winners and losers, and the relative gains and losses will have to be weighed against one another somehow.

9.2 | Moving out of a pay-as-you-go system

The effects on the capital stock from transitioning from a pay-as-you-go system to a fully funded system depend on how the transition is financed. If it is financed with taxes on the young, the capital stock increases. If it is funded by issuing debt, the capital stock may decrease.

There are several transitions associated with the introduction or revamping of pensions systems, and that we may want to analyze. For example, you could move from no pension system and implement a full capitalisation system. As aggregate saving behaviour does not change, we do not expect anything really meaningful to happen from such change in terms of capital accumulation and growth. (That is, of course, to the extent that rational behaviour is a good enough assumption when it comes to individual savings behaviour. We will get back to this pretty soon when we talk about consumption.) Alternatively, as discussed above, if we implement a pay-as-you-go system, the initial old are happy, while the effect for future generations remains indeterminate and depends on the dynamic efficiency of the economy.

However, in recent years it has become fashionable to move away from pay-as-you-go systems to fully funded ones. The reasons for such change is different in each country, but usually can be traced back to deficit and sometimes insolvent systems (sometimes corruption-ridden) that need to be revamped.[3] But one of the main reasons was to undo the capital depletion associated with pay-as-you-go systems. Thus, these countries hoped that going for a capitalisation system would increase the capital stock and income over time.

In what remains of this chapter we will show that what happens in such transitions from pay-as-you-go to fully funded systems depends very much on how the transition is financed. There are two options: either the transition is financed by taxing the current young, or it is financed by issuing debt. Both have quite different implications.

To make the analysis simple, in what follows we will keep $n = 0$. (Note that this puts us in the region where $r > n$, i.e. that of dynamic efficiency.)

Aggregate savings without pensions or with a fully funded system are

$$s_t^{agg} = \left(\frac{1}{2+\rho}\right) w_t. \tag{9.21}$$

With a pay-as-you-go system, they are

$$s_t^{agg} = s_t = \left(\frac{1}{2+\rho}\right) w_t - \frac{\left(1+r_{t+1}\right)d + (1+\rho)d}{(2+\rho)\left(1+r_{t+1}\right)}, \tag{9.22}$$

which is trivially lower (we knew this already). So now the question is how savings move when going from a pay-as-you-go to a fully funded system. You may think they have to go up, but we need to be careful: we need to take care of the old, who naturally will not be part of the new system, and their retirement income has to be financed. This, in turn, may have effects of its own on capital accumulation.

9.2.1 | Financing the transition with taxes on the young

If the transition is financed out of taxes, the young have to use their wages for consumption (c_{1t}), private savings (s_t), to pay for their contributions (d and also for taxes τ_t):

$$c_{1t} + s_t + d + \tau_t = w_t. \tag{9.23}$$

Future consumption is in turn given by

$$c_{2t+1} = \left(1 + r_{t+1}\right) s_t + \left(1 + r_{t+1}\right) d, \tag{9.24}$$

as we are in a fully funded system. Because taxes here are charged to finance the old, we have $\tau_t = d$ (remember we have assumed population growth to be equal to zero). If you follow the logic above, it can be shown that in this case we have

$$s_t^{agg} = \frac{(w_t - \tau_t)}{(2 + \rho)}. \tag{9.25}$$

You may notice that this is lower than the steady-state savings rate (next period, i.e. in 30 years, there are no more taxes), but you can also show that it is higher than in the pay-as-you-go system. To do so, replace τ_t with d in (9.25) and then compare the resulting expression with that of (9.22).

So savings goes up slowly, approaching its steady-state value. These dynamics are what supports World Bank recommendations that countries should move from pay-as-you-go to fully capitalised systems. Notice however that the reform hurts the current young that have to save for their own and for the current old generation. Then remember that one period here is actually one generation, so it's something like 30 years. What do you think would be the political incentives, as far as reforming the system, along those lines?

9.2.2 | Financing the transition by issuing debt

Now let's think about how things would change if the transition is financed by issuing debt. (Maybe that is a politically more palatable option!) In this case, for the current young there are no taxes, and debt is another asset that they can purchase:

$$c_{1t} + s_t + d + g_{debt} = w_t, \tag{9.26}$$

so consumption in old age can be

$$c_{2t+1} = \left(1 + r_{t+1}\right) s_t + \left(1 + r_{t+1}\right) d + \left(1 + r_{t+1}\right) g_{debt}. \tag{9.27}$$

Following the same logic as before, private savings are

$$s_t = \frac{w_t}{(2 + \rho)} - d - g_{debt}. \tag{9.28}$$

How about aggregate savings? Note that contributions to the fully funded system d, work as savings from an aggregate perspective: they are available to finance the accumulation of capital. However, the amount of debt issued by the government is in fact not used for capital accumulation, but rather for consumption, because it is a transfer to the old. As such, aggregate savings are given by

$$s_t^{agg} = s_t + d = \frac{w_t}{(2 + \rho)} - g_{debt} = \frac{w_t}{(2 + \rho)} - d, \tag{9.29}$$

where in the last step we use the fact that (under no population growth) the government issues $g_{debt} = d$ of debt to pay benefits to the current old.

Let's see how this compares to the pay-as-you-go savings. Rewriting equation (9.22) which shows the savings rate in a pay-as-you-go system

$$s_t^{agg} = s_t = \left(\frac{1}{2 + \rho}\right) w_t - d \frac{\left(1 + r_{t+1}\right) + (1 + \rho)}{(2 + \rho)\left(1 + r_{t+1}\right)}. \tag{9.30}$$

Notice that if

$$\frac{\left(1 + r_{t+1}\right) + (1 + \rho)}{(2 + \rho)\left(1 + r_{t+1}\right)} < 1, \tag{9.31}$$

then in this case savings is even lower than in the pay-as-you-go system, which happens because the government now pays r on its debt, which in this case is higher than n.

Another way to see this is if the government imposed a fully funded system but then makes the pension firms purchase government debt that is used for the current old (i.e. for consumption). There is no way this type of reform can increase the capital stock.

9.2.3 | Discussion

The above discussion embodies the dimensions of intergenerational equity, the potential efficiency effects, and also the importance of how policies are implemented. Moving from a pay-as-you-go system to a fully funded one is not immune to the way the transition is financed. This should capture your attention: you need to work out fully the effects of policies!

Pension reform has been an important debate in developed and developing countries alike. In the 1990s there was an emerging consensus that moving to a fully funded system would be instrumental in the development of local capital markets. This view triggered reforms in many countries. Here we want to discuss two cases that turned out very different: those of Argentina and Chile.[4]

Chile, for many years, was considered the poster-child for this reform. It implemented a change to a fully funded system in 1980. Furthermore, this was done at a time of fiscal consolidation. In the framework of the previous section, this is akin to the current working-age generation saving for their own retirement, as well as to pay for their contemporaneous old. As the theory suggested, the resources were deployed into investment, the savings rate, and Chile had a successful growth spurt, which many observers associated with the reform.

Argentina, on the other hand, also migrated to a fully funded system, but rather than streamlining the budget, the deficit increased. In fact, it increased by an amount not very different from the loss in pension funds that were now going to private accounts. In the framework of the previous section, this is akin to financing the transition with debt.

As we saw, in this case the reform reduces savings and, in fact, there was no discernible development of Argentine capital markets. The inflow of contributions into the pension funds went directly to buy government debt. But it was even worse: the bloating of the deficit increased the government's explicit debt. Of course, the counterpart was a reduction in future pension liabilities. But the market was not persuaded, and in 2001 Argentina plunged into a debt crisis. Many observers associated this macroeconomic crisis to the pension reform. A few years later, Argentina renationalized the pension system, moving away from a fully funded approach. The temptation to do so was big. The current generation basically ate up the accumulated, albeit little, capital stock, again, as predicted in our simple OLG specification.

While the contrast with Chile could not be starker, the system there eventually also came under attack. The math is simple. If the return to investments is 5%, an individual that contributes 10% of her wage to a pension system for say, 42 years, and has an expected pension life of 25 years, can actually obtain a replacement ratio of close to 100% (the exact number is 96%). But reality turned out to be far from that. When looking back at the evidence, the average retirement age in Chile has been around 62 years, and the pension life 25 years. However, people reach retirement with, on average, 20 years of contributions, not 42. This allows for a replacement ratio of only 24%. It is this low replacement ratio that has been the focus of complaints. Thus, most of these attempts eventually introduced some sort of low income protection for the elderly.

9.2.4 | Do people save enough?

The above setup assumes that agents optimise their savings to maximise intertemporal utility, with or without pensions. However, there are several reasons why this may not be the case. We will get into more detail in Chapters 11 and 12, but it is worth going over some of the possibilities here, in the context of pensions.

First and foremost, people may believe that if they don't save, the government will step in and bail them out. If you believe that, why would you save? This time inconsistency feature (the government may tell you to save but, if you don't, will feel tempted to help you out) may lead to suboptimal savings.

Even in the case of the U.S., where these considerations may not be so relevant, there has been ample discussion about the intensity with which people save for retirement. On the one hand, Scholz et al. (2006) shows that the accumulation of assets of people roughly matches the life cycle hypothesis (which we will see in detail in Chapter 11); on the other hand, there is evidence that suggests that consumption levels drop upon retirement (Bernheim et al. 2001), which is inconsistent with optimal savings. One possible reconciliation of these two facts is given by including the dimension of what type of assets people use for savings. Beshears et al. (2018) show that people save sizable amounts, but they tend to save in *illiquid* assets. Illiquid assets may provide unusually high returns (for example, owning your house provides steady rental income). Kaplan et al. (2014) estimate that housing services provides an after-tax risk adjusted rate of return of close to 8%. In such a world agents hold a large share of illiquid assets but consumption tracks income while they use some potentially expensive mechanisms to partially smooth consumption.

Present bias has also been mentioned as a reason why people tend to save less than the optimal level. In this case, imposing a pension system that forces people to save may be a ex ante optimal commitment device. We will discuss present bias in detail in Chapter 12.

Finally, recent research on savings for retirement has delivered some interesting new ideas and policy suggestions. One typical way of saving in the U.S. is the 401K programs, where you save with the benefit of a tax deferral: your income is taxed when withdrawing the funds. These programs are typically arranged with your employer, which matches the contributions with a vesting period to entice labour stability. Yet it has been found that matching is a fairly inefficient way to stimulate savings. Madrian (2013) finds that a matching contribution of 25% increases savings by 5%. In contrast default setting seems, to have a much stronger effect. Madrian and Shea (2001) show that when a company shifted from a default where, unless the worker would opt out, it would start contributing 3% of its salary to a 401K program, they found that fifteen months after the change, 85% of the workers participated, and 65% contributed 3% of their wages. This compared with only 49% participation for those workers hired previously in which only 4% contributed 3%. In short, default standards may be powerful (and cheap) tools for incentivizing savings.

9.3 | What have we learned?

In this chapter we applied the standard OLG model to study the issue of social security and pensions. We saw that the implications for capital accumulation can vary dramatically depending on the nature of the system. While fully-funded systems simply offer an alternative mechanisms to private savings, pay-as-you-go systems are essentially intergenerational transfers. These reduce the incentive for private savings, and reduce capital accumulation.

That said, we have also seen that the effects of policy reforms hinge very dramatically on implementation details. For instance, transitioning from pay-as-you-go to a fully funded system can even reduce capital accumulation, if the transition is financed with debt.

Very importantly, the welfare effects of policy interventions are hard to pin down, because there will be winners and losers. Things get even harder if we depart from fully rational behaviour. This also means that the political incentives can be tricky, and they must be taken into consideration.

9.4 | What next?

As we anticipated, the OLG framework has become increasingly used in macroeconomics. Many years ago, Auerbach and Kotlikoff (1987) provided an extension of this model to, realistically, allow for 50 generations of working age population. That model became the starting point of a more policy-oriented simulations, which were mostly applied to discussing taxations issues. Azariadis (1993) summarised our knowledge of these models, and is a good starting point for those interested in reviewing standard applications in macroeconomic theory, and understanding the potential of the OLG model to discuss business fluctuations and monetary policy. Ljungqvist and Sargent (2018) provide a more recent update.

But the interesting action has to do with the applications of the OLG model as a workhorse from modern macroeconomics in the age of low interest rates. As we will look into this in later chapters, we defer to the bibliography on this until then.

Notes

[1] See Feldstein and Bacchetta (1991) for a good non-technical introduction to some of the other issues, including distribution, risk, and labour market implications.

[2] As an example, check out this headline: 'China hopes social safety net will push its citizens to consume more, save less' (*Washington Post*, July 14, 2010).

[3] Chile is perhaps the best-known example, with its pioneering move in the early 1980s. (See also Feldstein's discussion.) For a discussion of the real-world pitfalls, Google this NYT article from January 2006: "Chile's Candidates Agree to Agree on Pension Woes".

[4] Maybe because two of us are from Argentina and Chile?

References

Auerbach, A. J. & Kotlikoff, L. J. (1987). Evaluating fiscal policy with a dynamic simulation model. *The American Economic Review, 77*(2), 49–55.

Azariadis, C. (1993). Intertemporal macroeconomics.

Bernheim, B. D., Skinner, J., & Weinberg, S. (2001). What accounts for the variation in retirement wealth among U.S. households? *American Economic Review, 91*(4), 832–857.

Beshears, J., Choi, J. J., Laibson, D., & Madrian, B. C. (2018). Behavioral household finance. *Handbook of behavioral economics: Applications and foundations 1* (pp. 177–276). Elsevier.

Feldstein, M. & Bacchetta, P. (1991). National saving and international investment. *National saving and economic performance* (pp. 201–226). University of Chicago Press.

Kaplan, G., Violante, G. L., & Weidner, J. (2014). *The wealthy hand-to-mouth.* (tech. rep.). National Bureau of Economic Research.

Ljungqvist, L. & Sargent, T. J. (2018). *Recursive macroeconomic theory*. MIT Press.

Madrian, B. C. & Shea, D. F. (2001). The power of suggestion: Inertia in 401 (k) participation and savings behavior. *The Quarterly Journal of Economics, 116*(4), 1149–1187.

Scholz, J. K., Seshadri, A., & Khitatrakun, S. (2006). Are Americans saving "optimally" for retirement? *Journal of Political Economy, 114*(4), 607–643.

CHAPTER 10

Unified growth theory

You will recall that among the key stylised facts we set out to explain in our study of economic growth was the very existence of growth in living standards: output per worker increases over time. This, however, has only been true for a very short span in human history, starting with the Industrial Revolution and the birth of modern economic growth.

For most of history, the prevailing situation was one that we may call Malthusian stagnation. In other words, there obviously were massive increases in productivity – the wheel, agriculture, domesticated animals, ships, double-entry bookkeeping – but these did not really translate into increased living standards, or into sustained productivity growth. Instead, as per the Malthusian assumption (recall our discussion of the Kremer (1993) paper in (Chapter 6), those increases in productivity mostly translated into increases in population.

Then at some point, around the 18th century, the Great Divergence happened (see Figure 10.1): a few Western European countries, and then the Western offshoots in the New World, took off and never looked back. They inaugurated the age of sustained economic growth, which eventually spread to most other countries around the world, and which has been the object of our study in this first part of the book.

But this begs the question: how did that transition happen? Is there any way in which we can understand within a single framework the growth process in the Malthusian and modern eras *combined*? Can we understand why the latter emerged in the first place, how, from stability, suddenly growth popped up?[1] This is the object of unified growth theory, a somewhat grandiosely named attempt at understanding growth from the perspective of millennia. This chapter constitutes a brief introduction to these ideas, following the presentation in Galor (2005). The fact that it uses some features of the OLG model explains why we have this discussion now.

10.1 | From Malthus to growth

Growth seems to have experienced a kink around the end of the 18th century, when it accelerated dramatically.

While we have argued above that technological progress and increases in productivity have been features of human history for millennia, it is pretty much undeniable that the pace at which such progress took place until the last couple of centuries was much, much slower than what we have come to expect

How to cite this book chapter:
Campante, F., Sturzenegger, F. and Velasco, A. 2021. *Advanced Macroeconomics: An Easy Guide.*
Ch. 10. 'Unified growth theory', pp. 147–158. London: LSE Press.
DOI: https://doi.org/10.31389/lsepress.ame.j License: CC-BY-NC 4.0.

Figure 10.1 The evolution of regional income per capita over the years 1–2008

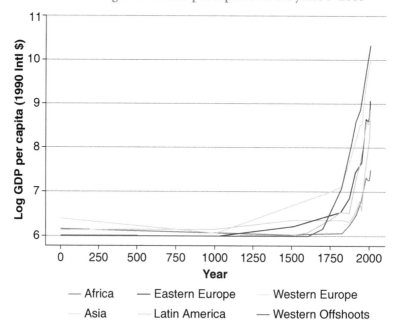

in recent times. The slow pace of productivity increases, combined with the Malthusian effect of those increases on population growth, meant that output per worker (i.e. living standards) grew very slowly over this period. Put simply, whenever things got a little better, people would starve less, live a little longer, have more kids, more of whom would reach adult age, etc. We would then simply end up sharing the increased output among a larger number of people, with essentially the same amount going for each of these people as before things had gotten better. In other words, increases in income per capita were essentially temporary, and eventually dissipated. It may sound odd to us today, but these were times when parents and sons lived in the same world, and so did their children and grandchildren. Progress was just too slow to be noticeable.

Mind you, stagnation doesn't mean that these were boring times when nothing particularly interesting happened. Much to the contrary, hovering around subsistence level meant that negative productivity shocks (say, droughts) were devastating. The flipside of the adjustment described above would clearly hold: bad shocks would mean people dying early, fewer kids reaching adulthood, etc., bringing population down.

By the same token, there were substantial differences across countries and regions. Naturally, some places were more productive (fertile land, natural resources, location) and technology varied substantially. However, more productive countries or regions were not richer on a per capita basis – they just had more people, as in China or the Indian subcontinent. In sum, this scenario had a natural implication for cross-country comparisons: population (or more precisely, population density) is the right measure of development in this era.

As such, how do we know that, from a global perspective, technological progress and economic performance were rather unimpressive? Because global population growth was very slow over the period, according to the best historical and archaeological evidence.

10.1.1 │ The post-Malthusian regime

Then industrialisation happened.[2] Gradually, first picking up steam (figuratively, but also literally!) in England in the mid- to late-18th century, and spreading over Western Europe and the U.S. through the 19th century, the growth rate of output per capita started a sustained increase by an order of magnitude. Eventually, this reached most other places in the world somewhere along the 20th century. Still, this initial takeoff was marked by the Great Divergence – a testament to the power of growth rates in changing living standards over time. The first countries to industrialise started to grow richer and richer, leaving behind the laggards (Figure 10.2). It also brought along a marked increase in urbanisation, with people flocking from rural areas to the more dynamic urban centers, which could now sustain substantially larger (and increasing) populations.

Still, this is not what we would call the full-on, modern, sustained growth regime. Why? Because a remnant of the Malthusian past remained. There remained a positive link between increased productivity and income per capita, on one side, and increased population on the other, as can be seen readily, for different parts of the world, in Figure 10.3. As such, part of the sustained increase in productivity growth was still being dissipated over more capitas.

However, a very important transition was taking place at the same time: the rise of human capital. The acceleration in productivity growth and income per capita was accompanied by rising literacy rates, schooling achievement, and improving health. This increase in human capital seems to be driven

Figure 10.2 The differential timing of the take-off across regions

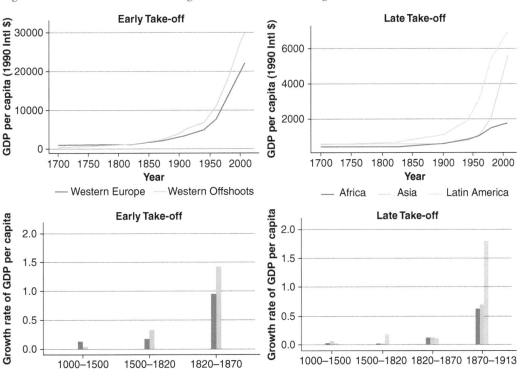

Figure 10.3   Regional growth of GDP per capita (green line) and population (red line) 1500–2000

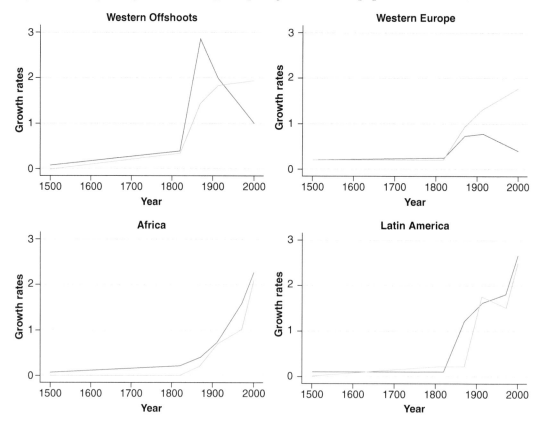

by the fact that the industrialisation process, particularly in its later stages, requires more and more "brain" relative to "brawn" – an educated, decently healthy workforce becomes a *sine qua non*.

10.1.2 | Sustained economic growth

Then the demographic transition happened. At some point, human societies escaped definitively from the Malthusian shackles. Population growth ceased to be positively related to income per capita, and the relationship was actually reversed, with sharp declines in fertility rates. Even from a basic arithmetic perspective, this opens up the way for a historically astonishing rate of increase in living standards. In fact, the regions that first went into this transition reach a sustained speed of about 2% annual growth in income per capita over the last century or so – a rate at which living standards double in the space of one generation (35 years). Simultaneously, the relative importance of human capital increased even further, which was met by the first efforts in mass public education.

The demographic transition, i.e. the decline in fertility rates (accompanied by lower mortality and higher life expectancy), happened first in the leading industrialised nations, but then eventually reached the latecomers, as illustrated in Figure 10.4. (The exception for the moment, as we can see, is still Africa.) It actually had a three-fold impact on the growth process. First, and most obviously,

Figure 10.4   The differential timing of the demographic transition across regions

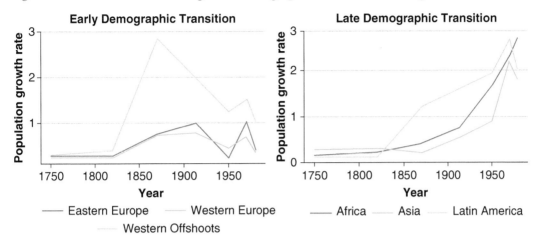

it ceased the dilution of capital (and land). Second, it actually enabled the increased investment in human capital. Put simply, the tradeoff between quantity of children and the quality of the investment made in each one of them turned decisively towards the latter. Third, and more temporarily, it yielded a demographic dividend: a relatively large labour force, with relatively few young dependents.

10.2 | A "unified" theory

Unified growth theory attempts to provide a single framework that can explain why growth may accelerate. One such mechanism relates to family decisions, i.e. whether to raise more kids or to raise fewer but more educated kids. Growth will force parents to educate their children at the expense of quantity of children, setting off an accelerating pattern.

The challenge is thus to come up with a framework that encompasses all the stylised facts spelled out in the previous section. In other words, we need a theory that has room for the Malthusian era, but then explains (i.e. endogenously generates) the transition to a post-Malthusian equilibrium with sustained productivity growth brought about by industrialisation and the attending increased importance of human capital. It must also account for the demographic transition and the possibility of sustained increases in living standards.

One could have told a story in which we combine the neoclassical growth model (which, after all, has zero growth in living standards in the long run) with the eventual takeoff of productivity being accounted for by the world of the endogenous growth models. However, how do we explain when and why we would move from one world to the other? And how do we incorporate the demographic aspect that seems to be such a central part of the story, and which lies thoroughly outside of the theories that we have seen so far?

We will start by sketching a model of parental investment that explains the links between demographic trends and productivity, while keeping the evolution of productivity exogenous. We will then endogenise productivity growth in order to complete our full very-long-run picture.

10.2.1 | A simple model of the demographic transition

Consider a discrete-time framework in which individuals live for two periods, as in our basic OLG model, but now each individual, instead of coming into the economy out of nowhere, has a single parent. In the first period of life (childhood), individuals consume a fraction of their parent's endowment of time (normalised to 1). This fraction will have to be greater to increase the child's quality. In the second period of life (parenthood), individuals are endowed with one unit of time, which they allocate between child-rearing and labour force participation. At this stage, the individual's problem is to choose the optimal mixture of quantity and quality of (surviving) children and supply their remaining time in the labour market, consuming their wages.

Let us consider the building blocks of this model in order.

Production

We assume that output is produced using land (exogenous and constant over time) and (efficiency units of) labour. We capture this using a constant returns to scale (CRS) production function:

$$Y_t = H_t^\alpha (A_t X)^{1-\alpha}, \tag{10.1}$$

where Y_t is total output, H_t is total efficiency units of labour, A_t is (endogenous) productivity, and X is land employed in production. We can write this in per worker terms as

$$y_t = h_t^\alpha x_t^{1-\alpha}, \tag{10.2}$$

where $y_t \equiv \frac{Y_t}{L_t}$, $h_t \equiv \frac{H_t}{L_t}$, and $x_t \equiv \frac{A_t X}{L_t}$ (we can think of x_t as effective (land) resources per worker).

Preferences

An individual who is a parent in time t cares about consumption c_t, and also about the number of children n_t, and their quality h_{t+1}. We summarise this in the following utility function:

$$u^t = c_t^{1-\gamma}(n_t h_{t+1})^\gamma. \tag{10.3}$$

We assume that individuals need to consume at least a subsistence level $\tilde{c}$, which will be very important for the results. Children are passive recipients of their parents' decisions. This means that this is not a full-fledged OLG model, such as the ones we have seen before, in which young and old made meaningful economic decisions, which in turn entailed intergenerational conflicts of interest. The OLG structure here is more meant to highlight the demographic structure of the problem.

Budget constraint

Let τ be the amount of time needed to raise a child, regardless of quality. Any additional quality that an individual parent in time t bestows upon each child (to be reflected in the quality h_{t+1}) requires some additional effort, e_{t+1} (education). Whatever is left of the unit time endowment will be supplied in the labour market, in exchange for a wage of w_t (per efficiency unit of labour). We assume that there are no property rights over land, so that the individual rate of return on that is zero.

For an individual who was given quality h_t by her parent, we thus have

$$c_t \le w_t h_t (1 - n_t \tau - n_t e_{t+1}). \tag{10.4}$$

This simply states that the individual can consume up to the level of income that she obtains from paid work.

Note that we can rearrange this budget constraint as follows:

$$c_t + w_t h_t n_t (\tau + e_{t+1}) \leq w_t h_t. \tag{10.5}$$

The RHS of this inequality, which we may call $z_t \equiv w_t h_t$, corresponds to total potential income, i.e. the income that the individual would obtain if all of her time were devoted to paid work. We can then reinterpret the budget constraint as stating that the individual can choose to devote her potential income to consumption or to raising her children, and the cost of raising children is the foregone income.

10.2.2 | Investing in human capital

We take human capital to be determined by a combination of individual quality and the technological environment. Specifically, we posit a function

$$h_{t+1} = h(e_{t+1}, g_{t+1}), \tag{10.6}$$

where $g_{t+1} \equiv \frac{A_{t+1} - A_t}{A_t}$ is the rate of technological progress. The idea is that $\frac{\partial h}{\partial e} > 0$ (more education leads to more human capital), and $\frac{\partial h}{\partial g} < 0$ (faster technological progress erodes previously acquired human capital by making it obsolete). We also assume that more education increases adaptability to technological progress, so that $\frac{\partial^2 h}{\partial g \partial e} > 0$. In the absence of investment in quality, each individual has a basic-level human capital that is normalised to 1 in a stationary technological environment: $h(0,0) = 1$.

Solution

We can substitute (10.4) and (10.6) into (10.3) to obtain:

$$u^t = (w_t[1 - n_t(\tau + e_{t+1})]h_t)^{1-\gamma} (n_t h(e_{t+1}, g_{t+1}))^\gamma. \tag{10.7}$$

Parents will choose n_t and e_{t+1} (how many children to have, and how much to invest in the education of each one of them) in order to maximise this utility. The FOC with respect to n_t will yield:

$$(1 - \gamma)c_t^{-\gamma}(n_t h(e_{t+1}, g_{t+1}))^\gamma w_t h_t(\tau + e_{t+1}) = \gamma c_t^{1-\gamma} n_t^{\gamma-1} h(e_{t+1}, g_{t+1})^\gamma \Rightarrow \tag{10.8}$$

$$\frac{c_t}{w_t h_t} = \frac{1 - \gamma}{\gamma} n_t(\tau + e_{t+1}). \tag{10.9}$$

Note, from (10.4), that the LHS of this equation is the fraction of time devoted to labour market activities, $1 - n_t(\tau + e_{t+1})$. It follows immediately that the individual will choose to devote a fraction γ of her time to child-rearing, and a fraction $1 - \gamma$ to labour.

The FOC characterises an interior solution, however, and we must take into account the subsistence consumption constraint. If $(1-\gamma)w_t h_t < \tilde{c}$, it follows that the interior solution would not be enough to sustain the individual. In that case, the subsistence constraint is binding, and the optimal thing to do is to work as much as needed to reach $\tilde{c}$, and devote whatever is left to child-rearing. In other words, any individual whose potential income is below $\tilde{z} \equiv \frac{\tilde{c}}{1-\gamma}$ will be constrained to subsistence consumption, and to limited investment in their kids.

This means that, below subsistence level, increases in potential income generate no increase in consumption, and an increase in the time spent raising kids (number and quality). After the subsistence threshold, it is consumption that increases, while the time spent in child-rearing stays flat.

How about the choice of education, e_{t+1}? With some algebra, you can show that the FOC with respect to e_{t+1} can be written as

$$\frac{\gamma}{1-\gamma}\frac{c_t}{n_t w_t h_t} = \frac{h(e_{t+1}, g_{t+1})}{\frac{\partial h}{\partial e}}. \tag{10.10}$$

Substituting the LHS using (10.9), we get the following:

$$\tau + e_{t+1} = \frac{h(e_{t+1}, g_{t+1})}{\frac{\partial h}{\partial e}}, \tag{10.11}$$

which implicitly defines e_{t+1} as a function of the productivity growth rate g_{t+1}. Using the implicit function theorem, we can see that, as long as h is decreasing in g, and concave in e, as we have assumed, e_{t+1} will be increasing in g_{t+1}. In other words, parents will choose to invest in more education when productivity grows faster, because education increases adaptability and compensates for the erosion of human capital imposed by technological change.

But how about the number of children? It is easy to see that there is no link between wages and the choice between quantity (n_t) and quality (e_{t+1}) in child-rearing: potential income doesn't show up in (10.11), and (10.9) only speaks to the overall amount of time (i.e. number times quality). However, (10.11) shows that productivity growth does affect that tradeoff: n_t doesn't show up in that equation, but e_{t+1} does. This means that an increase in g will increase the quality of kids, and reduce their quantity to keep consistency with (10.9).

In sum

This simple model therefore predicts a number of key stylised facts regarding the demographic transition:

1. An increase in (potential) income raises the number of children, but has no effect on their quality, as long as the subsistence constraint is binding.
2. An increase in (potential) income does not affect the number of children and their quality, as long as the subsistence constraint ceases to be binding.
3. An increase in the rate of technological progress reduces the number of children and increases their quality.

The first two results are driven by the subsistence requirement. As long as it is binding, any increase in potential income will imply that fewer hours of work are needed to obtain subsistence and more time can be devoted to having children. However, if the rate of technological change is constant, this will be translated into a greater number of kids, and not in higher quality: the point about investing in quality is to counteract the erosion of human capital imposed by faster technological change. When the subsistence constraint is no longer binding, then increased potential income will be reverted into increasing consumption.

10.2.3 | The dynamics of technology, education and population

In order to close the picture, we need to have a model of how technological progress takes place. Inspired by the models of endogenous growth that we have seen, we think of productivity growth being driven by the accumulation of knowledge, which is enhanced by human capital and by scale effects. Quite simply, we posit

$$g_{t+1} \equiv \frac{A_{t+1} - A_t}{A_t} = g(e_t, L_t), \tag{10.12}$$

where $g(\cdot, \cdot)$ is increasing and concave in both arguments: more and more educated people increase the rate of growth, at decreasing rates. (Remember that our discussion of scale effects argued that there is good evidence for their presence in this very long-run context, as per the models of innovation studied in Chapter 6 and synthesised in Kremer (1993).)

Obviously, the evolution of the size of the adult population is described by $L_{t+1} = n_t L_t$, since n_t is the number of children that each individual adult alive at time t chooses to have. The model of demographic decisions shows that n_t is a function of the rate of technological progress and, when the subsistence constraint is binding, also of potential income. Potential income, in turn, is a function of the existing technology, education levels, and the amount of effective resources per worker.

The one thing that is missing is the evolution of potential resources per worker, $x_t \equiv \frac{A_t X}{L_t}$, but that is easy to state: $x_{t+1} = \frac{1+g_{t+1}}{n_t} x_t$, that is, effective resources per worker grow at the rate of productivity, adjusted by the growth of population.

We now have a dynamic system in four variables: g_t, x_t, e_t, and L_t. These capture all of our variables of interest, namely productivity growth, productivity levels, human capital investment, and population.

Closing the model

The dynamics of the model can be analysed graphically, and we start by looking at the joint evolution of education and technology. Since the dynamics of education and technological progress are not affected by whether the subsistence constraint is binding, we can analyse then independently, as depicted in Figure 10.5. If population is small (Panel A), the rate of technological progress is slow because of scale effects. Then the only steady state is with zero levels of education: it is not worth investing in the quality of children, since the erosion caused by technological progress is really small. However, as population size grows, which the g curve shifts up, until we end up in the world of Panel B. Here there are two additional positive-education steady states (e_M and e_h, which is stable). As population grows even larger, we end up in Panel C, with a unique, stable steady state with high levels of educational investment.

10.3 | The full picture

Figure 10.5 encompasses all of our story, from the Malthusian regime to sustained growth. Consider an economy in early stages of development. Population size is relatively small and the implied slow rate of technological progress does not provide an incentive to invest in the education of children: this is the world of Figure 10.5A – the Malthusian Regime. Over time, the slow growth in population that takes place in the Malthusian Regime raises the rate of technological progress and shifts the g in

Figure 10.5 Dynamics of the model

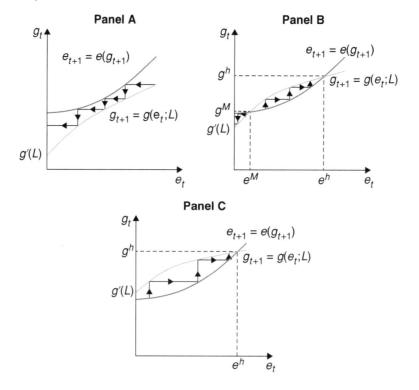

Panel A enough to generate a qualitative change to Panel B. This is characterised by multiple, history-dependent, stable steady-state equilibria: some countries may take off and start investing in human capital, while others lag behind. However, since the economy started in the Malthusian steady state, it initially sticks in the vicinity of that steady state, which is still stable in the absence of major shocks.

Eventually, the continued increase in population leads us to Panel C: the Malthusian steady state disappears, and the economy starts converging to the steady state with high education. The resulting increase in the pace of technological progress, due to the increased levels of education, has two opposing effects on the evolution of population. On the one hand, it allows for the allocation of more resources for raising children. On the other hand, it induces a reallocation of these additional resources toward child quality. Initially, there is low demand for human capital, and the first effect dominates: this is the Post-Malthusian Regime.

The interaction between investment in human capital and technological progress generates a virtuous circle: human capital formation pushes faster technological progress, which further raises the demand for human capital, which fosters more investment in child quality. Eventually, the subsistence constraint seizes to bind, triggering a demographic transition and sustained economic growth.

10.4 | What have we learned?

In sum, this theory explains growth over the very long run by marrying the insights of endogenous growth theory (the role of scale effects and human capital in increasing the growth rate of productivity) to a theory of endogenous population growth and human capital investment. In the presence of a subsistence level of consumption, this marriage produces an initial period of stagnation, and the eventual transition to sustained economic growth with high levels of human capital investment and the demographic transition.

10.5 | What next?

For those interested in this transition Galor (2005) is a great starting point.

Notes

[1] Notice that the Kremer model does not solve this riddle. Even though it starts from a Malthusian framework, by assuming a specific process of economic growth, it only explains the divergent part of the story.

[2] While industrialisation is considered the turning point for economic growth, arguably their impact was possible (or at least complemented) by two other world-changing events occurring at the same time. First, the French Revolution that dismantled the segmented labour market of the middle ages, opened up labour so that anybody could find his or her best use of their own abilities, thus increasing productivity dramatically. Second, the U.S. Constitution; a key attempt to have a government controlled by its citizens and not the other way around. Reigning in the authoritarian tendencies or the possibility of capricious use of resources also provided significant productivity gains through better infrastructure and better public goods provision.

References

Galor, O. (2005). From stagnation to growth: Unified growth theory. *Handbook of Economic Growth, 1,* 171–293.

Kremer, M. (1993). Population growth and technological change: One million B.C. to 1990. *The Quarterly Journal of Economics, 108*(3), 681–716.

Consumption and Investment

CHAPTER 11

Consumption

The usefulness of the tools that we have studied so far in the book goes well beyond the issue of economic growth and capital accumulation that has kept us busy so far. In fact, those tools enable us to think about all kinds of dynamic issues, in macroeconomics and beyond. As we will see, the same tradeoffs arise again and again: how do individuals trade off today vs tomorrow? It depends on the rate of return, on impatience, and on the willingness to shift consumption over time, all things that are captured by our old friend, the Euler equation! What are the constraints that the market imposes on individual behaviour? You won't be able to borrow if you are doing something unsustainable. Well, it's the no-Ponzi game condition! How should we deal with shocks, foreseen and unforeseen? This leads to lending and borrowing and, at an aggregate level, the current account!

All of these issues are raised when we deal with some of the most important (and inherently dynamic) issues in macroeconomics: the determinants of consumption and investment, fiscal policy, and monetary policy. To these issues we will now turn.

We start by looking at one of the most important macroeconomic aggregates, namely consumption. In order to understand consumption, we will go back to the basics of individual optimisation and the intertemporal choice of how much to save and consume. Our investigation into the determinants of consumption will proceed in two steps. First, we will analyse the consumer's choice in a context of full certainty. We will be careful with the algebra, so readers who feel comfortable with the solutions can skip the detail, while others may find the careful step-by-step procedure useful. Then, in the next chapter, we will add the realistic trait of uncertainty (however simply it is modelled). In the process, we will also see some important connections between macroeconomics and finance.

11.1 | Consumption without uncertainty

The main result of the consumption theory without uncertainty is that of *consumption smoothing*. People try to achieve as smooth a consumption profile as possible, by choosing a consumption level that is consistent with their intertemporal resources and saving and borrowing along the way to smooth the volatility in income paths.

Let's start with the case where there is one representative consumer living in a closed economy, and no population growth. All quantities (in small-case letters) are per-capita. The typical consumer-worker provides one unit of labour inelastically. Their problem is how much to save and how much to consume

How to cite this book chapter:
Campante, F., Sturzenegger, F. and Velasco, A. 2021. *Advanced Macroeconomics: An Easy Guide.*
Ch. 11. 'Consumption', pp. 161–170. London: LSE Press. DOI: https://doi.org/10.31389/lsepress.ame.k
License: CC-BY-NC 4.0.

over their lifetime of length T. This (unlike in the analysis of intertemporal choice that we pursued in the context of the Neoclassical Growth Model) will be partial equilibrium analysis: we take the interest rate r and the wage rate w as exogenous.

11.1.1 | The consumer's problem

This will be formally very similar to what we have encountered before. The utility function is

$$\int_0^T u(c_t)e^{-\rho t}dt, \tag{11.1}$$

where c_t denotes consumption and ρ (> 0) is the rate of time preference. Assume $u'(c_t) > 0, u''(c_t) \leq 0$, and that Inada conditions are satisfied.

The resource constraint is

$$\dot{b}_t = rb_t + w_t - c_t, \tag{11.2}$$

where w_t is the real wage and b_t is the stock of bonds the agent owns. Let us assume that the real interest rate r is equal to ρ.[1]

The agent is also constrained by the no-Ponzi game (NPG) or solvency condition:

$$b_T e^{-rT} \geq 0 \tag{11.3}$$

Solution to consumer's problem

The consumer maximises (11.1) subject to (11.2) and (11.3) for given and b_0. The current value Hamiltonian for the problem can be written as

$$H = u(c_t) + \lambda_t \left[rb_t + w_t - c_t \right]. \tag{11.4}$$

Note that c is a control variable (jumpy), b is the state variable (sticky), and λ is the costate variable (the multiplier associated with the intertemporal budget constraint, also jumpy). The costate has an intuitive interpretation: the marginal value as of time t of an additional unit of the state (assets b, in this case).

The optimality conditions are

$$u'(c_t) = \lambda_t, \tag{11.5}$$

$$\frac{\dot{\lambda}_t}{\lambda_t} = \rho - r, \tag{11.6}$$

$$\lambda_T b_T e^{-\rho T} = 0. \tag{11.7}$$

This last expression is the transversality condition (TVC).

11.1.2 | Solving for the time profile and level of consumption

Take (11.5) and differentiate both sides with respect to time

$$u''(c_t)\dot{c}_t = \dot{\lambda}_t. \tag{11.8}$$

Divide this by (11.5) and rearrange

$$\frac{u''(c_t)c_t}{u'(c_t)}\frac{\dot{c}_t}{c_t} = \frac{\dot{\lambda}_t}{\lambda_t}. \tag{11.9}$$

Now, as we've seen before, define

$$\sigma \equiv \left[-\frac{u''(c_t)c_t}{u'(c_t)}\right]^{-1} > 0 \tag{11.10}$$

as the elasticity of intertemporal substitution in consumption. Then, (11.9) becomes

$$\frac{\dot{c}_t}{c_t} = -\sigma\frac{\dot{\lambda}_t}{\lambda_t}. \tag{11.11}$$

Finally using (11.6) in (11.11) we obtain (what a surprise!):

$$\frac{\dot{c}_t}{c_t} = \sigma\left(r - \rho\right) = 0. \tag{11.12}$$

Equation (11.12) says that consumption is constant since we assume $r = \rho$. It follows then that

$$c_t = c^*, \tag{11.13}$$

so that consumption is constant.

We now need to solve for the level of consumption c^*. Using (11.13) in (11.2) we get

$$\dot{b}_t = rb_t + w_t - c^*, \tag{11.14}$$

which is a differential equation in b, whose solution is, for any time $t > 0$,

$$b_t = \int_0^t w_s e^{r(t-v)}ds - \left(e^{rt} - 1\right)\frac{c^*}{r} + b_0 e^{rt}. \tag{11.15}$$

where time v is any moment between 0 and t. Evaluating this at $t = T$ (the terminal period) we obtain the stock of bonds at the end of the agent's life:

$$b_T = \int_0^T w_s e^{r(T-s)}ds - \left(e^{rT} - 1\right)\frac{c^*}{r} + b_0 e^{rT}. \tag{11.16}$$

Dividing both sides by e^{rT} and rearranging, we have

$$b_T e^{-rT} = \int_0^T w_t e^{-rs}ds - \left(1 - e^{-rT}\right)\frac{c^*}{r} + b_0. \tag{11.17}$$

Notice that using (11.5), (11.7), and (11.13), the TVC can be written as

$$u'\left(c^*\right) b_T e^{-rT} = 0. \tag{11.18}$$

Since clearly $u'\left(c^*\right) \neq 0$ (this would require $c^* \to \infty$), for the TVC to hold it must be the case that $b_T e^{-rT} = 0$. Applying this to (11.17) and rearranging we have

$$\frac{c^*}{r}\left(1 - e^{-rT}\right) = b_0 + \int_0^T w_s e^{-rs}ds. \tag{11.19}$$

The LHS of this equation is the net present value (NPV) of consumption as of time 0, and the RHS the NPV of resources as of time 0.

11.2 | The permanent income hypothesis

Dividing (11.19) through by $\left(1 - e^{-rT}\right)$ and multiplying through by r we have

$$c^* = \frac{rb_0 + r\int_0^T w_t e^{-rt} dt}{1 - e^{-rT}}. \tag{11.20}$$

The RHS of this expression can be thought of as the permanent income of the agent as of time 0. That is what they optimally consume.

What is savings in this case? Define

$$s_t = w_t + rb_t - c_t$$

$$= r\left(b_t - \frac{b_0}{1 - e^{-rT}}\right) + \left(w_t - \frac{r\int_0^T w_t e^{-rt} dt}{1 - e^{-rT}}\right). \tag{11.21}$$

Hence, savings is high when a) bond-holdings are high relative to their permanent level, and b) current wage income is high relative to its permanent level. Conversely, when current income is less than permanent income, saving can be negative. Thus, the individual uses saving and borrowing to smooth the path of consumption. (Where have we seen that before?)

This is the key idea of Friedman (1957). Before then, economists used to think of a rule of thumb in which consumption would be a linear function of current disposable income. But if you think about it, from introspection, is this really the case? It turns out that the data also belied that vision, and Friedman (1957) gave an explanation for that.

11.2.1 | The case of constant labour income

Note also that if $w_t = w$, the expression for consumption becomes

$$c^* = \frac{rb_0 + rw\int_0^T e^{-rt} dt}{1 - e^{-rT}} = \frac{rb_0}{1 - e^{-rT}} + w. \tag{11.22}$$

Moreover, if $T \to \infty$, this becomes

$$c^* = rb_0 + w, \tag{11.23}$$

which has a clear interpretation: $rb_0 + w$ is what the agent can consume on a permanent (constant) basis forever.

What is the path of bond-holdings over time? Continue considering the case in which w is constant, but T remains finite. In that case the equation for bonds (11.15) becomes

$$b_t = \left(e^{rt} - 1\right)\frac{w - c^*}{r} + b_0 e^{rt}. \tag{11.24}$$

Using (11.22) in here we get

$$b_t = \left(\frac{1 - e^{-r(T-t)}}{1 - e^{-rT}}\right) b_0 < b_0. \tag{11.25}$$

Notice that

$$\frac{db_t}{dt} = -r\left(\frac{e^{-r(T-t)}}{1 - e^{-rT}}\right) b_0 < 0 \tag{11.26}$$

Figure 11.1 Bondholdings with constant income

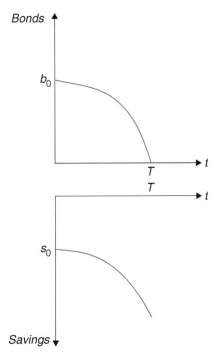

$$\frac{d^2 b_t}{dt^2} = -r^2 \left(\frac{e^{-r(T-t)}}{1 - e^{-rT}} \right) b_0 < 0, \tag{11.27}$$

so that bond-holdings decline, and at an accelerating rate, until they are exhausted at time T. Figure 11.1 shows this path.

11.2.2 | The effects of non-constant labour income

Suppose now that wages have the following path:

$$w_t = \begin{cases} w^H, 0 \leq t < T' \\ w^L, T' \leq t < T \end{cases}, \quad T' < T, w^H > w^L. \tag{11.28}$$

Then, we can use (11.20) to figure out what constant consumption is:

$$c^* = \frac{rb_0 + w^H r \int_0^{T'} e^{-rt} dt + w^L r \int_{T'}^{T} e^{-rt} dt}{1 - e^{-rT}} \tag{11.29}$$

$$= \frac{rb_0 + w^H \left(1 - e^{-rT'} \right) + w^L \left(e^{-rT'} - e^{-rT} \right)}{1 - e^{-rT}}. \tag{11.30}$$

For $t < T'$, saving is given by

$$s_t = w^H + rb_t - c_t \tag{11.31}$$

$$= r\left(b_t - \frac{b_0}{1 - e^{-rT}}\right) + \left(w^H - \frac{w^H\left(1 - e^{-rT'}\right) + w^L\left(e^{-rT'} - e^{-rT}\right)}{1 - e^{-rT}}\right).$$

What are bond-holdings along this path? In this case the equation for bonds (11.15) becomes, for $t < T'$

$$b_t = b_0 \frac{1 - e^{-r(T-t)}}{1 - e^{-rT}} + \left(e^{rt} - 1\right)\frac{w^H - w^L}{r}\left(\frac{e^{-rT'} - e^{-rT}}{1 - e^{-rT}}\right). \tag{11.32}$$

Notice

$$\frac{db_t}{dt} = \left\{-rb_0\frac{e^{-rT}}{1 - e^{-rT}} + \left(w^H - w^L\right)\left(\frac{e^{-rT'} - e^{-rT}}{1 - e^{-rT}}\right)\right\}e^{rt} \tag{11.33}$$

$$\frac{d^2 b_t}{dt^2} = \left\{-rb_0\frac{e^{-rT}}{1 - e^{-rT}} + \left(w^H - w^L\right)\left(\frac{e^{-rT'} - e^{-rT}}{1 - e^{-rT}}\right)\right\}re^{rt} \tag{11.34}$$

so that bond-holdings are increasing at an increasing rate for $t < T'$ if b_0 is sufficiently small.
Plugging this into (11.31) we obtain

$$s_t = -\left(\frac{e^{-r(T-t)}}{1 - e^{-rT}}\right)rb_0 + w^H$$

$$-w^H\left[1 - e^{rt}\left(\frac{e^{-rT'} - e^{-rT}}{1 - e^{-rT}}\right)\right] - w^L e^{rt}\left(\frac{e^{-rT'} - e^{-rT}}{1 - e^{-rT}}\right)$$

so that, yet again savings is high when current wage income is above permanent wage income.
Simplifying, this last expression becomes

$$s_t = \left\{-rb_0\frac{e^{-rT}}{1 - e^{-rT}} + \left(w^H - w^L\right)\left(\frac{e^{-rT'} - e^{-rT}}{1 - e^{-rT}}\right)\right\}e^{rt}. \tag{11.35}$$

Notice

$$\frac{ds_t}{dt} = \left\{-rb_0\frac{e^{-rT}}{1 - e^{-rT}} + \left(w^H - w^L\right)\left(\frac{e^{-rT'} - e^{-rT}}{1 - e^{-rT}}\right)\right\}re^{rt} \tag{11.36}$$

$$\frac{d^2 s_t}{dt^2} = \left\{-rb_0\frac{e^{-rT}}{1 - e^{-rT}} + \left(w^H - w^L\right)\left(\frac{e^{-rT'} - e^{-rT}}{1 - e^{-rT}}\right)\right\}r^2 e^{rt} \tag{11.37}$$

so that, if b_0 is sufficiently small, bond-holdings rise, and at an accelerating rate, until time T'.
Figure11.2 shows this path. This is consumption smoothing: since the current wage is higher than the future wage, the agent optimally accumulates assets.

Figure 11.2 Saving when income is high

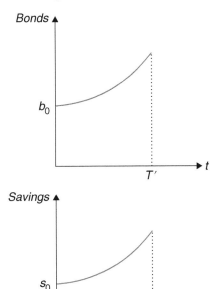

11.3 | The life-cycle hypothesis

The most notable application of the model with non-constant labour income is that of consumption over the life cycle. Assume $b_0 = 0$, and also that income follows

$$w_t = \begin{cases} w > 0, 0 \le t < T' \\ 0, T' \le t < T \end{cases}, \ T' < T$$

so that now the worker-consumer works for the first T' periods of his life, and is retired for the remaining $T - T'$ periods.

Then, consumption is simply given by (11.29) with $b_0 = 0$, $w^H = w$, $w^L = 0$:

$$c^* = w \left(\frac{1 - e^{-rT'}}{1 - e^{-rT}} \right) < w \tag{11.38}$$

so that consumption per instant is less than the wage.

Let us now figure out what bond-holdings are during working years ($t \le T'$). Looking at (11.32), and using (11.38), we can see that

$$b_t = \int_0^t we^{r(t-s)}ds - \left(e^{rt} - 1\right)\frac{w}{r}\left(\frac{1 - e^{-rT'}}{1 - e^{-rT}}\right) \Rightarrow$$

$$b_t = \frac{we^{rt}}{r}\left[1 - e^{-rt}\right] - \left(e^{rt} - 1\right)\frac{w}{r}\left(\frac{1 - e^{-rT'}}{1 - e^{-rT}}\right) \Rightarrow$$

$$b_t = \frac{w}{r}\left[e^{rt} - 1\right] - \left(e^{rt} - 1\right)\frac{w}{r}\left(\frac{1 - e^{-rT'}}{1 - e^{-rT}}\right) \Rightarrow$$

$$b_t = \frac{w}{r}\left[e^{rt} - 1\right]\left[\frac{\left(1 - e^{-rT}\right) - \left(1 - e^{rT'}\right)}{1 - e^{-rT}}\right] \Rightarrow$$

$$b_t = \frac{w}{r}\left(e^{rt} - 1\right)\left(\frac{e^{-rT'} - e^{-rT}}{1 - e^{-rT}}\right). \tag{11.39}$$

By the same token, savings during the working years ($t \le T'$) can be obtained simply by differentiating this expression with respect to time:

$$s_t \equiv \frac{db_t}{dt} = we^{rt}\left(\frac{e^{-rT'} - e^{-rT}}{1 - e^{-rT}}\right) \tag{11.40}$$

so that

$$\frac{ds_t}{dt} \equiv \frac{d^2b_t}{dt^2} = rwe^{rt}\left(\frac{e^{-rT'} - e^{-rT}}{1 - e^{-rT}}\right) > 0 \tag{11.41}$$

$$\frac{d^2s_t}{dt^2} = r^2we^{rt}\left(\frac{e^{rT'} - e^{-rT}}{1 - e^{-rT}}\right) > 0. \tag{11.42}$$

What happens after the time of retirement T'? To calculate bond-holdings, notice that for $t \ge T'$, (11.25) gives

$$b_t = \frac{w}{r}\left(1 - e^{r(t-T)}\right)\left(\frac{1 - e^{-rT'}}{1 - e^{-rT}}\right) \tag{11.43}$$

so that

$$s_t \equiv \frac{db_t}{dt} = -we^{r(t-T)}\left(\frac{1 - e^{-rT'}}{1 - e^{-rT}}\right) < 0 \tag{11.44}$$

$$\frac{ds_t}{dt} \equiv \frac{d^2b_t}{dt^2} = -rwe^{r(t-T)}\left(\frac{1 - e^{-rT'}}{1 - e^{-rT}}\right) < 0 \tag{11.45}$$

$$\frac{d^2s_t}{dt^2} = -r^2we^{r(t-T)}\left(\frac{1 - e^{-rT'}}{1 - e^{-rT}}\right) < 0 \tag{11.46}$$

so that savings decrease over time.

Figure 11.3 shows this path. The agent optimally accumulates assets until retirement time T', then depletes them between time T' and time of death T. This is the basic finding of the life-cycle hypothesis of Modigliani and Brumberg (1954).[2]

Figure 11.3 The life-cycle hypothesis

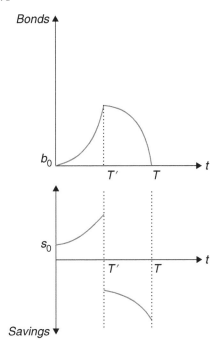

Of course, the life-cycle hypothesis is quite intuitive. One way or the other we all plan for retirement (or trust the government will). Scholz et al. (2006) show that 80% of the households over age 50 had accumulated at least as much wealth as a life-cycle model prescribes, and the the wealth deficit of the remaining 20% is relatively small, thus providing support for the model. On the other hand, many studies have also found that consumption falls at retirement. For example, Bernheim et al. (2001) show that there is a drop in consumption at retirement and that it is larger with families with a lower replacement rates from Social Security and pension benefits. This prediction is at odds with the life-cycle hypothesis.

Notes

[1] Do you remember our discussion of the open-economy Ramsey model, and the implications of $r > \rho$ or $r < \rho$?

[2] What explains the curvature? In other words, why is it that the individual accumulates at a faster rate as she approaches retirement, and then decumulates at a faster rate as she approaches death? The intuition is that, because of her asset accumulation, the individual's interest income increases as she approaches retirement – for a constant level of consumption, that means she saves more and accumulates faster. the flip-side of this argument happens close to the death threshold, as interest income gets lower and dissaving intensifies as a result.

References

Bernheim, B. D., Skinner, J., & Weinberg, S. (2001). What accounts for the variation in retirement wealth among U.S. households? *American Economic Review*, *91*(4), 832–857.

Friedman, M. (1957). The permanent income hypothesis. *A theory of the consumption function* (pp. 20–37). Princeton University Press.

Modigliani, F. & Brumberg, R. (1954). Utility analysis and the consumption function: An interpretation of cross-section data. *Franco Modigliani*, *1*(1), 388–436.

Scholz, J. K., Seshadri, A., & Khitatrakun, S. (2006). Are Americans saving "optimally" for retirement? *Journal of Political Economy*, *114*(4), 607–643.

CHAPTER 12

Consumption under uncertainty and macro finance

In the previous chapter we discussed optimal consumption in a world with certainty. The results basically came down to having people choose a consumption path as stable as possible. To estimate this sustainable level of consumption they take into account future income, net of the bequests they plan to hand over to their children.

There are two dimensions in which this strong result may be challenged. One has to do with uncertainty. Uncertainty may affect expected future income or the return of assets. The second is about preferences themselves. What happens if people have an unusually high preference for present consumption? We will discuss both problems in this chapter. We will see that uncertainty changes the conclusion in a fundamental way: it tilts the path upwards. Faced with uncertainty, people tend to be more cautious and save more than the permanent income hypothesis would suggest. Present bias delivers the opposite result, that people tend to overconsume and enter time inconsistent consumption paths. This rises a whole new set of policy implications.

We end this chapter by introducing a whole new topic, here succinctly sketched to get a flavour. In traditional finance, we typically study portfolio (the realm of asset management) or financing decisions (the realm of corporate finance) based on asset prices. But these asset prices have to make sense given the desired consumption and saving decisions of the individuals in the economy. The area of macro finance puts these two things together. Because asset demands derive directly from consumption decisions, we can flip the problem and ask: given the consumption decisions what are the equilibrium asset prices? The area of macro finance has been a very fertile area of research in recent years.

12.1 | Consumption with uncertainty

Consumption with uncertainty needs to deal with the uncertainty of future outcomes. The value function $V_t(b_t) = Max_{c_t} \left[u(c_t) + \frac{1}{1+\rho} E_t V_{t+1}(b_{t+1}) \right]$ will be a useful instrument to estimate optimal consumption paths.

The analysis of consumption under uncertainty is analogous to that under certainty with the difference that now we will assume that consumers maximise expected utility rather than just plain utility. As it

How to cite this book chapter:
Campante, F., Sturzenegger, F. and Velasco, A. 2021. *Advanced Macroeconomics: An Easy Guide.*
Ch. 12. 'Consumption under uncertainty and macro finance', pp. 171–188. London: LSE Press.
DOI: https://doi.org/10.31389/lsepress.ame.l License: CC-BY-NC 4.0.

turns out, it is more convenient to analyse the case with uncertainty in discrete, rather than continuous, time. The utility that the consumer maximises in this case is

$$maxE\left[\sum_{t=0}^{T}\frac{1}{(1+\rho)^t}u(c_t)\right],\qquad(12.1)$$

$$\text{s.t.}\quad b_{t+1}=(w_t+b_t-c_t)(1+r).\qquad(12.2)$$

The uncertainty comes from the fact that we now assume labour income w_t to be uncertain.[1] How do we model individual behaviour when facing such uncertainty? When we impose that individuals use the mathematical expectation to evaluate their utility we are assuming that they have *rational expectations*: they understand the model that is behind the uncertainty in the economy, and make use of all the available information in making their forecasts. (Or, at the very least, they don't know any less than the economist who is modelling their behaviour.) As we will see time and again, this will have very powerful implications.

Let us start with a two-period model, not unlike the one that we used when analysing the OLG model. As you will recall and can easily verify, the FOC looks like this:

$$u'\left(c_1\right)=\left(\frac{1+r}{1+\rho}\right)E_1\left[u'\left(c_2\right)\right].\qquad(12.3)$$

This FOC generalises to the case of many periods, with exactly the same economic intuition:

$$u'\left(c_t\right)=\left(\frac{1+r}{1+\rho}\right)E_t\left[u'\left(c_{t+1}\right)\right].\qquad(12.4)$$

This is our Euler equation for optimal consumption.

To see how this helps us find the consumption level in a multiperiod framework, we use the tools of dynamic programming, which you can briefly review in the math appendix at the end of the book. We show there that intertemporal problems can be solved with the help of a *Bellman equation*. The Bellman equation rewrites the optimisation problem as the choice between current utility and future utility. Future utility, in turn, is condensed in the value function that gives the maximum attainable utility resulting from the decisions taken today. In short:

$$V_t(b_t)=Max_{c_t}\left[u(c_t)+\frac{1}{1+\rho}E_tV_{t+1}(b_{t+1})\right].\qquad(12.5)$$

The optimising condition of the Bellman equation (maximise relative to c_t and use the budget constraint) is

$$u'(c_t)=E_t\left[\frac{1+r}{1+\rho}V'_{t+1}(b_{t+1})\right],\qquad(12.6)$$

but remember that $V'(b_t)=u'(c_t)$ along the optimal path. The intuition is that when the value function is optimised relative to consumption, the marginal value of the program along the optimised path has to be the marginal utility of consumption (see our mathematical appendix to refresh the intuition). But then (12.6) becomes (12.4). In a nutshell, the key intuition of dynamic programming, captured by the Bellman equation is that you can break a multi-period (potentially infinite) problem into a sequence of two-period problems where you choose optimally today, making sure that your decisions today make sense when measured against future utility, and then again all the way to eternity if necessary.

12.1.1 | The random walk hypothesis

With quadratic utility we find that $c_{t+1} = c_t + \varepsilon_{t+1}$, the *random walk* hypothesis of consumption. Changes in consumption levels should be unpredictable.

Suppose utility is quadratic[2], that is

$$u\left(c_t\right) = c_t - \frac{a}{2}c_t^2. \tag{12.7}$$

Here things become a bit simpler as marginal utility is linear:

$$u'\left(c_t\right) = 1 - ac_t. \tag{12.8}$$

This implies that

$$1 - ac_t = \frac{(1+r)}{(1+\rho)}E_t\left[1 - ac_{t+1}\right]. \tag{12.9}$$

If we keep assuming that $r = \rho$ as we've done before, it follows that

$$ac_t = E_t\left[ac_{t+1}\right], \tag{12.10}$$

or, more simply, that

$$c_t = E_t\left[c_{t+1}\right]. \tag{12.11}$$

Equation (12.11) can be depicted as the following stochastic process for consumption:

$$c_{t+1} = c_t + \varepsilon_{t+1}, \tag{12.12}$$

where ε_t is a zero-mean random disturbance (also called white noise).

A stochastic process that looks like this is called a *random walk*, for this reason this description of consumption (due to Hall 1978) is called the *random walk hypothesis* of consumption. It is a very strong statement saying that only unexpected events can change the consumption profile – all information that is already known must have already been taken into consideration and therefore will not change consumption when it happens. This result, one of the early applications of the rational expectations assumption, is a powerful empirical implication that can easily be tested.

12.1.2 | Testing the random walk hypothesis

Empirical evidence does not support fully the *random walk* hypothesis of consumption.

A large number of papers have tried to assess the random walk hypothesis. One classical contribution is the Shea (1995) test on whether predictable changes in income are or are not related to predictable changes in consumption. He looks into long-term union contracts which specified in advance changes in wages. He then runs the consumption growth on the income growth. The theory suggests the coefficient should be zero, but the number comes out to be .89.

Of course it can very well be that this is because people have liquidity constraints. So Shea runs the test on people that have liquid assets and could thus borrow from themselves. These people cannot have a liquidity constraint. Yet he still finds the same result. Then he splits people into two groups: those that are facing declining incomes and those for which income is growing. Those facing a future fall in income should reduce their consumption and save, so you should not find an effect of liquidity constraints. Yet, it seems that, again, changes in current income help predict changes in consumption.

This type of exercises has been replicated in many other contexts. Ganong and Noel (2019) for example, find that household consumption falls 13 percent when households receiving unemployment benefits reach the (anticipated) end of their benefits. Food stamp recipients and social security beneficiaries also show monthly patterns of consumption that are related to the payment cycle.

12.1.3 | The value function

The value function is a useful tool to estimate optimal paths. We review two approaches to solve for these paths: guess and replace and value function iteration.

While important, the quadratic case is a very special case that allows a simple characterisation of the consumption path. Can we solve for more general specifications? Here is where the value function approach comes in handy. There are several ways of using the value function to approximate the optimal path. If the problem is finite, one can work the problem backwards from the last period. But this is not very useful in problems with no terminal time, which is our typical specification. One way to approach the problem is to simply guess the value function. This can be done in simple cases, but is not typically available, particularly because no problem should rely on having a genius at hand that can figure out the solution beforehand. An alternative is to do an iteration process that finds the solution through a recursive estimation. This is easier, and may actually deliver a specific solution in some cases. However, this approach can also be implemented by a recursive estimation using computational devices. So that you get a sense of how these methods work, we will solve a very simple problem through the guess and replace solution, and then through the value function iteration method. It is a bit tedious but will allow you to get a feel of the methodology involved.

A guess and replace example

Imagine we take the special case of $u(c_t) = \log(c_t)$ and guess (spoiler: we already know it will work!) the form

$$V(b_t) = a \log(b_t) + d, \tag{12.13}$$

that is, with a form equal to utility and with constants a and d to be determined. If this is the value function, then consumption has to maximise

$$ln(c_t) + \frac{1}{1+\rho} E[a \log(b_{t+1}) + d]. \tag{12.14}$$

Remember that $b_{t+1} = (b_t - c_t)(1 + r)$, as in (12.2) where we just assumed w to be zero to lighten up notation. Now take the derivative of (12.14) relative to c_t. We leave this computation to you but it is easy and you should find that this gives

$$c_t = \frac{b_t}{1 + \frac{a}{1+\rho}}. \tag{12.15}$$

Are we done? No, because we need to find the value of a. To do this we are going to use our guess (12.13) using (12.5). This means writing

$$a \log(b_t) + d = \log\left(\frac{b_t}{1 + \frac{a}{1+\rho}}\right) + \frac{1}{1+\rho}\left[a \log\left[\left(b_t - \frac{b_t}{1 + \frac{a}{1+\rho}}\right)(1+r)\right] + d\right]. \qquad (12.16)$$

What we have done is write the value function on the left and replacing optimal consumption from (12.15), and b_{t+1} from the budget constraint (using optimal consumption again). The expectation goes because all variables are now dated at t. Now the log specification makes things simple. Just factor out the logs on the right hand side and pile up all the coefficients of b_t on the right-hand side. If the value function is right, these coefficients should be equal to a the coefficient of b_t in the value function on the left. After you clear this out, you will get the deceptively simple equivalence

$$a = 1 + \frac{a}{1+\rho}, \qquad (12.17)$$

which is an equation that you can use to solve for a. Trivial algebra gives that $a = \frac{1+\rho}{\rho}$ which, introduced in (12.15), gives our final solution

$$c_t = \frac{\rho}{1+\rho} b_t. \qquad (12.18)$$

This, by now is an expected result. You consume a fraction of your current wealth. (The log specification cancels the effect of returns on consumption and thus simplifies the solution).

Iteration

Now, let's get the intuition for the solution by iterating the value function. Let's imagine we have no idea what the value function could be, so we are going the make the arbitrary assumption that it is zero. Let us track the iteration by a subindex on the value function $1, 2, 3...$. So, with this assumption $V_0 = 0$. So our first iteration implies that

$$V_1(b_t) = Max_{c_t}\left[\log(c_t) + \frac{1}{1+\rho} 0\right], \qquad (12.19)$$

subject to the budget constraint in (12.2). The solution to this problem is trivial. As assets have no value going forward, $c_t = b_t$, so our $V_1 = \log(b_t)$. Now let's iterate to the second stage by defining V_2 using V_1. This means

$$V_2 = Max_{c_t}\left[\log(c_t) + \frac{1}{1+\rho}\log(b_{t+1})\right] = Max_{c_t}\log(c_t) + \frac{1}{1+\rho}\log[(b_t - c_t)(1+r)]. \qquad (12.20)$$

Again, maximise this value function relative to c_t. This is not complicated and you should get that $c_t^* = \frac{b_t(1+\rho)}{(2+\rho)}$. The more tricky part is that we will use this to compute our V_2 equation. Replace c_t^* in (12.20) to get

$$V_2 = \log(c_t^*) + \frac{1}{1+\rho}\log[(b_t - c_t^*)(1+r)]. \qquad (12.21)$$

Notice that the log will simplify things a lot so this will end up looking like

$$V_2 = (1 + \frac{1}{1+\rho})\log(b_t) + \log[\frac{1+\rho}{2+\rho}] + \frac{1}{1+\rho}\log[\frac{1}{2+\rho}(1+r)] = (1 + \frac{1}{1+\rho})\log(b_t) + \theta_2. \qquad (12.22)$$

The important part is the one that multiplies b_t the other is a constant which we see quickly becomes unwieldy. To finalise the solution let's try this one more time. Our last iteration uses our V_2 to compute V_3 (we omit the constant term):

$$V_3 = Max_{c_t} \left[\log(c_t) + \left(1 + \frac{1}{1+\rho} \right) \log(b_{t+1}) \right]. \tag{12.23}$$

Use again the budget constraint and maximise respect to c_t. You should be able to find that

$$c_t^* = \frac{1}{1 + \frac{1}{1+\rho} + \frac{1}{(1+\rho)^2}} b_t. \tag{12.24}$$

We leave, for the less fainthearted, the task of replacing this in (12.23) to compute the final version of V_3. Fortunately, we do not need to do this. You can see a clear pattern in the solutions for c_t^*. If you iterate and iterate to infinity, the denominator will add up to $\frac{1+\rho}{\rho}$. This implies that the solution is $c_t = \frac{\rho}{1+\rho} b_t$. Not surprisingly, the same as in (12.18).

12.1.4 | Precautionary savings

When faced with uncertainty consumers will be more precautionary, tilting the consumption profile upwards throughout their lifetimes. The Caballero model provides a simple specification that computes that slope and shows how it increases with volatility.

Let's ask ourselves how savings and consumption react when uncertainty increases. Our intuition suggests that an increase in uncertainty should tilt the balance towards more savings, a phenomenon dubbed precautionary savings. To illustrate how this works we go back to our Euler equation:

$$u' \left(c_t \right) = \frac{1}{1+\rho} E_t \left[\left(1 + r_{t+1}^i \right) u' \left(c_{t+1} \right) \right]. \tag{12.25}$$

Assume again that $r_{t+1}^i = \rho = 0$, to simplify matters. Thus, the condition reduces to (we've seen this before!):

$$u' \left(c_t \right) = E_t \left[u' \left(c_{t+1} \right) \right]. \tag{12.26}$$

Now assume, in addition to the typical $u' > 0$ and $u'' < 0$, that $u''' > 0$. This last condition is new and says that marginal utility is convex. This seems to be a very realistic assumption. It means that the marginal utility of consumption grows very fast as consumption approaches very low levels. Roughly speaking, people with convex marginal utility will be very concerned with very low levels of consumption. Figure 12.1 shows how marginal utility behaves if this condition is met.

Notice that for a quadratic utility

$$E \left[u' \left(c \right) \right] = u' \left(E \left[c \right] \right). \tag{12.27}$$

But the graph shows clearly that if marginal utility is convex then

$$E \left[u' \left(c \right) \right] > u' \left(E \left[c \right] \right), \tag{12.28}$$

and that the stronger the convexity, the larger the difference. The bigger $E[u'(c)]$ is, the bigger c_{t+1} needs to be to keep the expected future utility equal to $u'(c)$, the marginal utility of consumption today. Imagine, for example that you expect one of your consumption possibilities for next period

Figure 12.1   Precautionary savings

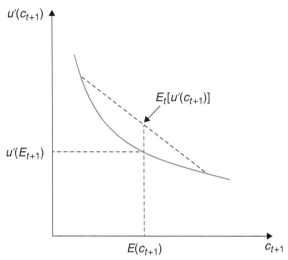

to be zero. If marginal utility at zero is ∞ then $E[u'(c)]$ will also be ∞, and therefore you want to increase future consumption as much as possible to bring this expected marginal utility down as much as possible. In the extreme you may choose not to consume anything today! This means that you keep some extra assets, a buffer stock, to get you through the possibility of really lean times. This is what is called *precautionary savings*. Precautionary savings represents a departure from the permanent income hypothesis, in that it will lead individuals to save more than would be predicted by the latter, because of uncertainty.

The Caballero model

Caballero (1990) provides a nice example that allows for a simple solution. Consider the case of a constant absolute risk aversion function.

$$u(c_t) = -\frac{1}{\theta}e^{-\theta c_t}. \tag{12.29}$$

Assuming that the interest rate is equal to the discount rate for simplification, this problem has a traditional Euler equation of the form

$$e^{-\theta c_t} = E_t\left[e^{-\theta c_{t+1}}\right]. \tag{12.30}$$

Caballero proposes a solution of the form

$$c_{t+1} = \Gamma_t + c_t + v_{t+1}, \tag{12.31}$$

were v is related to the shock to income, the source of uncertainty in the model. Replacing in the Euler equation gives

$$e^{-\theta c_t} = E_t\left[e^{-\theta[\Gamma_t + c_t + v_{t+1}]}\right], \tag{12.32}$$

which, taking logs, simplifies to

$$\theta\Gamma_t = \log E_t \left[e^{-\theta v_{t+1}} \right].$$
(12.33)

If v is distributed $N(0, \sigma^2)$, then we can use the fact that $Ee^x = e^{Ex + \frac{\sigma_x^2}{2}}$ to find the value of Γ (as the value is constant, we can do away with the subscript) in (12.33):

$$\theta\Gamma = \log \left[e^{\frac{\theta^2 \sigma_v^2}{2}} \right],$$
(12.34)

or, simply,

$$\Gamma = \frac{\theta \sigma_v^2}{2}.$$
(12.35)

This is a very simple expression. It says that even when the interest rate equals the discount rate the consumption profile is upward sloping. The higher the variance, the higher the slope.

The precautionary savings hypothesis is also useful to capture other stylised facts: families tend to show an upward-sloping consumption path while the uncertainties of their labour life get sorted out. Eventually, they reach a point were consumption stabilises and they accumulate assets. Gourinchas and Parker (2002) describe these dynamics. Roughly the pattern that emerges is that families have an increasing consumption pattern until sometime in the early 30s, after which consumption starts to flatten.

12.2 | New frontiers in consumption theory

Consumption shows significant deviations from the optimal intertemporal framework. One such deviation is explained by early bias, a tendency to give a stronger weight to present consumption. This leads to time inconsistency in consumption plans. Consumption restrictions, such as requesting a stay period before consumption, may solve the problem.

Though our analysis of consumption has taken us quite far, many consumption decisions cannot be suitably explained with the above framework as it has been found that consumers tend to develop biases that move their decisions away from what the model prescribes. For example, if a family receives an extra amount of money, they will probably allocate it to spending on a wide range of goods and maybe save at least some of this extra amount. Yet, if the family receives the same amount of extra money on a discount on food purchases, it is found that they typically increase their food consumption more (we could even say much more) than if they would have received cash. Likewise, many agents run up debts on their credit cards when they could pull money from their retirement accounts at a much lower cost.

One way of understanding this behaviour is through the concept of mental accounting, a term coined by Richard Thaler, who won the Nobel Prize in economics in 2017. In Thaler's view, consumers mentally construct baskets of goods or categories. They make decisions based on these categories not as if they were connected by a unique budget constraint, but as if they entailed totally independent decisions.

A similar anomaly occurs regarding defaults or reference points which we mentioned at the end of our Social Security chapter. Imagine organising the task of allocating yellow and red mugs to a group of people. If you ask people what colour they would like their mugs to be, you will probably get a uniform distribution across colours, say 50% choose yellow and 50% choose red. Now allocate the mugs randomly and let people exchange their mugs. When you do this, the number of exchanges is surprisingly low. The received mug has become a reference point which delivers utility *per-se*. This type of reference point explains why agents tend to stick to their defaults. Brigitte Madrian has shown that when a 3% savings contribution was imposed as default (but not compulsory), six months later 86% of the workers remained within the plan, relative to 49% if no plan had been included as default, and 65% stuck to the 3% contribution vs only 4% choosing that specific contribution when such percentage was not pre-established. (In fact, Madrian shows that the effect of defaults is much stronger than providing economic incentives for savings, and much cheaper!)

One of the biases that has received significant attention is what is called present bias. Present bias is the tendency to put more weight to present consumption relative to future consumption. Let's discuss the basics of this idea.

12.2.1 | Present bias

We follow (Beshears et al. 2006) in assuming a model with three periods. In period zero the consumer can buy (but not consume) an amount $c_0 \geq 0$ of a certain good. In period one, the consumer can buy more of this good ($c_1 \geq 0$) and now consume it. Total consumption is

$$c = c_0 + c_1. \tag{12.36}$$

In period 2, the consumer spends whatever was left on other goods x. The budget constraint can be written as

$$1 + T = c_0(1 + \tau_0) + c_1(1 + \tau_1) + x, \tag{12.37}$$

where τ_0 and τ_1 are taxes over c_0 and c_1 and T is a lump sum transfer. Income is assumed equal to 1. $T = \bar{c}_0\tau_0 + \bar{c}_1\tau_1$, where the bars indicate the average values for each variable. As the economy is large, these variables are unchanged by the individual decision to consume. Introducing taxes and lump sum transfers is not necessary, but will become useful below to discuss policy. Summing up, the structure is:

- Period 0: buys c_0 at after tax price of $(1 + \tau_0)$
- Period 1: buys an additional amount c_1 at an after tax price of $(1 + \tau_1)$. Consumes $c = c_0 + c_1$
- Period 2: buys and consumes good x at price 1 with the remaining resources $1 + T - c_0(1 + \tau_0) - c_1(1 + \tau_1)$.

Time inconsistency in consumer's behaviour

The key assumption is that the consumer has a quasi-hyperbolic intertemporal discount factor with sequence: $1, \beta\frac{1}{1+\rho}, \beta\left(\frac{1}{1+\rho}\right)^2, \beta\left(\frac{1}{1+\rho}\right)^3$. We assume $0 \leq \beta \leq 1$ to capture the fact that the consumer discounts more in the short run than the long run. As we will see, this will produce preferences that are not consistent over time. In addition, we will assume the good provides immediate satisfaction but a delayed cost (a good example would be smoking or gambling).

Let's assume that the utility of consuming c is

$$Eu_0(c, x) = E[\beta\frac{1}{1+\rho}(\alpha + \Delta)\log(c) - \beta\left(\frac{1}{1+\rho}\right)^2 \alpha\log(c) + \beta\left(\frac{1}{1+\rho}\right)^2 x], \tag{12.38}$$

where Δ and α are fixed *taste-shifters*. The utility from x is assumed linear, as it represents all other goods.

For simplicity, we assume $\frac{1}{1+\rho} = 1$. Expected utility as seen in period zero is

$$Eu_0(c, x) = E\beta[\Delta \log(c) + x]. \tag{12.39}$$

Notice that the delayed consumption penalty disappears when seen from afar. In period 1, the utility function is

$$u_1(c, x) = (\Delta + \alpha) \log(c) - \beta\alpha \log(c) + \beta x. \tag{12.40}$$

Notice that relative utility between the good c and x is not the same when seen at time 0 and when seen at time 1. At period zero, the other goods were not penalised relative to c, but from the perspective of period 1 the benefits of consumption are stronger because satisfaction is immediate relative to the delayed cost and relative to the utility of other goods to which the present bias applies. This will lead to time inconsistency.

Precommitment

Imagine consumption is determined at time zero and for now $\tau_0 = \tau_1 = 0$. This would give the optimal consumption *ex-ante*. Maximising (12.39) subject to (12.37) can easily be shown to give

$$\frac{\Delta}{c} = 1. \tag{12.41}$$

Notice that this implies $c = \Delta$ and $x = 1 - \Delta$. Thus, expected utility as of period 0 is

$$Eu_0(c, x) = E\beta[\Delta \log(\Delta)] + \beta(1 - \Delta). \tag{12.42}$$

This will be our *benchmark*.

The free equilibrium

Keeping $\tau_0 = \tau_1 = 0$, now imagine that consumption is chosen in period 1. This is obtained maximising (12.40) subject to (12.37). This gives

$$\frac{\alpha(1 - \beta) + \Delta}{c} = \beta. \tag{12.43}$$

Notice that now $c = \frac{\alpha(1-\beta)+\Delta}{\beta}$ which can easily be shown to be higher than the value obtained in the precommitment case. From the perspective of period 0, the marginal utility of c is now smaller than the utility of consuming x. Thus, this free equilibrium is not *first-best optimal* at least from the perspective of period zero.

Optimal regulation: Las Vegas or taxation?

Are there policies that may restore the first-best equilibrium from the perspective of period zero utility?

One option is an early decision rule that allows the purchase of c only during period zero. This is like having an infinite tax in period 1. A well-known application of this policy is, for example, to move gambling activities far away from living areas (e.g. Las Vegas). This way, the consumer decides on the consumption without the urgency of the instant satisfaction. This case trivially replicates the precommitment case above and need not be repeated here.

This outcome can also be replicated with optimal taxation. To see how, let's consider a tax policy of the form $\tau_0 = \tau_1 = \tau$. In order to solve this problem, let's revisit the maximisation of (12.40) subject to (12.37). The solution for c gives

$$c = \frac{\alpha(1-\beta) + \Delta}{\beta(1+\tau)}. \tag{12.44}$$

To obtain the optimal τ, replace (12.44) in (12.39) and maximise with respect to τ. The first order condition gives :

$$-\frac{\Delta}{1+\tau} + \frac{\alpha(1-\beta)+\Delta}{\beta(1+\tau)^2} = 0, \tag{12.45}$$

which gives the optimal tax rate

$$\tau = \left(\frac{\alpha}{\Delta}+1\right)\left(\frac{1}{\beta}-1\right), \tag{12.46}$$

which delivers $c = \Delta$, replicating the optimal equilibrium. So a tax policy can do the trick. In fact, with no heterogeneity both policies are equivalent.

Things are different if we allow for heterogeneity. Allow now for individual differences in Δ. We can repeat the previous steps replacing Δ with $E[\Delta]$, and get the analogous conditions

$$\beta\left[-\frac{E[\Delta]}{1+\tau} + \frac{\alpha(1-\beta)+E[\Delta]}{\beta(1+\tau)^2}\right] = 0, \tag{12.47}$$

which gives the same tax rate

$$\tau = \left(\frac{\alpha}{E(\Delta)}+1\right)\left(\frac{1}{\beta}-1\right). \tag{12.48}$$

With heterogeneity, consumers will move towards the first best but faced with a unique tax rate will consume different amounts. Notice that $\beta[\Delta\log(c) + (1-c)] < \beta[\Delta\log(\Delta) + (1-\Delta)]$ for all $c \neq \Delta$, which happens to the extent that $E[\Delta] \neq \Delta$. As this happens for a nonzero mass of consumers if heterogeneity is going to be an issue at all:

$$Eu_0 = E\beta[\Delta\log(c) + 1 + T - c(1+\tau)] = E\beta[\Delta\log(c) + 1 - c] \tag{12.49}$$

$$< E\beta[\Delta\log(\Delta) + 1 - \Delta]. \tag{12.50}$$

The result is quite intuitive, as each consumer knows its own utility an early decision mechanism is superior to a tax policy because each individual knows his own utility and attains the first best with the early decision mechanism.

These biases have generated significant attention in recent years, generating important policy recommendations.

12.3 | Macroeconomics and finance

While typical corporate finance uses asset prices to explain investment or financing decisions, macrofinance attempts to understand asset prices in a general equilibrium format, i.e. in a way that is consistent with the aggregate outcomes of the economy. The basic pricing equation $r_{t+1}^i - r_{t+1}^f = \frac{a \cdot cov(1+r_{t+1}^i, c_{t+1})}{E_t(u'(c_{t+1}))}$ is remarkable; expected returns are not associated with volatility but to the correlation with the stochastic discount factor.

We've come a long way in understanding consumption. Now it is time to see if what we have learnt can be used to help us understand what asset prices should be in equilibrium.

To understand this relationship, we can use Lucas's (1978) metaphor: imagine a tree that provides the economy with a unique exogenous income source. What is this tree worth? Optimal consumption theory can be used to think about this question, except that we turn the analysis upside down. Typically, we would have the price of an asset and have the consumer choose how much to hold of it. But in the economy the amount held and the returns of those assets are given because they are what the economy produces. So here we will use the FOCs to derive what price makes those exogenous holdings optimal. By looking at the FOCs at a given equilibrium point as an asset pricing equation allows us to go from actual consumption levels to asset pricing. Let's see an example.

Start with the first order condition for an asset that pays a random return r_{t+1}^i:

$$u'(c_t) = \frac{1}{1+\rho} E_t \left[\left(1 + r_{t+1}^i\right) u'(c_{t+1}) \right] \quad \forall i. \tag{12.51}$$

Remember that

$$cov(x, y) = E(xy) - E(x)E(y), \tag{12.52}$$

so, applying this equation to (12.51), we have that

$$u'(c_t) = \frac{1}{1+\rho} \left\{ E_t \left(1 + r_{t+1}^i\right) E_t \left(u'(c_{t+1})\right) + cov \left(1 + r_{t+1}^i, u'(c_{t+1})\right) \right\}. \tag{12.53}$$

This is a remarkable equation. It says that you really don't care about the variance of the return of the asset, but about the covariance of this asset with marginal utility. The variance may be very large, but, if it is not correlated with marginal utility, the consumer will only care about expected values. The more positive the correlation between marginal utility and return means a higher right-hand side, and, therefore, a higher value (more utility). Notice that a positive correlation between marginal utility and return means that the return is high when your future consumption is low. Returns, in short, are better if they are negatively correlated with your income; and if they are, volatility is welcomed!

As simple as it is, this equation has a lot to say, for example, as to whether you should own your house, or whether you should own stocks of the company you work for. Take the example of your house. The return on the house are capital gains and the rental value of your house. Imagine the economy booms. Most likely, prices of property and the corresponding rental value goes up. In these cases your marginal utility is going down (since the boom means your income is going up), so the correlation between returns and marginal utility is negative. This means that you should expect housing to deliver a very high return (because it's hedging properties are not that good). Well, that's right on the dot. Remember our mention to Kaplan et al. (2014) in Chapter 8, who show that housing has an amazingly high return. (There may be other things that play a role in the opposite direction, as home ownership provides a unique sense of security and belonging, which our discussion of precautionary savings indicates can be very valuable.).[3] Buying stocks of the firm you work in is a certain no go, so, to rationalise it, you need to appeal to asymmetric information, or to some cognitive bias that makes you think that knowing more about this asset makes you underestimate the risks. In fact, optimal policy would indicate you should buy the stock of your competitor.[4]

So far, we have been thinking of interest rates as given and consumption as the variable to be determined. However, if all individuals are optimising, equilibrium returns to assets will have to satisfy the same conditions. This means we can think of equation (12.53) as one of equilibrium returns. To make things simple, assume once again that $u(c) = c - \dfrac{ac^2}{2}$. Then (12.53) becomes:

$$u'\left(c_t\right) = \frac{1}{1+\rho}\left\{E_t\left(1+r^j_{t+1}\right) E_t\left(u'\left(c_{t+1}\right)\right) - a \cdot cov\left(1 + r^j_{t+1}, c_{t+1}\right)\right\}, \tag{12.54}$$

which can also be written as

$$E_t\left(1+r^j_{t+1}\right) = \frac{1}{E_t\left(u'\left(c_{t+1}\right)\right)}\left\{(1+\rho)\, u'\left(c_t\right) + a \cdot cov\left(1 + r^j_{t+1}, c_{t+1}\right)\right\}. \tag{12.55}$$

Notice that for a risk-free asset, for which $cov\left(1 + r^f_{t+1}, c_{t+1}\right) = 0$, we will have

$$\left(1+r^f_{t+1}\right) = \frac{(1+\rho)\, u'\left(c_t\right)}{E_t\left(u'\left(c_{t+1}\right)\right)}. \tag{12.56}$$

Before proceeding, you may want to ponder on an interesting result. Notice that in the denominator you have the expected marginal utility of future consumption. This produces two results. If consumption growth is high, the interest rate is higher (if c_{t+1} is big, its marginal utility is low). But at the same time, notice that if the volatility of consumption is big, then the denominator is bigger (remember our discussion of precautionary savings). To see this, imagine that under some scenarios c_{t+1} falls so much that the marginal utility becomes very large. In higher volatility economies, the risk-free rate will be lower!

So, using (12.55) in (12.56) we obtain

$$E_t\left(1+r^j_{t+1}\right) - \left(1+r^f_{t+1}\right) = \frac{a \cdot cov\left(1 + r^j_{t+1}, c_{t+1}\right)}{E_t\left(u'\left(c_{t+1}\right)\right)}, \tag{12.57}$$

$$E_t\left(r^j_{t+1}\right) - r^f_{t+1} = \frac{a \cdot cov\left(1 + r^j_{t+1}, c_{t+1}\right)}{E_t\left(u'\left(c_{t+1}\right)\right)}. \tag{12.58}$$

This equation states that the premia of an asset is determined in equilibrium by its covariance with aggregate consumption.

12.3.1 | The consumption-CAPM

We show that the basic pricing equation can be written as $r^j_{t+1} - r^f_{t+1} = \frac{cov(z^j_{t+1}, z^m_{t+1})}{var(z^m_{t+1})}\left[r^m_{t+1} - r^f_{t+1}\right]$. Risk premia depend on the asset's covariance with market returns with a coefficient called β that can be computed by running a regression between individual and market returns. This is the so-called capital asset pricing model (CAPM).

Consider now an asset called "the market" that covaries negatively with marginal utility of consumption (as the market represents the wealth of the economy, *consumption* moves with it, and therefore in the opposite direction as the marginal utility of consumption). That is,

$$u'\left(c_{t+1}\right) = -\gamma z_{t+1}^{m}. \tag{12.59}$$

Applying (12.58) to this asset, we have

$$r_{t+1}^{m} - r_{t+1}^{f} = \frac{\gamma \cdot var(z_{t+1}^{m})}{E_t\left(u'\left(c_{t+1}\right)\right)}. \tag{12.60}$$

Consider now an individual asset with return z_{t+1}^{i}. Applying the same logic we have that

$$r_{t+1}^{i} - r_{t+1}^{f} = \frac{\gamma \cdot cov\left(z_{t+1}^{i}, z_{t+1}^{m}\right)}{E_t\left(u'\left(c_{t+1}\right)\right)}. \tag{12.61}$$

Combining both equations (just replace $E_t\left(u'\left(c_{t+1}\right)\right)$ from (12.60) into (12.61), we have that

$$r_{t+1}^{i} - r_{t+1}^{f} = \frac{cov\left(z_{t+1}^{i}, z_{t+1}^{m}\right)}{var(z_{t+1}^{m})}\left[r_{t+1}^{m} - r_{t+1}^{f}\right]. \tag{12.62}$$

You may have seen something very similar to this equation: it is the so-called CAPM, used to determine the equilibrium return of an asset. The formula says that the asset will only get a premia for the portion of its variance that is not diversifiable. An asset can have a very large return, but if the correlation of the return with the market is zero, the asset will pay the risk-free rate in spite of all that volatility! Another way of saying this is that all idiosyncratic (i.e. diversifiable by holding a sufficiently large portfolio) risk is not paid for. This is the reason you should typically not want to hold an individual asset: it will carry a lot of volatility you are not remunerated for. The popularity of the CAPM model also hinges on how easy it is to compute the slope of the risk premia: it is just the regression coefficient obtained from running the return of the asset (relative to the risk free) and the market return. The value of that coefficient is called β.

This version, derived from the optimal behaviour of a consumer under uncertainty, is often referred to as Consumption-based CAPM (C-CAPM).

12.3.2 | Equity premium puzzle

The premia for equities is given by $E\left(r^{i}\right) - \bar{r} = \theta cov\left(r^{i}, g^{c}\right)$. But this does not hold in the data unless risk aversion is unreasonably high. This is the so-called equity premium puzzle.

Our asset pricing model can help us think about some asset pricing puzzles that have long left economists and finance practitioners scratching their heads. One such puzzle is the equity premium puzzle.

The puzzle, in the U.S., refers to the fact that equities have exhibited a large premia (around 6% on average) relative to bonds, and this premia has remained relatively constant for about 100 years. As equities are riskier than bonds a premia is to be expected. But does 6% make sense? If an asset earns 6% more than another, it means that the asset value will be 80% higher at the end of 10 years, 220% more at the end of 20 years, 1740% higher at the end of 50 years, and 33.800% higher at the end of 100

Figure 12.2 Equity premium puzzle, from Jorion and Goetzmann (1999)

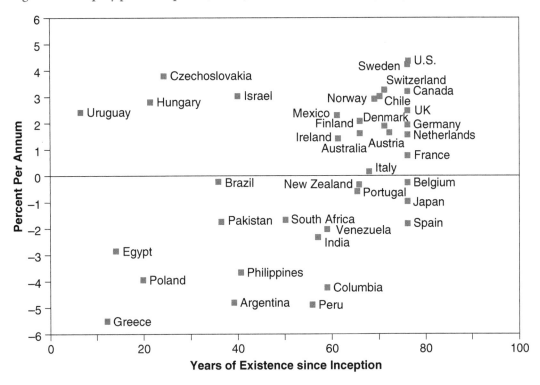

years! You get the point; there is no possible risk aversion coefficient that can deliver these differences as an equilibrium spread.

Figure 12.2, taken from Jorion and Goetzmann (1999), shows that the equity premium puzzle is a common occurrence, but does not appear in all countries. In fact the U.S. seems to be the country where its result is most extreme.

To have more flexibility, we need to move away from a quadratic utility function and use a more general CRRA utility function instead. Now our FOC looks like

$$c_t^{-\theta} = \frac{1}{1+\rho} E_t \left[\left(1 + r_{t+1}^j \right) c_{t+1}^{-\theta} \right], \tag{12.63}$$

which can be written as

$$1 + \rho = E_t \left[\left(1 + r_{t+1}^j \right) \frac{c_{t+1}^{-\theta}}{c_t^{-\theta}} \right] = E_t \left[\left(1 + r_{t+1}^j \right) \left(1 + g^c \right)^{-\theta} \right]. \tag{12.64}$$

Take a second order expansion of the term within the square brackets on the RHS at $g = r = 0$ (notice that in this case the usual Δr becomes r, and Δg becomes g)

$$1 + \left(1 + g^c \right)^{-\theta} r + (1 + r)(-\theta) \left(1 + g^c \right)^{-\theta-1} g^c + (-\theta) \left(1 + g^c \right)^{-\theta-1} g^c r +$$

$$+ \frac{1}{2} (1 + r)(-\theta)(-\theta - 1) \left(1 + g^c \right)^{-\theta-2} \left(g^c \right)^2. \tag{12.65}$$

At $r = g = 0$ (but keeping the deviations), this simplifies to

$$1 + r - \theta g^c - \theta g^c r + \frac{1}{2}\theta(\theta+1)\left(g^c\right)^2. \tag{12.66}$$

With this result, and using (12.52), we can approximate (12.64) as

$$\rho \cong E\left(r^i\right) - \theta E\left(g^c\right) - \theta\left\{E\left(r^i\right)E\left(g^c\right) + cov\left(r^i, g^c\right)\right\} + \frac{1}{2}\theta(\theta+1)\left\{E\left(g^c\right)^2 + var\left(g^c\right)\right\}, \tag{12.67}$$

where we can drop the quadratic terms $(E\left(r^i\right)E\left(g^c\right)$ and $E\left(g^c\right)^2)$ as these may be exceedingly small. This simplifies again to

$$\rho \cong E\left(r^i\right) - \theta E\left(g^c\right) - \theta cov\left(r^i, g^c\right) + \frac{1}{2}\theta(\theta+1)var\left(g^c\right). \tag{12.68}$$

For a risk free asset, for which $cov\left(r^i, g^c\right) = 0$, the equation becomes

$$\bar{r} = \rho + \theta E\left(g^c\right) - \frac{1}{2}\theta(\theta+1)var\left(g^c\right), \tag{12.69}$$

which again shows the result that the higher the growth rate, the higher the risk free rate, and that the bigger the volatility of consumption the lower the risk free rate! Using (12.69) in (12.68) we obtain

$$E\left(r^i\right) - \bar{r} = \theta cov\left(r^i, g^c\right). \tag{12.70}$$

This is the risk premia for an asset i. We will see that this equation is incompatible with the observed spread on equities (6% per year). To see this, notice that from the data we know that $\sigma_{g^c} = 3.6\%$, $\sigma_{r^i} = 16.7\%$, and $corr_{r^i, g^c} = .40$. This implies that

$$cov_{r^i, g^c} = (.40) \cdot (.036) \cdot (.167) = 0.0024. \tag{12.71}$$

Now we can plug this into (12.70) to get that the following relation has to hold,

$$0.06 = \theta \cdot 0.0024 \tag{12.72}$$

and this in turn implies $\theta = 25$, which is considered too high and incompatible with standard measures of risk aversion (that are closer to 2). Mehra and Prescott (1985) brought this issue up and kicked off a large influx of literature on potential explanations of the equity premium. In recent years the premium seemed, if anything, to have increased even further. But be careful, the increase in the premia may just reflect the convergence of the prices to their equilibrium without the premia. So we can't really say how it plays out from here on.

12.4 | What next?

Perfect or not, the idea of consumption smoothing has become pervasive in modern macroeconomics. Many of you may have been taught with an undergraduate textbook using a consumption function $C = a + bY$, with a so-called marginal propensity to consume from income equal to b. Modern macroeconomics, both in the version with and without uncertainty, basically states that this equation does not make much sense. Consumption is not a function of current income, but of intertemporal wealth. The distinction is important because it affects how we think of the response of consumption to shocks or taxes. A permanent tax increase will imply a one to one reduction in consumption with no effect on aggregate spending, while transitory taxes have a more muted effect on consumption. These intertemporal differences are indistinguishable in the traditional setup but essential when thinking about policy.

The theory of consumption has a great tradition. The permanent income hypothesis was initially stated by Milton Friedman who thought understanding consumption was essential to modern macroeconomics. Most of his thinking on this issue is summarised in his 1957 book *A Theory of the Consumption Function* (Friedman (1957)), though this text, today, would be only of historical interest. The life cycle hypothesis was presented by Modigliani and Brumberg (1954), again, a historical reference.

Perhaps a better starting point for those interested in consumption and savings is Angus Deaton's (1992) *Understanding Consumption*.

For those interested in exploring value function estimations you can start easy be reviewing Chiang's (1992) *Elements of Dynamic Optimization*, before diving into Ljungqvist and Sargent (2018) *Recursive Macroeconomic Theory*. Miranda and Fackler (2004) *Applied Computational Economics and Finance* is another useful reference. Eventually, you may want to check out Sargent and Stachurski (2014) *Quantitative Economics,* which is graciously available online at url:http://lectures. quantecon.org/.

There are also several computer programs available for solving dynamic programming models. The CompEcon toolbox (a MATLAB toolbox accompanying Miranda and Fackler (2004) textbook), and the quant-econ website by Sargent and Stachurski with Python and Julia scripts.

If interested in macrofinance, the obvious reference is Cochrane's *Asset Pricing* (2009) of which there have been several editions. Sargent and Ljungqvist provide two nice chapters on asset pricing theory and asset pricing empirics that would be a wonderful next step to the issues discussed in this chapter. If you want a historical reference, the original Mehra and Prescott (1985) article is still worth reading.

Notes

[1] Later on in the chapter we will allow the return r also to be stochastic. If such is the case it should be inside the square brackets. We will come back to this shortly.

[2] You can check easily that this specification has positive marginal utility (or can be so), and negative second derivative of utility relative to consumption.

[3] It might also be because policy, such as federal tax deductibility of mortgage interest (and not of rental payments), encourages excessive home ownership.

[4] We can also appeal to irrationality: people may convince themselves that the company they work for is a can't miss investment. And how often have you heard that paying rent is a waste of money?

References

Beshears, J., Choi, J. J., Laibson, D., & Madrian, B. (2006). *Early decisions: A regulatory framework.* National Bureau of Economic Research.

Caballero, R. J. (1990). Consumption puzzles and precautionary savings. *Journal of Monetary Economics, 25*(1), 113–136.

Friedman, M. (1957). *A theory of the consumption function.* Princeton University Press.

Ganong, P. & Noel, P. (2019). Consumer spending during unemployment: Positive and normative implications. *American Economic Review, 109*(7), 2383–2424.

Gourinchas, P.-O. & Parker, J. A. (2002). Consumption over the life cycle. *Econometrica, 70*(1), 47–89.

Hall, R. E. (1978). Stochastic implications of the life cycle-permanent income hypothesis: Theory and evidence. *Journal of Political Economy, 86*(6), 971–987.

Jorion, P. & Goetzmann, W. N. (1999). Global stock markets in the twentieth century. *The Journal of Finance, 54*(3), 953–980.

Kaplan, G., Violante, G. L., & Weidner, J. (2014). *The wealthy hand-to-mouth.* National Bureau of Economic Research. https://www.nber.org/system/files/working_papers/w20073/w20073.pdf.

Ljungqvist, L. & Sargent, T. J. (2018). *Recursive macroeconomic theory.* MIT Press.

Lucas Jr, R. E. (1978). Asset prices in an exchange economy. *Econometrica,* 1429–1445.

Mehra, R. & Prescott, E. C. (1985). The equity premium: A puzzle. *Journal of Monetary Economics, 15*(2), 145–161.

Miranda, M. J. & Fackler, P. L. (2004). *Applied computational economics and finance.* MIT Press.

Modigliani, F. & Brumberg, R. (1954). Utility analysis and the consumption function: An interpretation of cross-section data. *Post Keynesian Economics.* Rutgers University Press, 388–436.

Sargent, T. & Stachurski, J. (2014). *Quantitative economics.* http://lectures.quantecon.org/.

Shea, J. (1995). Myopia, liquidity constraints, and aggregate consumption: A simple test. *Journal of Money, Credit and Banking, 27*(3), 798–805.

CHAPTER 13

Investment

Investment is one of the most important macroeconomic aggregates, for both short-run and long-run reasons. In the short run, it turns out to be much more volatile than other components of aggregate demand, so it plays a disproportionate role in business cycles. In the long run, investment is capital accumulation, which we have seen is one of the main determinants of output and output growth. That is why we now turn to an inquiry into the determinants of investment.

We have often considered the problem of a firm in partial equilibrium, and analysed how it chooses its optimal level of capital. The firm owns or rents capital, and it can borrow and lend at a fixed interest rate. We saw over and over again that the optimal level of the capital stock for such a firm implies that the marginal product of capital (MPK) equals that interest rate. Investment will thus be whatever is needed to adjust the capital stock to that desired level.

But is that all there is to investment? There are many other issues: the fact that investments are often irreversible or very costly to reverse (e.g. once you decide to build a new plant, it is costly to get rid of it), and that there are costs of installing and operating new equipment. Because of such things, a firm will have a much harder problem than simply immediately increasing its capital stock in response to a fall in the interest rate.

We will now deal with some of these issues, and see how they affect some of the conclusions we had reached in different contexts. We will start by looking at standard practice in corporations and assess the role of uncertainty. We will then put aside the role of uncertainty to develop the Tobin's q theory of investment.

13.1 | Net present value and the WACC

The weighted average cost of capital (WACC) is defined as a weighted average of the firm's cost of financing through equity and debt. If a project yields a return higher than the WACC, it is more likely to be implemented.

The best place to start our understanding of investment is to go where all corporate finance books start: investment is decided on the basis of the net present value (NPV) of a project. If a project is started in period 0 and generates a (positive or negative) cash flow of W_t in any period t up until time T, the NPV will be given by:

How to cite this book chapter:
Campante, F., Sturzenegger, F. and Velasco, A. 2021. *Advanced Macroeconomics: An Easy Guide.*
    Ch. 13. 'Investment', pp. 189–202. London: LSE Press. DOI: https://doi.org/10.31389/lsepress.ame.m
    License: CC-BY-NC 4.0.

$$NPV = \sum_{t=0}^{T} \frac{1}{(1+r)^t} W_t, \qquad (13.1)$$

where r is the cost of capital. Typically, one would expect to have a negative cash flow initially, as investment is undertaken, before it eventually turns positive.

The key question is whether this NPV is positive or not. If NPV > 0, then you should invest; if NPV < 0, then you shouldn't. This sounds simple enough, but this immediately begs the question of what interest rate should be used, particularly considering that firms use a complex mix of financing alternatives, including both equity and debt to finance their capital expenditure (CAPEX) programs. In short, what is the cost of capital for a firm? A very popular measure of the cost of capital is the so-called weighted average cost of capital (WACC), which is defined as

$$WACC = \alpha_{eq} r_{eq} + \left(1 - \alpha_{eq}\right) r_{debt}, \qquad (13.2)$$

$$\alpha_{eq} = \left(\frac{\text{Net worth}}{\text{Total Assets}} \right). \qquad (13.3)$$

Here, r_{eq} is the return on equity (think dividends) and r_{debt} is the return on debt issued (think interest). This is a very popular model in part because it is easy to compute. Basically, it allocates the cost of equity using as weight the fraction of your assets that the firm finances with equity. The return on equity can, in turn, be easily derived, say from a CAPM regression, as explained in the previous chapter. With a weight equal to the share of assets that you finance with debt, the formula uses the cost of debt. For this, you may just take the interest cost of the company's issued debt.

In practice, typically firms go through a planning cycle in which the CFO sets a WACC for the following planning cycle and units decide on those projects that have a return higher than that WACC. Only those that have a return higher than the cost of capital get the green light to go ahead. There are several issues with this procedure. Units tend to exaggerate the benefits of their projects to obtain additional resources, projects take a lot of time, and there are many tax-induced distortions (such as reporting investments as expenses to get a tax credit). A lot of corporate finance is devoted to exploring these and other issues.

13.1.1 | Pindyck's option value critique

Investment is irreversible, so there is a significant option value when investing. This section illustrates how the value to wait can be essential in evaluating the attractiveness of investment projects.

Investment is a decision in which the presence of uncertainty makes a critical difference. This is because investment is mostly irreversible. It follows that there are option-like features to the investment decision that are extremely relevant. Consider, for example, a project with an NPV of zero. Would you pay more than zero for it? Most probably yes, if the return of the project is stochastic and you have the possibility of activating the project in good scenarios. In other words, a zero NPV project has positive value if it gives you the option to call it when, and only when, it makes you money. In that sense, it is just like a call option – i.e. one in which you purchase the right to buy an asset at some later date at a given price. People are willing to pay for a call option. This line of reasoning is critical, for example, in the analysis of mining rights and oil fields. Today an oil field may not be profitable, but it sure is worth more than zero if it can be tapped when energy prices go up.[1]

One of the most studied implications of this option-like feature is when there is an option value to waiting. This is best described by an example such as the following. Suppose you can make an initial investment of $2200, and that gives you the following stochastic payoff:

$$
\begin{array}{ccc}
t = 0 & t = 1 & t = 2 \\
& q \quad P_1 = 300 & \dots \\
P_0 = 200 & & \\
& 1 - q \quad P_1 = 100 & \dots
\end{array}
$$

That is, in the first period you make $200 for sure, but from then onward the payoff will be affected by a shock. If the good realisation of the shock occurs (and let's assume this happens with probability q), you get $300 forever. If you are unlucky, you get $100 forever instead. Suppose $q = 0.5$ and $r = 0.10$. Given this information, the expected NPV of the project, if it is considered at $t = 0$, is

$$
NPV = -2200 + \sum_{t=0}^{\infty} \frac{200}{(1.1)^t} = -2200 + 2200 = \$0. \tag{13.4}
$$

In other words, this is a really marginal investment opportunity. But now consider the option of waiting one period, so that the uncertainty gets resolved, and the project only happens if the good state gets realised (which happens with a 50% probability). Then we have

$$
NPV = 0.5 \left[-\frac{2200}{1.1} + \sum_{t=1}^{\infty} \frac{300}{(1.1)^t} \right] = 0.5 \left[-\frac{2200}{1.1} + \frac{300}{(1.1)} \left(\frac{1}{1 - \frac{1}{1.1}} \right) \right] = 500! \tag{13.5}
$$

As can readily be seen this is a much better strategy. What was missing in (13.4) was the option value (of $500) that the entrepreneur was foregoing by implementing the project in period 0. In other words, she should be willing to pay a substantial amount for the option of waiting until period 1.

This option value argument explains why a firm does not shut down in the first month it loses money – staying open has the value of keeping alive the potential for rewards when things get better. It also explains why people don't divorce whenever marriage hits its first crisis, nor do they quit their job when they have a bad month. These are all decisions that are irreversible (or at least very costly to reverse), and that have uncertain payoffs over time. In sum, they are very much like investment decisions!

A critical lesson from considering the option value entailed by irreversible (or costly reversible) decisions is that uncertainty increases the option value. If there is a lot of variance, then even though the business may be terrible right now, it makes sense to wait instead of shutting down because there is a chance that things could be very good tomorrow. This means that lots of uncertainty will tend to depress the incentive to make investments that are costly to reverse. A firm will want to wait and see instead of committing to building an extra plant; a farmer will want to wait and see before buying that extra plough, and so on. This idea underlies those claims that uncertainty is bad for investment.[2]

13.2 | The adjustment cost model

Why don't firms move directly to their optimal capital stock? Time to build or adjustment costs prevent such big jumps in capital and produce a smoother investment profile more akin to that observed in the data. This section introduces adjustment costs to capital accumulation delivering a smoother demand for investment.

Let us now go back to our basic framework of intertemporal optimisation, but introducing the crucial assumption that the firm faces adjustment costs of installing new capital. For any investment that the firm wants to make, it needs to pay a cost that varies with the size of that investment. That is to say, the firm cannot purchase whatever number of new machines it may desire and immediately start producing with them; there are costs to installing the new machines, learning how to operate them, etc. The more machines it buys, the greater the costs.[3]

If that is the case, how much capital should the firm install, and when? In other words, what is optimal investment?

13.2.1 | Firm's problem

The firm's objective function is to maximise the discounted value of profits:

$$\int_0^\infty \pi_t e^{-rt} dt, \tag{13.6}$$

where π_t denotes firm profits and $r > 0$ is (constant and exogenously-given) real interest rate. The profit function is[4]

$$\pi_t = y_t - \psi\left(i_t, k_t\right) - i_t, \tag{13.7}$$

where y_t is output and $\psi\left(i_t, k_t\right)$ is the cost of investing at the rate i_t, when the stock of capital is k_t. The term $\psi\left(i_t, k_t\right)$ is the key to this model; it implies adjustment costs, or costs of investing. Notice that if there are no costs of adjustment, given our assumption of a constant and exogenous interest rate, firms should go right away to their optimal stock. This would give an instantaneous investment function that is undefined, the investment rate either being zero or plus or minus infinite. However, in reality it seems that investment decisions are smoother and this has to mean that there are costs that make it very difficult if not impossible to execute large and instantaneous jumps in the stock of capital. Why would there be costs? We can think of several reasons. One is time-to-build; it simply takes time to build a facility, a dam, a power plant, a deposit, etc. This naturally smooths investment over time. Now, if you really want to hurry up, you can add double shifts, more teams, squeeze deadlines, etc., but all this increases the cost of investment expansions. We thus introduce the costs of adjustment equation as a metaphor for all these frictions in the investment process.

What is the equation of motion that constrains our firm? It is simply that the growth of capital must be equal to the rate of investment:

$$\dot{k}_t = i_t. \tag{13.8}$$

The production function is our familiar

$$y_t = Af\left(k_t\right), \tag{13.9}$$

where A is a productivity coefficient and where $f'\left(\cdot\right) > 0, f''\left(\cdot\right) < 0$, and Inada conditions hold.

Next, specialise the investment cost function to be

$$\psi\left(i_t, k_t\right) = \frac{1}{2\chi} \frac{\left(i_t\right)^2}{k_t},$$

(13.10)

where $\chi > 0$ is a coefficient. Figure 13.1 depicts this function.

Figure 13.1 Adjustment costs

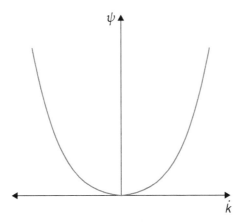

The important assumption is that the costs of adjustment are convex, with a value of zero at $i_t = 0$. The latter means that there is no fixed cost of adjustment, which is a simplifying assumption, while the former captures the idea that the marginal cost of adjustment rises with the size of that adjustment.

Solving this problem

The Hamiltonian can be written as

$$H = Af\left(k_t\right) - \frac{1}{2\chi} \frac{\left(i_t\right)^2}{k_t} - i_t + q_t i_t,$$

(13.11)

where q_t is the costate corresponding to the state k_t, and the control variable is i_t.
The first order condition with respect to the control variable is

$$\frac{\partial H}{\partial i_t} = 0 \Rightarrow \frac{1}{\chi} \frac{i_t}{k_t} = q_t - 1.$$

(13.12)

The law of motion for the costate is

$$\dot{q}_t = q_t r - \frac{\partial H}{\partial k_t} = q_t r - Af'\left(k_t\right) - \frac{1}{2\chi} \left(\frac{i_t}{k_t}\right)^2.$$

(13.13)

The transversality condition is

$$\lim_{T \to \infty} \left(q_T k_T e^{-rT}\right) = 0.$$

(13.14)

13.2.2 | Tobin's q

Our model of investment delivers the result that investment is positive if the value of capital is larger than the replacement cost of capital. This is dubbed Tobin's q theory of investment in honour of James Tobin, who initially proposed it.

Recall that the costate q_t can be interpreted as the marginal value (shadow price) of the state k_t. In other words, it is the value of adding an extra unit of capital. What does this price depend on? Solving (13.13) forward yields

$$q_T = q_t e^{r(T-t)} - \int_t^T \left[Af'(k_v) + \frac{1}{2\chi} \left(\frac{i_v}{k_v} \right)^2 \right] e^{r(T-v)} dv. \tag{13.15}$$

Dividing this by e^{rT} and multiplying by k_T yields

$$k_T q_T e^{-rT} = k_T \left\{ q_t e^{-rt} - \int_t^T \left[Af'(k_v) + \frac{1}{2\chi} \left(\frac{i_v}{k_v} \right)^2 \right] e^{-rv} dv \right\}. \tag{13.16}$$

Next, applying the TVC condition (13.14), we have

$$\lim_{T \to \infty} \left\{ k_T \left(q_t e^{-rt} - \int_t^T \left[Af'(k_v) + \frac{1}{2\chi} \left(\frac{i_v}{k_v} \right)^2 \right] e^{-rv} dv \right) \right\} = 0. \tag{13.17}$$

If $\lim_{T \to \infty} k_T \neq 0$ (it will not be – see below), this last equation implies

$$q_t e^{-rt} - \int_t^\infty \left[Af'(k_v) + \frac{1}{2\chi} \left(\frac{i_v}{k_v} \right)^2 \right] e^{-rv} dv = 0, \tag{13.18}$$

or

$$q_t = \int_t^\infty \left[Af'(k_v) + \frac{1}{2\chi} \left(\frac{i_v}{k_v} \right)^2 \right] e^{-r(v-t)} dv. \tag{13.19}$$

Hence, the price of capital is equal to the present discounted value of the marginal benefits of capital, where these have two components: the usual marginal product $(Af'(k_t))$ and the marginal reductions in investment costs that come from having a higher capital stock in the future.

The fact that q is the shadow value of an addition in the capital stock yields a very intuitive interpretation for the nature of the firm's investment problem. A unit increase in the firm's capital stock increases the present value of the firm's profits by q, and this raises the value of the firm by q. Thus, q is the market value of a unit of capital.

Since we have assumed that the purchase price of a unit of capital is fixed at 1, q is also the ratio of the market value of a unit of capital to its replacement cost. Tobin (1969) was the first to define this variable, nowadays known as Tobin's q.

Notice that (13.12) says that a firm increases its capital stock if the market value of the capital stock exceeds the cost of acquiring it, and vice versa. This is known as Tobin's q-theory of investment.

13.2.3 | The dynamics of investment

Rearranging (13.12) and using (13.8), we can obtain

$$\dot{k}_t = \chi \left(q_t - 1 \right) k_t. \tag{13.20}$$

Next, using (13.20) in (13.13) we have

$$\dot{q}_t = rq_t - Af' \left(k_t \right) - \frac{1}{2} \chi \left(q_t - 1 \right)^2. \tag{13.21}$$

Notice that (13.20) and (13.21) are a system in two differential equations in two unknowns, which can be solved independently of the other equations in the system. What is the interpretation of this system? Taking only a minor liberty, we can refer to this as a system in the capital stock and the price of capital.

Initial steady state

Return to the system given by equations (13.20) and (13.21). It is easy to show that, in a steady state (i.e. a situation where growth rates are constant), it must be the case that these growth rates must be zero.[5] Let * denote steady state variables. From (13.20), $\dot{k}_t = 0$ implies $q^* = 1$. In turn, setting $\dot{q}_t = 0$ in (13.21) implies $r = Af' \left(k^* \right)$, which shows that the marginal product of capital is set equal to the rate of interest. (Have we seen that before?) It follows that, in steady state, firm output is given by $y^* = Af(k^*)$. Note that this is true *only in steady state*, unlike what we had in previous models, where this was the optimality condition everywhere!

Dynamics

The system (13.20) and (13.21) can be written in matrix form as

$$\begin{bmatrix} \dot{k}_t \\ \dot{q}_t \end{bmatrix} = \Omega \begin{bmatrix} k_t - k^* \\ q_t - q^* \end{bmatrix}, \tag{13.22}$$

where

$$\Omega = \begin{bmatrix} \frac{\partial \dot{k}}{\partial k}\big|_{SS} & \frac{\partial \dot{k}}{\partial q}\big|_{SS} \\ \frac{\partial \dot{q}}{\partial k}\big|_{SS} & \frac{\partial \dot{q}}{\partial q}\big|_{SS} \end{bmatrix}. \tag{13.23}$$

Note that

$$\frac{\partial \dot{k}}{\partial k}\bigg|_{SS} = 0 \tag{13.24}$$

$$\frac{\partial \dot{k}}{\partial q}\bigg|_{SS} = \chi k^* \tag{13.25}$$

$$\frac{\partial \dot{q}}{\partial k}\bigg|_{SS} = -Af'' \left(k^* \right) \tag{13.26}$$

$$\left.\frac{\partial \dot{q}}{\partial q}\right|_{SS} = r,\tag{13.27}$$

so that

$$\Omega = \begin{bmatrix} 0 & \chi k^* \\ -Af''(k^*) & r \end{bmatrix}.\tag{13.28}$$

This means that

$$\text{Det}\,(\Omega) = Af''(k^*)\,\chi k^* < 0.\tag{13.29}$$

We know that Det(Ω) is the product of the roots of the matrix Ω. If this product is negative, the roots must have different signs. Note that q_t is a jumpy variable, and k_t is a sticky variable. With one positive root and one negative root, the system is saddle-path stable. Figure 13.2 shows the corresponding phase diagram.

Suppose starting at the steady state, the productivity parameter A falls to a lower permanent level $A' < A$. Let us focus on the evolution of the capital stock k_t and its price q_t, shown in Figure 13.3. The drop in A shifts the $\dot{q} = 0$ schedule to the left. The other locus is unaffected. The steady state of the economy also moves left. The new steady state capital stock is $k^{*\prime} < k^*$.

Dynamic adjustment is as follows. q falls on impact all the way to the saddle path that goes through the new steady state. Over time the system moves along the new saddle path until it reaches the new steady state. Along this trajectory the rate of investment is negative, eventually hitting $\dot{k}_t = 0$ as the economy lands on the new steady state. Notice that during the transition path the price of the asset *increases*. Why would it increase if the productivity of capital has fallen? Remember that at all times the asset has to deliver the opportunity cost of capital (r), if it does not you should sell the asset (this is the reason it's price falls). While the economy adjusts to its lower capital stock, the marginal product of capital is lower. Thus, you should expect a capital gain if you are to hold the asset. The price initially drops sufficiently to generate that capital gain.

Figure 13.2 The dynamics of investment

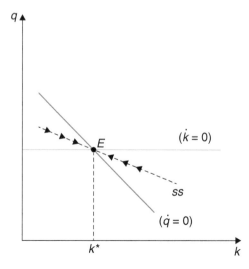

Figure 13.3 The adjustment of investment

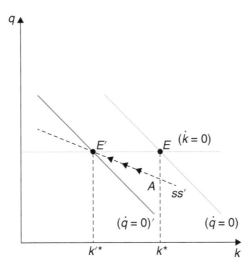

13.2.4 | The role of χ

We can see from the equations for the steady state that the parameter that indicates the costliness of adjustment does not matter for k^* or y^*. But it does matter for the dynamics of adjustment.

Note that as χ falls, costs of investment rise, and vice versa. In the limit, as χ goes to zero, capital never changes; we see from (13.20) that, in this, case $\dot{k}_t = 0$ always.

Consider what would happen to the reaction of capital and its price to the previous shock as χ rises. One can show (solving the model explicitly) that the higher χ, the lower the cost of adjustment and the flatter the saddle path. Intuitively, since with high χ adjustment will be fairly cheap and, therefore, speedy, the price of capital q does not have to jump by a lot to clear the market.

In the limit, as χ goes to infinity, adjustment is costless and instantaneous. The capital stock is no longer a sticky variable, and becomes a jumpy variable. Therefore, its price is always 1, and the system moves horizontally (along $\dot{k} = 0$) in response to any shocks that call for a different steady state capital stock.

13.3 | Investment in the open economy

In a small open economy, introducing a smooth adjustment of investment implies that the current account will change as a result of shocks. A somewhat counterintuitive result is that a negative productivity shock will lead to a surplus in the current account, as capital will fall gradually and consumption anticipates the future decline.

We can now embed the investment behaviour of the firm in a small open economy framework of Chapter 4. In other words, we revisit the open-economy Ramsey model that we have seen before, but now with the more realistic feature of adjustment costs. We want to understand how investment interacts with consumption and savings and how it matters for the trade balance and the current account. We will see that the assumption of adjustment costs has important implications, particularly for the latter.

Consider a small open economy perfectly integrated with the rest of the world in both capital and goods markets. There are two assets: the international bond and domestic capital, just as we have seen before.

In the small open economy, there is a representative consumer and a representative firm. The former can invest in international bonds or in shares of the firm. In fact the consumer owns all the shares of the firm, and receives all of its profits.

13.3.1 | The consumer's problem

The utility function is

$$\int_0^\infty u(c_t)e^{-\rho t}dt, \tag{13.30}$$

where c_t denotes consumption of the only traded good and $\rho(> 0)$ is the rate of time preference. We assume no population growth.

The consumer's flow budget constraint is

$$\dot{b}_t = rb_t + \pi_t - c_t, \tag{13.31}$$

where b_t is the (net) stock of the internationally-traded bond; r is the (constant and exogenously-given) world real interest rate; and π_t is firm profits. Notice that the consumer is small and, therefore, takes the whole sequence of profits as given when maximising his utility.

Notice that the LHS of the budget constraint is also the economy's current account: the excess of national income (broadly defined) over national consumption.

Finally, the solvency (No-Ponzi game) condition is

$$\lim_{T \to \infty} b_T e^{-rT} = 0. \tag{13.32}$$

The Hamiltonian can be written as

$$H = u\left(c_t\right) + \lambda_t \left[rb_t + \pi_t - c_t\right], \tag{13.33}$$

where λ_t is the costate corresponding to the state b_t, while control variables is c_t.

The first order condition with respect to the control variables is

$$u'(c_t) = \lambda_t. \tag{13.34}$$

The law of motion for the costate is

$$\dot{\lambda}_t = \lambda_t \left(\rho - r\right) = 0, \tag{13.35}$$

where the second equality comes from the fact that, as usual, we assume $r = \rho$.

Since λ cannot jump in response to anticipated events, equations (13.34) and (13.35) together say that the path of consumption will be flat over time. In other words, *consumption is perfectly smoothed over time*. Along a perfect foresight path the constant value of c_t is given by

$$c_0 = c_t = rb_0 + r\int_0^\infty \pi_t e^{-rt}dt, \qquad t \geq 0. \tag{13.36}$$

Consumption equals permanent income, defined as the annuity value of the present discounted value of available resources.

Notice that the second term on the RHS of (13.36) is the present discounted value of profits, which is exactly the object the firm tries to maximise. Hence, by maximising that, the firm maximises the feasible level of the consumer's consumption, and (indirectly) utility.

13.3.2 | Bringing in the firm

We now need to solve for the path of investment and output. But we have done that already, when we solved the problem of the firm. We know that the firm's behaviour can be summarised by the initial condition $k_0 > 0$, plus the pair of differential equations

$$\dot{k}_t = \chi \left(q_t - 1 \right) k_t. \tag{13.37}$$

and

$$\dot{q}_t = rq_t - Af' \left(k_t \right) - \frac{1}{2} \chi \left(q_t - 1 \right)^2. \tag{13.38}$$

Recall that (13.37) and (13.38) are a system of two differential equations in two unknowns, which can be solved independently of the other equations in the system.

Recall also that profits are defined as

$$\pi_t = Af \left(k_t \right) - \psi \left(\dot{k}_t, k_t \right) - \dot{k}_t. \tag{13.39}$$

- Once we have a solution (13.37) and (13.38), we know what k_t, $\dot{k}_t$, q_t and $\dot{q}_t$ are.
- With that information in hand, we can use (13.39) to figure out what the whole path for profits π_t will be.
- Knowing that, we can use equation (13.36) to solve for consumption levels.
- Knowing output levels $Af(k_t)$, investment rates $\dot{k}_t$, and consumption levels c_0, we can use this information plus the budget constraint (13.31) to figure out what the current account $\dot{b}_t$ is and, therefore, the path of bond-holdings b_t.

13.3.3 | Initial steady state

Consider the steady state at which debt holdings are b_0 and the capital stock is constant. Let stars denote steady state variables. From (13.37), $\dot{k}_t = 0$ implies $q^* = 1$. In turn, setting $\dot{q}_t = 0$ in (13.38) implies $r = Af'(k^*)$, which shows that the marginal product of capital is set equal to the world rate of interest. It follows that, in steady state, output is given by $y^* = Af(k^*)$. Finally, consumption is given by

$$c^* = rb_0 + y^*. \tag{13.40}$$

In the initial steady state, the current account is zero. The trade balance may be positive, zero, or negative depending on the initial level of net foreign assets:

$$TB \equiv y^* - c^* = -rb_0.$$

13.3.4 | The surprising effects of productivity shocks

Suppose again that, starting at this steady state, the productivity parameter A falls to a lower permanent level $A' < A$. To make life simpler, suppose that initially bond-holdings are zero ($b_0 = 0$).

Focus first on the evolution of the capital stock k_t and its price q_t, shown in Figure 13.3. The drop in A shifts the $\dot{q} = 0$ schedule to the left. The other locus is unaffected. The steady state of the economy also moves left. The new steady state capital stock is $k^{*\prime} < k^*$.

At time zero, q falls on impact all the way to the saddle path that goes through the new steady state. Over time the system moves along the new saddle path until it reaches the new steady state. Along this trajectory the rate of investment is negative, eventually hitting $\dot{k}_t = 0$ as the economy lands on the new steady state.

Notice that net output, defined as $y_t - \dot{k}_t - \psi\left(\dot{k}_t, k_t\right)$, may either go up or down initially, depending on whether the fall in gross output y_t is larger or smaller than the change in costs associated with the decline in investment. Over the long run, however, the effect is unambiguous: Net output is lower, since gross output falls and investment tends to zero. Figure 13.4 shows net output falling initially, and then declining further to its new steady state level.

The level of consumption is constant and given by

$$c_0' = r \int_0^{\infty} \left(A'f\left(k_t\right) - \dot{k}_t - \psi\left(\dot{k}_t, k_t\right)\right) e^{-rt} dt < c_0 \qquad t \geq 0. \tag{13.41}$$

Graphically (in terms of Figure 13.4), consumption is determined by the condition that the thatched areas above and below it be equal in present value.

What about the current account? Since initial bonds are zero, having consumption below net output (see Figure 13.4) must imply that the economy is initially running a current account surplus, saving in anticipation of the lower output in the future. In the new steady state, the net foreign asset position of the economy is that of a creditor: $b^{*\prime} > 0$ and the current account goes back to zero.

Figure 13.4 The effect on the current account

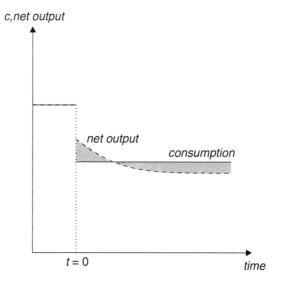

This result led to a novel and surprising interpretation of the current account. Imagine, for example, a fall in productivity that arises from an oil crisis (such as that in the 1970s), affecting an oil importing country.[6] Figure 13.4 suggests that this shock will lead to a surplus in the current account. Notice that this may challenge your intuition; if oil has become more expensive and this is an oil importing country, shouldn't the current account deteriorate? Why is this wrong? It is wrong because it fails to take into account the adjustment of aggregate spending in response to the shock. The oil shock not only makes imports more expensive, it lowers expected future income. As consumption smooths future decreases in income, it reacts strongly in the short run, in fact, ahead of the output decrease, leading to a surplus. By the same token, if you are an oil-exporting country, a positive shock to the price of oil would stimulate consumption and investment. As output will increase over time the reaction of consumption can be strong, leading to a deficit. Of course this result depends on a number or assumptions, for example that the shock be permanent and believed to be so. Changing any of these assumptions can change this result.

The bottom line is that these intuitions that are aided by our use of a general equilibrium format. In fact, when Sachs et al. (1981) tested these results by looking at the response of the current account to the oil shocks of the 1970's they found that the results of the theory held surprisingly well in the data. Oil exporting countries quickly (though not instantaneously) were experiencing deficits, while oil importing countries managed to show surpluses.

On a final note, you may recall that the adjustment process is quite different from what we had in the open-economy Ramsey model without adjustment costs in response to a permanent shock. There the current account of an economy in which $r = \rho$ was always zero. This was because all adjustments could be done instantaneously – if the shock led the economy to reduce its stock of capital, it could do so immediately by lending abroad. Now, because of adjustment costs, this process takes place over time, and we have current account dynamics in the transition.

13.4 | What next?

If you are interested in understanding better the investment process, a good starting point is, again, the Dixit and Pindyck (1994) masterpiece *Investment under Uncertainty*. The Bloom et al. (2007) paper provides a wonderful reference list with the most important pieces written to that date. In more recent years a debate has ensued on the nature of investment in an increasingly digitalised world where firms do not need so much capital as they do human capital. Crouzet and Eberly (2019) is a good entry point into this debate.

Notes

[1] The classical reference on this issue is Dixit and Pindyck (1994). See, for example, Brennan and Schwartz (1985) for mining projects. More recently, Schwartz has found that new reserves additions to oil companies *reduce* the value of the companies. In this case, they are an option to a loss! (See Atanasova and Schwartz (2019)).

[2] This issue has a long pedigree in economics. For a relatively recent reference, with many references thereof, you may want to check Bloom (2009).

[3] Careful with the use of the machines imagery! It brings to mind right away the role of indivisibilities – you can't purchase 3.36 machines – while we will assume that investment is perfectly divisible. Indivisibilities will bring in other issues that are beyond our present scope.

[4] We refer rather loosely here to profit, but really the equation depicts the free cash flow that the investment project will generate over it's lifetime.

[5] How can we show that? Note that (13.20) immediately implies that, for $\frac{k}{k}$ to be constant, we must have q constant. Using (13.21) to obtain $\frac{\dot{q}}{q}$, and using the fact that q is constant, we see that we must have the ratio $\frac{f'(k)}{q}$ constant, which requires that k is also constant.

[6] One way to think about this is by thinking of oil as an input that has become more costly, akin to a fall in labour or capital productivity.

References

Atanasova, C. & Schwartz, E. S. (2019). *Stranded fossil fuel reserves and firm value*. National Bureau of Economic Research.

Bloom, N. (2009). The impact of uncertainty shocks. *Econometrica, 77*(3), 623–685.

Bloom, N., Bond, S., & Van Reenen, J. (2007). Uncertainty and investment dynamics. *The Review of Economic Studies, 74*(2), 391–415.

Brennan, M. J. & Schwartz, E. S. (1985). Evaluating natural resource investments. *Journal of Business*, 135–157.

Crouzet, N. & Eberly, J. C. (2019). *Understanding weak capital investment: The role of market concentration and intangibles*. National Bureau of Economic Research.

Dixit, A. & Pindyck, R. S. (1994). *Investment under uncertainty*. Princeton University Press.

Sachs, J. D., Cooper, R. N., & Fischer, S. (1981). The current account and macroeconomic adjustment in the 1970s. *Brookings Papers on Economic Activity, 1981*(1), 201–282.

Tobin, J. (1969). A general equilibrium approach to monetary theory. *Journal of Money, Credit and Banking, 1*(1), 15–29.

Short Term Fluctuations

CHAPTER 14

Real business cycles

So far we have mostly talked about long-term dynamics, the process of capital accumulation, inter-generational issues, etc. However, a lot of macroeconomics focuses on the short term – the departures from the long-run trend that we've been mostly concerned about. This is, of course, particularly evident in recession times! Some of the biggest questions in macroeconomics revolve around this: how can we understand and influence the short-run, cyclical evolution of the economy? What can we (or should we) do about recessions?

These are obviously important questions, and they are very much at the heart of the development of macroeconomics as a discipline, as we discussed in the first chapter of the book. In fact, business cycles is where the distinction between macroeconomic schools of thought became more evident – giving credence to the idea that economists never agree with each other. Many of your policy recommendations will derive from which view of the world you have.

Essentially, one school is ingrained in the Keynesian perspective where there is scope for intervening on the cycle and that doing so is welfare-improving. Its modern version is the New Keynesian approach originated in the 1980s in response to the empirical and methodological challenges from the 1970s. The second approach is quite skeptical about what policy can or should do, as it views the cycle as the result of optimal adjustments to real shocks. Its modern version was born, also in the 1980s, with the so-called Real Business Cycle (RBC) framework, which argued that a perfectly competitive economy, with no distortions or aggregate imbalances of the Keynesian type, but subject to productivity shocks, could largely replicate the business-cycle frequency data for real-world economies.

Recent years have seen a great deal of methodological convergence, with both views adopting, to a large extent, the so-called dynamic stochastic general equilibrium (DSGE) framework that essentially implements the NGM with whatever exogenous shocks and market imperfections that you may feel are relevant. Because this model can be specified to work as a perfectly competitive distortion-free economy, or as one with more Keynesian-type characteristics, it has become the new workhorse of macroeconomics. This has allowed for a more unified conversation in recent decades.

In light of that, and because we have covered much of the ground when we studied the NGM, we will start by describing the RBC framework, which started the trend that turned the NGM into the workhorse of modern macroeconomics. This framework, from a theory standpoint, is, conceptually, a simple extension of the NGM to a context with stochastic shocks.

How to cite this book chapter:
Campante, F., Sturzenegger, F. and Velasco, A. 2021. *Advanced Macroeconomics: An Easy Guide.*
Ch. 14. 'Real business cycles', pp. 205–218. London: LSE Press.
DOI: https://doi.org/10.31389/lsepress.ame.n   License: CC-BY-NC 4.0.

Yet we will see that it has a sharp message. In particular, it delivers the ultimate anti-Keynesian statement: to the extent that business cycles are optimal responses to productivity shocks, policy interventions are worse than ineffective; they are bad, because they deviate the economy from its intertemporal optimum. From this benchmark, we will then turn to the Keynesian theories.

14.1 | The basic RBC model

The basic RBC model is simply the NGM (in discrete time) with two additions: stochastic shocks to productivity (to generate fluctuations in output) and a labour supply choice (to generate fluctuations in employment). Fluctuations come from optimal individual responses to the stochastic shocks.

The basic RBC model, first introduced by Kydland and Prescott (1982), is built around a typical NGM framework of intertemporal maximisation. There are three differences with what we've seen so far in the book. First, we introduce uncertainty in the form of exogenous productivity shocks, without which (as we've seen) no fluctuations emerge. Second, we also introduce a choice of how much labour will be supplied – in other words, there is a labour-leisure choice. This is what will enable us to say something about fluctuations in employment. Finally, RBC models typically use discrete time. This is so because the objective is to compare the simulated data from the model with that of the real data, which is always discrete, and also because the models quickly become too complicated for analytical solutions. One has to resort to numerical methods of solution, and computers can more easily handle discrete data.

The consumer's problem works as follows:

$$Max\, E\left[\sum_t \left(\frac{1}{1+\rho} \right)^t \left((1-\phi)\, u(c_t) + \phi v(h_t) \right) \right], \qquad (14.1)$$

subject to the household budget constraint in which individuals own the capital stock and labour endowment, and rent those out to the firms,

$$k_{t+1} = l_t w_t + (1+r_t)k_t - c_t, \qquad (14.2)$$

the production function,

$$f(k_t, l_t, z_t) = z_t k_t^\alpha l_t^{1-\alpha}, \qquad (14.3)$$

the labour endowment equation,

$$h_t + l_t = 1, \qquad (14.4)$$

and a productivity shock process

$$z_{t+1} = \varphi z_t + \varepsilon_{t+1}. \qquad (14.5)$$

c_t is consumption, h_t indicates leisure, r_t is the rate of return on capital (net of depreciation), k_t is the capital stock, l_t is the amount of labour devoted to market activities.[1] Finally, z_t is a productivity parameter which is subject to random shocks ε_t. The rest are parameters which should be relatively self-explanatory.

14.1.1 | The importance of labour supply

As we've pointed out, one of the RBC literature's main departures from the standard NGM is the presence of a labour supply choice. This is crucial to generate fluctuations in employment, which are a pervasive feature of actual business cycles. Let us consider this choice within the context of the basic model. With log utility, the consumer's objective function can be thought of as:

$$E\left[\sum_t \left(\frac{1}{1+\rho}\right)^t \left[(1-\phi)\log(c_t) + \phi\log(h_t)\right]\right].$$

Notice that the household has two control variables, consumption and leisure. We have seen before the solution to the problem of optimal intertemporal allocation of consumption; it is the familiar Euler equation:

$$u'(c_t) = \frac{1+r_{t+1}}{1+\rho} E\left[u'(c_{t+1})\right]. \tag{14.6}$$

Leaving aside uncertainty, for the moment, and using the log assumption, we can rewrite this as:

$$c_{t+1} = \frac{1+r_{t+1}}{1+\rho} c_t. \tag{14.7}$$

The labour-leisure choice, in contrast, is static; it takes place in each period with no implication for the next period. The FOC equates the marginal benefit of additional consumption to the marginal cost of lost leisure:

$$w_t(1-\phi)u'(c_t) = \phi v'(h_t). \tag{14.8}$$

Again using the log utility assumption, we get

$$w_t(1-\phi)h_t = \phi c_t. \tag{14.9}$$

To simplify things further, assume for the moment that r is exogenous – think of a small open economy. In this setup, we can use (14.9) into (14.7) to obtain

$$\frac{h_{t+1}}{h_t} = \frac{1+r}{1+\rho}\frac{w_t}{w_{t+1}} \Rightarrow \frac{1-l_{t+1}}{1-l_t} = \frac{1+r}{1+\rho}\frac{w_t}{w_{t+1}}. \tag{14.10}$$

This means that leisure will be relatively high in those periods when the wage is relatively low; in other words, a higher wage increases the supply of labour. We can also see the impact of the interest rate: a high interest rate will lead to a higher supply of labour. The intuition is that it is worth working more in the present the higher the interest rate, as it provides a higher return in terms of future leisure. These responses of the labour supply, driven by intertemporal substitution in labour and leisure, are at the very heart of the fluctuations in employment in RBC models.

The long-run labour supply

Let's pause for a minute to explore a bit deeper the shape of this labour supply curve. Consider the case when wages and income are constant, a case that would be akin to analysing the effect of permanent shocks to these variables. Let's see the form of the labour supply in this case.

Since consumption is constant at income level

$$c_t = w(1 - h_t),$$ (14.11)

substituting this into (14.8) we obtain

$$(1 - \phi)\, u'(w(1 - h_t)) = \frac{\phi v'(h_t)}{w}.$$ (14.12)

Using the log specification for consumption and allowing for $\phi = \frac{2}{3}$ allows us to simplify

$$\left(\frac{1}{3}\right) \frac{1}{w(1 - h_t)} = \frac{2}{3} \frac{1}{w h_t},$$ (14.13)

$$\frac{1}{(1 - h_t)} = \frac{2}{h_t} \Rightarrow h_t = \frac{2}{3}.$$ (14.14)

This is a strong result that says that leisure is independent of the wage level. You may think this is too strong but, surprisingly, it fits the data very well, at least when thinking about labour supply in the very, very long run.[2] It does seem that for humans income and substitution effects just cancel out (or maybe you prefer a more Leontieff setup in which people just can't work more than eight hours per day, or where the disutility of labour beyond eight hours a day becomes unbearable if repeated every day).

Does this mean that labour supply does not move at all? Not really. The above was derived under the assumption of the constancy of the wage. This is akin to assuming that any change in wages is permanent, which induces a very large response in the shadow value of consumption that works to offset the labour supply effect of the change in wages (totally cancelling it in the log case). But if the wage moves for a very short period of time we can assume the shadow value of consumption to remain constant, and then changes in the wage will elicit a labour supply response. Thus, while the long-run elasticity of labour supply may be zero, it is positive in the short run.

The basic mechanics

In its essence, the RBC story goes as follows: consider a positive productivity shock that hits the economy, making it more productive. As a result of that shock, wages (i.e. MPL) and interest rates (i.e. MPK) go up, and individuals want to work more as a result. Because of that, output goes up. It follows that the elasticity of labour supply (and the closely related elasticity of intertemporal substitution) are crucial parameters for RBC models. One can only obtain large fluctuations in employment, as needed to match the data, if this elasticity is sufficiently high. What is the elasticity of labour supply in this basic model? Consider the case when $\frac{(1+r)}{(1+\rho)} = 1$, in which consumption is a constant. We can read (14.8) as implying a labour supply curve (a relation between l_t and w_t):

$$\phi v'(1 - l_t) = \lambda w_t,$$ (14.15)

where λ is the (constant) marginal utility of consumption. Let's assume a slightly more general, functional form for the utility of leisure:

$$v(h) = \frac{\sigma}{1-\sigma} h^{\frac{\sigma-1}{\sigma}}, \qquad (14.16)$$

plugging this in (14.15) gives

$$\phi h_t^{-\frac{1}{\sigma}} = \lambda w_t \qquad (14.17)$$

or

$$h_t = \left(\frac{\lambda w_t}{\phi}\right)^{-\sigma}, \qquad (14.18)$$

which can be used to compute the labour supply:

$$l_t = 1 - \left(\frac{\lambda w_t}{\phi}\right)^{-\sigma}. \qquad (14.19)$$

This equation has a labour supply elasticity in the short run equal to

$$\frac{dl}{dw}\frac{w}{l} = \varepsilon_{l,w} = \frac{\sigma\left(\frac{\lambda w_t}{\phi}\right)^{-\sigma-1}\left(\frac{\lambda w_t}{\phi}\right)}{1-\left(\frac{\lambda w_t}{\phi}\right)^{-\sigma}} = \frac{\sigma\left(\frac{\lambda w_t}{\phi}\right)^{-\sigma}}{1-\left(\frac{\lambda w_t}{\phi}\right)^{-\sigma}} = \frac{\sigma h_t}{l_t}. \qquad (14.20)$$

If we assume that $\sigma = 1$ (logarithmic utility in leisure), and that ϕ and λ are such that $\frac{h}{l} = 2$ (think about an 8-hour workday), this gives you $\varepsilon_{l,w} = 2$. This doesn't seem to be enough to replicate the employment fluctuations observed in the data. On the other hand, it seems to be quite high if compared to micro data on the elasticity of labour supply. Do you think a decrease of 10% in real wages (because of inflation, for instance) would lead people to work 20% fewer hours?

14.1.2 | The indivisible labour solution

The RBC model thus delivers an elasticity of labour supply that is much higher than what micro evidence suggests, posing a challenge when it comes to matching real-world fluctuations in employment. One proposed solution for the conundrum is to incorporate the fact that labour decisions are often indivisible. This means that people may not make adjustments so much on the intensive margin of how many hours to work in your job, but more often on the extensive margin of whether to work at all. This implies that the aggregate elasticity is large even when the individual elasticity is small.

Hansen (1985) models that by assuming that there are fixed costs of going to work. This can actually make labour supply very responsive for a range of wage levels. The decision variables are both days of work: $d \leq \bar{d}$, and, then, the hours of work each day: n. We assume there is a fixed commuting cost in terms of utility κ, which you pay if you decide to work on that day, regardless of how many hours you work (this would be a sort of commuting time).

The objective function is now

$$MaxE\left[\sum_t \left(\frac{1}{1+\rho}\right)^t \left[u\left(c_t\right) - d_t v\left(n_t\right) - \kappa_t d_t\right]\right],$$ (14.21)

where we leave aside the term ϕ to simplify notation, and abuse notation to have $v(\cdot)$ be a function of hours worked, rather than leisure, entering negatively in the utility function. The budget constraint is affected in that now wage income is equal to $w_t d_t n_t$.

It is easy to see that we have the same FOCs, (14.7) – which is unchanged because the terms in consumption in both maximand and budget constraint are still the same –, and (14.8) – because the term in n_t is multiplied by d_t in both maximand and budget constraint, so that d_t cancels out. What changes is that now we have an extra FOC with respect to d_t:

$$\left[v(n_t) + k_t\right] \geq u'(c_t)w_t n_t.$$ (14.22)

Assume $\frac{(1+r)}{(1+\rho)} = 1$, so that c_t is constant. Then (14.8) simplifies to

$$v'(n_t) = \lambda w_t \Longrightarrow n^*(w),$$ (14.23)

which gives the optimal amount of hours worked (when the agent decides to work). Then (14.22) simplifies to

$$v(n^*) + k_t \geq \lambda w_t n^*.$$ (14.24)

If $v(n^*) + k > \lambda wn^*$, then $d = 0$, otherwise $d = \bar{d}$. This gives rise to a labour supply as shown in Figure 14.1

The important point is that this labour supply curve is infinitely elastic at a certain wage. The intuition is that on the margin at which people decide whether to work at all or not, the labour supply will be very sensitive to changes in wages.[3]

Figure 14.1   The Hansen labour supply

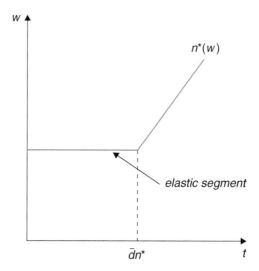

14.2 | RBC model at work

RBC models typically cannot be solved analytically, and require numerical methods. We discuss an example of a calibration approach to assess the success of the model in describing actual economic fluctuations.

Having discussed the basic intuition behind generating output and employment fluctuations from real shocks to the economy, let us now talk a little bit more generally about how RBC models are usually handled. The main challenge is that even simple specifications are impossible to solve analytically, so the alternative is to use numerical methods.

How is this done? In a nutshell, the strategy is to solve for the FOCs of the model which, in addition to the equations determining the nature of the stochastic shocks, will describe the dynamic path of the variables of interest. (This will often imply a step in which the FOCs are log-linearised around the balanced growth path, since it is easiest to analyse the properties of a linear system.) We then need to provide numbers for the computer to work with – this is done by calibrating the parameters. (Remember what we have discussed of calibration when talking about growth empirics – this approach was pretty much pioneered by the RBC literature.) Because the model is calibrated on the basis of parameters that are brought from "outside the model", the procedure provides somewhat of an independent test of the relevance of the model.

With this in hand, the model is simulated, typically by considering how the variables of interest responds after being exposed to a stochastic draw of exogenous productivity shocks. The results are then compared to the data. In both cases, the simulated and the real data, we work with the business cycle component, i.e. detrending the data. This is usually done using the Hodrick-Prescott filter, which is a statistical procedure to filter out the trend component of a time series. What output of the model is then compared to the data? Mostly second moments: variances and covariances of the variables of interest. A model is considered successful if it matches lots of those empirical moments.

14.2.1 | Calibration: An example

Let us consider the basic RBC model, and the calibration proposed by Prescott (1986) which is the actual kick-off of this approach and where Prescott tackles the issue of assigning parameters to the coefficients of the model. For example, at the time, he took as good a capital share of $\alpha = 0.36$.[4] To estimate the production function, he starts with a Cobb-Douglas specification we've used repeatedly

$$f(k) = k^{\alpha}. \tag{14.25}$$

Remember that the interest rate has to equal the marginal product of capital,

$$f'(k) = \alpha k^{\alpha-1}, \tag{14.26}$$

which means that we have an equation for the return on capital:

$$r = \alpha \frac{Y}{K} - \delta. \tag{14.27}$$

Now let's put numbers to this. What is a reasonable rate of depreciation? Let's use (14.27) itself to figure it out. If we assume that the rate of depreciation is 10% per year (14.27) becomes

$$0.04 = 0.36\frac{Y}{K} - 0.10 \tag{14.28}$$

$$0.14 = 0.36\frac{Y}{K} \tag{14.29}$$

$$\frac{0.36}{0.14} = \frac{K}{Y} = 2.6. \tag{14.30}$$

This value for the capital output ratio is considered reasonable, so the 10% rate of depreciation seems to be a reasonable guess.

How about the discount factor? It is assumed equal to the interest rate. (This is not as restrictive as it may seem, but we can skip that for now.) This implies a yearly discount rate of about 4% (the real interest rate), so that $\frac{1}{1+\rho} = 0.96$ (again, per year).

As for the elasticity of intertemporal substitution, he argues that $\sigma = 1$ is a good approximation, and uses the share of leisure equal to $2/3$, as we had anticipated (this gives a labour allocation of half, which is reasonable if we consider that possible working hours are 16 per day).

Finally, the productivity shock process is derived from Solow-residual-type estimations (as discussed in Chapter 6 when we talked about growth accounting), which, in the case of the U.S. at the time, yielded:

$$z_{t+1} = 0.9 * z_t + \varepsilon_{t+1}. \tag{14.31}$$

This is a highly persistent process, in which shocks have very long-lasting effects. The calibration for the standard deviation of the disturbance ε is 0.763.

So, endowed with all these parameters, we can pour them into the specification and run the model over time – in fact, multiple times, with different random draws for the productivity shock. This will give a time series for the economy in the theoretical model. We will now see how the properties of this economy compare to those of the real economy.

14.2.2 | Does it work?

Let's start with some basic results taken directly from Prescott's paper. Figure 14.2 shows log U.S. GDP and its trend. The trend is computed as a Hodrick-Prescott filter (think of this as a smoothed, but not fixed, line tracing the data). It is not a great way to compute the business cycle (particularly at the edges of the data set), but one that has become quite popular. Once the trend is computed, the cycle is easily estimated as the difference between the two and is showing in figure 14.3.

Figure 14.3 also shows the variation over the cycle in hours worked. As you can see, there is a large positive correlation between the two.

Real business cycle papers will typically include a table with the properties of the economy, understood as the volatility of the variables and their cross-correlation over time. Table 14.1 and 14.2 show this from Prescott's original paper for both the real data and the calibrated model.

As you can see, things work surprisingly well in the sense that most characteristics of the economy match. The volatility of output and the relative volatility of consumption and investment appear to be the optimal response to the supply shocks. The only caveat is that hours do not seem to move as much as in the data. This is why Prescott implemented Hansen's extension. Figure 14.4 shows how labour and output move in the Hansen economy (they seem to match better the pattern in Figure 14.1).

The Appendix to this chapter (at the end of the book) will walk you through an actual example so that you learn to numerically solve and simulate an RBC-style model yourself!

Figure 14.2 The U.S. output

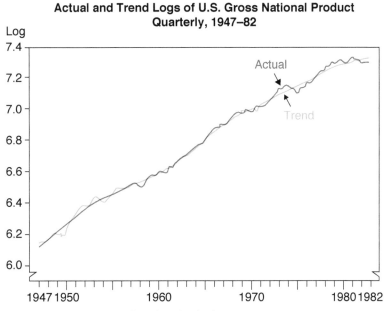

Actual and Trend Logs of U.S. Gross National Product Quarterly, 1947–82

Source of basic data: Citicorp's Citibase data bank

Figure 14.3 The cycle in the U.S.

Deviations From Trend of Gross National Product and Nonfarm Employee Hours in the United States Quarterly, 1947–82

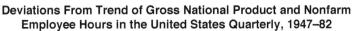

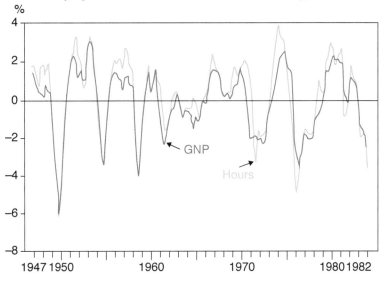

Source of basic data: Citicorp's Citibase data bank

Table 14.1 The data for the U.S. cycle, from Prescott (1986)

		Cross Correlation of GNP With		
Variable x	Standard Deviation	x(t − 1)	x(t)	x(t + 1)
Gross National Product	1.8%	.82	1.00	.82
Personal Consumption Expenditures				
Services	.6	.66	.72	.61
Nondurable Goods	1.2	.71	.76	.59
Fixed investment Expenditures	5.3	.78	.89	.78
Nonresidential Investment	5.2	.54	.79	.86
Structures	4.6	.42	.62	.70
Equipment	6.0	.56	.82	.87
Capital Stocks				
Total Nonfarm Inventories	1.7	.15	4.8	.68
Nonresidential Structures	.4	−.20	−.03	.16
Nonresidential Equipment	1.0	.03	.23	.41
Labor Input				
Nonfarm Hours	1.7	.57	.85	.89
Average Weekly Hours in Mfg.	1.0	.76	.85	.61
Productivity (GNP/Hours)	1.0	.51	.34	−.04

Source of basic data: Citicorp's Citibase data bank

Table 14.2 The variables in the Prescott model, from Prescott (1986)

Cyclical Behavior of the Kydland-Prescott Economy*

		Cross Correlation of GNP With		
Variable x	Standard Deviation	x(t − 1)	x(t)	x(t + 1)
Gross National Product	1.79%	.60	1.00	.60
	(.13)	(.07)	(—)	(.07)
Consumption	.45	.47	.85	.71
	(.05)	(.05)	(.02)	(.04)
Investment	5.49	.52	.88	.78
	(.41)	(.09)	(.03)	(.03)
Inventory Stock	2.20	.14	.60	.52
	(.37)	(.14)	(.08)	(.05)

Capital Stock	.47	−.05	.02	.25
	(.07)	(.07)	(.06)	(.07)
Hours	1.23	.52	.95	.55
	(.09)	(.09)	(.01)	(.06)
Productivity (GNP/Hours)	.71	.62	.86	.56
	(.06)	(.05)	(.02)	(.10)
Real Interest Rate (Annual)	.22	.65	.60	.36
	(.03)	(.07)	(.20)	(.15)

*These are the means of 20 simulations, each of which was 116 periods song. The numbers parentheses are standard errors.
Source: Kydland and Prescott 1984

Figure 14.4   The correlation of output and hours in the Hansen model

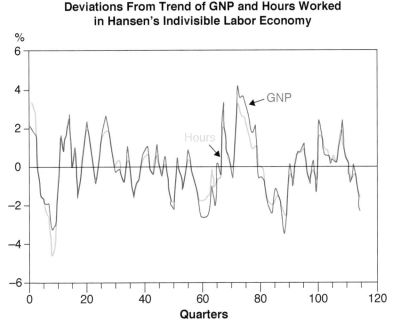

Deviations From Trend of GNP and Hours Worked
in Hansen's Indivisible Labor Economy

Source: Gray D. Hansen, Department of Economics, University of California, Santa Barbara

14.3 | Assessing the RBC contribution

The RBC approach led to a methodological revolution in macroeconomics; all macro models from then on have been expected to be framed as a dynamic stochastic general-equilibrium model with fully optimising agents and rational expectations. Whether or not you buy it as an explanation for business cycle fluctuations in general, and the associated critique of policy interventions, the approach can be useful in understanding at least some aspects of actual fluctuations.

Prescott (1986) summarises the claim in favour of the RBC model: "Economic theory implies that, given the nature of the shocks to technology and people's willingness and ability to intertemporally and intratemporally substitute, the economy will display fluctuations like those the U.S. economy displays." His claim is that his model economy matches remarkably well the actual data and, to the extent that it doesn't, it's probably because the real-world measurement does not really capture what the theory says is important – hence the title of 'Theory Ahead of Business Cycle Measurement'.

The startling policy implications of these findings are highlighted as follows: "Costly efforts at stabilization are likely to be counterproductive. Economic fluctuations are optimal responses to uncertainty in the rate of technological change." In other words, business cycle policy is not only useless, but harmful. One should focus on the determinants of the average rate of technological change.

The macro literature has vigorously pursued and refined the path opened by Prescott. Lots of different changes have been considered to the original specification, such as different sources for the shocks (for instance, government spending) or the inclusion of a number of market distortions (e.g. taxation). On the other hand, many objections have been raised to the basic message of RBCs. Do we really see such huge shifts in technology on a quarterly basis? Or, is the Solow residual capturing something else? (Remember, it is the measure of our ignorance...) Do we really believe that fluctuations are driven by people's willingness to intertemporally reallocate labour? If these are optimal, why do they feel so painful? How about the role of monetary policy, for which the RBC model has no role? Finally, it seems that the features of the fluctuations that are obtained are very close to the nature of the stochastic process that is assumed for the shocks – how much of an explanation is that?

Kydland and Prescott eventually received the Nobel Prize in Economics in 2004, partly for this contribution. (We will return to other contributions by the pair when we discuss monetary policy.) More importantly, the approach led to two developments. First, it generated a fierce counterattack to Keynesianism. The rational expectations revolution had stated that Keynesian policy was ineffective; Kydland and Prescott said it was wrong and harmful. Second, by validating the model, this calibrated stochastic version of the NGM became the workhorse of macroeconomics, so that the RBC approach won the methodological contest. In macro these days, people are pretty much expected to produce a DSGE model with fully optimising agents (with rational expectations) that is amenable to the discipline of calibration. Even the folks who believe in Keynesian-style business cycles are compelled to frame them in such models, though including some price rigidity, monetary disturbance, and so on, as we will see soon.

In addition, even if you believe that the Keynesian approach is a better description of business cycles in general, it may still be the case that a simple RBC framework can explain some important economic episodes. For instance, take a look at Figure 14.5, which depicts GDP, employment, consumption, and investment data for the U.S. over 2019–20. The sharp drop we see is, of course, the economic response to the Covid-19 pandemic, which fits well the supply shock paradigm. The response looks a lot like the kind of logic we have seen in this chapter: a shock to productivity – in this case, the threat posed by a virus – radically changes the intertemporal tradeoff, and leads to a postponement of labour supply and, consequently, to drops in employment and output. Notice that consumption in this case is not smoother than output even though investment is the most volatile variable, as the model predicts. Why is consumption more volatile in this context? Eichenbaum et al. (2020) provide an explanation. They make the realistic assumption that during the Covid-19 pandemic, people attached a risk of contagion to the act of consuming (consumption means going out to a restaurant, shopping mall, etc.) and, therefore, reduced consumption more than they would have done if only adjusting for the change in intertemporal wealth. The example illustrates that some specific changes in the setup may be required on occasion to adjust empirical observations.[5]

Figure 14.5   Trajectories of macro variables in response to Covid-19

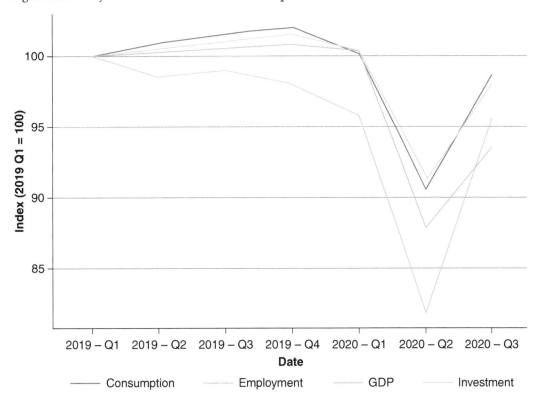

This particular example illustrates that real shocks actually exist, and shows, more broadly, that you do not have to be an RBC true believer to accept that the logic they illuminate has practical applications.

14.4 | What have we learned?

The RBC approach to business cycle fluctuations is conceptually very straightforward; take the basic NGM model, add productivity shocks (and a labour-supply choice), and you will get business cycle fluctuations. It highlights the importance of intertemporal substitution and labour supply elasticities as important potential driving factors behind these fluctuations, and can provide a useful lens with which to understand real-world fluctuations, at the very least, in some circumstances (as illustrated by the case of the Covid-19 pandemic).

The approach also has a very sharp message in terms of policy: you should not pursue counter-cyclical policy. If fluctuations are simply the optimal response of a distortion-free economy to real shocks, policy would only add noise to the process, and make adjustments harder. As we will see, the Keynesian approach has a very different, more policy-friendly message. The contraposition of these two traditions – and particularly the role they assign to policy intervention – is very much at the heart of macroeconomic policy debates.

But we also learned that, underpinning this policy divergence, is a substantial degree of methodological convergence. All of mainstream modern macroeconomics, to a first approximation, speaks the language that was first introduced by the RBC approach – that of dynamic, stochastic general equi-librium (DSGE) models.

14.5 | What next?

Readers who are interested in the RBC approach can go to McCandless (2008), *The ABCs of RCBs*, which, as the title indicates, provides a simple and practical introduction to solving RBC models. The paper by Prescott (1986) is also worth reading, as it provides a veritable manifesto of the original approach.

Those who want to dig deeper into the type of recursive methods that have become ubiquitous in macroeconomics, to solve models in the methodological tradition inaugurated by the RBC approach, should look into Ljungqvist and Sargent (2018). You will actually see many of the themes that we discuss in this book, but presented at a whole other level of formal rigor.

Notes

[1] You will often see *l* used to refer to leisure and *n* to labour, but we are going to stick with *l* for labour, for consistency. Think about *h* as standing for holidays.

[2] One way to think about this is asking yourself the following question: how many times higher are real wages today than, say, 300 years ago? And how many more hours do we work?

[3] Here is a weird little prediction from this model: note that consumption is constant regardless of the employment decision. This means that unemployed and employed workers have the same consumption. But, since work generates disutility, that means that unemployed workers are better off! For a discussion on the state-of-the-art of this debate, see Chetty et al. (2011).

[4] Remember that Parente and Prescott (2002) argue for $\alpha = .66$, but this was later...

[5] An alternative story is provided by Sturzenegger (2020). In his specification, *utility* changes and people, due to lockdowns, require fewer goods to obtain the same utility. The result is a sharp fall in optimal consumption as in Eichenbaum et al. (2020).

References

Chetty, R., Guren, A., Manoli, D., & Weber, A. (2011). Are micro and macro labor supply elastici-ties consistent? A review of evidence on the intensive and extensive margins. *American Economic Review*, *101*(3), 471–75.

Eichenbaum, M. S., Rebelo, S., & Trabandt, M. (2020). *The macroeconomics of epidemics* (tech. rep.). National Bureau of Economic Research.

Hansen, G. D. (1985). Indivisible labor and the business cycle. *Journal of Monetary Economics*, *16*(3), 309–327.

Kydland, F. E. & Prescott, E. C. (1982). Time to build and aggregate fluctuations. *Econometrica*, 1345–1370.

Ljungqvist, L. & Sargent, T. J. (2018). *Recursive macroeconomic theory*. MIT Press.

McCandless, G. (2008). *The ABCs of RBCs*. Cambridge, Massachusetts, London: Harvard.

Parente, S. L. & Prescott, E. C. (2002). *Barriers to riches*. MIT Press.

Prescott, E. C. (1986). Theory ahead of business-cycle measurement. *Carnegie-Rochester Conference Series on Public Policy*, *25*, 11–44.

Sturzenegger, F. (2020). Should we hibernate in a lockdown? *Economics Bulletin*, *40*(3), 2023–2033.

CHAPTER 15

(New) Keynesian theories of fluctuations: A primer

Keynesian thinking starts from a different viewpoint, at least compared with that of the RBC approach, regarding the functioning of markets. In this perspective, output and employment fluctuations indicate that labour markets, good markets, or both, are not working, leading to unnecessary unemployment. The idea is that, at least in some circumstances, the economy is demand-constrained (rather than supply-constrained), so that the challenge is to increase expenditure. If that could be done, then supply will respond automatically. (This is Keynes's Principle of Effective Demand.[1]) As a result, Keynesian models focus on aggregate demand management as opposed to supply-side policies. Later on in the book we will discuss specifically the role of fiscal and monetary policy in aggregate demand, but in this chapter we need to understand the framework under which this aggregate demand management matters.

Of course there is a lot of controversy among economists as to how is it possible that a situation where markets fail to clear may persist over time. Why is there unemployment? Can unemployment be involuntary? If it is involuntary, why don't people offer to work for less? Why are prices rigid? Why can't firms adjust their prices? How essential is price fixing in comparison with distortions on the labour market? And, in this setup, do consumers satisfy their intertemporal budget constraints?

These are difficult questions that have led to a large amount of literature trying to develop models with Keynesian features in a microfounded equilibrium framework with rational expectations. This line of work that has been dubbed New Keynesianism, emerged as a reaction to the challenge posed by the New Classical approach. Over time, and as New Classical thinking evolved into the RBC approach, the literature coalesced around the so-called DSGE models – with the New Keynesian literature building on these models while adding to them one or many market imperfections.

In any event, this is a very broad expanse of literature that we will not be able to review extensively here. We will thus focus on three steps. First, we will revisit the standard IS-LM model. This model captures the essence (or so most economists think) of the Keynesian approach, by imposing the assumption of price rigidities, which gives rise to the possibility of aggregate demand management. This simple approach, however, begs the question of what could explain those rigidities. Our second step therefore will be to provide a brief discussion of possible microfoundations for them. There may be many reasons for why a nominal price adjustment is incomplete: long-term client relationships, staggered price adjustment, long-term contracts, asymmetric information, menu costs, etc. Not all of

How to cite this book chapter:
Campante, F., Sturzenegger, F. and Velasco, A. 2021. *Advanced Macroeconomics: An Easy Guide.*
    Ch. 15. '(New) Keynesian theories of fluctuations: A primer', pp. 219–242. London: LSE Press.
    DOI: https://doi.org/10.31389/lsepress.ame.o   License: CC-BY-NC 4.0.

these lead to aggregate price rigidities, but we will not get into these details here. We will instead focus on a model where asymmetric information is the reason for incomplete nominal adjustments. This microfounded model highlights, in particular, the role of expectations in determining the reach of aggregate demand management.[2] Last but not least, we will see how these microfoundations combine to give rise to the modern New Keynesian DSGE models, which reinterpret the Keynesian insights in a rather different guise, and constitute the basis of most of macroeconomic policy analysis these days. (We include at the end of the book an appendix that takes you through the first steps needed so that you can run a DSGE model of your own!)

With at least some analytical framework that makes sense of the Keynesian paradigm and its modern interpretation, in later chapters we will discuss the mechanisms and policy levers for demand management, with an emphasis on monetary policy and fiscal policy.

15.1 | Keynesianism 101: IS-LM

We revisit the basic version of the Keynesian model that should be familiar from undergraduate macroeconomics: the IS-LM model.

In 1937, J.R. Hicks[3] provided a theoretical framework that can be used to analyse the *General Theory* Keynes had published the previous year. Keynes's book had been relatively hard to crack, so the profession embraced Hicks's simple representation that later became known as the IS-LM, model and went on to populate intermediate macro textbooks ever since (Hicks won the Nobel Prize in Economics in 1972 for this work). While much maligned in many quarters (particularly because of its static nature and lack of microfoundations), this simple model (and its open-economy cousin, the Mundell-Fleming model) is still very much in the heads of policy makers.

The model is a general equilibrium framework encompassing three markets: goods, money and bonds, though only two are usually described as the third will clear automatically if the other two do (remember Walras Law from micro!). It is standard to represent the model in terms of interest rates and output, and to look at the equilibrium in the money and goods market. The corresponding equations are:

A money market equilibrium locus called the *LM* curve:

$$\frac{M}{P} = L\left(\overset{(-)}{i}, \overset{(+)}{Y}\right),$$
(15.1)

and a goods market equilibrium called the *IS* curve:

$$Y = A\left(\overset{(-)}{r}, \underbrace{\overset{(+)}{Y}}_{<1}, \overset{(+)}{\text{Fiscal}}, \overset{(+)}{RER}\right)$$
(15.2)

where *Fiscal* stands for government expenditures and *RER* for the real exchange rate, or, alternatively,

$$Y = A\left(\overset{(-)}{r}, \overset{(+)}{\text{Fiscal}}, \overset{(+)}{RER}\right).$$
(15.3)

Finally, a relationship between nominal and real interest rates:

$$r = i - \pi^e.$$
(15.4)

15.1.1 | Classical version of the IS-LM model

In the classical version of the model, all prices are flexible, and so are real wages. Thus the labour market clears fixing the amount of labour as in Figure 15.1.

With full employment of labor and capital, output is determined by the supply constraint and becomes an exogenous variable, which we will indicate with a bar:

$$\bar{Y} = F\left(K, \bar{L}\right).\tag{15.5}$$

The *IS*, can then be used to determine r so that savings equals investment ($S = I$, thus the name of the curve). The nominal interest rate is just the real rate plus exogenous inflation expectations (equivalent to the expected growth rate of prices). With Y and i fixed, then the *LM* determines the price level P given a stock of nominal money:

$$P = \frac{\bar{M}}{L\left(i, \bar{Y}\right)},\tag{15.6}$$

which is an alternative way of writing the quantity equation of money:

$$MV = PY.\tag{15.7}$$

In short, the structure of the model is such that the labor market determines the real wage and output. The IS determines the real and nominal interest rate, and the money market determines the price level.

This is typically interpreted as a description of the long run, the situation to which the economy gravitates at any given moment. The idea is that prices eventually adjust so that supply ends up determining output. That is why we ignored aggregate demand fluctuations when discussing long-run growth. There we concentrated on the evolution of the supply capacity. In the classical version of the model (or in the long run) that supply capacity determines what is produced.

Figure 15.1 The classical model

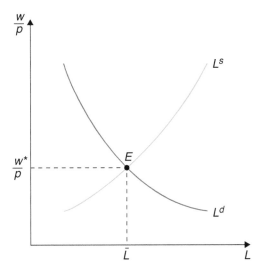

15.1.2 | The Keynesian version of the IS-LM model

However, as Keynes famously quipped, in the long run, we will all be dead. In the short run, the Keynesian assumption is that prices are fixed or rigid, and do not move to equate supply and demand:

$$P = \bar{P},$$ (15.8)

so now the *IS* and *LM* curves jointly determine Y and i as in Figure 15.2.

Notice that Y is determined without referring to the labour market, so the level of labour demand may generate involuntary unemployment.

It is typical in this model to think of the effects of monetary and fiscal policy by shifting the IS and LM curves, and you have seen many such examples in your intermediate macro courses. (If you don't quite remember it, you may want to get a quick refresher from any undergraduate macro textbook you prefer.) We will later show how we can think more carefully about these policies, in a dynamic, microfounded context.

15.1.3 | An interpretation: The Fed

Is the model useful? Yes, because policy makers use it. For example, when the Fed talks about expanding or contracting the economy it clearly has a Keynesian framework in mind. It is true that the Fed does not typically operate on the money stock, but one way of thinking about how the Fed behaves is to think of it as determining the interest rate and then adjusting the money supply to the chosen rate (money becomes somewhat endogenous to the interest rate). In our model, i becomes exogenous and M endogenous as in Figure 15.3:

$$\frac{M}{\bar{P}} = L\left(\bar{i}, Y\right)$$ (15.9)

$$Y = A\left(\bar{i} - \pi^e, \text{Fiscal}, ...\right).$$ (15.10)

Figure 15.2 The IS-LM model

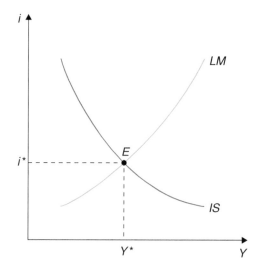

Figure 15.3 The IS-LM model with an exogenous interest rate

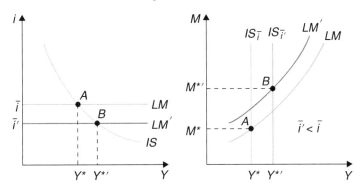

We can represent this using the same Y, i space, but the LM curve is now horizontal as the Fed sets the (nominal) interest rate. Alternatively, we can think about it in the Y, M space, since M is the new endogenous variable. Here we would have the same old LM curve, but now the IS curve becomes vertical in the Y, M space. Both represent the same idea: if the Fed wants to expand output, it reduces the interest rate, and this requires an expansion in the quantity of money.

As a side note, you may have heard of the possibility of a liquidity trap, or alternatively, that monetary policy may hit the zero interest lower bound. What does this mean? We can think about it as a situation in which interest rates are so low that the demand for money is infinitely elastic to the interest rate. In other words, because nominal interest rates cannot be negative (after all, the nominal return on cash is set at zero), when they reach a very low point an increase in the supply of money will be hoarded as cash, as opposed to leading to a greater demand for goods and services. In that case, the IS-LM framework tells us that (conventional) monetary policy is ineffective. Simply put, interest rates cannot be pushed below zero!

This opens up a series of policy debates. There are two big questions that are associated with this: 1) Is monetary policy really ineffective in such a point? It is true that interest rate policy has lost its effectiveness by hitting the zero boundary, but that doesn't necessarily mean that the demand for money is infinitely elastic. The Fed can still pump money into the economy (what came to be known as quantitative easing) by purchasing government (and increasingly private) bonds, and this might still have an effect (maybe through expectations). 2) In this scenario, can fiscal policy be effective? These are debates we'll come back to in full force in our discussions of fiscal and monetary policy.

15.1.4 | From IS-LM to AS-AD

Another way to understand the assumption on price rigidity in generating a role for aggregate demand management is to go from the IS-LM representation to one in which P is one of the endogenous variables. The LM curve implies that an increase in prices leads to a decrease in the supply of real money balances, which shifts LM to the left. Since IS is not affected, that means that a higher P leads to a lower level of output Y. This is the aggregate demand (AD) curve in Figure 15.4.

An increase in aggregate demand (through monetary or fiscal policy) will shift the AD curve to the right. The effect that this will have on equilibrium output will depend on the effect of this on prices, which in turn depends on the aggregate supply (AS) of goods and services. The classical case is one in

Figure 15.4 AS-AD model

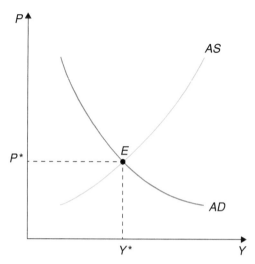

which this supply is independent of the price level – a vertical AS curve. This is the case where prices are fully flexible. The Keynesian case we considered, in contrast, is one in which AS is horizontal (P is fixed), and hence the shift in AD corresponds fully to an increase in output. This is an economy that is not supply constrained. In the intermediate case, where prices adjust but not completely, AS is positively sloped, and shifts in aggregate demand will have at least a partial effect on output.

The positively-sloped AS curve is the mirror image of the *Phillips curve* – the empirical observation of a tradeoff between output/unemployment and prices/inflation. We assume you are familiar with the concept from your intermediate macro courses, and we will get back to that when we discuss the modern New Keynesian approach.

15.2 | Microfoundations of incomplete nominal adjustment

We go over a possible explanation for the incomplete adjustment of prices or, more broadly, for why the AS curve may be upward-sloping. We study the Lucas model of imperfect information, which illustrates how we can solve models with rational expectations.

We have now reestablished the idea that, if prices do not adjust automatically, aggregate demand management can affect output and employment. The big question is, what lies behind their failure to adjust? Or, to put it in terms of the AS-AD framework, we need to understand why the AS curve is positively sloped, and not vertical. Old Keynesian arguments were built on things such as backward-looking (adaptive) expectations, money illusion, and the like. This in turn rubbed more classical-minded economists the wrong way. How can rational individuals behave in such a way? Their discomfort gained traction when the Phillips curve tradeoff seemed to break down empirically in the late 1960s and early 1970s. The model is also useful from a methodological point of view: it shows how a rational expectations model is solved. In other words, it shows how we use the model to compute the expectations that are an essential piece of the model itself. Let's see!

15.2.1 | The Lucas island model

The challenge to Keynesian orthodoxy, and hence the initial push from which modern Keynesian theories were built, took the shape of the pioneering model by Lucas (1973) – part of his Nobel-winning contribution. He derived a positively-sloped AS curve in a model founded at the individual level, and where individuals had rational expectations. This model also more explicit the role of expectations in constraining aggregate demand policy. The key idea was that of imperfect information: individuals can observe quite accurately the prices of the goods they produce or consume most often, but they cannot really observe the aggregate price level. This means that, when confronted with a higher demand for the good they produce, they are not quite sure whether that reflects an increase in its relative price – a case in which they should respond by increasing their output – or simply a general increase in prices – a case in which they should not respond with quantities, but just adjust prices. We will see that rational expectations implies that individuals should split the difference and attribute at least part of the increase to relative prices. (How much so will depend on how often general price increases occur.) This yields the celebrated *Lucas supply curve*, a positively-sloped supply curve in which output increases when the price increases *in excess of its expected level*.

The model is one with many agents (Lucas's original specification places each person on a different island, which is why the model is often referred to as the Lucas island model). Each agent is a consumer-producer that every period sees a certain level of demand. The basic question is to figure out if an increase in demand is an increase in real demand, which requires an increase in production levels, or if it is simply an increase in nominal demand, to which the optimal response is just an increase in prices. The tension between these two alternatives is what will give power to the model. In order to solve the model we will start with a specification with perfect information and, once this benchmark case is solved, we will move to the case of asymmetric information, which is where all the interesting action is.

15.2.2 | The model with perfect information

The representative producer of good i has production function

$$Q_i = L_i, \tag{15.11}$$

so that her feasible consumption is

$$c_i = \frac{P_i Q_i}{P}. \tag{15.12}$$

Utility depends (positively) on consumption and (negatively) on labour effort. Let's assume the specification

$$u_i = c_i - \frac{1}{\gamma} L_i^\gamma \qquad \gamma > 1. \tag{15.13}$$

If P is known (perfect information), the problem is easy; the agent has to maximize her utility (15.13) with respect to her supply of the good (which is, at the same time, her supply of labour). Replacing (15.11) and (15.12) in (15.13) gives

$$u_i = \frac{P_i L_i}{P} - \frac{1}{\gamma} L_i^\gamma. \tag{15.14}$$

The first order condition for L is

$$\frac{P_i}{P} - L_i^{\gamma-1} = 0, \tag{15.15}$$

which can be written as a labour supply curve

$$L_i = \left(\frac{P_i}{P}\right)^{\frac{1}{\gamma-1}}, \tag{15.16}$$

or, if expressed in logs (denoted in lower case letters), as

$$l_i = \left(\frac{1}{\gamma-1}\right)(p_i - p). \tag{15.17}$$

As expected, supply (production) increases with the relative price of the good.

Next, we need to think about demand for every good i, and about aggregate demand. The former takes a very simple form. It can be derived from basic utility but no need to do so here as the form is very intuitive. Demand depends on income, relative prices, and a good-specific taste shock – in log format it can be written as

$$q_i = y + z_i - \eta(p_i - p) \qquad \eta > 0, \tag{15.18}$$

where y is average income and p is the average price level. The taste shock z_i is assumed to affect relative tastes, hence it averages to zero across all goods. It is also assumed to be normally distributed, for reasons that will soon be clear, with variance v_z.

How about aggregate demand? We will assume that there is an aggregate demand shifter, a policy variable we can control, which in this case will be m. It can be anything that shifts the AD curve within the AS-AD framework developed above, but to fix ideas we can think about monetary policy. To introduce, it consider a money demand function in log form:

$$y = m - p. \tag{15.19}$$

We assume that m is also normally distributed, with mean $E(m)$ and variance v_m.

Equilibrium

To find the equilibrium we make demand equal to supply for each good. This is a model with market clearing and where all variables, particularly p, are known.

$$\left(\frac{1}{\gamma-1}\right)(p_i - p) = y + z_i - \eta(p_i - p), \tag{15.20}$$

from which we obtain the individual price

$$p_i = \frac{(\gamma-1)}{1+\eta\gamma-\eta}(y + z_i) + p, \tag{15.21}$$

and from which we can obtain the average price. Averaging (15.21) we get

$$p = \frac{(\gamma-1)}{(1+\eta\gamma-\eta)}y + p \tag{15.22}$$

which implies

$$y = 0.$$

You may find it strange, but it is not: remember that output is defined in logs. Replacing the solution for output in (15.19) we get that

$$p = m, \tag{15.23}$$

i.e. that prices respond fully to monetary shocks. In other words, the world with perfect information is a typical classical version with flexible prices and where aggregate demand management has no effect on real variables and full impact on nominal variables.

15.2.3 | Lucas' supply curve

When there is imperfect information, each producer observes the price of her own good, p_i, but cannot observe perfectly what happens to other prices. She will have to make her best guess as to whether a change in her price represents an increase in relative prices, or just a general increase in the price level. In other words, labour supply will have to be determined on the basis of expectations. Because we assume rational expectations, these will be determined by the mathematical expectation that is consistent with the model – in other words, individuals know the model and form their expectations rationally based on this knowledge.

Denote relative prices as $r_i = (p_i - p)$, then the analog to (15.17) is now[4]

$$l_i = \left(\frac{1}{\gamma - 1}\right) E\left(r_i | p_i\right). \tag{15.24}$$

It so happens that if the distribution of the shocks z_i and m is jointly normal, then so will be r_i, p_i, and p. Since r_i and p_i are jointly normally distributed, a result from statistics tells us that the conditional expectation is a linear function

$$E\left(r_i | p_i\right) = \alpha + \beta p_i. \tag{15.25}$$

More specifically, in this case, we have what is called a signal extraction problem, in which one variable of interest (r_i) is observed with noise. What you observe (p_i) is the sum of the signal you're interested in (r_i), plus noise you don't really care about (p). It turns out that, with the assumption of normality, the solution to this problem is

$$E\left(r_i | p_i\right) = \frac{v_r}{v_r + v_p}\left(p_i - E\left(p\right)\right), \tag{15.26}$$

where v_r and v_p are the variances of relative price and general price level, respectively. (They are a complicated function of v_z and v_m.) This expression is very intuitive; if most of the variance comes from the signal, your best guess is that a change in p_i indicates a change in relative prices. Substituting in (15.24) yields

$$l_i = \left(\frac{1}{\gamma - 1}\right) \frac{v_r}{v_r + v_p}\left(p_i - E\left(p\right)\right). \tag{15.27}$$

Aggregating over all the individual supply curves, and defining

$$b = \frac{1}{\gamma - 1}\frac{v_r}{v_r + v_p} \tag{15.28}$$

we have that

$$y = b\left(p - E\left(p\right)\right), \tag{15.29}$$

which is actually a Phillips curve, as you know from basic macro courses.

This became known as the *Lucas supply curve*. Note that this is a positively-sloped supply curve, in which output increases when the price increases *in excess of its expected level*. Why is it so? Because when facing such an increase, imperfectly informed producers rationally attribute some of that to an increase in relative prices. It also says that labour and output respond more to price changes if the relative relevance of nominal shocks is smaller. Why is this? Because the smaller the incidence of nominal shocks, the more certain is the producer that any price shock she faces is a change in real demand.

Solving the model

We know from the AS-AD framework that, with a positively-sloped supply curve, aggregate demand shocks affect equilibrium output. How do we see that in the context of this model? Plugging (15.29) into the aggregate demand equation (15.19) yields

$$y = b\left(p - E\left(p\right)\right) = m - p, \tag{15.30}$$

that can be used to solve for the aggregate price level and income:

$$p = \frac{m}{1+b} + \frac{b}{1+b}E\left(p\right), \tag{15.31}$$

$$y = \frac{bm}{1+b} - \frac{b}{1+b}E\left(p\right). \tag{15.32}$$

Now, rational expectations means that individuals will figure this out in setting their own expectations. In other words, we can take the expectations of (15.31) to obtain:[5]

$$E\left(p\right) = \frac{1}{1+b}E\left(m\right) + \frac{b}{1+b}E\left(p\right), \tag{15.33}$$

which implies, in turn, that

$$E\left(p\right) = E\left(m\right). \tag{15.34}$$

Using this and the fact that $m = E\left(m\right) + m - E\left(m\right)$ we have that

$$p = E\left(m\right) + \frac{1}{1+b}\left(m - E\left(m\right)\right), \tag{15.35}$$

$$y = \frac{b}{1+b}\left(m - E\left(m\right)\right). \tag{15.36}$$

In short, the model predicts that changes in aggregate demand (e.g. monetary policy) will have an effect on output, but only to the extent that they are unexpected. This is a very powerful conclusion in the sense that systematic policy will eventually lose its effects; people will figure it out, and come to expect it. When they do, they'll change their behaviour accordingly, and you won't be able to exploit it. This is at the heart of the famous *Lucas critique*: as the policy maker acts, the aggregate supply curve will change as a result of that, and you can't think of them as stable relationships independent of policy.

As we can see, the imperfect information approach highlights the role of expectations in determining the effectiveness of macro policy. This insight is very general, and lies behind a lot of modern policy making: inflation targeting as a way of coordinating expectations, the problem of time inconsistency, etc. In fact, we will soon see that this insight is very much underscored by the modern New Keynesian approach.

15.3 | Imperfect competition and nominal and real rigidities

We show that, with imperfect competition and nominal rigidities, there is a role for aggregate demand policy. Imperfect competition means that firms can set prices, and that output can deviate from the social optimum. Nominal rigidities mean that prices fail to adjust automatically. The two combined mean that output can be increased (in the short run), and that doing so can be desirable. We discuss how real rigidities amplify the impact of nominal rigidities.

The Lucas model was seen at the time as a major strike against Keynesian policy thinking. After all, while it illustrates how we can obtain a positively-sloped AS curve from a fully microfounded approach with rational agents, it also fails to provide a justification for systematic macro policy. The New Keynesian tradition emerged essentially as an attempt to reconcile rational expectations and the possibility and desirability of systematic policy.

Consider the desirability: in the Lucas model (or the RBC approach that essentially came out of that tradition), business cycles are the result of optimal responses by individuals to disturbances that occur in this economy, and aggregate demand policy can only introduce noise. If the market equilibrium is socially optimal, then any fluctuation due to aggregate demand shocks is a departure from the optimum, and thus undesirable. The New Keynesian view departs from that by casting *imperfect competition* in a central role. The key to justifying policy intervention is to consider the possibility that the market-determined level of output is suboptimal, and imperfect competition yields exactly that. In addition, this is consistent with the general impression that recessions are bad and booms are good.

Besides the issue of desirability, we have argued that the Lucas model also implies that systematic policy is powerless; rational agents with rational expectations figure it out, and start adjusting prices accordingly. The second essential foundation of New Keynesian thinking is thus the existence and importance of barriers to price adjustment. Note that this is also related to imperfect competition since price adjustment can only matter if firms are price-setters, which requires some monopoly power. It is not enough to have imperfect competition to have these rigidities, however, as monopolists will also want to adjust prices rather than output in response to nominal shocks.

We thus have to understand how barriers, that are most likely rather small at the micro level, and which have become known in the literature by the catch-all term *menu costs*, can still have large macroeconomic effects. Do we really think that in the real world the costs of adjusting prices are large enough to lead to sizeable consequences in output?

It turns out that the key lies once again with imperfect competition. Consider the effects of a decrease in aggregate demand on the behaviour of monopolist firms, illustrated in Figure 15.5. Taking the behaviour of all other firms as given, this will make any given firm want to set a lower price. If there were no costs of adjustment, the firm would go from point A in Figure 15.5 to point C. If the firm doesn't adjust at all, it would go to point B. It follows that its gain from adjusting would be the shaded triangle. If the menu cost is greater than that, the firm would choose not to adjust.

But what is the social cost of not adjusting? It is the difference in consumer surplus corresponding to a decrease in quantity from point C to point B. This is given by the area between the demand curve D' and the marginal cost curve, between B and C. This is *much* bigger than the shaded triangle! In other words, the social loss is much bigger than the firm's loss from not adjusting, and it follows that small menu costs can have large social effects.[6]

Another type of rigidity emphasised by New Keynesians are real rigidities (as distinct from the nominal kind). These correspond to a low sensitivity of the desired price to aggregate output. If the

Figure 15.5   Welfare effects of imperfect competition

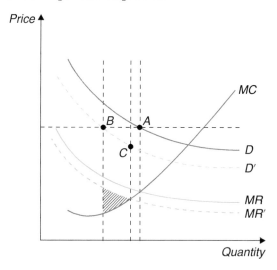

desired price doesn't change much with a change in output, the incentive to adjust prices will be lower. (Think about the slope of the marginal cost curve in Figure 15.5). If there are no costs of adjustment (i.e. nominal rigidities), that doesn't matter, of course; but the real rigidities amplify the effect of the nominal ones. These real rigidities could come from many sources, such as the labour market. If labour supply is relatively inelastic (think about low levels of labour mobility, for instance), we would have greater real rigidities. (This actually sets the stage for us to consider our next topic in the study of cyclical fluctuations: labour markets and unemployment.)

In sum, a combination of imperfect competition, nominal rigidities (menu costs), and real rigidities implies that aggregate demand policy is both desirable and feasible. We will now turn to a very brief discussion of how this view of the world has been embedded into full-fledged dynamic stochastic general equilibrium (DSGE) models such as those introduced by the RBC tradition to give birth to the modern New Keynesian view of fluctuations.[7]

15.4 | New Keynesian DSGE models

We express the modern New Keynesian DSGE (NK DSGE) model in its canonical (microfounded) version, combining the New Keynesian IS curve, the New Keynesian Phillips curve, and a policy rule. We show the continuous-time and discrete-time versions of the model.

New Keynesian DSGE models embody the methodological consensus underpinning modern macroeconomics. It has become impossible to work in any self-respecting Central Bank, for instance, without coming across a New Keynesian DSGE model. But modern, state-of-the-art DSGE models are very complicated. If you thought that RBC models were already intricate, consider the celebrated NK DSGE model by Smets and Wouters (2003), originally developed as an empirical model of the Euro area. It contains, in addition to productivity shocks, shocks to adjustment costs, the equity premium, wage markup, goods markup, labor supply, preferences, and the list goes on and on. Another difficulty is that there is little consensus as to which specific model is best to fit real-world fluctuations. So what we do here is consider a few of the key ingredients in NK DSGE models, and explain how they combine into what is often called the canonical New Keynesian model.

15.4.1 | The canonical New Keynesian model

We first develop the model in continuous time, which is simpler and allows for the use of phase diagrams, so that we can readily put the model to work and develop some intuition about its operation and dynamics. Later, we turn to discrete time, and write down the version of the model that is most commonly used in practical and policy applications.

The demand side of the canonical New Keynesian model is very simple. We start from our model of consumer optimisation, which by now we have seen many times. You will recall the Euler equation of the representative consumer.

$$\dot{C}_t = \sigma \left(r_t - \rho \right) C_t, \tag{15.37}$$

where C_t is consumption, $\sigma > 0$ is the elasticity of intertemporal substitution in consumption, and ρ is the rate of time discounting. In a closed economy with no investment, all output Y_t is consumed. Therefore,

$$C_t = Y_t, \tag{15.38}$$

and

$$\dot{Y}_t = \sigma \left(i_t - \pi_t - \rho \right) Y_t, \tag{15.39}$$

where we have used the definition $r_t \equiv i_t - \pi_t$, and i_t is the nominal interest rate, taken to be exogenous and constant for the time being. If we define the output gap as,

$$X_t \equiv \frac{Y_t}{\bar{Y}_t}, \tag{15.40}$$

where $\bar{Y}_t$ is the natural or long run level of output, then the output gap evolves according to

$$\frac{\dot{X}_t}{X_t} = \frac{\dot{Y}_t}{Y_t} - g, \tag{15.41}$$

where g is the percentage growth rate of the natural level of output, assumed constant for now. Finally, letting small-case letters denote logarithms, using the Euler equation (15.39), we have

$$\dot{x}_t = \sigma \left(i_t - \pi_t - r^n \right), \tag{15.42}$$

where $r^n \equiv \rho + \sigma^{-1} g$ is the natural or Wicksellian interest rate, which depends on both preferences and productivity growth. It is the interest rate that would prevail in the absence of distortions, and corresponds to a situation in which output is equal to potential.

This last equation, which we can think of as a dynamic New Keynesian IS equation (or NKIS) summarises the demand side of the model. The NKIS equation says that output is rising when the real interest rate is *above* its long-run (or natural) level. Contrast this with the conventional IS equation, which says that the *level* of output (as opposed to the *rate of change* of output in the equation above) is above its long-run level when the real interest is *below* its long-run (or neutral) level.

The NKIS differs from traditional IS in other important ways. First, it is derived from micro-founded, optimising household behaviour. Second, the relationship between interest rates and output emerges from the behaviour of consumption, rather than investment, as was the case in the old IS. Intuitively, high interest rates are linked to low output now because people decide that it is better to postpone consumption, thereby reducing aggregate demand.

Turn now to the supply side of the model. We need a description of how prices are set in order to capture the presence of nominal rigidities. There are many different models for that, which are typically classified as time-dependent or state-dependent. State-dependent models are those in which adjustment is triggered by the state of the economy. Typically, firms decide to adjust (and pay the menu cost) if their current prices are too far from their optimal desired level. Time-dependent models, in contrast, are such that firms get to adjust prices with the passage of time, say, because there are long-term contracts. This seems slightly less compelling as a way of understanding the underpinnings of price adjustment, but it has the major advantage of being easier to handle. We will thus focus on time-dependent models, which are more widely used.

There are several time-dependent models, but the most popular is the so-called Calvo model. Calvo (1983) assumes that the economy is populated by a continuum of monopolistically-competitive firms. Each of them is a point in the [0, 1] interval, thus making their 'total' equal to one. The key innovation comes from the price-setting technology: each firm sets its output price in terms of domestic currency and can change it only when it receives a price-change signal. The probability of receiving such a signal s periods from now is assumed to be independent of the last time the firm got the signal, and given by

$$\alpha e^{-\alpha s}, \quad \alpha > 0. \tag{15.43}$$

If the price-change signal is stochastically independent across firms, we can appeal to the 'law of large numbers' to conclude that a share α of firms will receive the price-change signal per unit of time. By the same principle, of the total number of firms that set their price at time $s < t$, a share

$$e^{-\alpha(t-s)} \tag{15.44}$$

will not have received the signal at time t. Therefore,

$$\alpha e^{-\alpha(t-s)} \tag{15.45}$$

is the share of firms that set their prices at time s and have not yet received a price-change signal at time $t > s$.

Next, let v_t be the (log of the) price set by an individual firm (when it gets the signal), and define the (log of the) price level p_t as the arithmetic average of all the prices v_t still outstanding at time t, weighted by the share of firms with the same v_t:

$$p_t = \alpha \int_{-\infty}^{t} v_s e^{-\alpha(t-s)} ds. \tag{15.46}$$

It follows that the price level is sticky, because it is a combination of pre-existing prices (which, because they are pre-existing, cannot jump suddenly).

How is v_t set? Yun (1996) was the first to solve the full problem of monopolistically-competitive firms that must set prices optimally, understanding that it and all competitors will face stochastic price-setting signals. Getting to that solution is involved, and requires quite a bit of algebra.[8]

Here we just provide a reduced form, and postulate that the optimal price v_t set by an individual firm depends on the contemporaneous price level p_t, the expected future paths of the (log of) expected relative prices, and of the (log of) the output gap:

$$v_t = p_t + \alpha \int_t^\infty \left[(v_s - p_s) + \eta x_s \right] e^{-(\alpha+\rho)(s-t)} ds, \qquad (15.47)$$

where, recall, ρ is the consumer's discount rate and $\eta > 0$ is a sensitivity parameter.[9] So the relative price the firm chooses today depends on a discounted, probability-weighted average of all future relative prices $(v_s - p_s)$ and all output gaps x_s. This is intuitive. For instance, if the output gap is expected to be positive in the future, then it makes sense for the firm to set a higher (relative) price for its good to take advantage of buoyant demand.

Note from this expression that along any path in which the future x_s and v_s are continuous functions of time (which we now assume), v_t is also, and necessarily, a continuous function of time. We can therefore use Leibniz's rule to differentiate the expressions for p_t and v_t with respect to time, obtaining[10]

$$\dot{p}_t = \pi_t = \alpha \left(v_t - p_t \right), \qquad (15.48)$$

and

$$\dot{v}_t - \dot{p}_t = -\alpha \eta x_t + \rho \left(v_t - p_t \right). \qquad (15.49)$$

Combining the two we have

$$\dot{v}_t - \dot{p}_t = -\alpha \eta x_t + \frac{\rho}{\alpha} \pi_t. \qquad (15.50)$$

Differentiating the expression for the inflation rate π_t, again with respect to time, yields

$$\dot{\pi}_t = \alpha \left(\dot{v}_t - \dot{p}_t \right). \qquad (15.51)$$

Finally, combining the last two expressions we arrive at

$$\dot{\pi}_t = \rho \pi_t - \kappa x_t, \qquad (15.52)$$

where $\kappa \equiv \alpha^2 \eta > 0$. This is the canonical New Keynesian Phillips curve. In the traditional Phillips curve, the rate of inflation was an increasing function of the output gap. By contrast, in the Calvo-Yun NKPC the *change* in the rate of inflation is a decreasing function of the output gap! Notice, also that while p_t is a sticky variable, its rate of change π_t is not; it is intuitive that π_t should be able to jump in response to expected changes in relevant variables.

Solving this equation forward we obtain

$$\pi_t = \int_t^\infty \kappa x_s e^{-\rho(s-t)} ds. \qquad (15.53)$$

So the inflation rate today is the present discounted value of all the future expected output gaps. The more "overheated" the economy is expected to be in the future, the higher inflation is today.

To complete the supply side of the model we need to specify why the output gap should by anything other than zero – that is, why firms can and are willing to supply more output than their long-term profit maximizing level. The standard story, adopted, for instance, by Yun (1996), has two components. Output is produced using labour and firms can hire more (elastically supplied) labour in the short-run to enlarge production when desirable. When demand rises (recall the previous section of this chapter), monopolistically-competitive firms facing fixed prices will find it advantageous to supply more output, up to a point.

This NKPC curve and the dynamic NKIS curve, taken together, fully describe this model economy. They are a pair of linear differential equations in two variables, π_t and x_t, with i_t as an exogenous policy variable. In this model there is no conflict between keeping inflation low and stabilising output. If $i = r^n$, then $\pi_t = x_t = 0$ is an equilibrium. Blanchard and Galí (2007) term this the divine coincidence.

The steady state is

$$\bar{\pi} = i - r^n \left(\text{from } \dot{x}_t = 0 \right) \tag{15.54}$$

$$\rho\bar{\pi} = \kappa\bar{x} \left(\text{from } \dot{\pi}_t = 0 \right) \tag{15.55}$$

where overbars denote the steady state. If, in addition, we assume $i = r^n$, then $\bar{\pi} = \bar{x} = 0$. In matrix form, the dynamic system is

$$\begin{bmatrix} \dot{\pi}_t \\ \dot{x}_t \end{bmatrix} = \Omega \begin{bmatrix} \pi_t \\ x_t \end{bmatrix} + \begin{bmatrix} 0 \\ \sigma \left(i - r^n \right) \end{bmatrix} \tag{15.56}$$

where

$$\Omega = \begin{bmatrix} \rho & -\kappa \\ -\sigma & 0 \end{bmatrix}. \tag{15.57}$$

It is straightforward to see that $\text{Det} (\Omega) = -\sigma\kappa < 0$, and $\text{Tr}(\Omega) = \rho > 0$. It follows that one of the eigenvalues of Ω is positive (or has positive real parts) and the other is negative. This means the system exhibits saddle path stability, in other words that for each π_t there is a value of x_t from which the system will converge asymptotically to the steady state. But remember that here both x and π are jump variables! This means that we have a continuum of perfect-foresight convergent equilibria, because we can initially choose both π_t and x_t.

The graphical representation of this result is as follows. When drawn in $\left[\pi_t, x_t\right]$ space, the Phillips curve is positively-sloped, while the IS schedule is horizontal, as you can see in the phase diagram in Figure 15.6. If $x_0 > \bar{x}$, there exists a $\pi_0 > \bar{\pi}$ such that both variables converge to the steady state in a south-westerly trajectory. The converse happens if $x_0 < \bar{x}$. Along a converging path, inflation and output do move together, as in the standard Phillips curve analysis. To see that, focus for instance on the south-west quadrant of the diagram. There, both output and inflation are below their long run levels, so that a depressed economy produces unusually low inflation. As output rises toward its long-run resting point, so does inflation.

But the important point is that there exists an infinity of such converging paths, one for each (arbitrary) initial condition! An exogenous path for the nominal interest, whichever path that may be, is not enough to pin down the rate of inflation (and the output gap) uniquely. What is the intuition for this indeterminacy or nonuniqueness? To see why self-fulfilling recessions may occur, suppose agents believe that output that is low today will gradually rise towards steady state. According to the NKPC, New Keynesian Phillips curve, a path of low output implies a path of low inflation. But with the nominal interest rate exogenously fixed, low expected inflation increases the real rate of interest and lowers consumption and output. The initial belief is thus self-fulfilling.

15.4.2 | A Taylor rule in the canonical New Keynesian model

In Chapter 19 we further discuss interest rate policy and interest rate rules. Here we simply introduce the best-known and most-widely used rule: the Taylor rule, named after Stanford economist John

Figure 15.6 Indeterminacy in the NK model

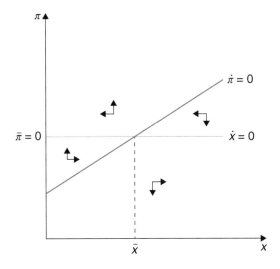

Taylor, who first proposed it as a description of the behaviour of monetary policy in the U.S. In Taylor (1993), the rule takes the form

$$i_t = r_t^n + \phi_\pi \pi_t + \phi_x x_t, \tag{15.58}$$

where ϕ_π and ϕ_x are two coefficients chosen by the monetary authority. The choice of r_t^n requires it be equal to the normal or natural real rate of interest in the steady state. In what follows we will often assume $\phi_\pi > 1$, so that when π_t rises above the (implicit) target of 0, the nominal interest rises more than proportionately, and the real interest goes up in an effort to reduce inflation. Similarly, $\phi_x > 0$, so that when the output gap is positive, i_t rises from its normal level. Using the Taylor rule in the NKIS equation (15.42) yields

$$\dot{x}_t = \sigma \left[\left(r_t^n - r^n \right) + \left(\phi_\pi - 1 \right) \pi_t + \phi_x x_t \right], \tag{15.59}$$

so that the rate of increase of the output gap is increasing in its own level and also increasing in inflation (because $\phi_\pi - 1 > 0$). The resulting dynamic system can be written as

$$\begin{bmatrix} \dot{\pi} \\ \dot{x}_t \end{bmatrix} = \Omega \begin{bmatrix} \pi_t \\ x_t \end{bmatrix} + \begin{bmatrix} 0 \\ \sigma \left(r_t^n - r^n \right) \end{bmatrix} \tag{15.60}$$

where

$$\Omega = \begin{bmatrix} \rho & -\kappa \\ \sigma \left(\phi_\pi - 1 \right) & \sigma \phi_x \end{bmatrix}. \tag{15.61}$$

Now $\mathrm{Det}(\Omega) = \rho \sigma \phi_x + \sigma \left(\phi_\pi - 1 \right) \kappa > 0$, and $\mathrm{Tr}(\Omega) = \rho + \sigma \phi_x > 0$. It follows that $\phi_\pi > 1$ is sufficient to ensure that both eigenvalues of Ω are positive (or have positive real parts). Because both π_t and x_t are jump variables, the steady state is now unique. After any permanent unanticipated shock, the system just jumps to the steady state and remains there!

As you can see in the phase diagram in Figure 15.7, the $\dot{x}_t = 0$ schedule (the NKIS) now slopes down. All four sets of arrows point away from the steady state point – which is exactly what you need to guarantee uniqueness of equilibrium in the case of a system of two jumpy variables!

Figure 15.7   Active interest rule in the NK model

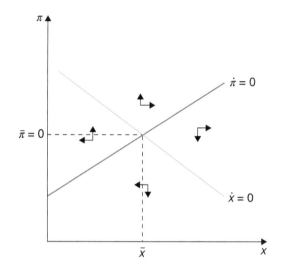

Go back to the expression Det $(\Omega) = \rho\phi_x + \sigma\left(\phi_\pi - 1\right)\kappa$, which reveals that if $\phi_\pi < 1$ and ϕ_x is not too large, then Det $(\Omega) < 0$. Since, in addition, Tr$(\Omega) > 0$, we would have a case of one positive and one negative eigenvalue, so that, again, multiplicity of equilibria (in fact, infinity of equilibria) would occur.

So there is an important policy lesson in all of this. In the canonical New Keynesian model, interest rate policy has to be sufficiently activist (aggressively anti-inflation, one might say), in order to guarantee uniqueness of equilibrium – in particular, to ensure that the rate of inflation and the output gap are pinned down. In the literature, policy rules where $\phi_\pi > 1$ are usually called active policy rules, and those where $\phi_\pi < 1$ are referred to as passive policy rules.

In this very simple model, which boils down to a system of linear differential equations, the uniqueness result is simple to derive and easy to understand. In more complex versions of the Keynesian model, –for instance, in non-linear models which need to be linearised around the steady state – or in circumstances in which the zero lower bound on the nominal interest rate binds, dynamics can be considerably more complicated, and the condition $\phi_\pi > 1$ in the Taylor rule need not be sufficient to guarantee uniqueness of equilibrium. For a more detailed treatment of these issues, see Benhabib et al. (2001a), Benhabib et al. (2001b), Benhabib et al. (2002), Woodford (2011), and Galí (2015).

Before ending this section, let us put this model to work by analysing a shock. Let's imagine a monetary tightening implemented through a transitory exogenous increase in the interest rate (think of the interest moving to $r_t^n + z$, with z the policy shifter), or, alternatively, imagine that at time 0, the natural rate of interest suddenly goes down from r^n to $\underline{r}^n$, where $0 < \underline{r}^n < r^n$, because the trend rate of growth of output, g, has temporarily dropped. After $T > 0$, either z goes back to zero, or the natural rate of interest goes back to r^n and remains there forever. How will inflation and output behave on impact, and in the time interval between times 0 and T? The phase diagram in Figure 15.8 below shows the answer to these questions in a simple and intuitive manner.

Notice that either of these changes imply a leftward shift of the $\dot{x}$ equation. So, during the transition the dynamics are driven by the original $\dot{\pi}$ and new $\dot{x}$ equations which intersect at point C.

Figure 15.8 A reduction in the natural rate

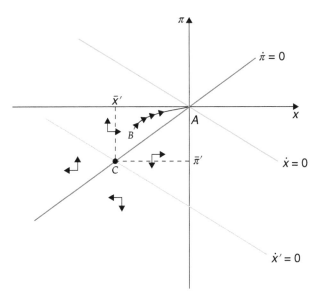

The system must return to A exactly at time T. On impact, inflation and the output jump to a point, such as B, which is pinned down by the requirement that between 0 and T dynamics be those of the system with steady state at point C. That is, during the temporary shock the economy must travel to the north-east, with inflation rising and the output gap narrowing, in anticipation of the positive reversion of the shock at T. Between 0 and T the negative shock, intuitively enough, causes output and inflation to be below their initial (and final, after T) steady-state levels. If initially $i^n = r^n$, so $\bar{\pi} = 0$ and $\bar{x} = 0$, as drawn below, then during the duration of the shock the economy experiences deflation and a recession (a negative output gap).[11]

What happens to the nominal interest rate? Between 0 and T, both inflation and the output gap are below their target levels of zero. So, the monetary authority relaxes the policy stance in response to both the lower inflation and the negative output gap. But that relaxation is not enough to keep the economy from going into recession and deflation. We return to this issue in Chapter 22.

15.4.3 | Back to discrete time

The canonical New Keynesian model has a natural counterpart in discrete time, which is more broadly used for practical applications. In discrete time the Phillips curve becomes (see Galí (2015) for the detailed derivation)

$$\pi_t = \beta E_t \pi_{t+1} + \kappa x_t, \tag{15.62}$$

where $0 < \beta = \frac{1}{1+\rho} < 1$ is the discount factor, E_t is the expectations operator (with expectations computed as of time t), and the output gap is again in logs. To derive the IS curve, again start from the Euler equation, which in logs can be written as

$$y_t = E_t y_{t+1} - \sigma \log\left(1 + r_t\right) + \sigma \log(1 + \rho), \tag{15.63}$$

where we have already used $c_t = y_t$. If we recall the fact that for small r_t and ρ, $\log\left(1 + r_t\right) \approx r_t$, and $\log(1 + \rho) \approx \rho$, equation (15.63) becomes

$$y_t = E_t y_{t+1} - \sigma\left(r_t - \rho\right). \tag{15.64}$$

Finally, subtracting $\bar{y}$ from both sides yields

$$x_t = E_t x_{t+1} - \sigma\left(i_t - E_t \pi_{t+1} - \rho\right), \tag{15.65}$$

where we have used the definition $r_t = i_t - E_t \pi_{t+1}$ and the fact that $x_t = y_t - \bar{y}$. If the natural rate of output is not constant, so that

$$\bar{y}_{t+1} = \bar{y}_t + \Delta, \tag{15.66}$$

(15.65) becomes

$$x_t = E_t x_{t+1} + \Delta - \sigma\left(i_t - E_t \pi_{t+1} - \rho\right) \tag{15.67}$$

or

$$x_t = E_t x_{t+1} - \sigma\left(i_t - E_t \pi_{t+1} - r^n\right), \tag{15.68}$$

where

$$r^n = \rho + \frac{\Delta}{\sigma}, \tag{15.69}$$

and again the variable r^n is the natural, or Wicksellian, interest rate, which can move around as a result of preference shocks (changes in ρ) or productivity growth (Δ). To close the model, we can again appeal to an interest rule of the form

$$i_t = i^n + \phi_\pi E_t \pi_{t+1} + \phi_x x_t. \tag{15.70}$$

As before, policy makers in charge of interest rate setting respond to deviations in expected inflation from the target (here equal to zero), and to deviations of output from the full employment or natural rate of output. Taylor argued that this rule (specifically, with $\phi_\pi = 1.5, \phi_x = 0.5$), and an inflation target of 2% is a good description of how monetary policy actually works in many countries -and, in particular, of how the Fed has behaved in modern times (since the mid-1980s).

There is an active research program in trying to compute optimal Taylor rules and also to estimate them from real-life data. In practice, no central bank has formally committed exactly to such a rule, but the analysis of monetary policy has converged onto some variant of a Taylor rule -and on interest rate rules more broadly — as the best way to describe how central banks operate.

Substituting the interest rate rule into the NKIS equation (15.70) (in the simple case of constant $\bar{y}$) yields

$$x_t = E_t x_{t+1} - \sigma\left[\left(\phi_\pi - 1\right) E_t \pi_{t+1} + \phi_x x_t + \left(i^n - r^n\right)\right]. \tag{15.71}$$

This equation plus the NKPC constitute a system of two difference equations in two unknowns. As in the case of continuous time, it can be shown that an interest rule that keeps i_t constant does not guarantee uniqueness of equilibrium. But, it again turns out that if $\phi_\pi > 1$, a Taylor-type rule does ensure that both eigenvalues of the characteristic matrix of the 2×2 system are larger than one. Since both π_t and x_t are jumpy variables, that guarantees a unique outcome; the system simply jumps to the steady state and stays there.

To analyse formally the dynamic properties of this system, rewrite the NKPC (15.62) as

$$E_t \pi_{t+1} = \beta^{-1} \pi_t - \beta^{-1} \kappa x_t. \tag{15.72}$$

Next, use this (15.71) to yield

$$E_t x_{t+1} = \sigma \left(\phi_\pi - 1\right) \beta^{-1} \pi_t + x_t + \sigma \left[- \left(\phi_\pi - 1\right) \beta^{-1} \kappa + \phi_x\right] x_t + \sigma \left(i^n - r^n\right). \tag{15.73}$$

(15.72) and (15.73) together constitute the canonical New Keynesian model in discrete time. In matrix form, the dynamic system is

$$\begin{bmatrix} E_t \pi_{t+1} \\ E_t x_{t+1} \end{bmatrix} = \Omega \begin{bmatrix} \pi_t \\ x_t \end{bmatrix} + \begin{bmatrix} 0 \\ \sigma \left(i^n - r^n\right) \end{bmatrix} \tag{15.74}$$

where

$$\Omega = \begin{bmatrix} \beta^{-1} & -\beta^{-1}\kappa \\ \sigma\beta^{-1} \left(\phi_\pi - 1\right) & 1 + \sigma \left[- \left(\phi_\pi - 1\right) \beta^{-1}\kappa + \phi_x\right] \end{bmatrix}. \tag{15.75}$$

Now

$$\text{Det}(\Omega) = \beta^{-1} \left(1 + \sigma\phi_x\right) = \lambda_1 \lambda_2 > 1 \tag{15.76}$$

and

$$\text{Tr}(\Omega) = \beta^{-1} + 1 + \sigma \left[\phi_x - \left(\phi_\pi - 1\right) \beta^{-1}\kappa\right] = \lambda_1 + \lambda_2, \tag{15.77}$$

where λ_1 and λ_1 are the eigenvalues of Ω. For both λ_1 and λ_2 to be larger than one, a necessary and sufficient condition is that

$$\text{Det}(\Omega) + 1 > \text{Tr}(\Omega) \tag{15.78}$$

which, using the expressions for the determinant and the trace, is equivalent to

$$\left(\phi_\pi - 1\right) x + (1 - \beta)\phi_x > 0. \tag{15.79}$$

This condition clearly obtains if $\phi_\pi > 1$. So, the policy implication is the same in both the continuous time and the discrete time of the model: an activist policy rule is required, in which the interest rate over-reacts to changes in the (expected) rate of inflation, in order to ensure uniqueness of equilibrium.

For a classic application of this model to monetary policy issues, see Clarida et al. (1999). In later chapters of this book we use the model to study a number of issues, some of which require the S to the DSGE acronym: shocks! As we saw in our discussion of RBC models, the business cycle properties we obtain from the model will depend on the properties we assume for those shocks.

The kind of DSGE model that is used in practice will add many bells and whistles to the canonical version, in the description of the behaviour of firms, households, and policy-makers. In doing so, it will open the door to a lot of different shocks as well. It will then try to either calibrate the model parameters, or estimate them using Bayesian techniques, and use the model to evaluate policy interventions. You will find in Appendix C a basic illustration of this kind of model, so you can do it for yourself!

These models will nevertheless keep the essential features of a firm grounding on household and firm optimisation, which is a way to address the Lucas Critique, and also of the consequent importance of expectations. We discuss the issues in greater detail in Chapter 17 and thereafter.

15.5 | What have we learned?

We have gone over the basics of the Keynesian view of the business cycle, from its old IS-LM version to the modern canonical New Keynesian DSGE model. We saw the key role of imperfect price adjustment, leading to an upward-sloping aggregate supply curve, under which aggregate demand shocks have real consequences. We showed how imperfect competition and nominal (and real) rigidities are crucial for that. We saw how the Euler equation of consumption gives rise to the modern New Keynesian IS curve, while the Calvo model of price setting gives rise to the New Keynesian Phillips curve. Finally, we saw how we need to specify a policy rule (such as the Taylor rule) to close the model.

There is no consensus among macroeconomists as to whether the Keynesian or classical (RBC) view is correct. This is not surprising since they essentially involve very different world views in terms of the functioning of markets. Are market failures (at least relatively) pervasive, or can we safely leave them aside in our analysis? This is hardly the type of question that can be easily settled by the type of evidence we deal with in the social sciences.

Having said that, it's important to stress the methodological convergence that has been achieved in macroeconomics, and that has hopefully been conveyed by our discussion in the last two chapters. Nowadays, essentially all of macro deals with microfounded models with rational agents, the difference being in the assumptions about the shocks and rigidities that are present (or absent) and driving the fluctuations. By providing a unified framework that allows policy makers to cater the model to what they believe are the constraints they face, means that the controversy about the fundamental discrepancies can be dealt, in a more flexible way within a unified framework. Imagine the issue of price rigidity, which is summarised by Calvo's α coefficient of price adjustment. If you believe in no price rigidities, α has a specific value, if you think there are rigidities you just change the value. And nobody is going to fight for the value of α, are they? Worst case scenario, you just run it with both parameters and look at the output. No wonder then that the DSGE models have become a workhorse, for example, in Central Banking.

15.6 | What next?

Any number of macro textbooks cover the basics of the Keynesian model, in its IS-LM version. The textbook by Romer (2018) covers the topics at the graduate level, and is a great introduction to the fundamentals behind the New Keynesian view. For the canonical, modern New Keynesian approach, the book by Galí (2015) is the key reference.

Notes

[1] This is what's behind Keynes oft-quoted (and misquoted) statement (from Ch. 16 of the *General Theory*) that "'To dig holes in the ground,' paid for out of savings, will increase, not only employment, but the real national dividend of useful goods and services." (Note, however that he immediately goes on to say that 'it is not reasonable, however, that a sensible community should be content to remain dependent on such fortuitous and often wasteful mitigation when once we understand the influences upon which effective demand depends.') Similarly, in Ch. 10 he states: "If the Treasury were to fill old bottles with banknotes, bury them at suitable depths in disused coalmines which are then filled up to the surface with town rubbish, and leave it to private enterprise on well-tried

principles of laissez-faire to dig the notes up again (the right to do so being obtained, of course, by tendering for leases of the note-bearing territory), there need be no more unemployment and, with the help of the repercussions, the real income of the community, and its capital wealth also, would probably become a good deal greater than it actually is. It would, indeed, be more sensible to build houses and the like; but if there are political and practical difficulties in the way of this, the above would be better than nothing."

[2] As we will see, this is not exactly a Keynesian model; it was actually the opening shot in the rational expectations revolution. The New Keynesian approach, however, is the direct descendant of that revolution, by incorporating the rational expectations assumption and championing the role of aggregate demand policy under those conditions.

[3] See Hicks (1937).

[4] This is a simplifying assumption of certainty equivalence behaviour.

[5] Note that this uses the law of iterated expectations, which states that $E(E(p)) = E(p)$: you cannot be systematically wrong in your guess.

[6] The mathematical intuition is as follows: because the firm is optimising in point A, the derivative of its income with respect to price is set at zero, and any gain from changing prices, from the firm's perspective, will be of second order. But point A does not correspond to a social optimum, because of imperfect competition, and that means that the effects of a change in prices on social welfare will be of first order.

[7] Somewhat confusingly, people often refer to the modern New Keynesian view of fluctuations and to DSGE models as synonyms. However, it is pretty obvious that RBC models are dynamic, stochastic, and general-equilibrium too! We prefer to keep the concepts separate, so we will always refer to New Keynesian DSGE models.

[8] See Benhabib et al. (2001b), appendix B, for a full derivation in continuous time.

[9] Implicit in this equation is the assumption that firms discount future profits at the household rate of discount.

[10] Leibniz's rule? Why, of course, you recall it from calculus: that's how you differentiate an integral. If you need a refresher, here it is: take a function $g(x) = \int_{a(x)}^{b(x)} f(x, s)ds$, the derivative of g with respect to x is: $\frac{dg}{dx} = f(x, b(x))\frac{db}{dx} - f(x, a(x))\frac{da}{dx} + \int_{a(x)}^{b(x)} \frac{df(x,s)}{dx}ds$. Intuitively, there are three components of the marginal impact of changing x on g: those of increasing the upper and lower limits of the integral (which are given by f evaluated at those limits), and that of changing the function f at every point between those limits (which is given by $\int_{a(x)}^{b(x)} \frac{df(x,s)}{dx}ds$). All the other stuff is what you get from your run-of-the-mill chain rule.

[11] Whatever i^n was initially, in drawing the figure below we assume the intercept does not change in response to the shock -- that is, it does not fall as the natural interest rate drops temporarily.

References

Benhabib, J., Schmitt-Grohé, S., & Uribe, M. (2001a). Monetary policy and multiple equilibria. *American Economic Review, 91*(1), 167–186.

Benhabib, J., Schmitt-Grohé, S., & Uribe, M. (2001b). The perils of Taylor rules. *Journal of Economic Theory, 96*(1-2), 40–69.

Benhabib, J., Schmitt-Grohé, S., & Uribe, M. (2002). Avoiding liquidity traps. *Journal of Political Economy, 110*(3), 535–563.

Blanchard, O. & Galí, J. (2007). Real wage rigidities and the New Keynesian model. *Journal of Money, Credit and Banking, 39*, 35–65.

Calvo, G. A. (1983). Staggered prices in a utility-maximizing framework. *Journal of Monetary Economics, 12*(3), 383–398.

Clarida, R., Gali, J., & Gertler, M. (1999). The science of monetary policy: A New Keynesian perspective. *Journal of Economic Literature, 37*(4), 1661–1707.

Galí, J. (2015). *Monetary policy, inflation, and the business cycle: An introduction to the New Keynesian framework and its applications.* Princeton University Press.

Hicks, J. R. (1937). Mr. Keynes and the "classics"; A suggested interpretation. *Econometrica*, 147–159.

Lucas, R. E. (1973). Some international evidence on output-inflation tradeoffs. *The American Economic Review, 63*(3), 326–334.

Romer, D. (2018). *Advanced macroeconomics.* McGraw Hill.

Smets, F. & Wouters, R. (2003). An estimated dynamic stochastic general equilibrium model of the Euro area. *Journal of the European Economic Association, 1*(5), 1123–1175.

Taylor, J. B. (1993). Discretion versus policy rules in practice. *Carnegie-Rochester Conference Series on Public Policy* (Vol. 39, pp. 195–214). Elsevier.

Woodford, M. (2011). *Interest and prices: Foundations of a theory of monetary policy.* Princeton University Press.

Yun, T. (1996). Nominal price rigidity, money supply endogeneity, and business cycles. *Journal of Monetary Economics, 37*(2), 345–370.

CHAPTER 16

Unemployment

16.1 | Theories of unemployment

One of the most prominent features of the business cycle is the fluctuation in the number of people who are not working. More generally, at any given point in time there are always people who say they would like to work, but cannot find a job. As a result, no book in macroeconomics would be complete without a discussion on what determines unemployment.

The question of why there is unemployment is quite tricky, starting with the issue of whether it exists at all. Every market has frictions, people that move from one job to the next, maybe because they want a change, their business closed, or they were fired. This in-between unemployment is called *frictional unemployment* and is somewhat inevitable, in the same way that at each moment in time there is a number of properties idle in the real estate market.[1]

Another difficulty arises when workers have very high reservation wages. This may come about because people may have other income or a safety net on which to rely.[2] When this happens, they report to the household survey that they want to work, and probably they want to, but the wage at which they are willing to take a job (their reservation wage) is off equilibrium.[3] How should we classify these cases? How involuntary is this unemployment?

Now, when people would like to work at the going wages and can't find a job, and more so when this situation persists, we say there is *involuntary unemployment*. But involuntary unemployment poses a number of questions: why wouldn't wages adjust to the point where workers actually find a job? Unemployed individuals should bid down the wages they offer until supply equals demand, as in any other market. But that does not seem to happen.

Theories of unemployment suggest an explanation of why the labour market may fail to clear. The original Keynesian story for this was quite simple; wages were rigid because people have money illusion, i.e. they confuse nominal with real variables. In that view, there is a resistance to have the nominal wage adjusted downwards, preventing an economy hit by a shock that would require the nominal (and presumably the real) wage to decrease to get there. There may be some truth to the money illusion story[4], but economists came to demand models with rational individuals. The money illusion story also has the unattractive feature that wages would be countercyclical, something that is typically rejected in the data.[5]

How to cite this book chapter:
Campante, F., Sturzenegger, F. and Velasco, A. 2021. *Advanced Macroeconomics: An Easy Guide.*
Ch. 16. 'Unemployment', pp. 243–258. London: LSE Press. DOI: https://doi.org/10.31389/lsepress.ame.p
License: CC-BY-NC 4.0.

The theories of unemployment we will see tell some more sophisticated stories. They can be classified as:

1. *Search/Matching models*: unemployment exists as a by-product of the process through which jobs that require different skills are matched with the workers who possess them.
2. *Efficiency-wage theories*: firms want to pay a wage above the market-clearing level, because that increases workers' productivity.
3. *Contracting/Insider-Outsider models*: firms cannot reduce the wage to market-clearing levels because of contractual constraints.

We will see that each of these stories (and the sub-stories within each class) will lead to different types of unemployment, for example frictional vs structural. They are not mutually exclusive, and the best way to think about unemployment is having those stories coexist in time and space. To what extent they are present is something that varies with the specific context. Yet, to tackle any of these models, we first need to develop the basic model of job search, to which we now turn.

A word of caution on unemployment data

Unemployment data is typically collected in *Permanent Household Surveys*. In these surveys, data collectors ask workers if they work (those that answer they do are called employed), if they don't work and have been looking for a job in the last x unit of time they are called unemployed. The sum of employed and unemployed workers comprise the labour force. Those that are not in the labour force are out of the labour force (this includes, children, the retired, students, and people who are just not interested in working). The key parameter here is the x mentioned above. It is not the same to ask about whether you looked for a job in the last minute (unemployment would probably be zero, considering that you are probably answering the survey!), in the last week or in the last year. The longer the span, the higher the labour force and the higher the unemployment rates. Methodological changes can lead to very significant changes in the unemployment figures.

16.2 | A model of job search

The theory of search solves the problem faced by an unemployed worker that is faced with random job offers. The solution takes the form of a reservation wage w_R. Only if the wage offer is larger than this reservation wage will the searcher take the job.

The specifics of the labour market have motivated the modelling of the process of job search. Obviously, how the market works depends on how workers *look* for a job. The theory of search tackles this question directly, though later on found innumerable applications in micro and macroeconomics.

Let's start with the basic setup. Imagine a worker that is looking for a job, and every period (we start in discrete time), is made an offer w taken from a distribution $F(w)$. The worker can accept or reject the offer. If he accepts the offer, he keeps the job forever (we'll give away with this assumption later). If he rejects the offer he gets paid an unemployment compensation b and gets a chance to try a new offer the following period. What would be the optimal decision? Utility will be described by the present discounted value of income, which the worker wants to maximise

$$\mathbb{E} \sum_{t=0}^{\infty} \beta^t x_t, \tag{16.1}$$

where $x = w$ if employed at wage w, and $x = b$ if unemployed and $\beta = \frac{1}{1+\rho}$. This problem is best represented by a value function that represents the value of the maximisation problem given your current state. For example, the value of accepting an offer with wage w is

$$W(w) = w + \beta W(w). \tag{16.2}$$

It is easy to see why. By accepting the wage w, he secures that income this period, but, as the job lasts forever, next period he still keeps the same value, so the second term is that same value discounted one period. On the other hand, if he does not accept an offer, he will receive an income of b and then next period will get to draw a new offer. The value of that will be the maximum of the value of not accepting and the value of accepting the offer. Let's call U the value of not accepting (U obviously is motivated by the word unemployment):

$$U = b + \beta \int_0^{\infty} \max\{U, W(w)\} dF(w). \tag{16.3}$$

Since,

$$W(w) = w/(1 - \beta), \tag{16.4}$$

is increasing in w, there is some w_R for which

$$W(w_R) = U. \tag{16.5}$$

The searcher then rejects the proposition if $w < w_R$, and accepts it if $w \geq w_R$. Replacing (16.4) in (16.5) gives

$$U = \frac{w_R}{(1 - \beta)}. \tag{16.6}$$

But then combining (16.3) and (16.4) with (16.6) we have

$$\frac{w_R}{1 - \beta} = b + \frac{\beta}{1 - \beta} \int_0^{\infty} \max\{w_R, w\} dF(w). \tag{16.7}$$

Subtracting $\frac{\beta w_R}{1-\beta}$ from both sides we get

$$w_R = b + \frac{\beta}{1 - \beta} \int_{w_R}^{\infty} (w - w_R) dF(w). \tag{16.8}$$

Equation (16.8) is very intuitive. The reservation wage needs to be higher than b, and how much depends on the possibility of eventually obtaining a good match; the better the prospects, the more demanding the searcher will be before accepting a match. On the other hand, a high discount factor, which means that waiting is painful will decrease the reservation wage.

An analogous specification can be built in continuous time. Here the value functions need to be understood as indicating the instantaneous payoff of each state. As time is valuable, these payoffs have to match the interest return of the value function. The analogous of the discrete time version are:

$$rW(w) = w, \tag{16.9}$$

$$rU = b + \alpha \int_0^\infty \max\{0, W(w) - U\} dF(w). \tag{16.10}$$

Notice how natural the interpretation for (16.9) is. The value of accepting a wage is the present discounted value of that wage $\frac{w}{r}$. The value of not accepting an offer is the instantaneous payment b plus α that needs to be interpreted as the probability with which a new opportunity comes along, times its expected value.[6] We can also use our standard asset pricing intuition, which we first encountered when analysing the Hamiltonian. The asset here is the state "looking for a job" that pays a dividend of b per unit of time. The capital gain (or loss) is the possibility of finding a job, which happens with probability α and yields a gain of $\int_0^\infty \max\{0, W(w) - U\} dF(w)$.

As still $W(w_R) = U$,

$$W(w) - U = \left(\frac{w - w_R}{r}\right), \tag{16.11}$$

which can be replaced in (16.10) to give an expression for the reservation wage

$$w_R = b + \frac{\alpha}{r} \int_{w_R}^\infty (w - w_R) \, dF(w). \tag{16.12}$$

16.2.1 | Introducing labour turnover

The model can be easily modified to introduce labour turnover. If the worker can lose his job, we need to introduce in the equation for the value of accepting an offer the possibility that the worker may be laid off and go back to the pool of the unemployed. We will assume this happens with probability λ:

$$rW(w) = w + \lambda[U - W(w)]. \tag{16.13}$$

The equation for the value of being unemployed remains (16.10), and still $W(w_R) = U$. Because $rW(w_R) = w_R$ we know that $rU = w_R$. (16.13) implies that $W(w) = \frac{w + \lambda U}{(r + \lambda)}$, which replacing in (16.10) gives

$$rU = b + \frac{\alpha}{r + \lambda} \int_{w_R}^\infty [w - w_R] dF(w), \tag{16.14}$$

or

$$rW(w_R) = w_R = b + \frac{\alpha}{r + \lambda} \int_{w_R}^\infty [w - w_R] dF(w). \tag{16.15}$$

The reservation wage falls the higher the turnover; as the job is not expected to last forever, the searcher becomes less picky.

This basic framework constitutes the basic model of functioning of the labour market. It's implications will be used in the remainder of the chapter.

16.3 | Diamond-Mortensen-Pissarides model

The Diamond-Mortensen-Pissarides model describes a two-way search problem: that of workers and that of firms. A matching function $M(U, V)$ that relates the number of matchings to the unemployment and vacancies rates allows us to build a model of frictional unemployment.

We will put our job search value functions to work right away in one very influential way of analysing unemployment: thinking the labour market as a matching problem in which sellers (job-seeking workers) and buyers (employee-seeking firms) have to search for each other in order to find a match. If jobs and workers are heterogeneous, the process of finding the right match will be costly and take time, and unemployment will be the result of that protracted process.[7]

Let us consider a simple version of the search model of unemployment. The economy consists of workers and jobs. The number of employed workers is E and that of unemployed workers is U ($E + U = \bar{L}$); the number of vacant jobs is V and that of filled jobs is F. (We will assume that one worker can fill one and only one job, so that $F = E$, but it is still useful to keep the notation separate.) Job opportunities can be created or eliminated freely, but there is a fixed cost C (per unit of time) of maintaining a job. An employed worker produces A units of output per unit of time ($A > C$), and earns a wage w, which is determined in equilibrium. We leave aside the costs of job search, so the worker's utility is w if employed or zero if unemployed; the firm's profit from a filled job is $A - w - C$, and $-C$ from a vacant job.

The key assumption is that the matching between vacant jobs and unemployed workers is not instantaneous. We capture the flow of new jobs being created with a matching function

$$M = M(U, V) = KU^{\beta}V^{\gamma}, \tag{16.16}$$

with $\beta, \gamma \in [0, 1]$. This can be interpreted as follows: the more unemployed workers looking for jobs, and the more vacant jobs available, the easier it will be to find a match. As such, it subsumes the searching decisions of firms and workers without considering them explicitly. Note that we can parameterise the extent of the thick market externalities: if $\beta + \gamma > 1$, doubling the number of unemployed workers and vacant jobs more than doubles the rate of matching; if $\beta + \gamma < 1$ the search process faces decreasing returns (crowding).

We also assume an exogenous rate of job destruction, which we again denote as b. This means that the number of employed workers evolves according to

$$\dot{E} = M(U, V) - bE. \tag{16.17}$$

We denote a as the rate at which unemployed workers find new jobs and α as the rate at which vacant jobs are filled. It follows from these definitions that we will have

$$a = \frac{M(U, V)}{U}, \tag{16.18}$$

$$\alpha = \frac{M(U, V)}{V}. \tag{16.19}$$

The above describes the aggregate dynamics of the labor market, but we still need to specify the value for the firm and for the worker associated with each of the possible states. Here is where we will use the intuitions of the previous section. Using the same asset pricing intuition that we used in (16.9) and (16.10), but now applied to both worker and firm, we can write

$$rV_E = w - b(V_E - V_U),$$ (16.20)
$$rV_U = a(V_E - V_U),$$ (16.21)
$$rV_V = -C + \alpha(V_F - V_V),$$ (16.22)
$$rV_F = A - w - C - b(V_F - V_V),$$ (16.23)

where r stands for the interest rate (which we assume to be equal to the individual discount rate). These equations are intuitive, so let's just review (16.20). The instantaneous value of being employed is the instantaneous wage. With probability b the worker can become unemployed in which case loses the utility $(V_E - V_U)$. The reasoning behind the other equations is similar, so we can just move on.

We assume that workers and firms have equal bargaining power when setting the wage, so that they end up with the same equilibrium rents:[8]

$$V_E - V_U = V_F - V_V.$$ (16.24)

16.3.1 | Nash bargaining

Let us start by computing the rents that will accrue to employed workers and employing firms, as a function of the wage, using (16.20)-(16.23):

$$r(V_E - V_U) = w - b(V_E - V_U) - a(V_E - V_U) \Rightarrow V_E - V_U = \frac{w}{a + b + r},$$ (16.25)

$$r(V_F - V_V) = A - w - C - b(V_F - V_V) + C - \alpha(V_F - V_V) \Rightarrow V_F - V_V = \frac{A - w}{\alpha + b + r}.$$ (16.26)

The assumption of equal bargaining power (16.24) implies that the equilibrium wage must satisfy

$$\frac{w}{a + b + r} = \frac{A - w}{\alpha + b + r} \Rightarrow w = \frac{(a + b + r)A}{a + \alpha + 2b + 2r}.$$ (16.27)

The intuition is simple: a and α capture how easy it is for a worker to find a job, and for a firm to find a worker; their relative size determines which party gets the bigger share of output.

The equilibrium will be pinned down by a free-entry condition: firms will create job opportunities whenever they generate positive value. In equilibrium, the value of a vacant job will be driven down to zero. But how much is a vacant job worth to a firm? Using (16.22), (16.26), and (16.27) yields

$$rV_V = -C + \alpha \frac{A - w}{\alpha + b + r} = -C + \alpha \frac{A - \frac{(a+b+r)A}{a+\alpha+2b+2r}}{\alpha + b + r}$$

$$\Rightarrow rV_V = -C + \frac{\alpha}{a + \alpha + 2b + 2r}A.$$ (16.28)

Now recall (16.18) and (16.19). We can turn these into functions of E, by focusing the analysis on steady states where E is constant. For this to be the case (16.17) implies that $M(U, V) = bE$, the numbers of jobs filled has to equal the number of jobs lost. It follows that

$$a = \frac{bE}{U} = \frac{bE}{\bar{L} - E}.$$ (16.29)

To find out what α is, we still need to express V in terms of E, which we do by using the matching function (16.16):

$$KU^\beta V^\gamma = bE \Rightarrow V = \left(\frac{bE}{KU^\beta}\right)^{\frac{1}{\gamma}} = \left(\frac{bE}{K(\bar{L}-E)^\beta}\right)^{\frac{1}{\gamma}}. \tag{16.30}$$

As a result, we obtain

$$\alpha = \frac{bE}{V} = \frac{bE}{\left(\frac{bE}{K(\bar{L}-E)^\beta}\right)^{\frac{1}{\gamma}}} = K^{\frac{1}{\gamma}}(bE)^{\frac{\gamma-1}{\gamma}}(\bar{L}-E)^{\frac{\beta}{\gamma}}. \tag{16.31}$$

Conditions (16.29) and (16.31) can be interpreted as follows: a is an increasing function of E because the more people are employed, the smaller will be the number of people competing for the new job vacancies and the easier it for an unemployed worker to find a job. Similarly, α is decreasing in E because the same logic will make it harder for a firm to fill a vacancy.

The final solution of the model imposes the free-entry condition, using (16.28), to implicitly obtain equilibrium employment:

$$rV_V(E) = -C + \frac{\alpha(E)}{a(E) + \alpha(E) + 2b + 2r}A = 0. \tag{16.32}$$

What does the function $V_V(E)$ look like? It is negatively sloped, because

$$V'_V(E) = \frac{A}{r}\frac{\alpha'(E)\left[a(E) + 2b + 2r\right] - a'(E)\alpha(E)}{(a(E) + \alpha(E) + 2b + 2r)^2} < 0. \tag{16.33}$$

Intuitively, more employment makes it harder and more expensive to fill vacant jobs, reducing their value to the firm. When E is zero, filling a job is very easy, and the firm gets all the surplus $A - C$; when E is equal to $\bar{L}$ (full employment), it is essentially impossible, and the value of the vacancy is $-C$. This can be plotted as in Figure 16.1.

Figure 16.1 Equilibrium employment in the search model

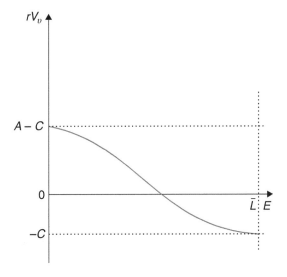

16.3.2 | Unemployment over the cycle

What happens when there is a negative shock in demand? We can illustrate this through analysing the effect of a drop in A, which a brief inspection of (16.28) shows corresponds to a leftward shift of the V_V curve in Figure 16.1 resulting in an increase in unemployment. Equation (16.27) in turn shows that the equilibrium wage will also fall as a result – though less than one for one, because of the effect of lower employment on the ease and cost of filling new vacancies. This means that the search models generate the kind of cyclical unemployment that characterises recessions.

We can also note that such a decrease in productivity will affect the equilibrium number of vacancies: (16.30) shows that there are fewer vacancies when employment is low. This seems to be consistent with the fact that you don't see many help wanted signs during recessions. (The negative link between unemployment and vacancies is often called Beveridge curve.) This happens in the model because a steady state with low employment is one in which the matching rate is low, and this means that firms will be discouraged from opening new vacancies that are likely to remain unfilled for a long time. This is precisely due to what is called thick market externalities: if there aren't many vacancies, people are unlikely to be looking for jobs, which discourages vacancies from being opened. People disregard the effect that their own job search or vacancy has on the thickness of the market, which benefits every other participant.

In any event, the unemployment described in these search models is what we call frictional unemployment – the by-product of the fact that it takes time to match heterogeneous workers and heterogenous jobs. It is hard to think that long-term unemployment of the sort that often happens in real life will be due to this mechanism. Thus, we need other stories to account for a more stable unemployment rate. To these we now turn.

16.4 | Efficiency wages

The efficiency wage story builds on the idea that effort increases with wages. The firm may find it optimal to charge an above equilibrium wage to induce workers to exert effort. The chosen wage may lead to aggregate unemployment without firms having an incentive to lower it. Efficiency wages provide then a model of steady state unemployment.

The idea behind efficiency wages is that the productivity of labour depends on effort, and that effort depends on wages. Because of these links, firms prefer to pay a wage that is higher than the market equilibrium wage. But at this wage there is unemployment. The most basic version of this story – one that applies to very poor countries – is that a higher wage makes workers healthier as they can eat better. But there are many other ways to make the argument. For example, it is mentioned that Henry Ford paid his workers twice the running wage to get the best and reduce turnover, and, as we will see in the next section, sometimes firms pay a higher wage to elicit effort because they have difficulty in monitoring workers' effort.[9]

To see this, let us consider a general model in which the firm's profits are

$$\pi = Y - wL,$$

where

$$Y = F(eL),$$

with $F' > 0$ and $F'' < 0$. We denote by e the effort or effectiveness of the worker. The crucial assumption is that this effectiveness is increasing in the real wage:

$$e = e(w),$$

with $e' > 0$. With all these assumption we can rewrite the firm problem as

$$Max_{L,w}F(e(w)L) - wL,$$

which has first-order conditions

$$\frac{\partial \pi}{\partial L} = F'e - w = 0, \qquad (16.34)$$

and

$$\frac{\partial \pi}{\partial w} = F'Le'(w) - L = 0. \qquad (16.35)$$

Combining (16.34) and (16.35) we have

$$\frac{we'(w)}{e(w)} = 1.$$

The wage that satisfies this condition is called the *efficiency wage*. This condition means that the elasticity of effort with respect to wage is equal to one: a 1% increase in the wage translates into an equal increase in effective labour.

Why does this create unemployment? Notice that (16.34) and (16.35) is a system that defines both the wage and employment. If the optimal solution is w^* and L^*, total labour demand is NL^* where N indicates the number of firms. If the supply of labour exceeds this number, there is unemployment because firms will not want to reduce their wages to clear the market.[10] We can also extend this model to include the idea that effort depends on the wage the firm pays relative to what other firms pay, or existing labour market conditions. Summers and Heston (1988) do this and the insights are essentially the same.

The model provides an intuitive explanation for a permanent disequilibrium in labour markets. What explains the relation between wages and effort? To dig a bit deeper we need a framework that can generate this relationship. Our next model does exactly that.

16.4.1 | Wages and effort: The Shapiro-Stiglitz model

The Shapiro-Stiglitz model builds a justification for efficiency wages on the difficulties for monitoring worker's effort. Labour markets with little monitoring problems will have market clearing wages and no unemployment. Markets with monitoring difficulties will induce worker's rents and steady state unemployment.

When you're at work, your boss obviously cannot perfectly monitor your effort, right? This means you have a moral hazard problem: the firm would like to pay you based on your effort, but it can only observe your production. It turns out that the solution to this moral hazard problem leads to a form of efficiency wages.

Following Shapiro and Stiglitz (1984), consider a model in continuous time with identical workers who have an instantaneous discount rate of ρ and a utility at any given instant that is given by

$$u(t) = \begin{cases} w(t) - e(t) \text{ , if employed} \\ \qquad 0 \qquad \text{, otherwise} \end{cases} \tag{16.36}$$

where again w is wage and e is effort. For simplicity, we assume that effort can take two values, $e \in \{0, \bar{e}\}$. At any given point in time, the worker can be in one of three states: E means that she is employed and exerting effort ($e = \bar{e}$), S means that she is employed and shirking ($e = 0$), and U denotes unemployment. We assume that there is an exogenous instantaneous probability that the worker will lose her job at any instant, which is given by b. In addition, there is an instantaneous probability q that a shirking worker will be caught by the firm, capturing the monitoring technology. Finally, the rate at which unemployed workers find jobs is given by a. This is taken to be exogenous by individual agents, but will be determined in equilibrium for the economy as a whole. Firms in this model will simply maximise profits, as given by

$$\pi(t) = F(\bar{e}E(t)) - w(t)\left[E(t) + S(t)\right], \tag{16.37}$$

where $F(\cdot)$ is as before, and $E(t)$ and $S(t)$ denote the number of employees who are exerting effort and shirking, respectively.

In order to analyse the choices of workers, we need to compare their utility in each of the states, E, S, and U. Let us denote V_i the intertemporal utility of being in state i; it follows that

$$\rho V_E = (w - \bar{e}) + b(V_U - V_E). \tag{16.38}$$

How do we know that? Again, we use our standard asset pricing intuition that we found in the first section of this chapter. The asset here is being employed and exerting effort, which pays a dividend of $w - \bar{e}$ per unit of time. The capital gain (or loss) is the possibility of losing the job, which happens with probability b and yields a gain of $V_U - V_E$. The rate of return that an agent requires to hold a unit of this asset is given by ρ. Using the intuition that that the total required return be equal to dividends plus capital gain, we reach (16.38). A similar reasoning gives us

$$\rho V_S = w + (b + q)(V_U - V_S), \tag{16.39}$$

because the probability of losing your job when shirking is $b + q$. Finally, unemployment pays zero dividends (no unemployment insurance), which yields[11]

$$\rho V_U = a(V_E - V_U). \tag{16.40}$$

Solving the model

If the firm wants workers to exert effort, it must set wages such that $V_E \geq V_S$. The cheapest way to do that is to satisfy this with equality, which implies

$$V_E = V_S \Rightarrow (w - \bar{e}) + b(V_U - V_E) = w + (b + q)(V_U - V_S),$$
$$\Rightarrow (w - \bar{e}) + b(V_U - V_E) = w + (b + q)(V_U - V_E),$$
$$\Rightarrow \bar{e} = q(V_E - V_U),$$
$$\Rightarrow V_E - V_U = \frac{\bar{e}}{q} > 0. \tag{16.41}$$

Note that wages are set such that workers are strictly better off being employed than unemployed. In other words, firms will leave rents to workers, so they are afraid of losing their jobs and exert effort as a result. What exactly is that wage? We can use (16.38), (16.40) and (16.41) to get

$$\rho V_E = (w - \bar{e}) - b\frac{\bar{e}}{q},$$

$$\rho V_U = a\frac{\bar{e}}{q}. \tag{16.42}$$

Subtracting these two equations yields

$$\rho\frac{\bar{e}}{q} = (w - \bar{e}) - b\frac{\bar{e}}{q} - a\frac{\bar{e}}{q} \Rightarrow w = \bar{e} + (\rho + a + b)\frac{\bar{e}}{q}. \tag{16.43}$$

Again this is very intuitive. The wage has to compensate effort, but then adds an extra which depends on the monitoring technology. For example if the monitoring technology is weak, the wage premia needs to be higher.

We know that a will be determined in equilibrium. What is the equilibrium condition? If we are in steady state where the rate of unemployment is constant, it must be that the number of workers losing their jobs is exactly equal to the number of workers gaining new jobs. If there are N firms, each one employing L workers (remember that all workers exert effort in equilibrium), and the total labour supply in the economy is $\bar{L}$, there are $a(\bar{L} - NL)$ unemployed workers finding jobs, and bNL employed workers losing theirs. The equilibrium condition can thus be written as:

$$a(\bar{L} - NL) = bNL \Rightarrow a = \frac{bNL}{\bar{L} - NL} \Rightarrow a + b = \frac{b\bar{L}}{\bar{L} - NL}. \tag{16.44}$$

Substituting this into (16.43) yields

$$w = \bar{e} + \left(\rho + \frac{b\bar{L}}{\bar{L} - NL}\right)\frac{\bar{e}}{q}. \tag{16.45}$$

This is the *no-shirking condition* (NSC), which the wage needs to satisfy in order to get workers to exert effort. Note that $\frac{\bar{L} - NL}{\bar{L}}$ is the unemployment rate in this economy, so that (16.45) implies that the efficiency wage will be decreasing in the unemployment rate; the greater the unemployment rate is, the more workers will have to fear, and the less their required compensation will be.[12] At full employment, an unemployed worker would instantly find a new job just like her old one, so she has nothing to fear from the threat of being fired. The premium is also decreasing in the quality of the monitoring technology, q, which also reduces the need for overcompensation.

We still need to figure out what L will be in equilibrium. Labor demand by firms will come from the maximisation of (16.37), which entails

$$\bar{e}F'(\bar{e}L) = w. \tag{16.46}$$

A graphic representation of the equilibrium is given in Figure 16.2.

In the absence of the moral hazard problem (or with perfect monitoring), the equilibrium occurs where the labour demand curve crosses the labour supply, which is horizontal at $\bar{e}$ up until the full employment point $\bar{L}$, at which it becomes vertical. (The figure assumes that $\bar{e}F'(\bar{e}\bar{L}/N) > \bar{e}$.) This frictionless equilibrium point is denoted E^W, and it entails full employment. However, because of the moral hazard problem, the firms will optimally choose to leave rents to workers, which in turn means that some workers will be left unemployed because the wage rate will not go down to market-clearing levels.

Figure 16.2   Shapiro-Stiglitz model

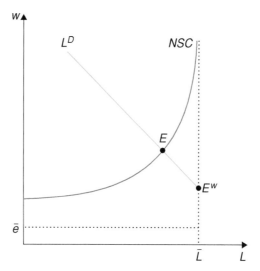

Figure 16.3   A decrease in labor demand

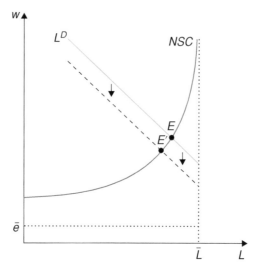

What happens when there is a negative shock to demand? This can be seen in Figure 16.3. We see that unemployment goes up, and the real wage goes down (as higher unemployment makes it cheaper to induce workers' effort).

Note that this unemployment is inefficient, as the marginal product of labour exceeds the marginal cost of effort. The first-best allocation is for everyone to be employed and to exert effort, but this cannot be simply implemented because of the informational failure.

This model, or rather a simple extension of it, is also consistent with a widespread feature of many labour markets, particularly (but not exclusively) in developing countries: the presence of dual labour markets. Suppose you have a sector where effort can be monitored more easily, say, because output is less subject to random noise, and another sector (say, the public sector) where monitoring is harder. Then those working in the latter sector would earn rents, and be very reluctant to leave their jobs.

This model has some theoretical difficulties (e.g. Why don't people resort to more complicated contracts, as opposed to a wage contract? What if the problem is one of adverse selection, e.g. unobservable abilities, as opposed to moral hazard?) and empirical ones (e.g. calibration suggests that the magnitude of employment effects would be quite small). But it is still one of the better-known stories behind efficiency wages.

16.5 | Insider-outsider models of unemployment

The insider-outsider story builds an institutional theory of unemployment: unionisation transforms the labour market into a bilateral wage negotiation that may lead to higher than equilibrium wages. The unemployed, however, cannot bid the wage down because they are excluded from the bargaining game.

The insider-outsider model also speaks of a dual labour market, but for different reasons. A standard model of a dual market occurs when governments impose a minimum wage above the equilibrium rate leaving some workers unemployed. Alternatively, in the formal market, unionised workers choose the wage jointly with the firm in a bargaining process. The key assumption is that the firm cannot hire outsiders before it has all insiders (e.g. union members) working, and insiders have little incentive to keep wages low so that outsiders can get a job. As a result the equilibrium wage is higher than the market-clearing wage.

In these dual labour market stories, we may want to ask what is going on in the labour market for outsiders. That, in fact, is a free market, so there should be full employment there. In fact, for most developing countries unemployment is not a big issue, though a privileged number of formal workers do have higher wages. In other words, for the insider-outsider story to generate high economy-wide unemployment, you need the economy to have a very small informal sector. Examples could be European countries or Southern African countries.

At any rate, to see the insider-outsider story in action as a model of unemployment, consider an economy where all workers are unionised so that aggregate labour demand faces a unique supplier of labour: the centralised union. In Figure 16.4 we show that, as with any monopolist, the price is driven above its equilibrium level, and at the optimal wage there is excess supply of labour (unemployment). Notice that if the demand for labour increases the solution is an increase in the wage and in employment, so the model delivers a procyclical wage.

The role of labour market regulations on the functioning of the labour market is a literature with strong predicament in Europe, where unionisation and labour regulation were more prevalent than, say, in the U.S. In fact, Europe showed historically a higher unemployment rate than the U.S., a phenomenon called Eurosclerosis.

The literature has produced a series of interesting contributions surrounding labour market rigidities. One debate, for example has do to with the role of firing costs on equilibrium unemployment. Increasing firing costs increases or decreases unemployment? It increases unemployment, some would claim because it makes hiring more costly. Others would claim it reduces unemployment because it makes firing more costly. Bentolila and Bertola (1990) calibrated these effects for European labour markets and found that firing costs actually decrease firing and reduce the equilibrium unemployment rate. The debate goes on.

Figure 16.4 The distortion created by the insider

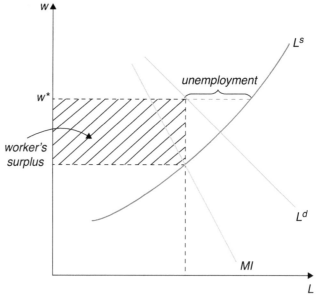

16.5.1 | Unemployment and rural-urban migration

Inspired by the slums of Nairobi, which swelled even further as the nation developed, Harris and Todaro (1970) developed the concept that unemployment was a necessary buffer whenever there were dual labour markets. It is a specific version of the insider-outsider interpretation. According to Harris and Todaro, there is a subsistence wage (back in the countryside) (w_s) that coexists with the possibility of a job in the formal sector (w_f). For the market to be in equilibrium, expected wages had to be equalised, i.e.

$$pw_f = w_s, \tag{16.47}$$

where p is the probability of finding a job in the formal sector. How is p determined? Assuming random draws from a distribution we can assume that

$$p = \frac{E}{E + U}, \tag{16.48}$$

where E stands for the total amount of people employed, and U for the total unemployed. Solving for U, using (16.47) in (16.48) we obtain that

$$U = E\left(\frac{w_f - w_s}{w_s}\right),$$

i.e. the unemployment rate is a function of the wage differential.

16.6 | What next?

The search theory of unemployment is well-covered in Rogerson et al. (2005) *Search-Theoretic Models of the Labor Market: A Survey*. Two textbooks you need to browse if you want to work on the topics discussed in this chapter are Pissarides (2000) *Equilibrium Unemployment Theory* and, of course, the graduate level textbook by Cahuc et al. (2014) *Labor Economics*. This will be more than enough to get you going.

Notes

[1] Lilien (1982) provides evidence that regions in the U.S. with larger sectorial volatility have higher unemployment rates, providing some evidence in favour of the frictional unemployment hypothesis.

[2] The running joke in the UK in the 70's claimed that if you were married and had three children you could not afford to be employed. In fact, there is ample evidence that the end of unemployment benefits strongly change the probability of someone finding a job.

[3] A relevant case of this would be South Africa, which has unemployment rates in the upper 20's. In South Africa, large portions of the population live in communities far away from city centers, a costly legacy of the Apartheid regime, making commuting costs expensive in money and time. At the same time, large transfers to lower income segments combine with transportation costs to generate large reservation wages. People look for a job but find it difficult to find one that covers these fixed costs, leading to high and persistent unemployment.

[4] A nice set of empirical experiments showing that nominal illusion is quite pervasive can be found in Shafir et al. (1997).

[5] Another reason why countercyclical real wages are problematic can be seen with a bit of introspection: if that were the case, you should be very happy during a recession, provided that you keep your job – but that doesn't seem to be the case!

[6] Technically, we would call this a *hazard rate* and not probability, as it is not limited to $[0,1]$. We abuse our language to aid in the intuition.

[7] This is but one example of a general kind of problem of two-sided markets, which can be used to study all sorts of different issues, from regulation to poverty traps. The unemployment version was worth a Nobel prize in 2010 for Peter Diamond, Dale Mortensen, and Chris Pissarides, and the analysis of two-sided markets is one of the main contributions of 2014 Nobel laureate Jean Tirole.

[8] This result is not arbitrarily imposed, but an application of the axiomatic approach to bargaining of Nash Jr (1950).

[9] Akerlof and Yellen (1986) provide a comprehensive review of the literature on efficiency wages.

[10] The mathematical intuition for why firms have a low incentive to adjust wages is similar to the argument for the effects of small menu costs under imperfect competition, which we saw in the last handout: because firms are in an interior optimum in the efficiency-wage case, the first-order gains from adjusting wages are zero.

[11] This assumes that, if employed, the wages will be enough that the worker will want to exert effort, which will be the case in equilibrium.

[12] This is not unlike the Marxian concept of the reserve army of labor!

References

Akerlof, G. A. & Yellen, J. L. (1986). *Efficiency wage models of the labor market*. Cambridge University Press.

Bentolila, S. & Bertola, G. (1990). Firing costs and labour demand: How bad is Eurosclerosis? *The Review of Economic Studies*, *57*(3), 381–402.

Cahuc, P., Carcillo, S., & Zylberberg, A. (2014). *Labor economics*. MIT Press.

Harris, J. R. & Todaro, M. P. (1970). Migration, unemployment and development: A two-sector analysis. *The American Economic Review*, *60*(1), 126–142.

Lilien, D. M. (1982). Sectoral shifts and cyclical unemployment. *Journal of Political Economy*, *90*(4), 777–793.

Nash Jr, J. F. (1950). The bargaining problem. *Econometrica*, 155–162.

Pissarides, C. A. (2000). *Equilibrium unemployment theory*. MIT Press.

Rogerson, R., Shimer, R., & Wright, R. (2005). Search-theoretic models of the labor market: A survey. *Journal of Economic Literature*, *43*(4), 959–988.

Shafir, E., Diamond, P., & Tversky, A. (1997). Money illusion. *The Quarterly Journal of Economics*, *112*(2), 341–374.

Shapiro, C. & Stiglitz, J. E. (1984). Equilibrium unemployment as a worker discipline device. *The American Economic Review*, *74*(3), 433–444.

Summers, R. & Heston, A. (1988). A new set of international comparisons of real product and price levels estimates for 130 countries, 1950–1985. *Review of Income and Wealth*, *34*(1), 1–25.

Monetary and Fiscal Policy

CHAPTER 17

Fiscal policy I: Public debt and the effectiveness of fiscal policy

We have now reached the point at which we can use our hard-earned theoretical tools to study in depth the main policy instruments of macroeconomics, and eventually their long-run and short-run effects. We will start by considering fiscal policy, which means we will now address some of the most pressing policy questions in both developing and developed countries: does an increase in government expenditure increase output, or does it reduce it? What are the determinants of fiscal policy? What are the views?

Fiscal policy can always be thought of under two lights. On one level, it is a component of aggregate demand and will interest us as a tool of macroeconomic stabilisation; on the other hand, it also has a role in terms of determining the provision of public goods which brings in a whole host of other long-run considerations associated with the quality of that spending.

As a tool of macroeconomic stabilisation it is fundamentally different from monetary policy because fiscal policy requires resources, in other words, it needs to be financed. The result is that whatever expansion is obtained by fiscal spending will be diluted by the negative effect produced by the fact that it needs to obtain resources from the economy to finance itself. As a result it will always unavoidably put in motion a countervailing effect that must be taken into account.

This chapter will deal with the first role of fiscal policy, it's role for demand management, which happens to be where we typically have our first encounter with the topic at the undergraduate level. In fact, our treatment of fiscal policy illustrates how the things we learn in undergraduate-level macro can be misleading. For instance, in the traditional Keynesian rendition, fiscal policy helps stabilise output – you may remember that an increase in G moves the IS to the right (see Figure 17.1). But this "undergraduate level" analysis is incomplete because it assumes that private consumption or investment are not affected by the increased expenditure. But how is the expenditure financed? Does this financing affect other components of aggregate demand? Imagine a permanent increase in expenditures financed with taxes. Our model of permanent income would anticipate a one to one decrease in private consumption, quite the opposite of a consumption function that is a rigid function of income.

In fact, if we ignore the financing side of the expenditure (be it through taxes or debt) it is evident that some budget constraint will be violated. Either the government is spending what it does not have, or consumers are spending what they cannot afford. Once we include the complete picture we realise

How to cite this book chapter:
Campante, F., Sturzenegger, F. and Velasco, A. 2021. *Advanced Macroeconomics: An Easy Guide.*
  Ch. 17. 'Fiscal policy I: Public debt and the effectiveness of fiscal policy', pp. 261–278. London: LSE Press.
  DOI: https://doi.org/10.31389/lsepress.ame.q   License: CC-BY-NC 4.0.

Figure 17.1 A fiscal expansion in the IS-LM model

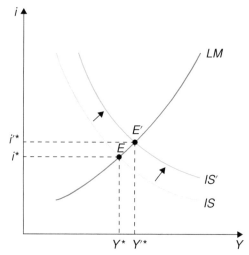

that some variables need to adjust – but when does this occur? And how? And by how much? It is these issues that make the analysis of fiscal policy so complex.

We will thus start our analysis by considering the government's intertemporal budget constraint. We have also explored the role of intertemporal budget constraints in analysing consumption and current account dynamics, the same analytical tools we used then will come in handy here. We will see the results that flow from this analysis in terms of the scope of fiscal policy and public debt dynamics.

17.1 | The government budget constraint

We must recognise that the government cannot create resources out of nothing, so it must respect an intertemporal budget constraint. This entails that the present value of government spending is limited by the present value of taxes (minus initial debt).

Let us start by looking carefully at the government budget constraint. Let g_t and τ_t denote the government's real purchases and tax revenues at time t, and d_0, its initial real debt outstanding. The simplest definition of the budget deficit is that it is the rate of change of the stock of debt. The rate of change in the stock of real debt equals the difference between the government's purchases and revenues, plus the real interest on its debt. That is,

$$\dot{d}_t = \left(g_t - \tau_t\right) + rd_t, \tag{17.1}$$

where r is the real interest rate.

The term in parentheses on the right-hand side of (17.1) is referred to as the primary deficit. It is the deficit excluding interest payments of pre-existing debt, and it is often a better way of gauging how fiscal policy at a given time is contributing to the government's budget constraint, since it leaves aside the effects of what was inherited from previous policies.

The government is also constrained by the standard solvency (no-Ponzi game) condition

$$\lim_{T \to \infty} \left(d_T e^{-rT}\right) \leq 0. \tag{17.2}$$

The government's budget constraint does not prevent it from staying permanently in debt, or even from always increasing the amount of its debt. Recall that the household's budget constraint in the Ramsey model implies that in the limit the present value of its wealth cannot be negative. Similarly, the restriction the budget constraint places on the government is that in the limit of the present value of its debt cannot be positive. In other words, the government cannot run a Ponzi scheme in which it raises new debt to pay for the ballooning interest on pre-existing debt. This condition is at the heart of the discussions on the solvency or sustainability of fiscal policy, and is the reason why sustainability exercises simply test that dynamics do not have government debt increase over time relative to GDP.

How do we impose this solvency condition on the government? We follow our standard procedure of solving the differential equation that captures the flow budget constraint. We can solve (17.1) by applying our familiar method of multiplying it by the integrating factor e^{-rt}, and integrating between 0 and T:

$$\dot{d}_t e^{-rt} - rd_t e^{-rt} = \left(g_t - \tau_t \right) e^{-rt} \Rightarrow$$

$$d_T e^{-rT} = d_0 + \int_0^T \left(g_t - \tau_t \right) e^{-rt} dt. \tag{17.3}$$

$$\lim_{T \to \infty} \left(d_T e^{-rT} \right) = d_0 + \int_0^\infty \left(g_t - \tau_t \right) e^{-rt} dt \leq 0, \tag{17.4}$$

Applying the solvency condition (17.2) and rearranging, this becomes

$$\int_0^\infty g_t e^{-rt} dt \leq -d_0 + \int_0^\infty \tau_t e^{-rt} dt. \tag{17.5}$$

A household's budget constraint is that the present value of its consumption must be less than or equal to its initial wealth plus the present value of its labour income. A government faces an analogous constraint: the present value of its purchases of goods and services must be less than or equal to its initial wealth plus the present value of its tax receipts. Note that because d_0 represents debt rather than wealth, it enters negatively into the budget constraint.

An alternative way of writing this constraint is

$$\int_0^\infty \left(\tau_t - g_t \right) e^{-rt} dt \geq d_0. \tag{17.6}$$

Expressed this way, the budget constraint states that the government must run primary surpluses large enough in present value to offset its initial debt.

17.2 | Ricardian equivalence

We add households to our problem, and derive a very important result in the theory of fiscal policy, namely Ricardian equivalence: given a path for government spending, it doesn't matter whether it is financed via taxes or debt. We discuss the conditions under which this result holds, and the caveats to its application in practice.

Let us now add households to the story, and ask questions about the effects of fiscal policy decisions on private actions and welfare. In particular, for a given path of spending, a government can choose to finance it with taxes or bonds. Does this choice make any difference? This question is actually at the heart of the issue of countercyclical fiscal policy. If you remember the standard Keynesian exercise, a fiscal stimulus is an increase in government spending that is not matched by an increase in current taxes. In other words, it is a debt-financed increase in spending. Is this any different from a policy that would raise taxes to finance the increased spending?

A natural starting point is the neoclassical growth model we have grown to know and love. To fix ideas, consider the case in which the economy is small and open, domestic agents have access to an international bond b which pays an interest rate r (the same as the interest rate on domestic government debt), and in which all government debt is held by domestic residents.

When there are taxes, the representative household's budget constraint is that the present value of its consumption cannot exceed its initial wealth plus the present value of its after-tax labour income:

$$\int_0^\infty c_t e^{-rt} dt = b_0 + d_0 + \int_0^\infty (y_t - \tau_t) e^{-rt} dt. \tag{17.7}$$

Notice that initial wealth now apparently has two components: international bond-holdings b_0 and domestic public debt holdings d_0.

17.2.1 | The effects of debt vs tax financing

Breaking the integral on the right-hand side of (17.7) in two gives us

$$\int_0^\infty c_t e^{-rt} dt = b_0 + d_0 + \int_0^\infty y_t e^{-rt} dt - \int_0^\infty \tau_t e^{-rt} dt. \tag{17.8}$$

It is reasonable to assume that the government satisfies its budget constraint, (17.5), with equality. If it did not, its wealth would be growing forever, which does not seem realistic. With that assumption, (17.5) implies that the present value of taxes, $\int_{t=0}^\infty \tau_t e^{-rt} dt$, equals initial debt d_0 plus the present value of government purchases, $\int_{t=0}^\infty g_t e^{-rt} dt$. Substituting this fact into (17.8) gives us

$$\int_0^\infty c_t e^{-rt} dt = b_0 + \int_0^\infty y_t e^{-rt} dt - \int_0^\infty g_t e^{-rt} dt. \tag{17.9}$$

Equation (17.9) shows that we can express the households' budget constraint in terms of the present value of government purchases without any reference to the division of the financing of those purchases at any point in time between taxes and bonds. Since the path of taxes does not enter either households' budget constraint or their preferences, it does not affect consumption. Thus, we have a key result: only the quantity of government purchases, not the division of the financing of those purchases between taxes and bonds, affects the economy. This was first pointed out by British economist David Ricardo, back in the 19th century, which is why it is called *Ricardian equivalence*. Barro (1974) revived this result, proving it in the context of the NGM.

To see the point more starkly, focus on the case in which the agent maximises

$$\int_0^\infty u(c_t) e^{-\rho t} dt, \tag{17.10}$$

where $\rho > 0$ is the rate of time preference. Assume moreover that $r = \rho$, as we have done in the past. This implies that the optimal consumption path is flat:

$$c_t = c \text{ for all } t \geq 0. \tag{17.11}$$

Applying this to (17.9) yields

$$c = rb_0 + r \int_0^\infty y_t e^{-rt} dt - r \int_0^\infty g_t e^{-rt} dt \qquad (17.12)$$

so that consumption is equal to permanent income. Again, since the path of taxes does not enter the RHS of (17.12), it does not affect consumption.

What is the intuition for this remarkable result? If a certain amount of spending is financed by issuing debt, the solvency condition implies that this debt must be repaid at some point. In order to do so, the government will have to raise taxes in the exact present value of that spending. This means that government bonds are not net wealth: for a given path of government expenditures, a higher stock of debt outstanding means a higher present value of taxes to be paid by households. In other words, the government cannot create resources out of nothing, it can only transfer them over time; rational, forward-looking consumers recognise this, and do not change their behaviour from what it would have been had that spending been financed with taxes immediately.

17.2.2 | Caveats to Ricardian equivalence

This very strong result was obtained under rather stringent assumptions, which we now underscore:

- Consumers live forever, so that a change in taxes even very far away in time matters to them. But note, if consumers had finite lives but acted altruistically in regards their sons and daughters, the result would still hold. This was the insight of Barro (1974).
- Taxes are lump-sum and therefore non-distortionary. If the present value of private income $\int_0^\infty y_t e^{-rt} dt$, for instance, fell if taxes increased (due to distortionary effects on investment or labour supply), then Ricardian equivalence would not hold.
- Consumers face no borrowing constraints so that all they care about is the present value of taxes. Consider, by contrast, an agent who cannot borrow and who has no initial wealth. Then, a tax increase today that was perfectly offset (in present value terms) by a tax break T periods later would reduce his income today – and therefore his consumption today– regardless of what happened in the future.
- Agents and the government can borrow at the same rate of interest r. If government could borrow more cheaply than consumers, for instance, by cutting taxes and running a larger deficit today, it would increase the wealth of consumers, enabling them to increase their consumption.

17.3 | Effects of changes in government spending

We show that changes in government spending have real effects, and that they are very different depending on whether they are temporary or permanent. Permanent increases are matched one-for-one by decreases in consumption. Temporary increases are matched less than one-for-one, with a current account deficit emerging as a result.

Now ask the opposite question. What is the effect of changes in government spending on consumption, savings, and the current account of the economy?

To get started, notice that the private budget constraint is

$$\dot{b}_t + \dot{d}_t = r\left(b_t + d_t\right) + y_t - \tau_t - c_t. \qquad (17.13)$$

Combining this with the government budget constraint (17.1) we have

$$\dot{b}_t = rb_t + y_t - g_t - c_t. \tag{17.14}$$

Suppose now that income is constant throughout, but government consumption can vary. In particular, suppose that g_t can take two values: g^H and g^L, with $g^H > g^L$. To gain further insights, we study the effects of permanent and temporary changes in government spending that take place at time 0.

17.3.1 | The initial steady state

Assume that just prior to the shock, spending is expected to remain constant forever; that is, $g_t = g^L$ for all t. The economy is thus in a steady state in which consumption is given by

$$c = rb_0 + y - g^L. \tag{17.15}$$

In the initial steady state, the current account is zero.

17.3.2 | Permanent increase in government spending

Suppose now that at time 0 there is an unanticipated and permanent increase in spending from g^L to g^H. From (17.12) it follows that consumption adjusts instantaneously to its new (and lower) value:

$$c' = rb_0 + y - g^H, \qquad t \geq 0. \tag{17.16}$$

Since consumption falls one-to-one with government spending, the trade and current accounts do not change. Hence, an unanticipated and permanent increase in spending has no impact on the current account.

17.3.3 | Temporary increase in spending

Suppose that the economy is in the initial steady state described above, with consumption given by (17.15). At time 0, there is an unanticipated and *temporary increase* in spending:

$$g_t = \begin{cases} g^H, & 0 \leq t < T \\ g^L, & t \geq T, \end{cases} \tag{17.17}$$

for some $T > 0$.

First compute the consumption path. From (17.12) it follows that consumption falls immediately to the level given by

$$c'' = rb_0 + y - g^H \left(1 - e^{-rT}\right) - g^L e^{-rT}, \qquad t \geq 0. \tag{17.18}$$

Next compute the current account path. Plugging (17.18) into (17.14) we have

$$\dot{b}_t = r \left(b_t - b_0\right) + \left(g^L - g^H\right) e^{-rT}, \qquad 0 \leq t < T. \tag{17.19}$$

Notice that at time $t = 0$ this implies

$$\dot{b}_0 = \left(g^L - g^H\right) e^{-rT} < 0. \tag{17.20}$$

The current account is negative ($\dot{b}_0 < 0$) from the start. It follows that $b_t - b_0 < 0$, and, from (17.19), that $\dot{b}_t < 0$ for all times between 0 and T. The current account worsens over time and then jumps back

Figure 17.2   Response to a transitory increase in government spending

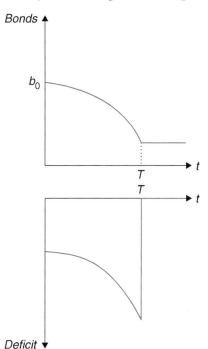

to zero at time T. Figure 17.2 shows the trajectory of the deficit and foreign assets in response to this temporary shock.

How do we know that the current account goes to 0 at time T? Recall the current account is given by

$$\dot{b}_t = rb_t + y_t - g_t - c_t. \tag{17.21}$$

Solving this for a constant path of income, spending, and consumption we have

$$b_T e^{-rT} = b_0 + \left(1 - e^{-rT}\right) \left(\frac{y - g^H - c''}{r}\right). \tag{17.22}$$

Plugging (17.18) into this expression we have

$$rb_T = rb_0 + \left(1 - e^{-rT}\right) \left(g^L - g^H\right). \tag{17.23}$$

Evaluating (17.14) at time T we have

$$\dot{b}_T = rb_T + y - g^L - c''. \tag{17.24}$$

Finally, using (17.18) and (17.23) in (17.24), we obtain

$$\dot{b}_T = rb_0 + \left(1 - e^{-rT}\right) \left(g^L - g^H\right) + y - g^L$$
$$- rb_0 - y + g^H \left(1 - e^{-rT}\right) + g^L e^{-rT} \tag{17.25}$$
$$= 0. \tag{17.26}$$

That is, the current account is zero at time T.

The key policy lesson of this discussion is that consumption does not fully offset the changes in government consumption when those changes are transitory. So, if government expenditure aims at changing aggregate demand, it has a much higher chance of achieving that objective if it moves in a transitory fashion. Here the excess spending affects the current account which can easily be governed by temporary changes in fiscal policy. This is why you may often hear mentions of twin deficits in policy debates, in reference to the idea that fiscal deficits can be accompanied by current account deficits.

17.4 | Fiscal policy in a Keynesian world

We go over how fiscal policy fits into the (New) Keynesian framework. When there is the possibility of increasing output via aggregate demand (that is, in the short run), fiscal policy can affect output. That depends, however, on the consumer and firm responses, which take into account the budget constraints.

We have seen that, once we consider the government's budget constraint, and its interaction with the households' budget constraint, the effects of fiscal policy are radically modified, compared to what you may have been used to in undergraduate discussions.

As a starter, the effectiveness of fiscal policy as a tool for managing aggregate demand, in a full employment economy, is clearly dubious. For example, think about the NGM in a closed economy. It should be immediately clear that government spending *cannot* have an effect on output from the demand side: the government cannot through aggregate management increase the productive capacity of the economy, and this means its increased spending must crowd out something else. (In a small open economy model, as we have seen, it crowds out mostly consumption; in a closed or large open economy, it would also crowd out investment.) This has the flavour of Ricardian equivalence.

Having said that, we are still left with the question: where is the role for Keynesian fiscal policy? Is the conclusion that such policy is impossible? Not quite. Recall that the models so far in this chapter had no room for aggregate demand policy by assumption: the economies we've seen were not demand constrained and output was exogenous. In other words, one might think of them as descriptions of long-term effects. However, in a recession, the government can try to engage those that are sitting idle because of insufficient aggregate demand. This is the view that lies behind the thinking of proponents of fiscal stimulus.

To think more systematically about this, let us look at the role of government in the context of the canonical (discrete-time) New Keynesian model we saw in Chapter 15. The key change that we incorporate is to include government spending, which (in a closed economy) entails the following resource constraint:

$$Y_t = C_t + G_t. \tag{17.27}$$

Expressing this in terms of (percentage) deviations from the steady state, it is easy to see that the log-linearised resource constraint is[1]

$$\hat{y}_t = (1 - \gamma)\hat{c}_t + \gamma\hat{g}_t, \tag{17.28}$$

where $\gamma = \frac{\bar{G}}{\bar{Y}}$ is the steady state share of government spending, and the hat above a variable z represents log deviations from the steady state: $\hat{z}_t = z_t - \bar{z}_t$.

Now take the Euler equation coming from consumer optimisation. Log-linearising around the (non-stochastic) steady state of the economy (and leaving aside the term in the discount rate ρ, for notational simplicity) yields our familiar

$$\hat{c}_t = E_t \hat{c}_{t+1} - \sigma r_t. \tag{17.29}$$

Now, we can't simply substitute output for consumption, as we did back in Chapter 15. Instead, substituting the new linearised resource constraint into (17.29) yields, after some simple manipulation.[2]

$$\hat{y}_t = E_t \hat{y}_{t+1} - \sigma(1 - \gamma) \left(i_t - E_t \pi_{t+1} - r_g^n \right), \tag{17.30}$$

where $r_g^n = -\frac{\gamma}{\sigma(1-\gamma)} \Delta \hat{g}_{t+1}$. This term r_g^n is the modified version of the natural interest rate – that is to say, the rate that would keep output stable – that we encountered in Chapter 15.[3] It is easy to see that a *transitory* increase in $\hat{g}_t$ corresponds to an increase in that natural interest rate. In other words, a transitory fiscal expansion increases aggregate demand.

Here's where you may ask: but isn't the resource constraint being violated? Well, no: we have used (17.28) explicitly in our derivation, after all. The trick is that the resource constraint embodies the possibility that output itself is not fixed (in the short run), but can increase. That is the key distinction that allows for a potential effect of fiscal policy on aggregate demand.

Does that mean that an increase in government spending will lead to an increase in output? Not necessarily.

First, consumption will change as well. Note that the Euler equation that underpins the NKIS in (17.29) does not pin down the full consumption path: for that we must incorporate the intertemporal budget constraint. And we know that an increase in government spending must correspond to an increase in taxes at some point, and consumers will respond to that. In particular, in a Ricardian world, that response will be a one-for-one decrease in consumption if the increase is permanent, thereby negating the impact of government spending on aggregate demand. That a permanent increase in g has no effect on aggregate demand can be seen by noticing that a permanent increase in g will not change r_g^n in (17.30). That permanent changes in g have no effect may come as a surprise, given what it typically portrayed in intermediate texts, but on a simple inspection is obvious. Countries differ radically in the amount of government expenditures, but there is no relation between aggregate demand, recessions, or macroeconomic performance between them. Permanent changes in government spending just crowd out other components of aggregate demand.

More generally, the impact of government spending on aggregate demand is thus predicated on it *being temporary*, or on departures from Ricardian assumptions, as we have discussed.

On top of that, there is also a supply-side effect, via the behaviour of firms: the New Keynesian Phillips Curve (NKPC) will also be affected. You will recall that the NKPC looks like this:

$$\pi_t = \beta E_t \pi_{t+1} + \kappa \hat{y}_t. \tag{17.31}$$

A shock to government spending will also have a supply-side effect via an increase in the output gap, thus affecting inflation expectations, which will feed back into the NKIS. In short, the fiscal multiplier – that is, the change in output in response to a change in government spending – will depend on the specification and parameters of the model.

Finally, the NKIS makes it clear that this will depend on the response of monetary policy – and remember, the full specification of the canonical New Keynesian DSGE model requires the specification of a monetary policy rule. For instance, if monetary policy responds by increasing the nominal interest rate, it undoes the impact of fiscal expansion.

Summing up, our point is that to assess the role of fiscal policy it's important to keep in mind that people will react to policy, and will consider (to a smaller or greater extent) its dynamic effects. Part of a fiscal stimulus will end up being saved to face future taxes, and the extent to which they will crowd out other sources of demand will depend on how demand-constrained the economy is. It must also take into account its effects on the perceived sustainability of current fiscal policies, as well as the response of monetary policy. All of these are empirical debates that take place, at least to some extent, within the context of this framework we've discussed. Let's finish our discussion by considering what happens in practice.

17.4.1 | The current (empirical) debate: Fiscal stimulus and fiscal adjustment

With all of these different effects in mind, we can look at some of the evidence regarding the effectiveness of fiscal policy and, closely related, on the implications of the kind of fiscal adjustment that might be needed in the face of soaring debt ratios.

The question on the effectiveness of fiscal policy as a tool for aggregate demand management is often subsumed in the discussion on the size of the multiplier: if I increase government spending a given amount, by what multiple of this amount will it increase output? The undergraduate text provides an unambiguous answer to this question: it goes up. But our model has led us to think of a number of things that might affect that multiplier: whether the increase is permanent or temporary and how agents react to it, the context in which it takes place, and what it entails for the future path of spending. There is a wide range of beliefs about that in the policy debate – as illustrated by the many countries in which proponents of fiscal expansion or austerity are pitched against one another. In practice, it is very hard to isolate that impact since there can obviously be reverse causality, and there are always lots of other things, besides the change in fiscal policy, that are going on at the same time and can also affect output. In sum, we have a classic identification challenge.

There are two main approaches to overcome that challenge. First, some people (e.g. Blanchard and Perotti 2002 and Ilzetzki et al. 2013) use what is called a structural vector autoregression (SVAR) econometric technique, which basically relies on the assumption that it takes time for fiscal policy to respond to news about the state of the economy. It uses VAR (regressing a vector of variables on their lags, essentially) to tease out predictable responses of fiscal policy to output and vice-versa, and attributes any correlation between the unpredicted components to the impact of government spending on output. The problem, of course, is that what is unpredicted by the econometrician need not be so for the agents themselves, so we can never be sure we're estimating the true impact. The second approach is to use natural experiments where government spending increases due to some credibly exogenous factor. A popular example is wars and associated military buildups (e.g. Ramey and Shapiro 1999, Ramey 2009, Barro and Redlick 2011), and, on a similar note, a recent paper by Nakamura and Steinsson (2014) looks at the differential effect of military buildup shocks across U.S. regions. (Another example, from Shoag (2013), uses variation induced by changes in state pension fund returns.) The problem is that exercises rely on specific sources of spending that may not be typical. In other words, it's hard to assess the external validity of these natural experiments.

The variation in the estimates is enormous. In the natural experiment literature, they range from 0.5 to 1.5, from military buildups, and reach above 2 in other approaches. The SVAR literature has wildly divergent numbers across time and countries and specific structural assumptions, ranging from −2.3 to 3.7! One state-of-the-art attempt, Ilzetzki et al. (2013), who use better (quarterly) data for a number of countries, also reached nuanced conclusions: (i) Short-run multiplier is negative in developing countries; (ii) Multiplier is zero or negative when debt level is high; (iii) Multiplier is zero under flexible exchange rates, but positive under fixed exchange rates, and is higher in closed economies than in open economies. Note that (i) and (ii) are quite consistent with the effects we have been talking about: if people believe that higher spending is unsustainable, they would expect higher taxes in the near future, dampening the effect of the expansion. By the same token, (iii) is consistent with a simple Mundell-Fleming model, which we haven't talked about in the book, but which you may recall from undergraduate macro: under flexible exchange rates, more government spending leads to a currency appreciation, which leads to a reduction in net exports that undoes the fiscal stimulus. These results share the flavour with our previous discussion of Ricardian equivalence: when deficits and debt levels become large, consumer behaviour seems to more clearly undo the effects of fiscal policy.

Of course, in practice, policymakers have to act even with all this uncertainty. Here's an example, Table 17.1, shows the estimates generated by the non-partisan Congressional Budget Office (CBO) for the impact of the 2009 stimulus in the U.S. One can see patterns that are broadly in line with our discussion: (temporary) spending has a larger effect than tax cuts, tax cuts to people who are more likely to be credit-constrained have a larger effect. (Note that this short-term estimate keeps at a minimum the possible supply-side effects that might come from distortionary taxation. We will get to this in the next chapter.)

This discussion on the effectiveness of fiscal policy also colours the debate on the desirability and implications of fiscal adjustments aimed at putting the debt situation under control. As discussed in Alesina et al. (2019), the conventional wisdom that these adjustments would necessarily be contractionary is too simplistic. The inherent intertemporal nature of fiscal policy sees to that: maybe a fiscal contraction, by convincing people that a previously unsustainable debt trajectory is now sustainable, will "crowd in" private spending, as people anticipate lower taxes (or no tax hikes) in the future. It may also have the supply-side effects that will be the focus of our next chapter.

Alesina et al. evidence suggests, that in practice, many fiscal contractions have indeed been expansionary! It seems that this is particularly likely if the adjustment is about cutting spending rather than increasing taxes – perhaps because the former are deemed to be more sustainable in the long run. While there is controversy about the evidence – who would have thought? (see Ball et al. (2013) – particularly with respect to what is selected as an episode of major fiscal contraction), the point remains that the practice is more complex than what the simple undergraduate textbook view would have suggested.

17.5 | What have we learned?

The key lesson from this chapter is that evaluating the macroeconomic impact of fiscal policy requires considering its dynamic implications and the existence of budget constraints. The fact that economic agents understand that means that any change in fiscal policy will meet with a response from the private sector, which in turn immediately affects the impact of that change.

The first expression of this logic is the Ricardian equivalence result: it does not matter whether a certain path of spending is financed via debt or taxes, because in the end it all has to come from taxes at some point. As a result, changes in government spending create a counteracting adjustment in private spending, because of future taxes. The size of the adjustment depends on whether the change is permanent or temporary – in the later case, the adjustment by consumption is less than one-for-one, and aggregate demand moves accordingly.

Table 17.1 Estimating the multiplier for the 2009 U.S. fiscal stimulus

	Estimated Output Multipliers[a]		Major Provisions of ARRA	Total Budgetary Cost of Provisions, 2009–2019[b]
Type of Activity	Low Estimate	High Estimate		
Purchases of Goods and Services by the Federal Government	1.0	2.5	Division A, Title II: Other; Title IV: Energy Efficiency and Renewable Energy; Title IV: Innovative Technology Loan Guarantee Program; Title IV: Other Energy Programs; Title V: Federal Buildings Fund; Title VIII: National Institutes of Health; Title VIII: Other Department of Health and Human Services	$88 billion
Transfer Payments to State and Local Governments for Infrastructure	1.0	2.5	Division A, Title VII: Clean Water and Drinking Water State Revolving Funds; Title XI: Other Housing Assistance; Title XII: Highway Construction; Title XII: Other Transportation	$44 billion
Transfer Payments to State and Local Governments for Other Purposes	0.7	1.9	Division A, Title VIII: Education for the Disadvantaged; Title VIII: Special Education; Title IX: State Fiscal Stabilization Fund; Division B, Title V: State Fiscal Relief Fund	$215 billion
Transfer Payments to Individuals	0.8	2.2	Division A, Title I: Supplemental Nutrition Assistance Program; Title VIII: Student Financial Assistance; Division B, Title II: Unemployment Compensation; Title III: Health Insurance Assistance	$100 billion
One-Time Payments to Retirees	0.2	1.2	Division B, Title II: Economic Recovery Payments, Temporary Aid to Needy Families, and Child Support[c]	$18 billion
Two-Year Tax Cuts for Lower- and Middle-Income People	0.5	1.7	Division B, Title I: Refundable Tax Credits; Making Work Pay Credit;[d] American Opportunity Tax Credit[d]	$168 billion
One-Year Tax Cut for Higher-Income People	0.1	0.5	Increase in Individual AMT Exemption Amount[d]	$70 billion
Extension of First-Time Homebuyer Credit	0.2	1.0	Extension of First-Time Homebuyer Credit[d]	$7 billion

Still, we saw that fiscal policy can affect output in the short run, in a Keynesian world. But even in this case, understanding the impact of fiscal policy requires thinking about the private sector adjustments – driven by the shadow of the intertemporal budget constraints – as well as the response of monetary policy.

17.6 | What next?

If you are interested in learning more about the debate on the impact of fiscal policy, a great starting point is the book *Fiscal Policy After The Financial Crisis*, edited by Alesina and Giavazzi (2013). It contains a thorough overview of different perspectives in that debate.

17.7 | Appendix

17.7.1 | Debt sustainability

Let us now turn to some practical issues when analysing fiscal policy from a dynamic perspective. Our discussion in this chapter has talked about how fiscal policy has to fit into an intertemporal budget constraint. But that raises the question: how do we know, in practice, whether a certain fiscal trajectory fits into the intertemporal budget constraint? If it does not we say the debt level is unsustainable, and we must expect some sort of change. We deal with this issue first. We then turn to some problems related to measurement, which are particularly important given the inherently dynamic nature of fiscal policy.

17.7.2 | A simplified framework

An important issue in macroeconomic analysis is to figure out if the debt dynamics are sustainable. Strictly speaking, sustainability means satisfying the NPG condition: the present discounted value of debt in the long run has to be zero. This restriction is relatively imprecise as to short term debt dynamics. Debt can grow, and grow very fast, and still satisfy the NPG condition. There is an ample literature on this, but a very practical, though primitive, way of answering this question is by asking whether the debt-to-GDP ratio is increasing or not. According to this stark definition debt sustainability is achieved when the debt-to-GDP ratio is constant or declining over time.

With this in mind a typical debt sustainability analysis would start with the dynamic equation for debt:

$$D_t = \left(1 + r_t\right) D_{t-1} + \overbrace{\left(G_t - T_t\right)}^{\text{primary deficit}}. \tag{17.32}$$

(Note that this is the discrete-time equivalent of (17.1).) Divide this by GDP_t (we also multiply and divide the first term to the right of the equal sign by GDP_{t-1}) to obtain

$$\frac{D_t}{GDP_t} = \left(1 + r_t\right) \frac{D_{t-1}}{GDP_{t-1}} \frac{GDP_{t-1}}{GDP_t} + \left(\frac{G_t}{GDP_t} - \frac{T_t}{GDP_t}\right). \tag{17.33}$$

Denoting with lower cases the variables relative to GDP, the above becomes

$$d_t = \frac{(1 + r_t)}{(1 + \gamma)} d_{t-1} + \left(\underbrace{g_t - t_t}_{pd_t} \right) \tag{17.34}$$

or

$$d_t = \frac{(1 + r_t)}{(1 + \gamma)} d_{t-1} - \left(\underbrace{t_t - g_t}_{ps_t} \right),$$

where pd and ps stand for primary deficit and surplus (again, the difference between government expenditure and income, and vice versa, respectively, prior to interest payments), γ is the growth rate of GDP. Assume that we are in a steady state such that everything is constant. In this case

$$d = \frac{(1 + r)}{(1 + \gamma)} d - ps, \tag{17.35}$$

which can be solved for the primary surplus needed for debt to GDP ratios to be stable:

$$ps = d \left[\frac{(1 + r)}{(1 + \gamma)} - 1 \right] = d \left[\frac{1 + r - 1 - \gamma}{1 + \gamma} \right] = d \left[\frac{r - \gamma}{1 + \gamma} \right]. \tag{17.36}$$

Any surplus larger than that in (17.36) will also do. In order to make this equation workable, practitioners typically try to estimate expected growth in the medium term (growth has to be assessed in the same denomination of the debt, so if debt is, say, in U.S. dollars, you should use the growth rate of GDP in current U.S. dollars), the interest rate can be estimated from the average interest payments, and debt to GDP ratios are typically available. Table 17.2 makes this computation for a series of values of g and d given a specific r (in this table we use 7%).

The table shows the primary surplus required to stabilise the debt to GDP ratio. It can also be used to estimate restructuring scenarios. Imagine a country (Greece?) with a debt to GDP ratio of 150% and an expected growth rate of 2%. The table suggests it needs to run a budget surplus of 7.6% of GDP. If only a 2.5% surplus is feasible debt, sustainability obtains (at this interest rate) if debt is 50% of GDP. To obtain debt sustainability the country needs a haircut of 66%.

Recent models have emphasized the stochastic nature of fiscal revenues and expenditures. Simulating these processes, rather than estimating a single number, they compute a distribution function for fiscal results thus allowing to compute the value at risk in public debt.

17.8 | Measurement issues

The government budget constraint (17.5) involves the present values of the entire paths of purchases and revenues, and not the deficit at a point in time. As a result, conventional measures of either the primary or total deficit can be misleading about the real evolution of fiscal accounts. We illustrate this with three examples.

Table 17.2 Required primary surpluses

Public debt	GDP growth rate (%)					
to GDP (%)	1	2	3	4	5	6
35	2.1	1.7	1.4	1.0	0.7	0.3
40	2.4	2.0	1.6	1.2	0.8	0.4
45	2.7	2.2	1.7	1.3	0.9	0.4
50	3.0	2.5	1.9	1.4	1.0	0.5
55	3.3	2.7	2.1	1.6	1.0	0.5
60	3.6	2.9	2.3	1.7	1.1	0.6
65	3.9	3.2	2.5	1.9	1.2	0.6
70	4.2	3.4	2.7	2.0	1.3	0.7
75	4.5	3.7	2.9	2.2	1.4	0.7
80	4.8	3.9	3.1	2.3	1.5	0.8
85	5.0	4.2	3.3	2.5	1.6	0.8
90	5.3	4.4	3.5	2.6	1.7	0.8
95	5.6	4.7	3.7	2.7	1.8	0.9
100	5.9	4.9	3.9	2.9	1.9	0.9
110	6.5	5.4	4.3	3.2	2.1	1.0
120	7.1	5.9	4.7	3.5	2.3	1.1
130	7.7	6.4	5.0	3.8	2.5	1.2
140	8.3	6.9	5.4	4.0	2.7	1.3
150	8.9	7.4	5.8	4.3	2.9	1.4
160	9.5	7.8	6.2	4.6	3.0	1.5

17.8.1 | The role of inflation

The first example is the effect of inflation on the measured deficit. The change in nominal debt out-standing – that is, the conventionally measured budget deficit – equals the difference between nominal purchases and revenues, plus the nominal interest on the debt. If we let D denote the nominal debt, the nominal deficit is thus

$$\dot{D}_t = P_t\left(g_t - \tau_t\right) + i_t D_t, \qquad (17.37)$$

where P is the price level and i is the nominal interest rate. When inflation rises, the nominal interest rate rises for a given real rate. Thus, interest payments and the deficit increase. Yet the higher interest payments are just offsetting the fact that the higher inflation is eroding the value of debt. The behaviour of the real stock of debt, and thus the government's budget constraint is not affected.

To see this formally, we use the fact that, by definition, the nominal interest rate equals the real rate plus inflation. This allows us to rewrite our expression for the nominal deficit as

$$\dot{D}_t = P_t\left(g_t - \tau_t\right) + \left(r + \pi_t\right) D_t. \qquad (17.38)$$

Dividing through by P_t this yields

$$\frac{\dot{D}_t}{P_t} = g_t - \tau_t + \left(r + \pi_t\right)\frac{D_t}{P_t}. \qquad (17.39)$$

Next define real debt as

$$d_t = \frac{D_t}{P_t},$$

(17.40)

so that (17.39) becomes

$$\frac{\dot{D}_t}{P_t} = g_t - \tau_t + (r + \pi_t) d_t.$$

(17.41)

But recall next from (17.1) that

$$\dot{d}_t = g_t - \tau_t + rd_t.$$

(17.42)

Using this in (17.41) we finally have

$$\frac{\dot{D}_t}{P_t} = \dot{d}_t + \pi_t d_t.$$

(17.43)

Higher inflation raises the conventional (nominal) measure of the deficit even when it is deflated by the price level. This was Brazil's problem for many years.

17.8.2 | Asset sales

The second example is the sale of an asset. If the government sells an asset, it increases current revenue and thus reduces the current deficit. But it also forgoes the revenue the asset would have generated in the future. In the natural case where the value of the asset equals the present value of the revenue it will produce, the sale has no effect on the present value of the government's revenue. Thus, the sale affects the current deficit but does not affect the government's net worth. It follows that the effect of privatisation on the fiscal position of the government has to be analysed carefully, as it is not given by the bump in measured current revenue. If there is a positive impact it should be predicated on the idea that the present value of the revenues to the private sector is greater than what would be the case for the government (say, because the government runs it inefficiently), so that the buyer would be willing to pay more than the present value of the revenues the government would obtain from it. But this argument, not to speak of the computation, is seldom done.

17.8.3 | Contingent liabilities

The third example is a contingent liability. A contingent liability is a government commitment to incur expenses in the future that is made without provision for corresponding revenues. (Did anyone say Social Security?) In contrast to an asset sale, a contingent liability affects the budget constraint without affecting the current deficit. If the government sells an asset, the set of policies that satisfy the budget constraint is unchanged. If it incurs a contingent liability, on the other hand, satisfying the budget constraint requires higher future taxes or lower future purchases. In industrialised countries, the largest contingent or unfunded liabilities are entitlement programs, particularly social security and health insurance. These unfunded liabilities are typically larger than the conventionally measured stock of government debt; they are the main reason that fiscal policies in these countries do not appear to be on sustainable paths.

One way to compute these contingent liabilities is to do a debt decomposition exercise, decomposing the evolution of the debt-to-GDP ratio into its components: the primary deficit, economic growth, etc. The residual in this computation is the recognition of contingent liabilities over the years.

17.8.4 | The balance sheet approach

Another alternative to look into fiscal accounts is to work out the whole balance sheet of the government. This requires understanding that the main asset of the government is the NPV of its taxes, and that the main liability is not explicit debt, but the NPV of future wages and pensions. If so, the budget constraint can be written as

Assets	Liabilities
NPV of future taxes	Explicit debt
Liquid assets	NPV of future pensions and wages
Other assets	Contingent liabilities

This so-called balance sheet approach has been shown to qualify quite dramatically the role played by explicit liabilities in determining the vulnerability or currency exposure of governments. For example, for many countries that issue debt in foreign currency, it is believed that a real exchange rate depreciation compromises fiscal sustainability because it increases the real value of debt. However, this statement should consider what other liabilities it has in domestic currency (say, wages), and how a real depreciation may increase its tax base. If the government collects a sizable fraction of its income, say, from export taxes, then its net worth may actually increase with a devaluation. An example is provided in Figure 17.3, by looking at the histogram of the NPV of government and its reaction to a real depreciation for Argentina and Chile.

Argentina, for example, shows an improvement in the net worth of the government as a result of a devaluation, in contrast with the results from the literature that focuses on explicit debt.

Figure 17.3 Net worth: Argentina vs Chile, from Levy-Yeyati and Sturzenegger (2007)

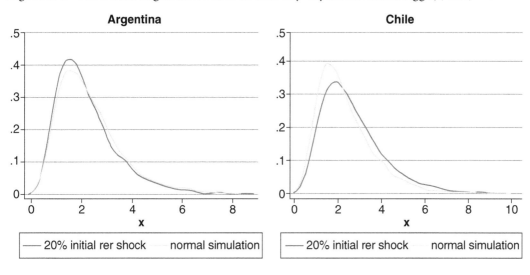

Notes

[1] Is it really that easy? Let $\bar{Y}$ be the steady state level of output, and, similarly, for C and G. Now subtract $\bar{Y}$ from both sides of the equation, and divide both sides by $\bar{Y}$. Recognising that $\bar{Y} = \bar{C} + \bar{G}$, this gives you $\frac{Y_t - \bar{Y}}{\bar{Y}} = \frac{C_t - \bar{C}}{\bar{Y}} + \frac{G_t - \bar{G}}{\bar{Y}}$. Now multiply and divide the first term on the RHS by $\bar{C}$, and the second term by $\bar{G}$, and you will get the result.

[2] Here's how that one goes: note from the resource constraint that $\hat{c}_t = \frac{1}{1-\gamma}\hat{y}_t - \frac{\gamma}{1-\gamma}\hat{g}_t$, and plug this into (17.29). Multiplying both sides by $(1-\gamma)$ yields $\hat{y}_t = E_t\hat{y}_{t+1} - \gamma\left(E_t\hat{g}_{t+1} - \hat{g}_t\right) - \sigma(1-\gamma)r_t$. Define $\Delta\hat{g}_{t+1} = \left(E_t\hat{g}_{t+1} - \hat{g}_t\right)$ and collect terms, and the result follows.

[3] Recall that, for notational simplicity, we are leaving aside the terms in the discount rate and the productivity shock that shifts the natural rate of output, which is implicit within the log deviation term.

References

Alesina, A., Favero, C., & Giavazzi, F. (2019). Effects of austerity: Expenditure-and tax-based approaches. *Journal of Economic Perspectives*, *33*(2), 141–62.

Alesina, A. & Giavazzi, F. (2013). *Fiscal policy after the financial crisis*. University of Chicago Press.

Ball, L., Furceri, D., Leigh, D., & Loungani, P. (2013). *The distributional effects of fiscal austerity* (tech. rep.) DESA Working Paper No. 129.

Barro, R. J. (1974). Are government bonds net wealth? *Journal of Political Economy*, *82*(6), 1095–1117.

Barro, R. J. & Redlick, C. J. (2011). Macroeconomic effects from government purchases and taxes. *The Quarterly Journal of Economics*, *126*(1), 51–102.

Blanchard, O. & Perotti, R. (2002). An empirical characterization of the dynamic effects of changes in government spending and taxes on output. *The Quarterly Journal of Economics*, *117*(4), 1329–1368.

Ilzetzki, E., Mendoza, E. G., & Végh, C. A. (2013). How big (small?) are fiscal multipliers? *Journal of Monetary Economics*, *60*(2), 239–254.

Levy-Yeyati, E. & Sturzenegger, F. (2007). A balance-sheet approach to fiscal sustainability. *CID Working Paper Series*.

Nakamura, E. & Steinsson, J. (2014). Fiscal stimulus in a monetary union: Evidence from U.S. regions. *American Economic Review*, *104*(3), 753–92.

Ramey, V. A. (2009). Defense news shocks, 1939–2008: Estimates based on news sources. *Unpublished paper, University of California, San Diego*.

Ramey, V. A. & Shapiro, M. D. (1999). *Costly capital reallocation and the effects of government spending*. National Bureau of Economic Research.

Shoag, D. (2013). Using state pension shocks to estimate fiscal multipliers since the Great Recession. *American Economic Review*, *103*(3), 121–24.

CHAPTER 18

Fiscal policy II: The long-run determinants of fiscal policy

In our previous chapter we learned that it may be quite misleading to think about fiscal policy without thinking about the budget constraint. Our overarching question was whether fiscal policy can actually affect aggregate demand, and the central message was that the existence of budget constraints limits substantially what fiscal policy can do in that domain. In particular, all fiscal policy interventions will have to be eventually paid for, and rational individuals will understand that and adjust their consumption in ways that might undo the effects of those interventions – completely or partially, depending on the nature of the latter. Fiscal policy is more constrained than our old IS-LM world had led us to believe.

This relatively muted effect on aggregate demand, led to skepticism with respect to the prospects of government spending as a tool for macroeconomic stabilisation, with monetary policy taking over as the go-to aggregate demand management tool. In fact, over the years, Central Bankers have taken a much more prominent role in managing stabilisation policies than fiscal policy. (The very low interest rates of recent times changed more than a few minds on this point, particularly because of the zero-rate lower bound issue. We will turn to that in due course.)

In any event, this leads us to think of fiscal policy as it relates to the needs for public good provision, the second angle we highlighted at the start of the last chapter. We can think of this as a long-run view: that of setting up a system aimed at providing these public goods (though keeping in mind that some of these may depend on the cycle, such as unemployment insurance). With this view in mind, how should the level of government spending and taxes move over time? How stable should they be?

In order to think that optimal long-run fiscal policy we will initially consider a government that faces an exogenous stream of government expenditures (public goods and entitlements, which may be shocked by natural disasters, wars, pandemics, etc.) How should it finance them? What should the path of taxes and borrowing be?

As it turns out, with non-distortionary taxation, long-lived individuals, and perfect capital markets, we know that this choice is inconsequential: it's the world of Ricardian equivalence! But assume now that taxes are in fact distortionary, so that a high tax rate is costly – for instance, because it reduces incentives to work and/or to invest. What should the government do? After analysing this problem,

How to cite this book chapter:
Campante, F., Sturzenegger, F. and Velasco, A. 2021. *Advanced Macroeconomics: An Easy Guide.*
    Ch. 18. 'Fiscal policy II: The long-run determinants of fiscal policy', pp. 279–294. London: LSE Press.
    DOI: https://doi.org/10.31389/lsepress.ame.r   License: CC-BY-NC 4.0.

we will discuss the decision of how government spending itself may react to shocks. If income falls, should government expenditure remain the same?

We then go over the question of whether fiscal policy, in practice, behaves in the way that theory would prescribe. The answer is that, of course, there are significant departures, because policy makers are often not behaving in the way our simple theory suggests – in particular, they are not benevolent planners, but rather part of an often messy political process. We need to get into the political economy of fiscal policy to think through these issues.

Finally, we briefly address the issue of what type of taxes should be raised to finance government expenditure, in particular whether it makes sense to finance expenditures with taxes on labor or taxes on capital. While this is a topic that overlaps with issues discussed in the field of public finance, it delivers a remarkable result with implications for capital accumulation, and therefore for the macroeconomics discussion.

But let's start at the beginning by looking at the optimal path for aggregate taxes.

18.1 | Tax smoothing

We establish the tax smoothing principle, that suggests a countercyclical pattern for fiscal policy: one should run deficits when spending needs are higher than normal, and surpluses when they are below normal. By the same token, temporary expenditures should be financed by deficits.

Let g_t and τ_t denote the government's real purchases and tax revenues at time t, and d_0 is the initial real debt outstanding. The budget deficit is

$$\dot{d}_t = \left(g_t - \tau_t\right) + rd_t, \tag{18.1}$$

where r is the real interest rate.

The government is also constrained by the standard solvency condition:

$$\lim_{T\to\infty}\left(d_T e^{-rT}\right) \leq 0, \tag{18.2}$$

In the limit the present value of its debt cannot be positive.

18.1.1 | The government objective function

The government wants to minimise tax distortions:

$$L = \int_0^\infty y_t \ell\left(\frac{\tau_t}{y_t}\right) e^{-rt} dt, \tag{18.3}$$

where $\ell(0) = 0$, $\ell(.)' > 0$ and $\ell''(.) > 0$. This function is a shorthand to capture the fact that taxes usually distort investment and labour-supply decisions, such that the economy (the private sector) suffers a loss, which is higher the higher is the ratio of tax revenues to income. Notice that we can think of the ratio $\frac{\tau_t}{y_t}$ as the tax rate. The loss function is also convex: the cost increases at an increasing rate as the tax rate $\frac{\tau_t}{y_t}$ rises. Notice also that these are pecuniary losses, which the government discounts at the rate of interest.

18.1.2 | Solving the government's problem

Assume that the government controls tax revenue τ_t (which becomes the control variable) while government spending g_t is given. The Hamiltonian for the problem is

$$H = y_t \ell \left(\frac{\tau_t}{y_t} \right) + \lambda_t \left(g_t - \tau_t + r d_t \right),$$ (18.4)

where debt d_t is the state variable and λ_t the costate. The FOCs are

$$\ell' \left(\frac{\tau_t}{y_t} \right) = \lambda_t,$$ (18.5)

$$\dot{\lambda}_t = \lambda_t \left(r - r \right) = 0,$$ (18.6)

$$\lim_{T \to \infty} \left(\lambda_T d_T e^{-rT} \right) = 0.$$ (18.7)

18.1.3 | The time profile of tax distortions

The combination of (18.5) and (18.6) implies that tax revenue as a share of output should be constant along a perfect foresight path:

$$\ell' \left(\frac{\tau_t}{y_t} \right) = \lambda \text{ for all } t \geq 0.$$ (18.8)

We call this tax smoothing. The intuition is the same as in consumption smoothing. With the rate of interest equal to the rate at which loss is discounted, there is no incentive to have losses be higher in one moment than in another. The intuition is that, because the marginal distortion cost per unit of revenue raised is increasing in the tax rate (the ratio $\frac{\tau_t}{y_t}$), a smooth tax rate minimises distortion costs.

Denote the implicit tax rate by

$$\phi_t = \frac{\tau_t}{y_t}.$$ (18.9)

Expression (18.8) says that along a perfect foresight path, the tax rate should be constant:

$$\phi_t = \frac{\tau_t}{y_t} = \phi \text{ for all } t.$$ (18.10)

This is known as the "tax smoothing" principle, and is the key result of the paper by Barro (1979).[1]

Notice also that, if λ is constant and non-zero, the TVC (18.7) implies that

$$\lim_{T \to \infty} \left(d_T e^{-rT} \right) = 0.$$ (18.11)

That is, the solvency condition will hold with equality. Since the shadow value of debt is always positive, the government will choose to leave behind as much debt as possible (in present value) – that is to say, zero.

18.1.4 | The level of tax distortions

Solving (18.1) forward starting from some time 0 yields

$$d_T e^{-rT} = d_0 + \int_0^T (g_t - \tau_t)\, e^{-rt} dt. \tag{18.12}$$

Next, apply to this last equation the transversality/solvency condition (18.11) to get

$$\lim_{T \to \infty} \left(d_T e^{-rT} \right) = d_0 + \int_0^\infty (g_t - \tau_t)\, e^{-rt} dt = 0. \tag{18.13}$$

Rearranging, this becomes

$$\int_0^\infty \tau_t e^{-rt} dt = d_0 + \int_0^\infty g_t e^{-rt} dt. \tag{18.14}$$

But, given (18.10), this can be rewritten as

$$\phi \int_0^\infty y_t e^{-rt} dt = d_0 + \int_0^\infty g_t e^{-rt} dt, \tag{18.15}$$

or

$$\phi = \frac{d_0 + \int_0^\infty g_t e^{-rt} dt}{\int_0^\infty y_t e^{-rt} dt}. \tag{18.16}$$

That is to say, the optimal flat tax rate equals the ratio of the present value of the revenue the government must raise to the present value of output.

18.1.5 | The steady state

Imagine that initially both output and expenditures are expected to remain constant, at levels $g_t = g^L$ and $y_t = y$. Then, (18.16) implies

$$\tau = \phi y = r d_0 + g^L, \tag{18.17}$$

so that the chosen tax revenue is equal to the permanent expenditures of government. Using this result in budget constraint (18.1) we have

$$\dot{d}_t = r d_t + g^L - \tau_t = r d_t + g^L - r d_0 - g^L = r \left(d_t - d_0 \right). \tag{18.18}$$

Evaluating this expression at time 0 we obtain

$$\dot{d}_0 = r \left(d_0 - d_0 \right) = 0. \tag{18.19}$$

Hence, the stock of debt is constant as well.

18.1.6 | Changes in government expenditures

Suppose now that at time 0 there is an unanticipated and permanent increase in spending from g^L to g^H. From (18.17) it follows that tax revenue adjusts instantaneously to its new (and higher) value:

$$\tau' = \phi' y = rd_0 + g^H, \qquad t \geq 0. \tag{18.20}$$

The adjustment takes place via an increase in the tax rate ϕ, to a higher level ϕ'. Since revenues increases one-to-one with government spending, fiscal deficit does not change. Hence, an unanticipated and permanent increase in spending has no impact on the deficit nor on government debt.

How about temporary shocks? Suppose that the economy is in the initial steady-state described above, with revenue given by (18.17). At time 0, there is an unanticipated and *temporary increase* in spending:

$$g_t = \begin{cases} g^H, & 0 \leq t < T \\ g^L, & t \geq T, \end{cases} \tag{18.21}$$

for some $T > 0$.

First compute the revenue path. Expression (18.16) becomes

$$\phi = \frac{rd_0 + r\int_0^\infty g_t e^{-rt} dt}{y}. \tag{18.22}$$

Combining (18.21) and (18.22) we have that revenue rises immediately to the level given by:

$$\tau'' = \phi'' y = rd_0 + g^H \left(1 - e^{-rT}\right) + g^L e^{-rT}, \qquad t \geq 0. \tag{18.23}$$

where $\phi'' > \phi$ is now the new and constant tax rate.

Note that, quite naturally, the increase in the tax rate is lower under the temporary increase in spending than under the permanent increase:

$$\phi' - \phi'' = \frac{\left(g^H - g^L\right) e^{-rT}}{y} > 0. \tag{18.24}$$

Next, compute the path for the fiscal deficit. Plugging (18.23) into (18.1) we have

$$\dot{d}_t = r\left(d_t - d_0\right) + \left(g^H - g^L\right) e^{-rT}, \qquad 0 \leq t < T. \tag{18.25}$$

Notice that at time $t = 0$ this implies

$$\dot{d}_0 = \left(g^H - g^L\right) e^{-rT} > 0. \tag{18.26}$$

There is a fiscal deficit ($\dot{d}_0 > 0$) from the start. From (18.25), this means that $d_t > d_0$ for all times between 0 and T. The fiscal deficit worsens over time and then jumps back to zero at time T. Figure 18.1 shows the evolution of the deficit and government debt in response to this temporary spending shock.

How do we know that the fiscal deficit goes to 0 at time T? Recall from (18.12) that

$$d_T e^{-rT} = d_0 + \left(1 - e^{-rT}\right) \left(\frac{g^H - \tau''}{r}\right). \tag{18.27}$$

Plugging (18.23) into this expression we have

$$rd_T = rd_0 + \left(1 - e^{-rT}\right) \left(g^H - g^L\right). \tag{18.28}$$

Figure 18.1 Response to an increase in government spending

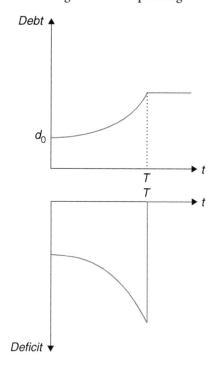

Evaluating (18.1) at time T we have

$$\dot{d}_T = r d_T + g^L - \tau''. \tag{18.29}$$

Finally, using (18.23) and (18.28) in (18.29) we obtain

$$\begin{aligned}
\dot{d}_T &= r d_0 + \left(1 - e^{-rT}\right)\left(g^H - g^L\right) + g^L \\
&\quad - r d_0 - g^H \left(1 - e^{-rT}\right) - g^L e^{-rT} \\
&= 0.
\end{aligned} \tag{18.30}$$

Hence, debt is constant at time T and thereafter.

18.1.7 | Countercyclical fiscal policy

The pattern we have just established gives us a standard framework for thinking about how fiscal policy should respond to fluctuations: you should run deficits when expenditure needs are unusually high, and compensate with surpluses when they are relatively low. In short, the logic of tax smoothing provides a justification for running a *countercyclical* fiscal policy, based on long-run intertemporal optimisation.

This basic principle can be even stronger under plausible alternative assumptions, relative to what we have imposed so far. Consider, for instance, the case of a loss function for the deadweight loss of taxes that depends uniquely on the tax rate (i.e. eliminating the factor y_t that multiplies $\ell(\cdot)$ in (18.3) above). Then it is easy to see that the FOC is

$$\ell'\left(\frac{\tau_t}{y_t}\right)\frac{1}{y_t} = \lambda, \tag{18.31}$$

which means that the tax rate should be higher in booms and lower in recessions. The same happens if, plausibly, distortions are higher in recessions.[2] Or if government expenditure has a higher value in recessions than in booms – say, because of unemployment insurance. All of these changes further strengthen the countercyclical nature of fiscal policy.

18.1.8 | Smoothing government spending

The opposite happens if there is a desire to smooth government spending over time. Consider, for example, a case where tax revenues are now exogenous, though maybe hit by exogenous shocks. This may capture important cases, such as those in which economies are heavily reliant on the proceeds from natural resources, on whose prices they may not have much influence.[3] How should such an economy plan its spending profile?

To discuss this question imagine the case of a country where the government maximises

$$\int_0^\infty \left(\frac{\sigma}{1-\sigma}\right) g_t^{\frac{\sigma-1}{\sigma}} e^{-\rho t} dt, \tag{18.32}$$

subject to the budget constraint:

$$\dot{b}_t = rb_t + \tau_t + \epsilon_t - g_t, \tag{18.33}$$

where b stands for government assets, plus the NPG condition that we omit for brevity. Notice that this is identical to our standard consumption optimisation in an open economy, and, therefore, we know that the government has a desire to smooth government expenditures over time. We assume, though, that the shock to income ϵ_t follows:

$$\epsilon_t = \epsilon_0 e^{-\delta t}. \tag{18.34}$$

This embeds a full range of cases – for instance, if $\delta \to \infty$ then we have a purely transitory shock, but if $\delta \to 0$, the shock would be permanent.

Assuming, for simplicity, as we've done before, that $\rho = r$, the FOC for this problem is $\dot{g} = 0$: it is now government spending that should remain constant over time. This means that

$$g = r\left[b_0 + \frac{\tau}{r} + \frac{\epsilon_0}{r+\delta}\right]. \tag{18.35}$$

Notice that the final two terms give the present discounted value of taxes and of the income shock. Using (18.33) in (18.35) (and allowing $b_0 = 0$):

$$\dot{b}_t = \frac{\delta}{r+\delta}\epsilon_t. \tag{18.36}$$

Notice that if the shock is permanent ($\delta = 0$), the change in debt is zero, and government spending adjusts immediately to its new level. If shocks are transitory and positive then the government accumulates assets along the converging path. What is the implication of this result? That if the government wants to smooth its consumption, it will actually decrease its expenditures when hit by a negative shock. How persistent the shock is determines the impact on government expenditures. In other words, the desire to smooth this response somewhat weakens the countercyclical results we have discussed above.

18.1.9 | Summing up

If taxation is distortionary, then a government should endeavor to smooth the path of taxes as much as possible. That means that taxes respond fully to permanent changes in government expenditure, but only partially to transitory changes. The government borrows in bad times (when its expenditure is unusually high) and repays in good times (when its expenditure is unusually low).

If you think about it, this is exactly the same logic of consumption-smoothing, for the exact same reasons. But it has very important policy consequences: any extraordinary expenditure – e.g. a war, or a big infrastructure project – should be financed with debt, and not with taxes. The path followed by debt, however, ought to satisfy the solvency constraint; in other words, it must be sustainable.

This implies a *countercyclical* pattern for fiscal policy: you should run deficits when expenditure needs are unusually high, and compensate with surpluses when they are relatively low. This may interact with the business cycle as well: to the extent that spending needs go up in cyclical downturns (e.g. because of unemployment insurance payments), and the revenue base goes up when income goes up, the tax smoothing principle will suggest that deficits increase during recessions, and decrease when times are good. It doesn't make sense to increase tax rates to deal with higher unemployment insurance needs.

Yet this is different from using fiscal policy as an aggregate demand management tool, which is often the sense in which one may hear the term countercyclical fiscal policy being deployed. That said, there is a clear complementarity between the two angles: running the optimal fiscal policy, from a tax smoothing perspective, will also operate in the right direction when needed for aggregate demand management purposes, to the extent that it has an effect on aggregate demand, as per the previous chapter.

18.2 | Other determinants of fiscal policy

We discuss how political considerations may explain why, in practice, we see departures from the tax smoothing prescriptions. We also talk about how rules and institutions might address that.

While tax smoothing is a good starting point to understand and plan fiscal policy, tax smoothing can't explain many of the observed movements in fiscal policy. What are we missing? Alesina and Passalacqua (2016) provide a comprehensive literature review that you should read to understand the political subtleties of how fiscal policy gets determined in practice. They start by acknowledging that Barro's tax smoothing theory works very well when it comes to explaining U.S. and UK's last 200 years of debt dynamics. For these two countries, we see, generally speaking, debt increase during wars and then decline in the aftermath.[4]

More generally, tax smoothing is less descriptively useful when thinking about the short term. First of all, the prescriptions of tax smoothing depend strongly on expectations. When is an increase in spending temporary, thereby requiring smoothing? For a practitioner, it becomes an informed guess at best. Beyond that, however, there are many fiscal episodes that cannot be reconciled with tax smoothing: burgeoning debt-to-GDP ratios, protracted delays in fiscal adjustments, differences in how countries respond to the same shocks, etc.

Such episodes require a political economy story – namely, the realisation that policy makers in practice are not benevolent social planners.[5] The literature has come up with a menu of alternative possibilities.

18.2.1 | The political economy approach

The first one is called *fiscal illusion* which basically claims that people don't understand the budget constraint. Voters overestimate the benefits of current expenditure and underestimate the future tax burden. Opportunistic politicians (you?) may take advantage of this. If so, there is a bias towards deficits. A derivation of this theory is the so-called political business cycle literature, which looks at the timing of spending around elections. Even with rational voters, we can still have cycles related to the different preferences of politicians from different parties or ideological backgrounds. There is evidence of electoral budget cycles across countries, but that evidence suggests that they are associated with uninformed voters, and, hence, that they tend to disappear as a democracy consolidates or as transparency increases. The main conclusion is that these factors may explain relatively small and short-lived departures from optimal fiscal policy, but not large and long-lasting excessive debt accumulation.

Another issue has to do with *intergenerational redistribution.* The idea is that debt redistributes income across generations. Obviously, if there is Ricardian equivalence (for example, because through bequests there are intertemporal links into the infinite future), this is inconsequential. But there are models where this can easily not be the case. For example, imagine a society with poor and rich people. The rich leave positive bequests, but the poor would like to have negative bequests. Because this is not possible, running budget deficits is a way of borrowing on future generations. In this case, the poor vote or push for expansionary fiscal policies. This effect will be stronger the more polarised society is, where the median voter has a lower income relative to average income.

The distributional conflicts may not be across time but actually at the same time. This gives rise to the theory of deficits as the result of distributive conflicts. Alesina and Drazen (1991) kicked off the literature with their model on deficits and *wars of attrition.* The idea is that whichever group gives in (throws the towel) will pay a higher burden of stabilisation costs. Groups then wait it out, trying to signal their toughness in the hope the other groups will give in sooner. Notice that appointing extremists to fight for particular interest groups can be convenient, though this increases the polarisation of the political system. In this setup, a crisis triggers a stabilisation and fiscal adjustment by increasing the costs of waiting. Drazen and Grilli (1993) show the surprising result that, in fact, a crisis can be welfare enhancing! Laban and Sturzenegger (1994) argue that delays occur because adjustment generates uncertainty, and therefore, there is value in waiting, even if delaying entails costs. Imagine a sick person who fears the risk of an operation to cure his ailment. Under a broad range of parameters, he may choose to wait in the certain state of poor health and put off the chances of an unsuccessful operation. This literature has opened the room to analyse other issues. Signalling, for example, is an important issue. Cukierman and Tommasi (1998) explain that it takes a Nixon to go to China: political preferences opposite to the policies implemented convey more credibly the message of the need for reform (Sharon or Rabin, Lula, etc. are all examples of this phenomenon).

Yet another story related to conflicting preferences about fiscal policy refers to *debt as a commitment,* or *strategic debt.* (See Persson and Svensson (1989) and Alesina and Tabellini (1990)). The idea is that a government who disagrees with the spending priorities of a possible successor chooses to overburden it with debt so it restricts its spending alternatives. Then, the more polarised a society, the higher its debt levels. If the disagreement is on the size of government, the low spender will reduce taxes and increase debt. (Does this ring any bells?)

Another version has to do with externalities associated with the provision of local public goods, a version of what is called the tragedy of commons. Battaglini and Coate (2008) consider a story where a legislature decides on public good provision, but with two kinds of public goods: one that benefits all citizens equally, and another that is local (i.e. benefits only those who live in the locality where it is provided). If decisions are made by a legislature where members are elected in local districts, an externality arises: a member's constituents get all the benefits of the bridge their representative got built, but everyone in the country shares in the cost. They show that, in this case, debt will be above the efficient level, and tax rates will be too volatile.

Departures from optimal fiscal policy can also be due to rent-seeking. Acemoglu et al. (2011) or Yared (2010) consider scenarios where there is an agency problem between citizens and self-interested politicians, and the latter can use their informational advantage to extract rents. The tension between the need to provide these incentives to politicians (pushing to higher revenue and lower spending on public goods), on the one hand, and the needs of citizens (lower taxes and higher spending) on the other – and how they fluctuate in response to shocks – can lead to volatility in taxes and over-accumulation of debt.

Finally, an interesting failure of the tax smoothing prediction that is widespread in developing countries is the issue of procyclical fiscal policy. As we have noted, the intuition suggests that fiscal policy should be countercyclical, saving in good times to smooth out spending in bad times. However, Gavin and Perotti (1997) noted that Latin American governments, in particular, have historically tended to do the exact opposite, and the evidence was later extended to show that most developing countries do the same. One explanation is that these countries are credit-constrained: when times are bad, they lose all access to credit, and this prevents them from smoothing. This explanation again begs the question of why these governments don't save enough so that they eventually don't need to resort to capital markets for smoothing. Another explanation, proposed by Alesina et al. (2008), builds on a political economy story: in countries with weak institutions and corruption, voters will rationally want the government to spend during booms, because any savings would likely be stolen away. This predicts that the procyclical behaviour will be more prevalent in democracies, where voters exert greater influence over policy, a prediction that seems to hold in the data.

18.2.2 | Fiscal rules and institutions

Since there are so many reasons why politicians may choose to depart from optimal fiscal policy prescriptions – and impose costs on society as a result – it is natural to ask whether it might be possible to constrain their behaviour in the direction of optimal policy.

One type of approach in that direction is the adoption of specific rules – the most typical example of which is in the form of balanced-budget requirements. These impose an obvious cost in terms of flexibility: you do want to run deficits and surpluses, as a matter of optimal fiscal policy! The question is whether the political distortions are so large that this may be preferable. One key insight from the literature on such rules is that the costs of adopting them tend to arise in the short run, while the benefits accrue in the longer term. This in itself raises interesting questions about their political sustainability.

You could imagine a variety of rules and institutions, among different dimensions: do you want to decentralise your fiscal decisions? If so, how do you deal with tax sharing? Do you want to delegate decisions to technocrats? Does it all make a difference? The general conclusions is that, even taking into account the endogeneity of institutional arrangements, institutions matter to some extent. Yet there is room for skepticism. After all, many countries have passed balanced-budget rules and yet have never mastered fiscal balance. Chile, on the other hand, had no law, but run a structural, full employment,

1% surplus for many years to compensate for its depletion of copper reserves. In the end, the policy question of how you build credibility is still there: is it by passing a law that promises you will behave, or simply by behaving?

All in all, we can safely conclude that fiscal policy is heavily affected by political factors, which is another reason why the reach of the fiscal instrument as a tool for macroeconomic policy may be blunted in most circumstances. This is particularly so in developing countries, which tend to be more politically (and credit) constrained. As a result, our hunch is that you want transparent, simple, stable (yet *flexible*), predictable rules for governing fiscal policy. Your success will hinge on convincing societies to stick to these simple rules!

18.3 | Optimal taxation of capital in the NGM

We end with a public finance detour: what should be the optimal way of taxing capital in the context of the NGM? We show that even a planner who cares only about workers may choose to tax capital very little. The optimal tax on capital can grow over time, or converge to zero, depending on the elasticity of intertemporal substitution.

Let's end our discussion of fiscal policy with an application of the NGM. Our exercise will have more the flavour of public finance (what kinds of taxes should we use to fund a given path of government expenditure) rather than the macroeconomic perspective we have focused on so far. We develop it here to show the wealth of questions the framework we have put so much effort to develop throughout the book can help us understand. It will also allow us to present an additional methodological tool: how to solve for an optimal taxation rule.

Imagine that you need to finance a certain amount of public spending within the framework of the NGM. What would be the optimal mix of taxes? Should the central planner tax labour income, or should it tax capital? The key intuition to solving these problems is that the tax will affect behaviour, so the planner has to include this response in his planning problem. For example, if a tax on capital is imposed, you know it will affect the Euler equation for the choice of consumption, so the planner needs to *add* this modified Euler equation as an additional constraint in the problem. Adding this equation will allow the planner to internalise the response of agents to taxes, which needs to be done when computing the optimal level of taxation.

To make things more interesting, let's imagine the following setup which follows Judd (1985) and Straub and Werning (2020). There are two types of agents in the economy: capitalists that own capital, earn a return from it, and consume C_t; and workers that only have as income their labour, which they consume (c_t).[6] We will assume the central planner cares only about workers (it is a revolutionary government!), which is a simplification for exposition. However, we will see that even in this lopsided case some interesting things can happen, including having paths where, asymptotically, workers decide not to tax capitalists!

So let's get to work. The planner's problem (in discrete time) would be to maximise

$$\sum_{t=0}^{\infty} \left(\frac{1}{1+\rho} \right)^t u\left(c_t\right),$$

(18.37)

subject to

$$u'(C_t) = \frac{(1 + r_{t+1})}{1 + \rho}(1 - \tau_{t+1})u'(C_{t+1}),$$ (18.38)

$$C_t + b_{t+1} = (1 - \tau_t)(1 + r_t)b_t,$$ (18.39)

$$c_t = w_t + T_t,$$ (18.40)

$$C_t + c_t + k_{t+1} = f(k_t) + (1 - \delta)k_t,$$ (18.41)

$$k_t = b_t.$$ (18.42)

The first equation (18.38) is the Euler condition for capitalists. As we said above, this equation needs to hold and, therefore, has to be considered by the planner as a constraint. The following two equations (18.39) and (18.40) define the budget constraint of capitalists and workers. Capitalist earn income from their capital, though this may be taxed at rate τ. Workers are just hand-to-mouth consumers: they eat all their income. They receive, however, all the proceeds of the capital tax $T_t = \tau_t k_t$. Equation (18.41) is the resource constraint of the economy where we assume capital depreciates at rate δ. Finally equation (18.42) states that in equilibrium the assets of the capitalists is just the capital stock. We have omitted the transversality conditions and the fact that wages and interest rates are their marginal products – all conditions that are quite familiar by now.

Before proceeding you may think that, if the planner cares about workers, and not at all about capitalists, the solution to this problem is trivial: just expropriate the capital and give it to workers. This intuition is actually correct, but the problem becomes relatively uninteresting.[7] To rule that out, we will add the extra assumption that workers would not know what to do with capital. You actually have to live with the capitalists so they can run the capital.

Something else you may notice is that we have not allowed for labour taxation. Labour taxation creates no distortion here, but would be neutral for workers (what you tax is what you return to them), so the interesting question is what is the optimal tax on capital.

Typically, you would just set out your Bellman equation (or Hamiltonian, if we were in continuous time) to solve this problem, simply imposing the Euler equation of capitalists as an additional constraint. However, if their utility is log, the solution is simpler because we already know what the optimal consumption of capitalists is going to be: their problem is identical to the consumption problem we solved in Chapter 12! You may recall that the solution was that consumption was a constant share of assets $C_t = \frac{\rho}{(1+\rho)}(1 + r_t)b_t = (1 - s)(1 + r_t)b_t$, where the second equality defines s. Capitalists consume what they don't save. In our case, this simplifies the problem quite a bit. We can substitute for the capitalists' consumption in the resource constraint, knowing that this captures the response function of this group to the taxes.[8] Using the fact that

$$C_t = (1 - s)(1 - \tau_t)(1 + r_t)b_t,$$ (18.43)

and that

$$b_{t+1} = s(1 - \tau_t)(1 + r_t)b_t,$$ (18.44)

it is easy to show (using the fact that $b_t = k_t$) that

$$C_t = \frac{(1 - s)}{s}k_{t+1}.$$ (18.45)

We can replace this in the resource constraint to get

$$\frac{k_{t+1}}{s} + c_t = f(k_t) + (1 - \delta)k_t.$$ (18.46)

Notice that this is equivalent to the standard growth model except that the cost of capital is now increased by $\frac{1}{s}$. Capital has to be intermediated by capitalists, who consume part of the return, thus making accumulation more expensive from the perspective of the working class.

Solving (18.37) subject to (18.46) entails the first order condition

$$u'(c_t) = \frac{s}{1+\rho} u'(c_{t+1})(f'(k_t) + 1 - \delta). \tag{18.47}$$

In steady state, this equation determines the optimal capital stock:

$$1 = \frac{s}{1+\rho}(f'(k^*) + 1 - \delta) = s\frac{1}{1+\rho}R^*, \tag{18.48}$$

where R^* is the interest rate before taxes. Notice that in steady state we must also have that the savings are sufficient to keep the capital stock constant,

$$sRk = k, \tag{18.49}$$

where R is the after-tax return for capitalists. Using (18.48) and (18.49), it is easy to see that

$$\frac{R}{R^*} = \frac{1}{1+\rho} = (1-\tau), \tag{18.50}$$

or simply that $\tau = \frac{\rho}{1+\rho}$.

In short: the solution is a constant tax on capital, benchmarked by the discount rate. In particular, the less workers (or the planner) discount the future, the smaller the tax: keeping the incentives for capitalists to accumulate pays of in the future and therefore is more valuable the less workers discount future payoffs. In the limit, with very patient workers/planner, the tax on capital approaches zero, and this happens even though the planner does not care about the welfare of capitalists! This is a powerful result.

Yet, this result relies heavily on the log utility framework. In fact, Straub and Werning (2020) solve for other cases, and show that things can be quite different. As you may have suspected by now, this is all about income versus substitution effects. Consider a more general version of the utility function of capitalists: $U(C_t) = \frac{C_t^{1-\sigma}}{(1-\sigma)}$. If $\sigma > 1$, the elasticity of intertemporal substitution is low, and income effects dominate. If $\sigma < 1$, in contrast, substitution effects dominate. Does the optimal tax policy change? It does – in fact, Straub and Werning show that, in the first case, optimal taxes on capital grow over time! In the second case, on the other hand, they converge to zero.

The intuition is pretty straightforward: workers want capitalists to save more since, the larger the capital stock, the larger the tax they collect from it. If taxes are expected to increase, and income effects prevail, capitalists will save more in expectation of the tax hike, which makes it optimal from the perspective of the workers to increase taxes over time. The opposite occurs when substitution effects prevail. As we can see, even this simple specification provides interesting and complex implications for fiscal policy.

18.4 | What have we learned?

We have seen that, from the standpoint of financing a given path of government spending with a minimum of tax distortions, there is a basic principle for optimal fiscal policy: tax smoothing. Optimal fiscal policy will keep tax rates constant, and finance temporarily high expenditures via deficits, while running surpluses when spending is relatively low. This countercyclical fiscal policy arises not because of aggregate demand management, but from a principle akin to consumption smoothing. Because high taxes entail severe distortions, you don't want to have to raise them too high when spending needs arise. Instead, you want to tax at the level you need to finance the permanent level of expenditures, and use deficits and surpluses to absorb the fluctuations.

As it turns out, in practice there are many important deviations from this optimal principle – more often than not in the direction of over-accumulation of debt. We thus went over a number of possible political economy explanations for why these deviations may arise. We can safely conclude that fiscal policy is heavily affected by political factors, which gives rise to the question of whether rules and institutions can be devised to counteract the distortions.

Finally, we briefly went over the public finance question of optimal taxation of capital in the context of the NGM model. We obtained some surprising results – a social planner concerned only with workers may still refrain from taxing capital to induce more capital accumulation, which pays off in the long run. Yet, these results are very sensitive to the specification of preferences, particularly in the elasticity of intertemporal substitution, further illustrating the power of our modelling tools in illuminating policy choices.

18.5 | What next?

The survey by Alesina and Passalacqua (2016) is a great starting point for the literature on the determinants of fiscal policy.

Notes

[1] In a model with uncertainty the equivalent to equation (18.10) would be $\phi_t = E(\phi_{t+1})$, that is, that the tax rates follow a random walk.

[2] A good application of this is to think about the optimal response to the Covid-19 pandemic of 2020. In a forced recession, taxes became almost impossible to pay, in some cases leading to bankruptcies and thus promoting policies of tax breaks during the outbreak.

[3] Take the case of Guyana, which one day found oil and saw its revenues grow by 50% in one year – this actually happened in 2020.

[4] Even in these countries, however, there are anomalies, such as the U.S. accumulating debt over the relatively peaceful 1980s – more on this later...

[5] In fact, the need for a political economy story strikes even deeper. Suppose we had a truly benevolent and farsighted government, what should it do in the face of distortionary taxation? Well, Aiyagari et al. (2002) have the answer: it should accumulate assets gradually, so that, eventually, it would have such a huge pile of bonds that it could finance any level of spending just with the interest it earned from them – no need for any distortionary taxes! In that sense, even the tax smoothing logic ultimately hinges on there being some (binding) upper bound on the level of assets that can be held by the government, often referred to as an ad hoc asset limit.

[6] The problem for capitalists is to maximise $\sum_{t=0}^{\infty} \left(\frac{1}{1+\rho}\right)^t u\left(C_t\right)$, subject to $C_t + b_{t+1} = (1 + r_t)b_t$. Notice that this problem is virtually identical, but not exactly the same, to the consumer problem we solved in Chapter 12. The difference is a timing convention. Before savings at time t did not generate interest income in period t, here they do. Thus what before was b_t will now become $b_t(1 + r_t)$.

[7] Though in the real world this option sometimes is implemented. Can you think of reasons why we don't see it more often?

[8] The log case is particularly special because the tax rate does not affect the capitalist's consumption path – more on this in a bit.

References

Acemoglu, D., Golosov, M., & Tsyvinski, A. (2011). Political economy of Ramsey taxation. *Journal of Public Economics*, 95(7-8), 467–475.

Aiyagari, S. R., Marcet, A., Sargent, T. J., & Seppälä, J. (2002). Optimal taxation without state-contingent debt. *Journal of Political Economy*, 110(6), 1220–1254.

Alesina, A. & Drazen, A. (1991). Why are stabilizations delayed? *American Economic Review*, 81(5), 1170–1188.

Alesina, A., Campante, F. R., & Tabellini, G. (2008). Why is fiscal policy often procyclical? *Journal of the European Economic Association*, 6(5), 1006–1036.

Alesina, A. & Passalacqua, A. (2016). The political economy of government debt. *Handbook of Macroeconomics*, 2, 2599–2651.

Alesina, A. & Tabellini, G. (1990). A positive theory of fiscal deficits and government debt. *The Review of Economic Studies*, 57(3), 403–414.

Barro, R. J. (1979). On the determination of the public debt. *Journal of Political Economy*, 87(5, Part 1), 940–971.

Battaglini, M. & Coate, S. (2008). A dynamic theory of public spending, taxation, and debt. *American Economic Review*, 98(1), 201–36.

Cukierman, A. & Tommasi, M. (1998). When does it take a Nixon to go to China? *American Economic Review*, 180–197.

Drazen, A. & Grilli, V. (1993). The benefit of crises for economic reforms. *The American Economic Review*, 83(3), 598–607.

Gavin, M. & Perotti, R. (1997). Fiscal policy in Latin America. *NBER Macroeconomics Annual*, 12, 11–61. https://www.journals.uchicago.edu/doi/pdf/10.1086/654320.

Judd, K. L. (1985). Redistributive taxation in a simple perfect foresight model. *Journal of Public Economics*, 28(1), 59–83.

Laban, R. & Sturzenegger, F. (1994). Distributional conflict, financial adaptation and delayed stabilizations. *Economics & Politics*, 6(3), 257–276.

Persson, T. & Svensson, L. E. (1989). Why a stubborn conservative would run a deficit: Policy with time-inconsistent preferences. *The Quarterly Journal of Economics*, 104(2), 325–345.

Straub, L. & Werning, I. (2020). Positive long-run capital taxation: Chamley-Judd revisited. *American Economic Review*, 110(1), 86–119.

Yared, P. (2010). Politicians, taxes and debt. *The Review of Economic Studies*, 77(2), 806–840.

CHAPTER 19

Monetary policy: An introduction

19.1 | The conundrum of money

We have finally reached our last topic: monetary policy (MP), one of the most important topics in macroeconomic policy, and perhaps the most effective tool of macroeconomic management. While among practitioner's there is a great deal of consensus over the way monetary policy should be implemented, it always remains a topic where new ideas flourish and raise heated debates. Paul Krugman tweeted,

> Nothing gets people angrier than monetary theory. Say that Trump is a traitor and they yawn; say that fiat money works and they scream incoherently.

Our goal in these final chapters is to try to sketch the consensus, its shortcomings, and the ongoing attempts to rethink MP for the future, even if people scream!

We will tackle our analysis of monetary policy in three steps. In this chapter we will start with the basics: the relation of money and prices, and the optimal choice of inflation. This will be developed first, in a context where output is exogenous. This simplifies relative to the New Keynesian approach we discussed in Chapter 15, but will provide some of the basic intuitions of monetary policy. The interaction of money and output creates a whole new wealth of issues. Is monetary policy inconsistent? Should it be conducted through rules or with discretion? Why is inflation targeting so popular among central banks? We will discuss these questions in the next chapter. Finally, in the last two chapters we will discuss new frontiers in monetary policy, with new challenges that have become more evident in the new period of very low interest rates. In Chapter 21 we discuss monetary policy when constrained by the lower bound, and the new approach of quantitative easing. In Chapter 22 we discuss a series of topics: secular stagnation, the fiscal theory of the price level, and bubbles. Because these last two chapters are more prolific in referencing this recent work, we do not add the what next section at the end of the chapter, as the references for future exploration are already plenty within the text.

But before we jump on to this task, let us briefly note that monetary economics rests on a fairly shaky foundation: the role of money – why people hold it, and what are its effects on the economy – is one of the most important issues in macroeconomics, and yet it is one of the least understood. Why is this? For starters, in typical micro models – and pretty much in all of our macro models as well – we did not deal with money: the relevant issues were always discussed in terms of relative prices,

How to cite this book chapter:
Campante, F., Sturzenegger, F. and Velasco, A. 2021. *Advanced Macroeconomics: An Easy Guide.*
  Ch. 19. 'Monetary policy: An introduction', pp. 295–314. London: LSE Press.
  DOI: https://doi.org/10.31389/lsepress.ame.s License: CC-BY-NC 4.0.

not nominal prices. There was no obvious (or, at least, essential) role for money in the NGM that we used throughout this book. In fact, the *non plus ultra* of micro models, the general equilibrium Arrow-Debreu framework, not only does not need money, it also does not have trading! (Talk about outrageous assumptions.) In that model, all trades are consummated at the beginning of time, and then you have the realisation of these trades, but no new trading going on over time. Of course, the world is not that complete, so we need to update our trading all the time. We use money as an insurance for these new trades. However, it is much easier to say people use money for transactions than to model it, because we need to step into the world of incomplete markets, and we do not know how to handle that universe well.

The literature has thus taken different paths for introducing money into general equilibrium models. The first is to build a demand for money from micro-foundations. The question here is whether one commodity (maybe gold, shells, salt?) may become a vehicle that people may naturally choose for transactions, i.e. what we usually refer to as money. Kiyotaki and Wright (1989), for example, go this way. While nice, by starting from first principles, this approach is intractable and did not deliver models which are sufficiently flexible to discuss other issues, so this research has only produced a plausible story for the existence of money but not a workable model for monetary policy.

The other alternative is to introduce money in our typical overlapping generations model. Money serves the role of social security, and captures the attractive feature that money has value because you believe someone down the road will take it. Unfortunately, the model is not robust. Any asset that dominates money in rate of return will simply crowd money out of the system, thus making it impossible to use this model to justify the use of money in cases in which the inflation rate is minimally positive when money is clearly dominated in rate of return.

A third approach is to just assume that money needs to be used for purchases, the so-called cash in advance constraints. In this framework the consumer splits itself at the beginning of each period into a consumer self and a producer self. Given that the consumer does not interact with the producer, she needs to bring cash from the previous period, thus the denomination of cash in advance. This is quite tractable, but has the drawback that gives a very rigid money demand function (in fact, money demand is simply equal to consumption).

A more flexible version is to think that the consumer has to devote some time to shopping, and that shopping time is reduced by the holdings of money. This provides more flexibility about thinking in the demand for money.

Finally, a take-it-all-in alternative is just to add money in the utility function. While this is a reduced form, it provides a flexible money demand framework, and, therefore, has been used extensively in the literature. At any rate, it is obvious that people demand money, so we just postulate that it provides utility. An additional benefit is that it can easily be accommodated into the basic framework we have been using in this book, for example, by tacking it to an optimisation problem akin to that of the NGM.

Thus, we will go this way in this chapter. As you will see, it provides good insights into the workings of money in the economy.

19.1.1 | Introducing money into the model

Let's start with the simplest possible model. Output exogenous, and a government that prints money and rebates the proceeds to the consumer. We will lift many of these assumptions as we go along. But before we start we need to discuss the budget constraints.

Assume there is only one good the price of which in terms of money is given by P_t. The agent can hold one of two assets: money, whose nominal stock is M_t, and a real bond, whose real value is given, as in previous chapters, by b_t. Note that we now adopt the convention that real variables take on small-case letters, and nominal variables are denoted by capital letters. The representative agent's budget constraint is given by

$$\frac{\dot{M}_t}{P_t} + \dot{b}_t = rb_t + y_t - \tau_t - c_t, \tag{19.1}$$

where τ_t is real taxes paid to the government and, as usual, y_t is income and c_t consumption. Define the real quantity of money as

$$m_t = \frac{M_t}{P_t}. \tag{19.2}$$

Taking logs of both sides, and then time derivatives, we arrive at:

$$\dot{m}_t = m_t \frac{\dot{M}_t}{M_t} - m_t \frac{\dot{P}_t}{P_t} = \frac{M_t}{P_t}\frac{\dot{M}_t}{M_t} - m_t\frac{\dot{P}_t}{P_t}. \tag{19.3}$$

Defining $\pi_t \equiv \frac{\dot{P}_t}{P_t}$ as the rate of inflation and rearranging, we have:

$$\frac{\dot{M}_t}{P_t} = \dot{m}_t + \pi_t m_t. \tag{19.4}$$

The LHS of (19.4) is the real value of the money the government injects into the system. We call this total revenue from money creation, or seigniorage. Notice from the RHS of (19.4) that this has two components:

- The term $\dot{m}_t$ is the increase in real money holdings by the public. (It is sometimes referred to as seigniorage as well; we'll keep our use consistent).
- The term $m_t \pi_t$ is the inflation tax: the erosion, because of inflation, of the real value of the money balances held by the public. We can think of m_t as the tax base, and π_t as the tax rate.

Using (19.4) in (19.1) we have that

$$\dot{m}_t + \dot{b}_t = rb_t + y_t - \tau_t - c_t - \pi_t m_t. \tag{19.5}$$

On the LHS we have accumulation by the agent of the two available financial assets: money and bonds. The last term on the RHS is an additional expense: taxes paid on the real balances held.

Let us consider a steady state in which all variables are constant, then (19.5) becomes

$$rb + y = \tau + c + \pi m. \tag{19.6}$$

Hence, total income on the LHS must be enough to finance total expenditures (including regular taxes τ and the inflation tax πm).

A useful transformation involves adding and subtracting the term rm_t to the RHS of (19.5):

$$\dot{m}_t + \dot{b}_t = r\left(m_t + b_t\right) + y_t - \tau_t - c_t - \left(r + \pi_t\right)m_t. \tag{19.7}$$

Now define

$$a_t = m_t + b_t \tag{19.8}$$

as total financial assets held by the agent, and

$$i_t = r + \pi_t \tag{19.9}$$

as the nominal rate of interest. Using these two relationships in (19.7) we get

$$\dot{a}_t = ra_t + y_t - \tau_t - c_t - i_t m_t. \tag{19.10}$$

The last term on the RHS shows that the cost of holding money, in an inflationary environment, is the nominal rate of interest i_t.

19.2 | The Sidrauski model

Following Sidrauski (1967), we assume now the representative agent's utility function is

$$\int_0^\infty [u\left(c_t\right) + v(m_t)]e^{-\rho t} dt. \tag{19.11}$$

Here $v(m_t)$ is utility from holdings of real money balances. Assume $v'(m_t) \geq 0$, $v''(m_t) < 0$ and that Inada conditions hold. The agent maximises (19.11) subject to (19.10), which we repeat here for clarity, though assuming, without loss of generality, that output remains constant

$$\dot{a} = ra_t + y - \tau_t - c_t - i_t m_t,$$

plus the standard solvency condition

$$\lim_{T \to \infty} \left[a_T e^{-rT}\right] \geq 0, \tag{19.12}$$

and the initial condition a_0. The Hamiltonian is

$$H = [u(c_t) + v(m_t)] + \lambda_t \left(ra_t + y - \tau_t - c_t - i_t m_t\right), \tag{19.13}$$

where m_t and c_t are control variables, a_t is the state variable and λ_t is the co-state. First order conditions for a maximum are

$$u'(c_t) = \lambda_t, \tag{19.14}$$

$$v'(m_t) = \lambda_t i_t, \tag{19.15}$$

$$\dot{\lambda}_t = \lambda_t (\rho - r) = 0, \tag{19.16}$$

where the last equality comes from assuming $r = \rho$ as usual. Equations (19.14) and (19.16) together imply that c_t is constant and equal to c for all t. Using this fact and combining (19.14) and (19.15) we have

$$v'(m_t) = i_t u'(c). \tag{19.17}$$

We can think of equation (19.17) as defining money demand: demand for real balances is decreasing in the nominal interest rate i_t and increasing in steady state consumption c. This is a way to microfound the traditional money demand functions you all have seen before, where demand would be a positive function of income (because of transactions) and a negative function of the nominal interest rate, which is the opportunity cost of holding money.

19.2.1 | Finding the rate of inflation

What would the rate of inflation be in this model? In order to close the model, notice that

$$\frac{\dot{m}_t}{m_t} = \sigma - \pi_t, \tag{19.18}$$

where σ is the rate of money growth. We will also assume that the money printing proceeds are rebated to the consumer, which means that

$$\tau = -\sigma m_t. \tag{19.19}$$

Replacing (19.18) and (19.19) into (19.10), using $\rho = r$, and realizing the agent has no incentive to hold debt, gives that $c = y$, so that marginal utility is also constant and can be normalised to 1. Using (19.9), equation (19.17) becomes

$$v'(m_t) = \rho + \pi_t, \tag{19.20}$$

which substituting in (19.18) gives

$$\dot{m}_t = (\rho + \sigma)m_t - v'(m_t)m_t. \tag{19.21}$$

Equation (19.21) is a differential equation that defines the equilibrium. Notice that because $v'(m_t) < 0$, this is an unstable differential equation. As the initial price level determines the initial point (m is a jump variable in our definitions of Chapter 3), the equilibrium is unique at the point where $\dot{m}_t = 0$. The dynamics are shown in Figure 19.1.

This simple model provides some of the basic intuitions of monetary theory.

- An increase in the quantity of nominal money will leave m unchanged and just lead to a jump in the price level. This is the quantitative theory of money that states that any increase in the stock of money will just result in an equivalent increase in prices.

Figure 19.1 The Sidrausky model

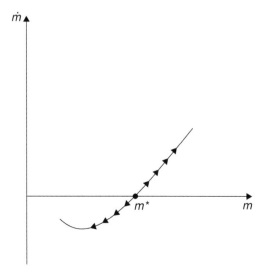

- The rate of inflation is the rate of growth of money (see equation (19.18)). Inflation is a monetary phenomenon.
- What happens if, suddenly, the rate of growth of money is *expected* to grow in the future? The dynamics entail a jump in the price level today and a divergent path which places the economy at its new equilibrium when the rate of growth finally increases. In short, increases in future money affect the price and inflation levels today. The evolution of m and π are shown in Figure 19.2.
- Does the introduction of money affect the equilibrium? It doesn't. Consumption is equal to income in all states of nature. This result is called the neutrality of money.

19.2.2 | The optimal rate of inflation

Let's assume now that we ask a central planner to choose the inflation rate in order to maximise welfare. What σ, and, therefore, what inflation rate would be chosen?

Figure 19.2   An anticipated increase in the money growth

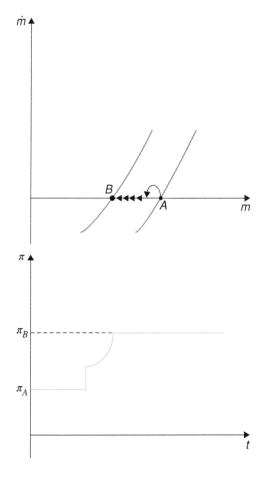

We know from (19.20) and (19.17) that the steady-state stock of money held by individuals solves the equation

$$v'(m) = (\rho + \pi) = (\rho + \sigma). \tag{19.22}$$

This means that the central bank can choose σ to maximise utility from money-holdings. This implies choosing

$$\pi^{best} = \sigma^{best} = -\rho < 0, \tag{19.23}$$

so that

$$v'(m^{best}) = 0. \tag{19.24}$$

This means that m^{best} is the satiation stock of real balances and you achieve it by choosing a *negative* inflation rate. This is the famous Friedman rule for optimal monetary policy. What's the intuition? You should equate the marginal cost of holding money from an individual perspective (the nominal interest rate) to the social cost of printing money, which is essentially zero. A zero nominal rate implies an inflation rate that is equal to minus the real interest rate.

In practice, we don't see a lot of central banks implementing deflationary policy. Why is it so? Probably because deflation has a lot of costs that are left out of this model: its effect on debtors, on aggregate demand, etc., likely in the case when prices and wages tend to be sticky downwards.

We should thus interpret our result as meaning that policy makers should aim for low levels of inflation, so as to keep social and private costs close. In any case, there is a huge literature on the costs of inflation that strengthens the message of this result, we will come back to this at the end of the chapter.

19.2.3 | Multiple equilibria in the Sidrauski model

In the previous section we analysed the steady state of the model, but, in general, we have always been cautious as to check if other equilibria are possible. In this monetary model, as it happens, they are.

Figure 19.3 shows the possible configurations for equation (19.21), for all m. We know that

$$\left.\frac{\partial \dot{m}}{\partial m}\right|_{SS} = -v''(m) > 0, \tag{19.25}$$

so that the curve crosses the steady state with a positive slope. But what happens to the left of the steady state? Figure 19.3, shows two paths depending on whether the value of the term $v'(m)m$ approaches zero or a positive number as m approaches zero. If money is very essential and it's marginal utility is very high as you reduce your holdings of money, then $v'(m)m > 0$ as m approaches zero. This case corresponds to the path denoted by the letter B. If $v'(m)m \to 0$, as $m \to 0$ then the configuration is of the path leading to A.

With this we can now study other equilibria. The paths to the right are deflationary paths, where inflation is negative and real balances increase without bound. We do not see these increasing deflationary paths, so, from an empirical point of view, they do not seem very relevant (mathematically they are feasible, and some people resorted to these equilibria to explain the low inflation rates in the U.S. in recent years, see Sims (2016)). The paths to the left of the steady state are inflationary paths. Paths along the B curve are inconsistent, as they require $\dot{m} < 0$ when m hits zero, which is unfeasible. However, paths that do end up at zero, denoted A in Figure 19.3, are feasible. In these cases money is not so essential, so it is wiped out by a hiperinflationary process. In a classical paper, Cagan (1956)

Figure 19.3 Multiple equilibria in the Sidrauski model

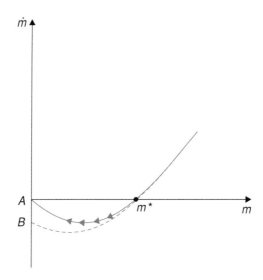

speculated on the possibility of these self-sustaining inflationary dynamics in which the expectation of higher inflation leads to lower money demand, fuelling even higher inflation. So these feasible paths to the left of the steady state could be called Cagan equilibria. The general equilibrium version of the Cagan equilibria described here was first introduced by Obstfeld and Rogoff (1983).

19.2.4 | Currency substitution

The model is amenable to discussing the role of currency substitution, that is, the possibility of phasing out the currency and being replaced by a sounder alternative.

The issue of understanding how different currencies interact, has a long tradition in monetary economics. Not only because, in antiquity, many objects operated as monies, but also because, prior to the emergence of the Fed, currency in the U.S. were issued by commercial banks, so there was an innumerable number of currencies circulating at each time. A popular way to think this issue is Gresham's Law; faced with a low quality currency and a high quality currency, Gresham's Law argues that people will try to get rid of the low quality currency while hoarding the high quality currency, *bad money displaces good money*. Of course while this may be true at the individual level, it may not be so at the aggregate level because prices may increase faster when denominated in units of the bad-quality currency debasing its value. Sturzenegger (1994) discusses this issue and makes two points.

- When there are two or more currencies, it is more likely that the condition $v'(m)m=0$ is satisfied (particularly for the low quality currency). Thus, the hyperinflation paths are more likely.
- If the dynamics of money continue are described by an analogous to (19.21) such as

$$\dot{m}_1 = (\rho + \sigma_1)m_1 - v'(m_1, m_2)m_1, \tag{19.26}$$

notice that if the second currency m_2 reduces the marginal utility of the first one, then the inflation rate on the equilibrium path is lower: less inflation is needed to wipe out the currency.

This pattern seems to have occurred in a series of hyperinflations in Argentina in the late 80s, each new wave coming faster but with *lower* inflation. Similarly, at the end of the 2000s, also in Argentina, very tight monetary conditions during the fixed exchange regime led to the development of multiple private currencies. Once the exchange rate regime was removed, these currencies suffered hyperinflations and disappeared in a wink (see Colacelli and Blackburn 2009).

19.2.5 | Superneutrality

How do these results extend to a model with capital accumulation? We can see this easily also in the context of the Sidrauski model (we assume no population growth), but where we give away the assumption of exogenous output and allow for capital accumulation. Consider now the utility function

$$\int_0^\infty u\left(c_t, m_t\right) e^{-\rho t} dt, \tag{19.27}$$

where $u_c, u_m > 0$ and $u_{cc}, u_{mm} < 0$. However, we'll allow the consumer to accumulate capital now. Defining again $a = k + m$, the resource constraint can be written as

$$\dot{a}_t = r_t a_t + w_t - \tau_t - c_t - i_t m_t. \tag{19.28}$$

The Hamiltonian is

$$H = u\left(c_t, m_t\right) + \lambda_t \left[ra_t + w_t - \tau_t - c_t - i_t m_t\right]. \tag{19.29}$$

The FOC are, as usual,

$$u_c(c_t, m_t) = \lambda_t, \tag{19.30}$$

$$u_m(c_t, m_t) = \lambda_t i_t, \tag{19.31}$$

$$\dot{\lambda}_t = (\rho - r)\lambda_t. \tag{19.32}$$

The first two equations give, once again, a money demand function $u_m = u_c i$, but the important result is that because the interest rate now is the marginal product of capital, in steady state $r = \rho = f'(k^*)$, where we use the $*$ superscript to denote the steady state. We leave the computations to you, assuming $\tau = -\sigma m$, and using the fact that w is the marginal product of labour, replacing in (19.28) we find that

$$c = f(k^*). \tag{19.33}$$

But this is the level of income that we would have had in the model with no money! This result is known as superneutrality: not only does the introduction of money not affect the equilibrium, neither does the inflation rate.

Later, we will see the motives for why we believe this is not a good description of the effects of inflation, which we believe in the real world are harmful for the economy.

19.3 | The relation between fiscal and monetary policy

If inflation originates in money printing, the question is, what originates money printing? One possible explanation for inflation lies in the need of resources to finance public spending. This is called the public finance approach to inflation and follows the logic of our tax smoothing discussion in the previous chapter. According to this view, taxes generate distortions, and the optimal taxation mix entails equating these distortions across all goods, and, why, not money. Thus, the higher the cost of collecting other taxes (the weaker your tax system), the more you should rely on inflation as a form of collecting income. If the marginal cost of taxes increases with recessions, then you should use more inflation in downturns.

Another reason for inflation is to compensate the natural tendency towards deflation. If prices were constant, we would probably have deflation, because we know that price indexes suffer from an upward bias. As new products come along and relative prices move, people change their consumption mix looking for cheaper alternatives, so their actual basket is always "cheaper" than the measured basket. For the U.S., this bias is allegedly around 1% per year, but it has been found larger for emerging economies.[1] Thus an inflation target of 1 or 2% in fact aims, basically, at price stability.

However, the main culprit for inflation, is, obviously, fiscal needs regardless of any optimisation consideration. The treasury needs resources, does not want to put with the political pain of raising taxes, and simply asks the central bank to print some money which eventually becomes inflation.

19.3.1 | The inflation-tax Laffer curve

The tax collected is the combination of the inflation rate and the money demand that pays that inflation tax. Thus, a question arises as to whether countries may choose too high an inflation rate. May the inflation rate be so high that discouraging money demand actually reduces the amount collected through the inflation tax? In other words are we on the wrong side of the Laffer curve?[2]

To explore this question let's start with the budget constraint for the government,

$$\dot{m}_t = rd_0 + g - \tau - \pi_t m_t, \tag{19.34}$$

which, in steady state, becomes

$$rd_0 + g - \tau = \pi m. \tag{19.35}$$

Assuming a typical demand function for money

$$m = ye^{-\gamma i}, \tag{19.36}$$

we can rewrite this as

$$rd_0 + g - \tau = \pi ye^{-\gamma(r+\pi)}. \tag{19.37}$$

Note that

$$\frac{\partial \left(\pi e^{-\gamma(r+\pi)} \right)}{\partial \pi} = ye^{-\gamma(r+\pi)}(1 - \gamma\pi), \tag{19.38}$$

so that revenue is increasing in π for $\pi < \gamma^{-1}$, and decreasing for $\pi > \gamma^{-1}$. It follows that $\pi = \gamma^{-1}$ is the revenue maximising rate of inflation. Empirical work, however, has found, fortunately, that government typically place themselves on the correct side of the Laffer curve.[3]

19.3.2 | The inflation-tax and inflation dynamics

What are the dynamics of this fiscally motivated inflation? Using (19.36), we can write,

$$\pi_t = \gamma^{-1}(\log(y) - \log(m_t)) - r. \tag{19.39}$$

This in (19.34) implies

$$\dot{m}_t = rd_0 + g - \tau - \gamma^{-1}\left(\log(y) - \log(m_t)\right)m_t + rm_t. \tag{19.40}$$

Notice that,

$$\left.\frac{\partial \dot{m}_t}{\partial m_t}\right|_{SS} = -\gamma^{-1}(\log(y) - \log(m)) + \gamma^{-1} + r, \tag{19.41}$$

which using (19.39)

$$\pi_t = \gamma^{-1}(\log(y) - \log(m_t)) - r. \tag{19.42}$$

simplifies to,

$$\left.\frac{\partial \dot{m}_t}{\partial m_t}\right|_{SS} = \gamma^{-1} - \pi_t. \tag{19.43}$$

Hence, $\left.\frac{\partial \dot{m}_t}{\partial m_t}\right|_{SS} > 0$ for the steady state inflation below γ^{-1}, and $\left.\frac{\partial \dot{m}_t}{\partial m_t}\right|_{SS} < 0$ for the steady state inflation rate above γ^{-1}.

This means that the high inflation equilibrium is stable. As m is a jumpy variable, this means that, in addition to the well-defined equilibrium at low inflation, there are infinite equilibria in which inflation converges to the high inflation equilibria.

Most practitioners disregard this high inflation equilibria and focus on the one on the good side of the Laffer curve, mostly because, as we said, it is difficult to come up with evidence that countries are on the wrong side. However, the dynamics should be a reminder of the challenges posed by stabilisation.

19.3.3 | Unpleasant monetary arithmetic

In this section we will review one of the most celebrated results in monetary theory, the unpleasant monetarist arithmetic presented initially by Sargent and Wallace (1981). The result states that a monetary contraction may lead to higher inflation in the future. Why? Because, if the amount of government spending is exogenous and is not financed with seigniorage, it has to be financed with bonds. If eventually seigniorage is the only source of revenue, the higher amount of bonds will require more seigniorage and, therefore, more inflation. Of course, seigniorage is not the only financing mechanism, so you may interpret the result as applying to situations when, eventually, the increased cost of debt is not financed, at least entirely, by other revenue sources. Can it be the case that the expected future inflation leads to higher inflation now? If that were the case, the contractionary monetary policy would be ineffective even in the short run! This section discusses if that can be the case.

The tools to discuss this issue are all laid out in the Sidrauski model discussed in section 19.2, even though the presentation here follows Drazen (1985).

Consider the evolution of assets being explicit about the components of a,

$$\dot{b}_t + \dot{m}_t = -\pi_t m_t + y + \rho b_t - c_t. \tag{19.44}$$

Where we assume $r = \rho$ as we've done before. The evolution of real money follows

$$\dot{m}_t = (\sigma - \pi_t)m_t. \tag{19.45}$$

Replacing (19.45) into (19.44), we get

$$\dot{b}_t = -\sigma m_t + y - c_t + \rho b_t, \tag{19.46}$$

where the term $y - c$ can be interpreted as the fiscal deficit.[4] Call this expression D. Replacing (19.20) in (19.45) we get

$$\dot{m}_t = (\sigma + \rho - v'(m_t))m_t. \tag{19.47}$$

Equations (19.46) and (19.47) will be the dynamic system, which we will use to discuss our results. It is easy to see that the $\dot{b}$ equation slopes upwards and that the $\dot{m}$ is an horizontal line. The dynamics are represented in Figure 19.4. A reduction in σ shifts both curves upwards.

Notice that the system is unstable. But b is not a jump variable. The system reaches stability only if the rate of money growth is such that it can finance the deficit stabilising the debt dynamics. It is the choice of money growth that will take us to the equilibrium. b here is not the decision variable.

Our exercise considers the case where the rate of growth of money falls for a certain period of time after which it moves to the value needed to keep variables at their steady state. This exercise represents well the case studied by Sargent and Wallace.

To analyse this we first compute all the steady state combinations of m and b for different values of σ. Making $\dot{b}$ and $\dot{m}$ equal to zero in (19.46) and (19.47) and substituting σ in (19.46) using (19.47), we get

$$b = \frac{mv'(m)}{\rho} - m - \frac{D}{\rho}. \tag{19.48}$$

This is the SS locus in Figure 19.5. We know that eventually the economy reverts to a steady state along this line. To finalize the analysis, show that the equation for the accumulation of assets can be written as

$$\dot{a}_t = \rho a_t - v'(m_t)m_t + D. \tag{19.49}$$

Figure 19.4 The dynamics of m and b

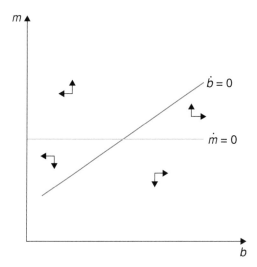

Figure 19.5   Unpleasant monetarist arithmetic

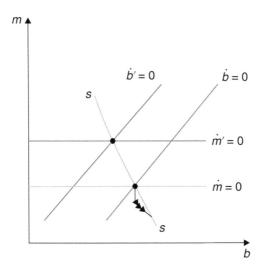

notice, however, that if $\dot{a} = 0$ this equation coincides with (19.48). This means that above the steady states locus the dynamic paths have a slope that is less than one (so that the sum of m and b grows as you move) and steeper than one below it (so that the total value of assets falls).

We have now the elements to discuss our results. Consider first the case where $v(m) = \log(m)$. In this case the inflation tax is constant and independent of the inflation rate. Notice that this implies from (19.44) that the $\dot{b} = 0$ line is vertical. In this case, the reduction in the growth rate of money implies a jump to the lower inflation rate, but the system remains there and there is no unpleasant monetary arithmetic. A lowering of the rate of growth of money, does not affect the collection of the inflation tax and thus does not require more debt financing, so the new lower inflation equilibrium can sustain itself, and simply jumps back to the original point when the growth rate of money reverts to its initial value.

Now consider that case where the demand for money is relatively inelastic, which implies that, in order to increase seigniorage, a higher inflation rate is required and the slope of the SS curve is negative.[5] Now the policy of reducing seigniorage collection for some time will increase inflation in the long run as a result of the higher level of debt. This is the soft version of the Sargent-Wallace result.

But the interesting question is whether it may actually increase inflation even in the short run, something we call the hard version of the unpleasant monetarist arithmetic, or, in Drazen's words, the spectacular version.

Whether this is the case will depend on the slope of the SS curve. If the curve is flat then a jump in m is required to put the economy on a path to a new steady state. In this case, only the soft, and not the hard, version of the result holds (an upwards jump in m happens only if inflation falls). However, if the SS curve is steeper than negative one (the case drawn in (19.5), only a downwards jump in m can get us to the equilibrium. Now we have Sargent and Wallace's spectacular, unpleasant monetary result: lowering the rate of money growth can actually increase the inflation rate in the short run! The more inelastic money demand, then the more likely this is to be in this case.

Of course these results do not carry to all bond issues. If, for example, a central bank sells bonds B_t to buy foreign reserves Re_t (where e_t is the foreign currency price in domestic currency units), the central bank income statement changes by adding an interest cost $i\Delta B_t$ but also adds a revenue equal to i^*Re_t where i and i^* stand for the local and foreign interest rates. If $\Delta B = Re$, to the extent that $i = i^* + \frac{\dot{e}}{e}$ (uncovered interest parity), there is no change in net income, and therefore no change in the equilibrium inflation rate.

This illustrates that the Sargent-Wallace result applies to bond sales that compensate money printed to finance the government (i.e. with no backing). In fact, in Chapter 21 we will discuss the policy of quantitative easing, a policy in which Central Banks issue, substantial amount of liquidity in exchange for real assets, such as corporate bonds, and other financial instruments, finance with interest bearing reserves. To the extent that these resources deliver an equilibrium return, they do not change the monetary equilibrium.

19.3.4 | Pleasant monetary arithmetic

Let's imagine now that the government needs to finance a certain level of government expenditure, but can choose the inflation rates over time. What would be the optimal path for the inflation tax? To find out, we assume a Ramsey planner that maximises consumer utility, internalising the optimal behaviour of the consumer to the inflation tax itself, much in the same way we did in the previous chapter in our discussion of optimal taxation; and, of course, subject to it's own budget constraint.[6] The problem is then to maximise

$$\int_0^\infty [u\left(y\right) + v(L(i_t, y)]e^{-\rho t}dt, \tag{19.50}$$

where we replace c for y and m_t for $L(i_t, y)$, as per the results of the Sidrausky model. The government's budget constraint is

$$\dot{a}_t = \rho a_t - i_t m_t + \tau_t, \tag{19.51}$$

where $a_t = \frac{B_t + M_t}{P_t}$ is the real amount of liabilities of the government, d_t is the government deficit and we've replaced $r = \rho$. The Ramsey planner has to find the optimal sequence of interest rates, that is, of the inflation rate. The FOCs are

$$v_m L_i + \lambda_t \left[L(i_t, y) + i_t L_i\right] = 0, \tag{19.52}$$

plus

$$\dot{\lambda}_t = \rho \lambda_t - \rho \lambda_t. \tag{19.53}$$

The second FOC show that λ is constant. Given this the first FOC shows the nominal interest is constant as well. Optimal policy smooths the inflation tax across periods, a result akin to our tax smoothing result in the previous chapter (if we include a distortion from taxation, we would get that the marginal cost of inflation should equal the marginal cost of taxation, delivering the result that inflation be countercyclical).

What happens now if the government faces a decreasing path for government expenditures, that is

$$d_t = d_0 e^{-\delta t}. \tag{19.54}$$

The solution still requires a constant inflation rate but now the seigniorage needs to satisfy

$$i^* m^* = \rho a_0 + \rho \frac{d_0}{\rho + \delta}. \tag{19.55}$$

Integrating (19.51) gives the solution for a_t

$$a_t = \frac{i^* M^*}{\rho} - \frac{d_0}{\rho + \delta} e^{-\delta t}. \tag{19.56}$$

Notice that debt increases over time: the government smoothes the inflation tax by running up debt during the high deficit period. This debt level is higher, of course, relative to a policy of financing the deficit with inflation in every period (this would entail a decreasing inflation path pari passu with the deficit). At the end, the level of debt is higher under the smoothing equilibrium than under the policy of full inflation financing, leading to higher steady state inflation. This is the monetaristic arithmetic at work. However, far from being unpleasant, this is the result of an optimal program. The higher long run inflation is the cost of smoothing the inflation in other periods.

19.4 │ The costs of inflation

The Sidrauski model shows that inflation does not affect the equilibrium. But somehow we do not believe this result to be correct. On the contrary, we believe inflation is harmful to the economy. In their celebrated paper, Bruno and Easterly (1996) found that, beyond a certain threshold inflation was negatively correlated with growth, a view that is well established among practicioners of monetary policy. This result is confirmed by the literature on growth regressions. Inflation always has a negative and significant effect on growth. In these regressions it may very well be that inflation is capturing a more fundamental weakness as to how the political system works, which may suggest that for these countries it is not as simple as "choosing a better rate of inflation".

However, to make the point on the costs of inflation more strongly, we notice that even disinflation programs are expansionary. This means that the positive effects of lowering inflation are strong, so much so that they even undo whatever potential costs a disinflation may have. Figures 19.6 and 19.7 show all recent disinflation programs for countries that had reached an inflation rate equal to or higher than 20% in recent years. The figure is split in two panels, those countries that implemented disinflation with a floating regime and those that used some kind of nominal anchor (typically the exchange rate), and shows the evolution of inflation (monthly) in 19.6 and GDP (quarterly) in 19.7 since the last time they reached 20% anual inflation. The evidence is conclusive: disinflations are associated with higher growth.

So what are these costs of inflation that did not show up in the Sidrausky model? There has been a large literature on the costs of inflation. Initially, these costs were associated with what were dubbed shoe-leather costs: the cost of going to the bank to get cash (the idea is that the higher the inflation, the lower your demand for cash, and the more times you needed to go to the bank to get your cash). This was never a thrilling story (to say the least), but today, with electronic money and credit cards, simply no longer makes any sense. On a more benign note we can grant it tries to capture all the increased transaction costs associated with running out (or low) of cash.

Other stories are equally disappointing. Menu costs (the idea that there are real costs of changing prices) is as uneventful as the shoe-leather story. We know inflation distorts tax structures and redistributes incomes across people (typically against the poorest in the population), but while these are undesirable consequences they on their own do not build a good explanation for the negative impact of inflation on growth.

Figure 19.6 Recent disinflations (floating and fixed exchange rate regimes)

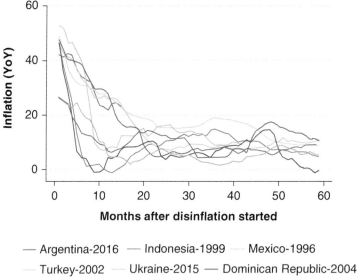

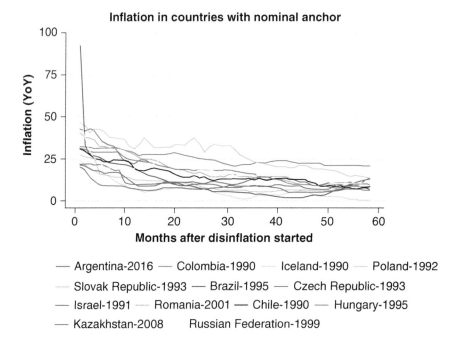

Figure 19.7   GDP growth during disinflations

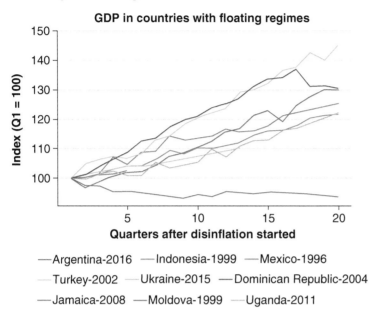

—Argentina-2016   —Indonesia-1999   —Mexico-1996
—Turkey-2002   —Ukraine-2015   —Dominican Republic-2004
—Jamaica-2008   —Moldova-1999   —Uganda-2011

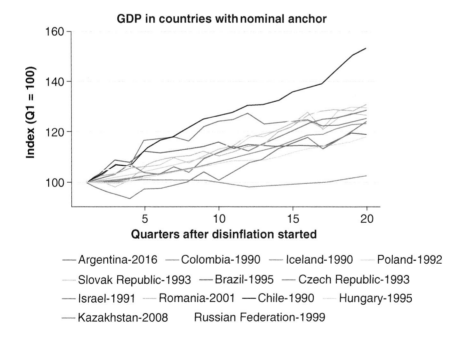

—Argentina-2016   —Colombia-1990   —Iceland-1990   —Poland-1992
—Slovak Republic-1993   —Brazil-1995   —Czech Republic-1993
—Israel-1991   —Romania-2001   —Chile-1990   —Hungary-1995
—Kazakhstan-2008   Russian Federation-1999

19.4.1 | The Tommasi model: Inflation and competition

So the problem with inflation has to be significant and deep. An elephant in the room that seems difficult to see. Tommasi (1994) provides what we believe is a more plausible story based on the role of inflation in messing up the price system. Tommasi focuses on a well-known fact: increases in inflation increase the volatility in relative prices (this occurs naturally in any model where prices adjust at different times or speed). Tommasi argues that relative prices changes, not only generate economic inefficiencies but also change the relative power of sellers and purchasers pushing the economy away from its competitive equilibrium. To see this, let's draw from our analysis of search discussed in Chapter 16.

Imagine a consumer that is searching for a low price. Going to a store implies finding a price, the value of which can be described by

$$rW(p) = (\bar{x} - p) + \rho[U - W(p)]. \tag{19.57}$$

Having a price implies obtaining a utility $\bar{x} - p$. If relative prices were stable, the consumer could go back to this store and repurchase, but if relative prices change, then this price is lost. This occurs with probability ρ. If this event occurs, the consumer is left with no offer (value U). The ρ parameter will change with inflation and will be our object of interest. If the consumer has no price, he needs to search for a price with cost C and value U as in

$$rU = -C + \alpha \int_0^\infty max(0, W(p) - U)dF(p). \tag{19.58}$$

Working analogously as we did in the case of job search, remember that the optimal policy will be determined by a reservation price p_R. As this reservation price is the one that makes the customer indifferent between accepting or not accepting the price offered, we have that $rW(p_R) = \bar{x} - p_R = rU$, which will be handy later on. Rewrite (19.57) as

$$W(p) = \frac{\bar{x} - p + \rho U}{r + \rho}. \tag{19.59}$$

Subtracting U from both sides (and using $rU = \bar{x} - p_R$), we have

$$W(p) - U = \frac{\bar{x} - p + \rho U}{r + \rho} - U = \frac{\bar{x} - p - rU}{r + \rho} = \frac{p_R - p}{r + \rho}. \tag{19.60}$$

We can now replace rU and $W(p) - U$ in (19.58) to obtain

$$\bar{x} - p_R = -C + \frac{\alpha}{r + \rho} \int_0^{p_R} (p_R - p)dF(p), \tag{19.61}$$

or, finally,

$$p_R = C + \bar{x} - \underbrace{\frac{\alpha}{r + \rho} \int_0^{p_R} (p_R - p)\, dF(p)}_{(+)}. \tag{19.62}$$

The intuition is simple. The consumer is willing to pay up to his valuation of the good $\bar{x}$ plus the search cost C that can be saved by purchasing this unit. However, the reservation price falls if there is expectation of a better price in a new draw.

The equation delivers the result that if higher inflation implies a the higher ρ, then the higher is the reservation price. With inflation, consumers search less thus deviating the economy from its competitive equilibrium.

Other stories have discussed possible other side effects of inflation. There is a well documented negative relation between inflation and the size of the financial sector (see for example Levine and Renelt (1991) and Levine and Renelt (1992)). Another critical feature is the fact that high inflation implies that long term nominal contracts disappear, a point which becomes most clear if inflation may change abruptly. Imagine a budget with an investment that yields a positive or negative return x or $-x$, in a nominal contract this may happen if inflation moves strongly. Imagine that markets are incomplete and agents cannot run negative net worth (any contract which may run into negative wealth is not feasible). The probability of eventually running into negative wealth increases with the length of the contract. [7] The disappearance of long term contracts has a negative impact on productivity.

19.4.2 | Taking stock

We have seen how money and inflation are linked in the long run, and that a simple monetary model can help account for why central banks would want to set inflation at a low level. We haven't really talked about the short run, in fact, in our model there are no real effects of money or monetary policy. However, as you anticipate by now, this is due to the fact that there are no price rigidities. To the extent that prices are flexible in the long run, the main concern of monetary policy becomes dealing with inflation, and this is how the practice has evolved in recent decades. If there are rigidities, as we have seen previously, part of the effect of monetary policy will translate into output, and not just into the price dynamics. It is to these concerns that we turn in the next chapter.

Notes

[1] de Carvalho Filho and Chamon (2012) find a 4.5% annual bias for Brazil in the 80s. Gluzmann and Sturzenegger (2018) find a whopping 7% bias for 85–95 in Argentina, and 1% for the period 95–2005.

[2] You may know this already, but the Laffer curve describes the evolution of tax income as you increase the tax rate. Starts at zero when the tax rate is zero, and goes back to zero when the tax rate is 100%, as probably at this high rates the taxable good has disappeared. Thus, there is a range of tax rates where increasing the tax rate decreases tax collection income.

[3] See Kiguel and Neumeyer (1995).

[4] If $y = c + g$ then $y - c = g$, and as there are no tax resources, it indicates the value of the deficit.

[5] We disregard the equilibria where the elasticity is so high that reducing the rate of money growth increases the collection of the inflation tax. As in the previous section, we disregard these cases because we typically find the inflation tax to operate on the correct side of the Laffer curve.

[6] This section follows Uribe (2016).

[7] For a contract delivering a positive or negative return x with equal probabilities in each period, the possibility of the contract eventually hitting a negative return is .5 if it lasts one period and $.5 + \sum_{3,5,\ldots}^{\infty} \frac{1}{n+1} \frac{(n-2)!!}{(n-1)!!}$ if it lasts n periods. This probability is bigger than 75% after nine periods, so, quickly long term contracts become unfeasible. See Neumeyer (1998) for a model along these lines.

References

Bruno, M. & Easterly, W. (1996). Inflation and growth: In search of a stable relationship. *Federal Reserve Bank of St. Louis Review, 78*(May/June 1996).

Cagan, P. (1956). The monetary dynamics of hyperinflation. *Studies in the Quantity Theory of Money.*

Colacelli, M. & Blackburn, D. J. (2009). Secondary currency: An empirical analysis. *Journal of Monetary Economics, 56*(3), 295–308.

de Carvalho Filho, I. & Chamon, M. (2012). The myth of post-reform income stagnation: Evidence from Brazil and Mexico. *Journal of Development Economics, 97*(2), 368–386.

Drazen, A. (1985). Tight money and inflation: Further results. *Journal of Monetary Economics, 15*(1), 113–120.

Gluzmann, P. & Sturzenegger, F. (2018). An estimation of CPI biases in Argentina 1985–2005 and its implications on real income growth and income distribution. *Latin American Economic Review, 27*(1), 8.

Kiguel, M. A. & Neumeyer, P. A. (1995). Seigniorage and inflation: The case of Argentina. *Journal of Money, Credit and Banking, 27*(3), 672–682.

Kiyotaki, N. & Wright, R. (1989). On money as a medium of exchange. *Journal of Political Economy, 97*(4), 927–954.

Levine, R. & Renelt, D. (1991). *Cross-country studies of growth and policy: Methodological, conceptual, and statistical problems* (Vol. 608). World Bank Publications.

Levine, R. & Renelt, D. (1992). A sensitivity analysis of cross-country growth regressions. *The American Economic Review*, 942–963.

Neumeyer, P. A. (1998). Inflation-stabilization risk in economies with incomplete asset markets. *Journal of Economic Dynamics and Control, 23*(3), 371–391.

Obstfeld, M. & Rogoff, K. (1983). Speculative hyperinflations in maximizing models: Can we rule them out? *Journal of Political Economy, 91*(4), 675–687.

Sargent, T. J. & Wallace, N. (1981). Some unpleasant monetarist arithmetic. *Federal Reserve Bank of Minneapolis Quarterly Review, 5*(3), 1–17.

Sidrauski, M. (1967). Rational choice and patterns of growth in a monetary economy. *The American Economic Review, 57*(2), 534–544.

Sims, C. A. (2016). Fiscal policy, monetary policy and central bank independence. https://bit.ly/3BmMJYE.

Sturzenegger, F. A. (1994). Hyperinflation with currency substitution: Introducing an indexed currency. *Journal of Money, Credit and Banking, 26*(3), 377–395.

Tommasi, M. (1994). The consequences of price instability on search markets: Toward understanding the effects of inflation. *The American Economic Review*, 1385–1396.

Uribe, M. (2016). *Is the monetarist arithmetic unpleasant? (tech. rep.).* National Bureau of Economic Research.

CHAPTER 20

Rules vs Discretion

Now, let's move back to the new keynesian world of Chapter 15 where the existence of nominal rigidities implies that monetary policy (MP) can have real effects. Most central banks believe this a more realistic description of the environment, at least in the short run. In such a world, MP has to assess the trade-offs when it comes to stabilising inflation versus stabilising output. In this chapter we develop a framework that will let us analyse this.

20.1 | A basic framework

Fortunately, we have already developed most of the ingredients of such framework: it's the canonical New Keynesian model! As you may recall, it is founded on two basic equations, the New Keynesian IS curve (NKIS), and the New Keynesian Phillips curve (NKPC), which we rewrite here for your convenience. First, the NKIS:

$$y_t = E_t[y_{t+1}] - \sigma \left(i_t - E_t[\pi_{t+1}] - \rho \right) + u_t^{IS}. \tag{20.1}$$

This is exactly as we had before, with u_t^{IS} corresponding to an (aggregate demand) shock. We specify shocks being a random, white-noise disturbance.

Now, the NKPC:

$$\pi_t = \kappa(y_t - y_t^n) + \beta E_t[\pi_{t+1}] + u_t^\pi, \tag{20.2}$$

with u_t^π corresponding to an (aggregate supply) shock. If you check this against the specification of previous chapters, the main difference you will notice is the existence of these demand and supply shocks.

You will recall that, when we discussed the canonical NK model, we talked about an interest rate rule, namely the celebrated Taylor rule. Now is the time to think about the nature of monetary policy rules more broadly.

20.1.1 | Time inconsistency

The first thing we have to do is to think about what the central bank/policy-maker (CB, for shorthand) wants to do. We assume that, when it comes to inflation, it wants to minimise departures from the optimal level, which we normalize to zero. (Again, it could be positive, could be negative – it's just

How to cite this book chapter:
Campante, F., Sturzenegger, F. and Velasco, A. 2021. *Advanced Macroeconomics: An Easy Guide.*
Ch. 20. 'Rules vs Discretion', pp. 315–322. London: LSE Press.
DOI: https://doi.org/10.31389/lsepress.ame.t   License: CC-BY-NC 4.0.

a normalization.) When it comes to output, we will introduce a more consequential assumption: we take that the CB wants to minimise deviations not from the natural rate (y), but rather from what we may call the Walrasian rate of output, which we call y^*. Think of this as the output level that would prevail in the absence of any market distortions, such as monopoly power or distortionary taxation. The idea is that it is almost surely the case that $y^* > y$ – monopolies produce suboptimal quantities, distortionary taxes lead to suboptimal effort, etc.

In order to capture this idea, we will usually think of the CB as minimising a loss function like this:

$$L = \frac{1}{2}\left[\alpha \pi_t^2 + \left(y_t - y^*\right)^2\right],\tag{20.3}$$

where $\alpha > 0$ denotes the relative importance of inflation as compared to output deviations.

To discuss the implications, let's develop a model to deal with this issue in the spirit of Rogoff (1985). The details follow Velasco (1996) which uses a simpler Phillips curve, but which captures the spirit of (20.2). In this simplified version the economy is fully characterised by the expectational Phillips curve

$$y_t - y = \theta\left(\pi_t - \pi_t^e\right) + z_t, \quad \theta > 0,\tag{20.4}$$

where π is the actual rate of inflation, π^e is the expected rate, y_t is actual output, y is steady state (or natural rate) output, and z_t is a random shock (which should be interpreted here as a supply shock) with mean zero and variance σ^2. The term $\theta\left(\pi_t - \pi_t^e\right)$ implies that whenever actual inflation is below expected inflation, output falls. Notice that the supply shock is the only shock here (we assume away demand shocks, whether of the nominal or real kind).

The social loss function is

$$L = \left(\frac{1}{2}\right)\left(\alpha \pi_t^2 + \left(y_t - \gamma y\right)^2\right), \quad \alpha > 0, \gamma > 1.\tag{20.5}$$

The function (20.5) indicates that society dislikes fluctuations in both inflation and output. Notice that the bliss output rate is $y^* = \gamma y$, is above the natural rate of y. This will be a source of problems.

The timing of actions is as follows. The economy has a natural output rate y which is known by all players. The public moves first, setting its expectations of inflation. The shock z_t is then realised. The policymaker moves next, setting π to minimise (20.5) subject to (20.4), the realisation of the shock (known to the policymaker) and the public's expectations of inflation. Notice this timing implies the policymaker has an informational advantage over the public.

By assuming that the policymaker can control π_t directly, we are finessing the issue of whether that control is exercised via a money rule (and, therefore, flexible exchange rates), an interest rate rule, or an exchange rate rule. What is key is that the authorities can set whatever policy tool is at their disposal once expectations have been set.

The policy maker, acting with discretion sets, π_t optimally, taking π_t^e (which has been already set) as given. Substituting (20.4) into (20.5) the objective function becomes

$$L = \left(\frac{1}{2}\right)\alpha \pi_t^2 + \left(\frac{1}{2}\right)\left[\theta\left(\pi_t - \pi_t^e\right) + z_t - y(\gamma - 1)\right]^2.\tag{20.6}$$

Minimising with respect to π_t yields

$$\alpha \pi_t + \theta\left[\theta\left(\pi_t - \pi_t^e\right) + z_t - y(\gamma - 1)\right] = 0.\tag{20.7}$$

Rearranging we arrive at

$$\theta \pi_t = (1 - \lambda) \left[\theta \pi_t^e - z_t + y(\gamma - 1) \right],\tag{20.8}$$

where $\lambda \equiv \frac{\alpha}{\alpha + \theta^2} < 1$.

If, in addition, we impose the rational expectations condition that $\pi_t^e = E\pi_t$, we have from (20.8) that

$$\theta \pi_t^e = \left(\frac{1 - \lambda}{\lambda} \right) (\gamma - 1) y.\tag{20.9}$$

Hence, under discretion, inflation expectations are positive as long as $(\gamma - 1) y$ is positive. Since $(\gamma - 1) y$ is the difference between the natural rate of output and the target rate in the policymaker's loss function, we conclude that, as long as this difference is positive, the economy exhibits an inflation bias: expected inflation is positive.

Using (20.9) in (20.8) yields

$$\theta \pi_t = \left(\frac{1 - \lambda}{\lambda} \right) (\gamma - 1) y - (1 - \lambda) z_t,\tag{20.10}$$

or, more simply,

$$\pi_t = \left(\frac{1 - \lambda}{\theta \lambda} \right) (\gamma - 1) y - \frac{(1 - \lambda)}{\theta} z_t,\tag{20.11}$$

so that actual inflation depends on the shock as well as on the fixed inflation bias term. The fact that the CB wants to boost output above its natural level leads to a problem of dynamic inconsistency and inflationary bias that was originally pointed out by Kydland and Prescott (1977), and Barro and Gordon (1983). This is one of the most important and influential results for modern macroeconomic policy-making, and its intuition points squarely at the limits of systematic policy in a world where people are rational and forward-looking: they will figure out the CB's incentives, and, because of that, the tradeoff that the CB would like to exploit vanishes. Rational expectations implies that the equilibrium will occur at an inflation rate sufficiently high so that the cost of increasing inflation further would not be desirable to the CB. Once this anticipation is included in the model, discretion does not help expand output. In fact, if all could agree to a lower inflation, everybody would be better off.

The main takeaway is that *credibility* is a key element of monetary policy practice: if people believe the CB's commitment to fight inflation and not to exploit the inflation-output tradeoff systematically, the terms of the tradeoff in the short run become more favourable. This idea has been encapsulated in the mantra of *rules vs discretion*: policy-makers are better off in the long run if they are able to commit to rules, rather than trying to make policy in discretionary fashion.

20.1.2 | A brief history of monetary policy

In common policy parlance, the lesson is that being subject to time inconsistency, the CB needs to find an anchor for monetary policy. This anchor helps keep inflation expectations in check, and ameliorate the time inconsistency problem. The drawback is that the anchor may be too rigid, and make monetary policy less effective or have other side effects. Therefore the key issue is how to find an anchor that delivers credibility while not jeopardising the ability to react to shocks. One such mechanism is to appoint conservative central bankers,[1] who would have a low γ; or insuring the independence of the CB and having it focus squarely on inflation. These two policies, now widely used, have helped to reduce the inflation bias as shown in Figure 20.1. But in addition to these obvious solutions, the quest to

Figure 20.1   Inflation: advanced economies (blue line) and emerging markets (red line)

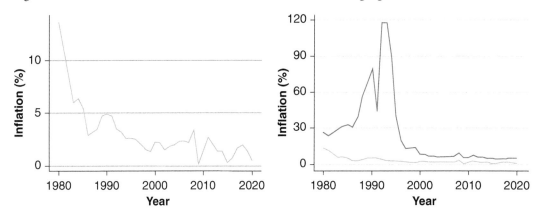

build a monetary framework that provides credibility and flexibility has gone on for decades. Mishkin (1999)) provides a nice narrative that we summarize as follows:

- The age of discretion lasted until the early 70s when there was a belief that there was a long term tradeoff between inflation and output. During this period there were no major objections to the use of monetary policy. The Keynesian/monetarist debate focused on the relative merits of fiscal vs. monetary policy.
- The rise of inflation in the 1970s led to increased skepticism on the role of monetary policy, and led to the acknowledgement that a nominal anchor was required. The discussion took place mostly in the U.S., as most other countries still had a fixed exchange rate that they carried over from the Bretton Woods system (and therefore no monetary policy of their own). But once countries started recovering their monetary policies by floating the exchange rate, monetary aggregates became the prime nominal anchor. Central banks committed to a certain growth in monetary aggregates over the medium term, while retaining flexibility in the short run.
- By the 1980s, it was clear that monetary aggregate targeting was not working very well, mostly due to instability in the demand for money. Gerald Bouey, then governor of the Bank of Canada, described the situation in his famous quote "We didn't abandon monetary aggregates, they abandoned us."
- Starting in the 1990s, central banks have increasingly used inflation itself as the nominal target. This is the so called inflation targeting regime. Other central banks (the Fed in the U.S.) have remained committed to low inflation, but without adopting an explicit target (though Fed governors embrace openly the idea of a 2% target for annual inflation recently updated to "an average of 2% over time"). Other countries remained using fixed exchange rates, while monetary targeting went in disuse.
- Inflation targeting, however, has a drawback: it magnifies output volatility when the economy is subject to substantial supply shocks. As a response many central bankers do not run a strict inflation targeting but a flexible inflation targeting, where the target is a long run objective retaining substantial flexibility in the short run.[2]
- More recently, some central banks have veered away from targeting inflation and started targeting inflation expectations instead (see Adrian et al. (2018)).

20.2 | The emergence of inflation targeting

Given its increasing popularity, let's spend some time analysing the monetary framework of inflation targeting. We laid the framework above which gave us a solution for the inflation rate.

Recall that using (20.9) in (20.8) yields

$$\theta \pi_t = \left(\frac{1-\lambda}{\lambda}\right)(\gamma - 1)\,y - (1 - \lambda)\,z_t, \tag{20.12}$$

so that actual inflation depends on the shock as well as on the fixed inflation bias term. Subtracting (20.9) from (20.12) yields

$$\theta\left(\pi_t - \pi_t^e\right) = -(1 - \lambda)\,z_t, \tag{20.13}$$

or

$$y_t = y + \lambda z_t. \tag{20.14}$$

That is, deviations of output from the natural rate are random and depend on the shock and on the parameter λ.

Finally, using (20.12) and (20.14) in (20.5) yields

$$L = \left(\frac{1}{2}\right)\left(\frac{1-\lambda}{\lambda}\right)\left[(\gamma - 1)\,y - \lambda z_t\right]^2 + \left(\frac{1}{2}\right)\left(y(1 - \gamma) + \lambda z_t\right)^2, \tag{20.15}$$

and taking expectations we have

$$L = \left(\frac{1}{2}\right)\left(\frac{1}{\lambda}\right)\left[(\gamma - 1)^2\,y^2 + \lambda^2 E z_t^2\right], \tag{20.16}$$

or

$$EL^{disc} = \left(\frac{1}{2}\right)\left[\frac{(\gamma - 1)^2\,y^2}{\lambda} + \lambda\sigma^2\right], \tag{20.17}$$

where σ^2 is the variance of z_t and the expectation is unconditional – that is, taken without knowing the realisation of z_t. Hence, expected social loss is increasing in the natural rate y, in the difference between γ and 1, and in the variance of the shock.

20.2.1 | A rigid inflation rule

Consider what happens, on the other hand, if the policymaker has precommitted not to manipulate inflation, therefore setting $\pi_t = 0$. The Phillips curve dictates that

$$y_t = y - \theta\pi_t^e + z_t. \tag{20.18}$$

If, in addition, the rule is credible, so that $\pi_t^e = 0$, we have

$$y_t = y + z_t. \tag{20.19}$$

Notice that, unlike the case of discretionary policy (see expression (20.14)), here output absorbs the full impact of the shock (the coefficient λ is missing).

The corresponding loss is

$$L^{rule} = \left(\frac{1}{2}\right)\left[-y(\gamma - 1) + z_t\right]^2. \tag{20.20}$$

The unconditional expectation of (20.20) is

$$EL^{rule} = \left(\frac{1}{2}\right)\left[y^2\,(\gamma - 1)^2 + \sigma^2\right]. \tag{20.21}$$

20.2.2 | Which regime is better?

If the unconditional expectation of the loss is the welfare criterion, then deciding which regime is better depends on parameter values. Expressions (20.17) and (20.21) reveal that $EL^{rule} < EL^{disc}$ if and only if $(\gamma - 1)y > \sigma\sqrt{\lambda}$. The LHS is a proxy for the inflation bias under discretion; the RHS is a proxy for the variability cost under a rigid rule. The rigid rule is better when the former is larger, and vice versa. In short, you prefer a fixed rule if your inflation bias is large and the supply shocks small.

20.2.3 | The argument for inflation targeting

Suppose now that the social objective function is still given by (20.5), but that now the policymaker is given the objective function

$$L^p = \left(\frac{1}{2}\right)\alpha\left(\pi_t + \pi\right)^2 + \left(\frac{1}{2}\right)\left(y_t - \gamma y\right)^2, \tag{20.22}$$

where $-\pi$ is the bliss rate of inflation for the policymaker. We can interpret this as the target assigned to the policymaker by society.

Substituting (20.4) into (20.22), one gets

$$L^p = \left(\frac{1}{2}\right)\alpha\left(\pi_t + \pi\right)^2 + \left(\frac{1}{2}\right)\left[\theta\left(\pi_t - \pi_t^e\right) + z_t - (\gamma - 1)y\right]^2. \tag{20.23}$$

Minimising with respect to π_t yields

$$\alpha\left(\pi_t + \pi\right) + \theta\left[\theta\left(\pi_t - \pi_t^e\right) + z_t - (\gamma - 1)y\right] = 0. \tag{20.24}$$

Rearranging we arrive at

$$\theta\pi_t = (1 - \lambda)\left[\theta\pi_t^e - z_t + y(\gamma - 1)\right] - \lambda\theta\pi. \tag{20.25}$$

Taking expectations we have

$$\theta\pi_t^e = \left(\frac{1 - \lambda}{\lambda}\right)(\gamma - 1)y - \theta\pi, \tag{20.26}$$

so the inflation bias is positive or negative depending on the setting of π. Suppose the target is set so that the inflation bias is zero. Having $\theta\pi_t^e = 0$ implies

$$\lambda\theta\pi = (1 - \lambda)(\gamma - 1)y. \tag{20.27}$$

Using this in (20.25) yields

$$\theta\pi_t = -(1 - \lambda)z_t. \tag{20.28}$$

Using this and $\pi_t^e = 0$ in (20.4) yields

$$y_t - y = \lambda z_t, \tag{20.29}$$

so that deviations of output from its long run level are the same as under discretion.

Finally, using (20.28) and (20.29) into the public's loss function (20.5) yields

$$L = \left(\frac{1}{2}\right) \lambda (1 - \lambda) z_t^2 + \left(\frac{1}{2}\right) \left[\lambda z_t - (\gamma - 1) y\right]^2. \tag{20.30}$$

Taking expectations and rearranging

$$EL^{target} = \left(\frac{1}{2}\right) \left[\lambda \sigma^2 + (\gamma - 1)^2 y^2\right]. \tag{20.31}$$

It is easy to check that EL^{target} is smaller than either EL^{disc} or EL^{rule}. That is, inflation targeting is better for welfare than fully discretionary policy and a rigid rule. The intuition should be simple: targeting enjoys the flexibility benefits of discretion and the credibility benefits of a rule (the inflation bias is zero).

20.2.4 | In sum

As inflation in the world decreased, monetary policy entered into a happy consensus by the 2000s. Credibility had been restored, and even those central banks that did not explicitly target inflation were widely understood to be essentially doing the same. The short-term interest rate was the policy tool of choice. Enhanced credibility, or the so called "flattening of the Phillips curve" made monetary policy more powerful as a stabilisation mechanism, and as a result became the tool of choice for steering the business cycle. Some central bankers even acquired heroic, pop-culture status.

But then, the 2008/2009 crisis hit. The consensus was revealed inadequate to deal with the crisis at its worst, and questions were raised as to the extent to which monetary policy had failed to prevent (and perhaps contributed to) the Great Recession and, later on, the European Crisis. Perhaps with the benefit of hindsight, the challenge proved to be central bank's finest hour: the recoveries were relatively swift and inflation remained low. The hard-gained credibility provided the room for massive increases in liquidity, that shattered not a bit the credibility of the central banks and allowed to counteract the drainage of liquidity during the crises. This was perhaps best epitomised in a celebrated quote by Mario Draghi, then governor of the European Central Bank who, in July 2012, announced that the Central Bank would do "whatever it takes". This phrase, as of today, is the symbol of the coming of age of modern CB when full discretion can be pursued without rising an eyebrow or affecting expectations!

Notes

[1] One way of illustrating this debate is to remember the discussion surrounding the creation of the European Central Bank. As a novel institution whose governance was in the hands of a number of countries, it was not clear how it would build its credibility. Someone suggested to locate it in Frankfurt, so it could absorb (by proximity?) Germany's conservative approach to monetary policy. The french wanted to control the presidency, but this was considered not sufficiently strong at least at the beginning, so they compromised on a two year presidency with a Dutch. However, after two years, when French Jean Marie Trichet took over, he still had to be overly conservative to build his, and the institution's, credibility.

[2] We should also keep in mind that inflation targeting does not mean that the central bank or policy maker does not care about anything other than inflation. As we show in the model in the next section, the central bank's objective function may take deviations of output into account – the relative weight of output will affect the tolerance of the central bank to deviations of inflation from the target as a result of shocks.

References

Adrian, T., Laxton, M. D., & Obstfeld, M. M. (2018). *Advancing the frontiers of monetary policy*. International Monetary Fund.

Barro, R. J. & Gordon, D. B. (1983). Rules, discretion and reputation in a model of monetary policy. *Journal of Monetary Economics*, *12*(1), 101–121.

Kydland, F. E. & Prescott, E. C. (1977). Rules rather than discretion: The inconsistency of optimal plans. *Journal of Political Economy*, *85*(3), 473–491.

Mishkin, F. S. (1999). International experiences with different monetary policy regimes. *Journal of Monetary Economics*, *43*(3), 579–605.

Rogoff, K. (1985). The optimal degree of commitment to an intermediate monetary target. *The Quarterly Journal of Economics*, *100*(4), 1169–1189.

Velasco, A. (1996). Fixed exchange rates: Credibility, flexibility and multiplicity. *European Economic Review, 40*, 1023–1035.

CHAPTER 21

Recent debates in monetary policy

In the last two chapters we presented the basic analytics of monetary policy in the long and in the short run. For the short run, we developed a simple New Keynesian model that can parsimoniously make sense of policy as it has been understood and practised over the last few decades.

Before the 2008 financial crisis, most advanced-country central banks, and quite a few emerging-market central banks as well, carried out monetary policy by targeting a short-term interest rate. In turn, movements in this interest rate were typically guided by the desire to keep inflation close to a pre-defined target — this was the popular policy of inflation targeting. This consensus led to a dramatic decrease in inflation, to the point of near extinction in most economies, over the last two or three decades.

But this benign consensus was shaken by the Great Financial Crisis of 2008-2009. First, there was criticism that policy had failed to prevent (and perhaps contributed to unleashing) the crisis. Soon, all of the world´s major central banks were moving fast and courageously into uncharted terrain, cutting interest rates sharply and all the way to zero. A first and key issue, therefore, was whether the conventional tools of policy had been rendered ineffective by the zero lower bound.

In response to the crisis, and in a change that persists until today, central banks adopted all kinds of unconventional or unorthodox monetary policies. They have used central bank reserves to buy Treasury bonds and flood markets with liquidity, in a policy typically called quantitative easing. And they have also used their own reserves to buy private sector credit instruments (in effect lending directly to the private sector) in a policy often referred to as credit easing.

Interest rate policy has also become more complex. Central banks have gone beyond controlling the contemporary short rate, and to announcing the future path of short rates (for a period of time that could last months or years), in an attempt at influencing expectations a policy known as forward guidance. Last but not least, monetary authorities have also begun paying interest on their own reserves — which, to the extent that there is a gap between this rate and the short-term market rate of interest (say, on bonds), gives central bankers an additional policy tool.

These policies can be justified on several grounds. One is the traditional control of inflation — updated in recent years to include avoidance of deflation as well. Another is control of aggregate demand and output, especially when the zero lower bound on the nominal interest limits the effectiveness of traditional monetary policy. A third reason for unconventional policies is financial stability: if

How to cite this book chapter:
Campante, F., Sturzenegger, F. and Velasco, A. 2021. *Advanced Macroeconomics: An Easy Guide.*
  Ch. 21. 'Recent debates in monetary policy', pp. 323–344. London: LSE Press.
  DOI: https://doi.org/10.31389/lsepress.ame.u   License: CC-BY-NC 4.0.

spikes in spreads, for instance, threaten the health of banks and other financial intermediaries (this is exactly what happened in 2007-09), then monetary policy may need to act directly on those spreads to guarantee stability and avoid runs and the risk of bankruptcy.

Do these policies work, in the sense of attaining some or all of these objectives? How do they work? Why do they work? What does their effectiveness (or lack of effectiveness) hinge on?

A massive academic literature on these questions has emerged during the last decade. Approaches vary, but the most common line of attack has been to append a financial sector to the standard New Keynesian model (yes, hard to believe, but, until the crisis, finance was largely absent from most widely-used macro models), and then explore the implications.

This change brings at least two benefits. First, finance can itself be a source of disturbances, as it occurred in 2007-09 and had also occurred in many earlier financial crises in emerging markets. Second, the enlarged model can be used to study how monetary policy can respond to both financial and conventional disturbances, with the financial sector also playing the role of potential amplifier of those shocks.

Here we cannot summarise that literature in any detail (but do look at Eggertsson and Woodford (2003), Gertler and Karadi (2011), and the survey by Brunnermeier et al. (2013) for a taste). What we do is extend our standard NK model of earlier sections and chapters to include a role for liquidity and finance, and we use the resulting model to study a few (not all) varieties of unconventional monetary policy.

The issues surrounding conventional and unconventional monetary policies have taken on new urgency because of the Covid-19 crisis. In the course of 2020, central banks again resorted to interest, cutting it all the way to the zero lower bound, coupled with quantitative easing and credit easing policies that are even more massive than those used over a decade ago. And in contrast to the Great Financial Crisis, when only advanced-country central banks experimented with unconventional policies, this time around many emerging-economy central banks have dabbled as well. So understanding how those policies work has key and urgent policy relevance — and that is the purpose of this chapter.

21.1 | The liquidity trap and the zero lower bound

John Hicks, in the famous paper where he introduced the IS-LM model, Hicks (1937), showed how monetary policy in occasions might become ineffective. These "liquidity traps" as he called them, occurred when the interest rate fell to zero and could not be pushed further down. In this section we model this liquidity trap in our New Keynesian framework.

Until not too long ago, economists viewed the liquidity trap as the stuff of textbooks, not reality. But then in the 1990s Japan got stuck in a situation of very low or negative inflation and no growth. No matter what the Japanese authorities tried, nothing seemed to work. In 1998, Paul Krugman pointed out that "here we are with what surely looks a lot like a liquidity trap in the world's second-largest economy". And then he proceeded to show that such a trap could happen not just in the static IS-LM model, but in a more sophisticated, dynamic New Keynesian model.

Of course, the experience of Japan was not the only one in which a liquidity trap took center stage. During the world financial crisis of 2008-09, the world's major central banks cut their interests to zero or thereabouts, and found that policy alone was not sufficient to contain the collapse of output. The same, perhaps with greater intensity and speed, has occurred during the Covid-19 crisis of 2020-21, with monetary authorities cutting rates to zero and searching for other policy tools to contain the destruction of jobs and the drop in activity. So, the issues surrounding the zero lower bound and liquidity traps are a central concern of macroeconomists today[1].

To study such traps formally, let us return to the two-equation canonical New Keynesian model of Chapter 15

$$\dot{\pi}_t = \rho \pi_t - \kappa x_t, \tag{21.1}$$

$$\dot{x}_t = \sigma \left(i_t - \pi_f - r^n \right), \tag{21.2}$$

where, recall, π_t is inflation, x_t is the output gap, i_t is the policy-determined nominal interest rate, $r^n \equiv \rho + \sigma^{-1} g$ is the natural or Wicksellian interest rate, which depends on both preferences (the discount rate ρ and the elasticity σ) and trend productivity growth (g).

To close the model, instead of simply assuming a mechanic policy rule (of the Taylor type or some other type, as we did in Chapter 15), we consider alternative paths for the interest rate in response to an exogenous shock. Werning (2011), in an influential and elegant analysis of the liquidity trap, studies formal optimisation by the policymaker, both under rules and under discretion. Here we take a somewhat more informal approach, which draws from his analysis and delivers some of the same policy insights.[2]

Define a liquidity trap as a situation in which the zero lower bound is binding and monetary policy is powerless to stabilise inflation and output. To fix ideas, consider the following shock:

$$r^n_t = \begin{cases} \underline{r^n} < 0 & \text{for } 0 \leq t < T \\ r^n > 0 & \text{for } t \geq T. \end{cases} \tag{21.3}$$

Starting from r^n, at time 0 the natural rate of interest unexpectedly goes down to $\underline{r^n}$, and it remains there until time T, when it returns to r^n and stays there forever. The key difference between this shock and that studied in Chapter 15 in the context of the same model, is that now the natural rate of interest is *negative* for an interval of time. Recall that this rate depends on preferences and on trend growth in the natural rate of output. So if this productivity growth becomes sufficiently negative, r^n_t could be negative as well.

Notice that the combination of flagging productivity and a negative natural rate of interest corresponds to what Summers (2018) has labelled secular stagnation. The point is important, because, if secular stagnation, defined by Summers precisely as a situation in which the natural rate of interest falls below zero for a very long time (secular comes from the Latin *soeculum*, meaning *century*), then economies will often find themselves in a liquidity trap.

The other novel component of the analysis here, compared to Chapter 15, is that now we explicitly impose the zero lower bound on the nominal interest rate, and require that $i_t \geq 0 \forall t$.

If the central bank acts with discretion, choosing its preferred action at each instant, the zero lower bound will become binding as it responds to the shock. To see this, let us first ask what the central bank will optimally do once the shock is over at time T. Recall the canonical New Keynesian model displays, what Blanchard and Galí (2007) called the divine coincidence: there is no conflict between keeping inflation low and stabilising output. If $i = r^n$, then $\pi_t = x_t = 0$ is an equilibrium. So starting at time T, any central bank that is happiest when both inflation and the output gap are at zero will engineer exactly that outcome, ensuring $\pi_t = x_t = 0 \quad \forall t \geq T$.

In terms of the phase diagram in Figure 21.1, we assume that initially (before the shock) $i = r^n$, so that $\pi_t = 0 \forall t < 0$. Therefore, the initial steady state was at point A, and to that point exactly the system must return at time T. What happens between dates 0 and T? Trying to prevent a recession and the

Figure 21.1 Monetary policy in the ZLB

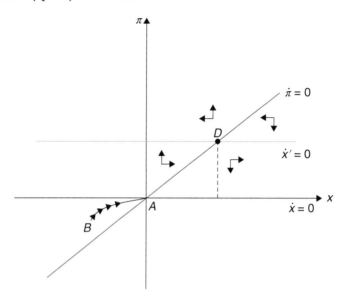

corresponding deflation, the central bank will cut the nominal interest all the way to zero. That will mean that between dates 0 and T, dynamics correspond to the system with steady state at point D, but because of the zero lower bound, policy cannot take the economy all the way back to the pre-shock situation and keep $\pi_t = x_t = 0$ always. So, on impact the system jumps to point B, and both inflation and the output gap remain negative (deflation and depression or at least recession take hold) in the aftermath of the shock and until date T [3].

Both Krugman (1998) and Werning (2011) emphasise that the problem is the central bank's lack of credibility: keeping the economy at $\pi_t = x_t = 0$ is optimal starting at time T, and so people in this economy will pay no attention to announcements by the central bank that claim something else. In technical language, the monetary authority suffers from a time inconsistency problem of the kind identified by Kydland and Prescott (1977) and Calvo (1978) (see Chapter 20): from the point of view of any time before time T, engineering some inflation after T looks optimal. But when time T arrives, zero inflation and a zero output gap become optimal.

What is to be done? This is Krugman's (1998) answer: The way to make monetary policy effective, then, is for the Central Bank to credibly promise to be irresponsible – to make a persuasive case that it will permit inflation to occur, thereby producing the negative real interest rates the economy needs. In fact, there are simple paths for the nominal interest rate that, if the central bank could commit to them, would deliver a better result. Consider a plan, for instance, that keeps inflation and the output gap constant at

$$\pi_t = -\underline{r}^n > 0 \ \text{ and } \ x_t = -\frac{\underline{r}^n}{\kappa} > 0 \quad \forall t \geq 0. \tag{21.4}$$

Since $i_t = r_t^n + \pi_t$, it follows that $i_t = 0 \quad \forall t < T$, and $i_t = r^n - \underline{r}^n > 0 \quad \forall t \geq T$. Although this policy is not fully optimal, it may well (depending on the social welfare function and on parameter values) deliver higher welfare than the policy of $i_t = 0$ forever, which causes recession and deflation between

0 and T. And note that as prices become less sticky (in the limit, as κ goes to infinity), the output gap goes to zero, so this policy ensures no recession (and no boom either)[4].

Notice, strikingly, that this policy - just like the one described in the phase diagram above - also involves keeping the nominal interest stuck against the zero lower bound during the whole duration of the adverse shock, between times 0 and T. So if the policy is the same over that time interval, why are results different? Why is there no recession as a result of the shock? Crucially, the difference arises because now people expect there will be inflation and a positive output gap after time T, and this pushes up inflation before T (recall from Chapter 15 that inflation today increases with the present discounted value of the output gaps into the infinite future), reducing the real interest rate and pushing up consumption demand and economic activity.

Of course, the alternative policy path just considered is just one such path that avoids recession, but not necessarily the optimal path. Werning (2011) and, before that, Eggertsson and Woodford (2003) characterised the fully optimal policies needed to get out of a liquidity trap. Details vary, but the main message is clear: during the shock, the central bank needs to be able to persuade people (to pre-commit, in the language of theory) it will create inflation *after* the shock is over.

What can central banks do to acquire the much-needed credibility to become "irresponsible"? One possibility is that they try to influence expectations through what has become known as "forward guidance". One example, is the Fed's repeated assertion that it anticipates that "weak economic conditions are likely to warrant exceptionally low levels of the federal funds rate for some time". Alternatively, central bankers can stress that they will remain vigilant and do whatever it takes to avoid a deep recession. For instance, on 28 February 2020, when the Covid 19 pandemic was breaking out, Fed Chairman Jerome Powell issued this brief statement:

> The fundamentals of the U.S. economy remain strong. However, the coronavirus poses evolving risks to economic activity. The Federal Reserve is closely monitoring developments and their implications for the economic outlook. We will use our tools and act as appropriate to support the economy.

When put this way, the problem seems relatively simple to solve: the CB needs only to use these additional tools to obtain a similar result to what it would obtain by simply playing around with the short-term nominal interest rate, as in normal times. Unfortunately, this is not that easy precisely because of the crucial role played by expectations and credibility. The crucial point is that the central bankers need to convince the public that it will pursue expansionary policies in the future, even if inflation runs above target, and this runs counter to their accumulated credibility as hawkish inflation-fighters and committed inflation-targeters.

Recent thinking on these issues - and on other policy alternatives available to policymakers when against the zero lower bound - is summarised in Woodford (2016). He argues that, when it comes to forward guidance, what is needed are explicit criteria or rules about what would lead the central bank to change policy in the future - criteria that would facilitate commitment to being irresponsible.

One way to do that is to make policy history-dependent: the central bank commits to keep a certain path for interest rates unless certain criteria, in terms of a certain target for the output gap or unemployment or nominal GDP, for instance, are met. The Fed has actually moved recently towards that approach, stating that current low rates will be maintained unless unemployment falls below a certain level, or inflation rises above a certain level. The recent inflation targeting shift by the Bank of Japan can also be interpreted in line with this approach.

Another way forward is to move from an inflation target to a price level target (see Eggertsson and Woodford (2003) and Eggertsson and Woodford (2004)). The benefit of a price-level target over an inflation target to fight deflation is that it meets enhanced deflationary pressure with an intensified commitment to pursue expansionary policy in the future (even if the target price level is unchanged). An inflation target, on the other hand, lets bygones be bygones: a drop in prices today does not affect the course of policy in the future, since, under inflation targeting, the central bank is focused only on the current rate of change in prices. Thus, inflation targeting does not induce the same kind of stabilising adjustment of expectations about the future course of policy as does price-level targeting[5].

And if a rethinking of the traditional inflation targeting framework is called for, another rule that has gained adherents recently is the so-called NGDP or nominal GDP level targeting (see Sumner (2014) and Beckworth (2019)). In targeting nominal GDP the central bank could commit to compensate for falls in output by allowing for higher inflation. The underlying point is that NGDP would provide a better indicator, compared to inflation alone, of the kind of policy intervention that is needed.

21.2 | Reserves and the central bank balance sheet

As we mentioned, the Great Financial Crisis introduced a wealth of new considerations for monetary policy. In this section we develop a model of quantitative easing where the Central Bank pays money on its reserves, adding a new variable to the policy tool which was not present in our traditional monetary models where the rate of return on all Central Bank liabilities was fixed at zero. We will see this introduces a number of new issues. While the modelling does not make this necessarily explicit, underlying the new paradigm is the understanding that there is a financial sector that intermediates liquidity. Thus, before going into the full fledged optimisation problem, we lay out a more pedestrian approach to illustrate some of the issues.

21.2.1 | Introducing the financial sector

To introduce these new issues we can start from a simple IS-LM type of model, as in the lower panel of Figure 21.2.[6]

If there are financial intermediaries, there must be multiple interest rates – one that is paid to savers (i^s), and another that is charged from borrowers (i^b). Otherwise, of course, how would those intermediaries make any money? This market, depicting the supply of loans and the demand for loans, is shown in the upper panel of Figure 21.2. The IS curve below is drawn for a given level of spread.

As a result, the role of intermediation introduces a new channel for the amplification and propagation of economic shocks. For instance, suppose a high level of economic activity affects asset prices, and hence the net worth of financial intermediaries and borrowers. This will allow for additional borrowing at any level of spread (a shift of the XS curve to the right). This makes the IS curve flatter than what it would otherwise be: the same change in income would be associated with a smaller change in the interest rate paid to savers. This amplifies the effects on output of any shift in the LM/MP curves.

Even more interestingly, this lets us consider the effects of direct shocks to intermediation – beyond the amplification of other shocks. An upward shift of the XS curve (less credit available for any level of spread) means a downward shift to the IS curve – a larger equilibrium spread translated into less interest being paid to savers. This shock, illustrated in Figure 21.2, leads (in the absence of monetary policy compensating for the negative shock) to an output contraction with falling interest rates. Anything that impairs the capital of financial intermediaries (say, a collapse in the prices of mortgage-backed

Figure 21.2 Effects of a disruption of credit supply

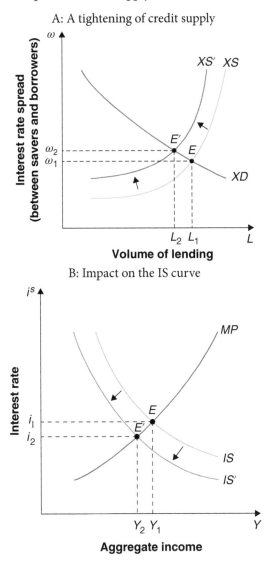

A: A tightening of credit supply

B: Impact on the IS curve

securities they hold) or that tighten leverage constraints (say, they are required to post more collateral when raising funds because the market is suspicious of their solvency) will correspond to such an upward shift of the XS curve. If the IS curve is shifted far enough to the left, monetary policy may be constrained by the zero lower bound on interest rates. Does all of that sound familiar?

Needless to say, a simple IS-LM type of framework leaves all sorts of questions open in terms of the microfoundations behind the curves we've been fiddling around with. To that point we now turn.

21.2.2 | A model of quantitative easing

Now we focus on the role of the central bank balance and, more specifically, on the role of central bank reserves in the conduct of unconventional monetary policy. This emphasis has a practical motivation. As Figure 21.3 makes clear, the Federal Reserve (and other central banks) have issued reserves to purchase government bonds, private-sector bonds and other kinds of papers, dramatically enlarging the size of central bank balance sheets.

The assets in Figure 21.3 have been financed mostly with overnight interest paying voluntarily held deposits by financial institutions at the central bank. We call these deposits reserves for short.

As Reis (2016) emphasises, reserves have two unique features that justify this focus. First, the central bank is the monopoly issuer of reserves. As a monopoly issuer, it can choose the interest to pay on these reserves. Second, only banks can hold reserves. This implies that the aggregate amount of reserves in the overall banking system is determined by the central bank.

The liability side of a central bank balance sheet has two main components: currency (think of it as bank notes) and reserves. Together, currency and reserves add up to the monetary base. The central bank perfectly controls their sum, even if it does not control the breakdown between the two components of the monetary base.

These two properties of the central bank imply that the central bank, can in principle, choose both the quantity of the monetary base and the nominal interest rate paid on reserves. Whether it can also control the quantity of reserves, and do so independently of the interest rate that it pays, depends on the demand for reserves by banks[7].

Figure 21.3   Assets held by FED, ECB, BOE and BOJ

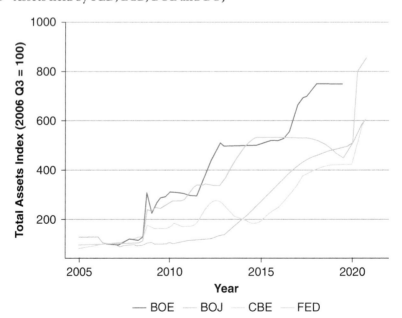

Before the 2008 financial crisis, central banks typically adjusted the volume of reserves to influence nominal interest rates in interbank markets. The zero lower bound made this policy infeasible during the crisis. Post-crisis, many central banks adopted a new process for monetary policy: they set the interest rate on reserves, and maintained a high level of reserves by paying an interest rate that is close to market rates (on bonds, say). In turn, changes in the reserve rate quickly feed into changes in interbank and other short rates.

Let D_t be the real value of a central bank-issued means of payment. You can think of it as central bank reserves. But following Diba and Loisel (2020) and Piazzesi et al. (2019), you can also think of it as a digital currency issued by the monetary authority and held directly by households[8]. In either case, the key feature of D_t is that it provides liquidity services: it enables parties to engage in buying, selling, and settling of balances. In what follows, we will refer to D_t using the acronym MP (means of payment, not be confused with our earlier use of MP for monetary policy), but do keep in mind both feasible interpretations. Later in this chapter we will show that the model developed here can also be extended (or reinterpreted, really) to study a more conventional situation in which only commercial banks have access to accounts at the central bank and households only hold deposits at commercial banks.

The simplest way to model demand for MP is to include it in the utility function of the representative household:

$$u_t = \left(\frac{\sigma}{\sigma-1}\right) Z_t^{\left(\frac{\sigma-1}{\sigma}\right)}, \quad Z_t = C_t^\alpha D_t^{1-\alpha}, \tag{21.5}$$

where $\sigma > 0$ is the interemporal elasticity of substitution in consumption, and is a Cobb-Douglas weight with α that lies between 0 and 1. The representative household maximises the present discounted value of this utility flow subject to the following budget constraint:

$$\dot{D}_t + \dot{B}_t = Y_t + \left(i_t^b - \pi_t\right) B_t + \left(i_t^d - \pi_t\right) D_t - C_t, \tag{21.6}$$

where B_t is the real value of a nominal (currency-denominated) bond, issued either by the government or by the private sector, i_t^b is the nominal interest rate paid by the bond, and i_t^d is the nominal interest rate paid by the central bank to holders of D_t. (Income Y_t comprises household income and government transfers.) In accordance with our discussion above, the monetary authority controls this interest rate and the supply of MP [9].

Since we do not want to go into the supply side of the model in any detail here, we simply include a generic formulation of household income, which should include wage income but could have other components as well. Government transfers must be included because governments may wish to rebate to agents any seigniorage collected from currency holders.

Let total assets be $A_t = B_t + D_t$. Then we can write the budget constraint as

$$\dot{A}_t = Y_t + \left(i_t^b - \pi_t\right) A_t - \left(i_t^b - i_t^d\right) D_t - C_t. \tag{21.7}$$

In the household's optimisation problem, A_t is a state variable and D_t and C_t are the control variables. First order conditions are

$$\alpha Z_t^{\left(\frac{\sigma-1}{\sigma}\right)} = C_t \lambda_t \tag{21.8}$$

$$(1-\alpha) Z_t^{\left(\frac{\sigma-1}{\sigma}\right)} = \lambda_t D_t \left(i_t^b - i_t^d\right) \tag{21.9}$$

$$\dot{\lambda}_t = -\lambda_t \left(i_t^b - \pi_t - \rho\right), \tag{21.10}$$

where λ_t is the shadow value of household assets (the co-state variable in the optimisation problem). These conditions are standard for the Ramsey problem, augmented here by the presence of the MP. It follows from (21.8) and (21.9) in logs, denoted by small case letters, the demand function for MP is

$$d_t = c_t - \Delta_t, \tag{21.11}$$

where

$$\Delta_t = \log\left[\left(\frac{\alpha}{1-\alpha}\right)\left(i_t^b - i_t^d\right)\right]. \tag{21.12}$$

So, intuitively, demand for MP is proportional to consumption and decreasing in the opportunity cost $\left(i_t^b - i_t^d\right)$ of holding MP. Notice that this demand function does not involve satiation: as $i_t^b - i_t^d$ goes to zero, d_t does not remain bounded. From a technical point of view, it means that we cannot consider here a policy of $i_t^d = i_t^{b\,10}$.

The appendix shows that in logs, the Euler equation is

$$\dot{c}_t = \sigma\left(i_t^b - \pi_t - \rho\right) + (1-\sigma)(1-\alpha)\dot{\Delta}_t. \tag{21.13}$$

Differentiating (21.11) with respect to time yields

$$\dot{c}_t - \dot{d}_t = \dot{\Delta}_t. \tag{21.14}$$

To close the model we need two more equations. One is the law of motion for real MP holdings, also in logs:

$$\dot{d}_t = \mu - \pi_t, \tag{21.15}$$

where μ is the rate of growth of the nominal stock of MP. Intuitively, the real stock rises with μ and falls with π. So μ and i_t^d are the two policy levers, with i_t^b endogenous (market-determined).

From (21.14) and (21.15) it follows that

$$\dot{c}_t = \mu - \pi_t + \dot{\Delta}_t. \tag{21.16}$$

This equation and the Euler equation (21.13) can be combined to yield

$$\dot{\Delta}_t = \frac{\sigma\left(i_t^b - \rho\right) - \mu + (1-\sigma)\pi_t}{\alpha + \sigma(1-\alpha)}. \tag{21.17}$$

Now, given the definition of Δ_t in (21.12),

$$i_t^b = \left(\alpha^{-1} - 1\right)e^{\Delta_t} + i_t^d, \tag{21.18}$$

which can trivially be included in (21.17)

$$\dot{\Delta}_t = \frac{\sigma\left[\left(\alpha^{-1} - 1\right)e^{\Delta_t} + i_t^d - \rho\right] - \mu + (1-\sigma)\pi_t}{\alpha + \sigma(1-\alpha)}. \tag{21.19}$$

Recall next that because the economy is closed all output is consumed, so $c_t = y_t$. If we again define $x_t \equiv y_t - \bar{y}$ as the output gap, the Euler equation becomes

$$\dot{x}_t = \sigma\left(i_t^b - \pi_t - r^n\right) + (1-\sigma)(1-\alpha)\dot{\Delta}_t, \tag{21.20}$$

where, as in previous sections, the natural rate of interest is $r^n \equiv \rho + \sigma^{-1}g$, and g is the exogenous rate of growth of the natural rate of output $\bar{y}$.

Next, with $c_t = y_t$ the MP demand function (21.11) becomes

$$d_t = y_t - \Delta_t,$$ (21.21)

which, in deviations from steady state, is

$$x_t = \left(d_t - \bar{d}\right) + \left(\Delta_t - \bar{\Delta}\right).$$ (21.22)

We close the model with the Phillips curve, using the same formulation as in this chapter and earlier:

$$\dot{\pi}_t = \rho\pi_t - \kappa x_t.$$ (21.23)

Replacing (21.22) in (21.23) we get

$$\dot{\pi}_t = \rho\pi_t - \kappa\left(d_t - \bar{d}\right) - \kappa\left(\Delta_t - \bar{\Delta}\right).$$ (21.24)

That completes the model, which can be reduced to a system of three differential equations in 3 unknowns, π_t, d_t and Δ_t, whose general solution is quite complex. But there is one case, that of log utility, which lends itself to a simple and purely graphical solution. On that case we focus next.

If $\sigma = 1$, then (21.19) simplifies to:

$$\dot{\Delta}_t = \left(\alpha^{-1} - 1\right) e^{\Delta_t} + i_t^d - \rho - \mu.$$ (21.25)

This is an unstable differential equation in Δ_t and exogenous parameters or policy variables. Thus, when there is a permanent shock, Δ_t jumps to the steady state. This equation does not depend on other endogenous variables $\left(x_t, d_t, \pi_t \text{ or } i_t^b\right)$, so it can be solved separately from the rest of the model. The evolution over time of Δ_t depends on itself and the policy parameters i_t^d and μ[11].

Now the Phillips curve and the law of motion for MP are a system of two differential equations in two unknowns, π_t and d_t, with $\left(\Delta_t - \bar{\Delta}\right)$ exogenously given. In matrix form the system is

$$\begin{bmatrix} \dot{\pi}_t \\ \dot{d}_t \end{bmatrix} = \Omega \begin{bmatrix} \pi_t \\ d_t \end{bmatrix} + \begin{bmatrix} \kappa\bar{d} - \kappa\left(\Delta_t - \bar{\Delta}\right) \\ \mu \end{bmatrix},$$ (21.26)

where

$$\Omega = \begin{bmatrix} \rho & -\kappa \\ -1 & 0 \end{bmatrix}.$$ (21.27)

It is straightforward to see that $\text{Det}(\Omega) = -\kappa < 0$, and $\text{Tr}(\Omega) = \rho > 0$. It follows that one of the eigenvalues of Ω is positive and the other is negative. Since π_t is a jumpy variable and d_t is a sticky or state variable, we conclude that the 2×2 system is saddle-path stable, as seen in Figure 21.4.

Before considering the effects of shocks on the dynamics of this system, let us ask: why this model? What does it add to the standard NK formulation?

The first is realism. Since the Great Financial Crisis, many central banks have begun using the interest paid on reserves as an instrument of monetary policy. This policy alternative is not something one can study in conventional NK models.

Second, and more important, not only different interest rates, but the size and composition of the central bank's balance sheet now matter. Changes in the speed of MP creation and open market operations involving MP can affect both inflation and output. For a more general discussion of the role of the central bank's balance sheet, see Curdia and Woodford (2011).

Third, a technical but policy-relevant point: this model does not suffer from the problem of nonuniqueness of equilibrium that plagues NK models with an exogenous nominal interest rate, as we saw in Chapter 15. For further discussion, see Hall and Reis (2016) and Diba and Loisel (2020).

Figure 21.4 A model of central bank reserves

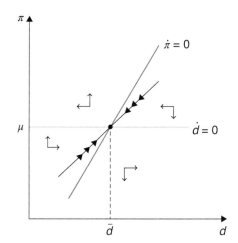

Figure 21.5 Reducing the rate on reserves

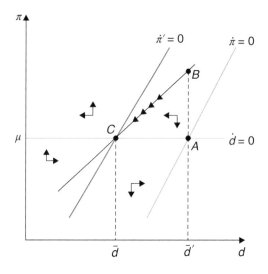

21.2.3 | Effects of monetary policy shocks

Consider first the effects of an unexpected and permanent reduction in i_t^d, one of the two policy tools the central bank has. Suppose that at time 0, i_t^d moves from i^d to $\underline{i^d}$, where $\underline{i^d} < i^d$. We show this in Figure 21.5.

Recall that in steady state the market rate of interest on bonds is pinned down by $i^b = \rho + \mu$. So, as i_t^d falls, $\bar{\Delta}$, the steady state gap between the two interest rates rises. We saw that in response to a permanent policy shock, Δ_t will immediately jump to its new (higher, in this case) steady state level. This means that we can look at the dynamics of π_t and d_t independently of Δ_t.

The other thing to notice is that as the steady state gap $\left(i^b - i^d\right)$ goes up, steady state demand for MP falls. In the phase diagram in Figure 21.5, this is reflected in the fact that the $\dot{\pi} = 0$ schedule moves to the left, and the new steady state is at point C. On impact, the system jumps up to point B, with inflation temporarily high. Thereafter, both inflation and real stocks of MP fall toward their new steady state levels.

What happens to consumption and output? The cut in i^d_t makes people want to hold less MP, but the stock of MP cannot fall immediately. What equilibrates the market for MP is a an upward jump in consumption (and output, given that prices are sticky). The temporary boom causes an increase in inflation above the rate μ of nominal MP growth, which over time erodes the real value of the stock of MP outstanding, until the system settles onto its new steady state.

In summary: the permanent cut in the interest rate paid on MP causes a temporary boom. Inflation rises and then gradually falls and so does output. All of this happens without modifying the pace of nominal MP growth. So, changes in the interest rate paid on central bank reserves (or on a digital means of payment) do serve as tool of monetary policy, with real effects.

Consider next the effects of an unexpected and permanent increase in μ, the other tool the central bank has at its disposal. Suppose that at time 0, policy moves from μ to $\bar{\mu}$, where $\bar{\mu} > \mu$. Recall again that in steady state the market rate of interest on bonds is pinned down by $i^b = \rho + \mu$. So, as μ rises and i^d remains constant, $\bar{\Delta}$, the steady state gap between the two interest rates will go up. But Δ_t will jump right away to $\bar{\Delta}$, so again we can look at the dynamics of the 2×2 system independently of Δ_t.

As the steady state gap $\left(i^b - i^d\right)$ rises, steady state demand for MP goes down. In the phase diagram in Figure 21.6, this is reflected in the fact that the $\dot{\pi} = 0$ schedule moves to the left. But now the $\dot{d} = 0$ schedule also shifts (upward), so that the new steady state is at point F. On impact, the system jumps up to point E, with inflation overshooting its new, higher, steady state level. Thereafter, both inflation and the real stock of MP fall toward their new steady state levels.

Figure 21.6 Increasing money growth

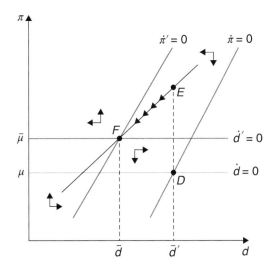

Figure 21.7 The dynamics of the interest rate spread

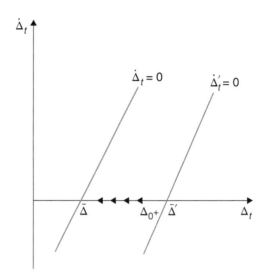

Note that the overshoot is necessary to erode the real value of MP, since in the new steady state agents will demand less of it. As in the previous case, inflation rises since consumption and output are temporarily above their steady state levels.

Finally, consider the effects of a temporary drop in i_t^d, the interest rate paid on MP. To fix ideas, consider the following unexpected shock occurring at time 0:

$$i_t^d = \begin{cases} i^d < i^d & \text{for} \ \ 0 \le t < T \\ \ i^d & \text{for} \ \ \ \ t \ge T. \end{cases} \tag{21.28}$$

To sort out what happens it helps to begin by asking what is the trajectory of Δ_t. It rises on impact, but it does not go all the way up to $\bar{\Delta}'$, the level it would take on if the change were permanent. The differential Δ_t falls thereafter, so that it can jump at T when i_t^d goes back to its initial level, ensuring that Δ_t is back to its initial steady state level $\bar{\Delta}$ an instant after T (in contrast to the policy variable, i^b cannot jump).

Let Δ_{0+} be the value of Δ_t once the unexpected shock happens at $t = 0$. It must be the case, by the arguments above, that $\bar{\Delta} < \Delta_0+ < \bar{\Delta}'$. You can see this evolution in the phase diagram in Figure 21.7, where we show the (linearised version of) the $\dot{\Delta}_t = 0$ schedule.

What are the implications for the dynamic behaviour of inflation and the real stock of MP? We can study that graphically in Figure 21.8 below. If the policy change were permanent, the $\dot{\pi} = 0$ schedule would have moved all the way to $\dot{\pi}'' = 0$, giving rise to a steady state at H. But the fact that $\Delta_0 - \bar{\Delta}' < 0$ offsets some of that leftward movement. So, the $\dot{\pi} = 0$ schedule moves to $\dot{\pi}' = 0$, creating a temporary (for an instant) steady state at G.

Ask what would happen if Δ_t were to remain at Δ_0 until time T. Inflation would jump up on impact. But it cannot go beyond point K, because if it did the system would diverge to the northwest afterwards. So, inflation would jump to a point like N. After the jump, the economy would begin to move following the arrows that correspond to the system with steady state at G.

Figure 21.8 A temporary decline in the rate on reserves

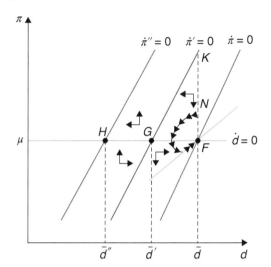

Of course, an instant after T, and because of the movement in Δ_t, the locus $\dot{\pi}' = 0$ begins to shift to the right. But this does not affect the qualitative nature of the adjustment path, because the system always lies to the right of the shifting $\dot{\pi}' = 0$ locus, and thus obeys the same laws of motion as it did an instant earlier. The evolution of inflation and real MP is guided by the need that, at T, the system must be on the saddle path leading to the initial steady state at point F.

You can see from the phase diagram that after the initial jump up, inflation falls between times 0 and T, and rises thereafter. The real value of MP drops initially due to the high inflation, but then gradually recovers as π_t falls below μ. One can show also that output goes through a boom between times 0 and T, takes a discrete drop at T when the interest rate i_t^d rises again, and recovers gradually until returning to its initial steady state level.

21.3 | Policy implications and extensions

21.3.1 | Quantitative easing

We emphasised above that in this model the monetary authority has access to two policy levers: an interest rate (i^d) and a quantity tool (μ) —or potentially, two interest rates, if the central bank chooses to engage in open market operations and use changes in quantities to target i^b. So we have gone beyond the realm of conventional policy, in which control of the single interest rate on bonds is the only alternative.[12]

We saw earlier that a dilemma arises when the nominal interest rate is against the zero lower bound. Can we use the model we have just built to study that conundrum? Is there a policy that can stabilise output and inflation when the lower bound binds? The answer is yes (subject to parameter values), and in what follows we explain how and why.

To fix ideas, let us go back to the situation studied earlier in this chapter, in which, because of lagging productivity growth, the natural rate of interest drops. Suppose initially $i^b = r^n > 0$, $i_t^d = 0$

and $\mu = \pi = 0$. Then the following shock hits

$$r_t^n = \begin{cases} \underline{r}^n < 0 & \text{for} \quad 0 \leq t < T \\ \bar{r}^n > 0 & \text{for} \quad t \geq T. \end{cases} \tag{21.29}$$

So starting from $\bar{r}^n$, at time 0 the natural rate of interest unexpectedly drops down to $\underline{r}^n < 0$ and it remains there until time T, when it returns to $\bar{r}^n$ and stays there forever.

Notice first that if $\sigma = 1$, during the duration of the shock the NKIS curve (21.20) becomes:

$$\dot{x}_t = (i_t^b - \pi_t - \underline{r}^n) \tag{21.30}$$

So $\dot{x}_t = \pi_t = 0$ would require $i_t^b = \underline{r}^n < 0$. But this is impossible if the zero lower bound is binding and hence i_t^b must be non-negative. Our first conclusion, therefore, is that for monetary policy to get around the zero lower bound problem we must focus on the case in which $\sigma \neq 1$. This is the case in which the utility function is not separable in consumption and liquidity (MP), so that that changes in the opportunity cost of holding liquidity have an impact on the time profile of consumption and aggregate demand.

If we go back to the case in which $\sigma \neq 1$, during the duration of shock the NKIS curve (21.20) becomes:

$$\dot{x}_t = \sigma(i_t^b - \pi_t - \underline{r}^n) + (1 - \sigma)(1 - \alpha)\dot{\Delta}_t \tag{21.31}$$

It follows from (21.31) that $\dot{x}_t = x_t = 0$ and $\pi_t = 0$ if and only if

$$\dot{\Delta}_t = \frac{\sigma\left[(\alpha^{-1} - 1)e^{\Delta_t} + i_t^d - \underline{r}^n\right]}{(\sigma - 1)(1 - \alpha)}. \tag{21.32}$$

where we have used $i_t^b = (\alpha^{-1} - 1)e^{\Delta_t} + i_t^d$. For simplicity, focus on the case $\sigma > 1$. In that case, the RHS of this equation is positive (recall $\underline{r}^n < 0$), so the interest gap Δ_t must rise gradually during the period of the shock.

At this point we have to take a stance on a difficult question: does the zero lower bound apply to i_t^d as well? If we interpret d_t narrowly, as reserves commercial banks hold at the central bank, the answer may be negative: it is not hard to think of liquidity or safety reasons why banks would want to hold reserves at the central bank even if they have to pay a cost to do so. But if we interpret i_t^d more broadly as a digital currency, then the answer could be yes, because if the nominal interest rate on reserves is negative, households could prefer to hold their liquidity under the mattress and look for substitutes as a means of payment. This is the standard "disintermediation" argument for the zero lower bound. To avoid wading into this controversy, in this section we assume $i_t^d \geq 0$.

Moreover, and to keep things very simple, we assume the central bank keeps i_t^d at its steady state level of zero throughout. In that case, the equation for the evolution of Δ_t (21.32) reduces to

$$\dot{\Delta}_t = \frac{\sigma\left[(\alpha^{-1} - 1)e^{\Delta_t} - \underline{r}^n\right]}{(\sigma - 1)(1 - \alpha)}. \tag{21.33}$$

Next, recall the liquidity demand function $d_t = c_t - \Delta_t$, which implies that if consumption is to be constant during the period of the shock, then $\dot{d}_t = -\dot{\Delta}_t$ That is to say, the interest gap can be rising only if the (real) stock of MP is falling. But since we are also requiring zero inflation during that period, real MP decline is the same as nominal MP decline, implying $\mu_t = -\dot{\Delta}_t < 0$.

So now we know what the time profile of Δ_t and d_t must be between times 0 and T. What about the initial and terminal conditions? Suppose we require $i_T^b = \bar{r}^n$, so that the interest rate on bonds will be exactly at its steady state level at time T. Since i_t^d is constant at zero and Δ_t must be falling, it follows that i_t^b must be rising during the length of the shock. So i_t^b must have jumped down at time 0, which in turn means d_t must have jumped up at the same time.

In summary: if $\sigma > 1$, a policy that keeps output at "full employment" and inflation at zero, in spite of the shock to the natural interest rate, involves: a) discretely increasing the nominal and real stock of MP at the time of the shock, causing the interest rate on bonds to fall on impact in response to the shock, in what resembles QE;[13] b) allowing the nominal and real stock of MP to fall gradually during the period of the shock, in what resembles the "unwinding" of QE; c) once the shock is over, ensuring policy variables return to (or remain at) their steady state settings: $\mu = 0$ and $i_t^d = 0$ for all $t \geq T$.[14]

The intuition for why this policy can keep the economy at full employment is as follows. With two goods (in this case, consumption and liquidity services) entering the utility function, what matters for the optimal intertemporal profile of expenditure is not simply the real interest rate in units of consumption, but in units of the bundle Z_t that includes both the consumption good and the real value of MP. Because the nominal rate on bonds cannot fall below zero, what brings the real "utility-based" interest rate down to the full employment level is the behaviour of the "relative price" Δ_t. When $\sigma > 1$, Δ_t has to rise to achieve the desired effect. If, on the contrary, we assumed $\sigma < 1$, then Δ_t would have to fall over time the period of the shock.[15]

In the case $\sigma > 1$, the gradual increase in Δ_t follows an initial drop in the same variable, caused by a discrete increase in the nominal and real stock of MP. This "quantitative easing", if feasible, manages to keep the economy at full employment and zero inflation in spite of the shock to the natural rate of interest and the existence of a zero lower bound for both nominal interest rates.

21.3.2 | Money and banking

An objection to the arguments so far in this chapter is that digital currencies do not yet exist, so households do not have accounts at the central bank. In today's world, the only users of central bank reserves are commercial banks. But most households do use bank deposits for transactions.

This does not mean that our previous analysis is useless. On the contrary, with relatively small modifications, it is straightforward to introduce a banking system into the model. Piazzesi et al. (2019) carry out the complete analysis. Here, we just sketch the main building blocks.

A simplified commercial bank balance sheet has deposits and bank equity on the liability side, and central bank reserves and other assets (loans to firms, government bonds) on the asset side. Banks are typically borrowing-constrained: they can issue deposits only if they have enough collateral - where central bank reserves and government bonds are good collateral.

So now d_t can stand for (the log of) the real value of deposits held in the representative commercial bank, and i_t^d is the interest rate paid on those deposits. Because deposits provide liquidity services, i_t^d can be smaller than the interest rate on bonds, i_t^b.

The central bank does not control i_t^b or i_t^d directly. But banks do keep reserves at the central bank, and this gives the monetary authority indirect control over market rates. Denote by i_t^h the interest rate paid on central bank reserves. It is straightforward to show (see Piazzesi et al. (2019) for details) that optimal behaviour by banks leads to

$$\left(i_t^b - i_t^d\right) = \ell \left(i_t^b - i_t^h\right), \tag{21.34}$$

where $\ell < 1$ if banks are borrowing-constrained and/or have monopoly power.[16] Whenever $\ell < 1$, $\left(i_t^b - i_t^h\right)(1 - \ell) = i_t^d - i_t^h > 0$ so that the rate on deposits and on central bank reserves are linked, with the former always above the latter. The central bank can affect the rate on deposits by adjusting both the quantity of reserves and the interest rate paid on them. Demand for deposits, as in the previous subsection, depends on the opportunity cost of holding deposits:

$$d_t = c_t - \log\left[\left(\frac{\alpha}{1-\alpha}\right)\left(i_t^b - i_t^d\right)\right]. \tag{21.35}$$

Using the equation above we have

$$d_t = c_t - \log\left[\left(\frac{\alpha}{1-\alpha}\right)\ell\left(i_t^b - i_t^h\right)\right] = c_t - \log\left[\left(\frac{\alpha}{1-\alpha}\right)\ell\right] - \log\left(i_t^b - i_t^h\right). \tag{21.36}$$

With this expression in conjunction with the dynamic NKIS curve, the NKPC, and the corresponding policy rules, we have a macro model almost identical to that of the earlier sections, and which can be used to analyse the effects of exogenous shocks and policy changes.

Aside from realism, this extended version has one other advantage: shocks to financial conditions can now become another source of business cycle variation that needs to be counteracted by monetary (and perhaps fiscal) policy. The parameter ℓ, reflecting conditions in the financial markets, the quality of the collateral, the extent of competition, etc., enter as shifters in the expression for deposit demand. To fix ideas, consider what happens if we continue with the policy arrangement of the previous subsection, with $i_t^b = 0$ and the interest rate on reserves (now labelled i_t^h) exogenously given. Then, and since d_t is a sticky variable that cannot jump in response to shocks, an unexpected change in ℓ would imply a change in consumption, and, therefore, in aggregate demand and output. So, in the presence of shocks to financial market conditions, monetary policymakers have to consider whether and how they want to respond to such shocks.

21.3.3 | Credit easing

So far the focus of this chapter has been on unconventional policies that involve changing the quantity of reserves by having the central bank carry out open market operations involving safe assets like government bonds. But at the zero lower bound, and if the interest rate on reserves is brought down to the level of the interest rate on bonds (a case of liquidity satiation, not considered above), then from the point of view of the private sector (of a commercial bank, say), central bank reserves and short-term, liquid government bonds become identical: they are both i.o.u´s issued by the state (or the consolidated government, if you wish), paying the same rate of interest. So, operations that involve swapping one for the other cannot have any real effects.

That is why, in the face of financial markets frictions and distortions, over the last decade and particularly since the Great Financial Crisis, central banks have turned to issuing reserves to purchase other kinds of assets, from corporate bonds to loans on banks´ balance sheets, in effect lending directly to the private sector. As mentioned at the outset, these are usually labelled credit easing policies, in contrast to the "quantitative easing" policies that only involve conventional open market operations.

Credit easing can be incorporated into a simple model like the one we have been studying in this chapter, or also into more sophisticated models such as those of Curdia and Woodford (2011) and Piazzesi et al. (2019). There are many obvious reasons why such policies can have real effects: one is that they can get credit flowing again when the pipes of the financial system become clogged or frozen in a crisis.

A related reason is that in this context policy can not only address aggregate demand shortfalls, but also help alleviate supply constraints — if, for instance, lack of credit keeps firms from having the necessary working capital to operate at the optimal levels of output. This all begs the question of what policy rules ought to look like in such circumstances, a fascinating subject we cannot address here, but about which there is a growing literature — beginning with the 2009 lecture at LSE in which Ben Bernanke, then Fed Chair, explained the Fed's approach to fighting the crisis, which stressed credit easing policies (Bernanke (2009).

21.4 | Appendix

The FOC, (21.8)-(21.10) repeated here for convenience, are

$$\alpha Z_t^{\left(\frac{\sigma-1}{\sigma}\right)} = C_t \lambda_t \tag{21.37}$$

$$(1-\alpha)Z_t^{\left(\frac{\sigma-1}{\sigma}\right)} = \lambda_t D_t \left(i_t^b - i_t^d\right) \tag{21.38}$$

$$\dot{\lambda}_t = -\lambda_t \left(i_t^b - \pi_t - \rho\right), \tag{21.39}$$

where we have defined

$$C_t^\alpha D_t^{1-\alpha} \equiv Z_t. \tag{21.40}$$

Combining the first two, we have demand for MP:

$$D_t = \frac{C_t}{\left(\frac{\alpha}{1-\alpha}\right)\left(i_t^b - i_t^d\right)}, \tag{21.41}$$

which in logs is

$$d_t = c_t - \Delta_t, \tag{21.42}$$

where

$$\Delta_t = \log\left[\left(\frac{\alpha}{1-\alpha}\right)\left(i_t^b - i_t^d\right)\right]. \tag{21.43}$$

Next, differentiating (21.38) with respect to time and then combining with (21.40) yields

$$\left(\frac{\sigma-1}{\sigma}\right)\frac{\dot{Z}_t}{Z_t} = \frac{\dot{C}_t}{C_t} - \left(i_t^b - \pi_t - \rho\right). \tag{21.44}$$

Or, in logs

$$\left(\frac{\sigma-1}{\sigma}\right)\dot{z}_t = \dot{c}_t - \left(i_t^b - \pi_t - \rho\right). \tag{21.45}$$

Using demand for MP from (21.42) in the definition of Z_t (21.41) yields

$$Z_t = C_t^\alpha D_t^{1-\alpha} = C_t \left(\frac{\alpha}{1-\alpha}\right)^{-(1-\alpha)} \left(i_t^b - i_t^d\right)^{-(1-\alpha)}. \tag{21.46}$$

Or, in logs

$$z_t = c_t - (1-\alpha)\Delta_t. \tag{21.47}$$

Differentiating (21.48) with respect to time yields

$$\dot{z}_t = \dot{c}_t - (1 - \alpha)\dot{\Delta}_t. \tag{21.48}$$

Replacing the expression for $\dot{z}_t$ from (21.46) in (21.49) we obtain the Euler equation (21.13) used in the text:

$$\dot{c}_t = \sigma \left(i_t^b - \pi_t - \rho \right) + (1 - \sigma)(1 - \alpha)\dot{\Delta}_t, \tag{21.49}$$

which can be also written, perhaps more intuitively, as

$$\dot{c}_t = \sigma \left[i_t^b - \pi_t - \left(\frac{\sigma - 1}{\sigma} \right) (1 - \alpha)\dot{\Delta}_t - \rho \right]. \tag{21.50}$$

This way of writing it emphasises that the relevant real interest rate now includes the term $\left(\frac{\sigma - 1}{\sigma} \right)(1 - \alpha)\dot{\Delta}_t$, which corrects for changes in the relative price of the two items that enter the consumption function.

Notes

[1] On monetary policy during the pandemic, see Woodford (2020).

[2] A good review of the discussion can be found in Rogoff (2017).

[3] A technical clarification: in Chapter 15 we claimed that, in the absence of an activist interest rule, the canonical 2− equation New Keynesian model does not have a unique equilibrium. So why have no multiplicity issues cropped up in the analysis here? Because, to draw the phase diagram the way we did we assumed the central bank would do whatever it takes to keep $\pi_t = x_t = 0$ starting at T (including, perhaps, the adoption of an activist rule starting at that time). That is enough to pin down uniquely the evolution of the system before T_j because it must be exactly at the origin $(\pi_t = x_t = 0)$ at T. See Werning (2011) for the formal details behind this argument.

[4] Recall from Chapter 14 that $\kappa \equiv \alpha^2 \eta > 0$, and α^{-1} is the expected length of a price quotation in the Calvo (1983) model. So as prices become perfectly flexible, κ goes to infinity.

[5] For details, see the discussion by Gertler on the paper by Eggertsson and Woodford (2003).

[6] See Woodford (2010) from which this discussion is taken.

[7] In particular, on whether banks' demand for liquidity has been satiated or not. See the discussion in Reis (2016).

[8] We will see later that, under some simple extensions, D_t can also be thought of as deposits issued by commercial banks. But let us stick with the digital currency interpretation for the time being.

[9] You may be wondering where currency is in all of this. We have not modelled it explicitly, but we could as long as it is an imperfect substitute for MP (meaning they are both held in equilibrium even though they have different yields — zero in nominal terms in the case of currency).

[10] According to Reis (2016), this is more or less what the Federal Reserve has tried to do since the Great Financial Crisis of 2007-09, thereby satiating the demand for liquidity.

[11] This very helpful way of solving a model of this type is due to Calvo and Végh (1996).

[12] Notice, however, that all the analysis so far (and what follows as well) assumes $i^d < i^b$. That is, there is an opportunity cost of holding reserves (or MP, if you prefer) and therefore liquidity demand by banks (or households, again, if you prefer) is not satiated. The situation is different when the interest rate on reserves is the same as the interest rate on government bonds. Reserves are a liability issued by one branch of government — the central bank. Bonds or bills are a liability issued by another

branch of government — the Treasury. The issuer is the same, and therefore these securities ought to have the same (or very similar) risk characteristics. If they also pay the same interest rate, then they become perfect substitutes in the portfolios of private agents. An operation involving exchanging reserves for bonds, or vice-versa, would have no reason to deliver real effects. A Modigliani-Miller irrelevance result would kick. However, there may be some special circumstances (fiscal or financial crisis, for instance) in which this equivalence breaks down. See the discussion in Reis (2016).

[13] QE involves issuing reserves to purchase bonds, and that is exactly what is going on here.

[14] Notice this policy is not unique. There are other paths for MP and i_t^d that could keep output and inflation constant. We have just chosen a particularly simple one. Notice also that in the sequence we described, the interest gap Δ_t jumps down on impact and then rises gradually until it reaches its steady level $r^n > 0$ at time T, but this trajectory is feasible as long as the shock does not last too long (T is not too large) and the shock is not too deep ($\underline{r}^n$ is not too negative). The constraints come from the fact that on impact Δ_t drops but can never reach zero (because in that case demand for MP would become unbounded). In other words, the central bank is not free to pick any initial condition for Δ_t, in order to ensure that, given the speed with which it must rise, it will hit the right terminal condition at time T. Part of the problem comes from the fact that we have assumed that the inflation rate in the initial steady state is zero, so the initial nominal interest rate on bonds is equal to the natural rate of interest. But, in practice, most central banks target inflation at 2 percent per year, which gives Δ_t "more room" to drop, so that central bankers can freely engage in the kind of policy we have described. Moreover, in the aftermath of the 2007-09 global financial crisis there were suggestions to raise inflation targets higher, to give central banks even "more room" in case of trouble.

[15] Dornbusch (1983) was the first to make this point.

[16] By contrast, in the absence of financial frictions and with perfect competition, $\ell = 1$ and $i_t^d = i_t^h$, so that the interest rate on deposits is equal to the rate paid on central bank reserves.

References

Beckworth, D. (2019). Facts, fears, and functionality of NGDP level targeting: A guide to a popular framework for monetary policy. *Mercatus Research Paper*.

Bernanke, B. S. (2009). The crisis and the policy response. Stamp Lecture, London School of Economics, January, 13, 2009.

Blanchard, O. & Galí, J. (2007). Real wage rigidities and the New Keynesian model. *Journal of Money, Credit and Banking*, 39, 35–65.

Brunnermeier, M., Eisenbach, T., & Sannikov, Y. (2013). Macroeconomics with financial frictions: A survey. *Advances in Economics and Econometrics*.

Calvo, G. A. (1978). On the time consistency of optimal policy in a monetary economy. *Econometrica*, 1411–1428.

Calvo, G. A. (1983). Staggered prices in a utility-maximizing framework. *Journal of Monetary Economics*, 12(3), 383–398.

Calvo, G. A. & Végh, C. A. (1996). Disinflation and interest-bearing money. *The Economic Journal*, 106(439), 1546–1563.

Curdia, V. & Woodford, M. (2011). The central-bank balance sheet as an instrument of monetarypolicy. *Journal of Monetary Economics*, 58(1), 54–79.

Diba, B. & Loisel, O. (2020). Pegging the interest rate on bank reserves: A resolution of New Keynesian puzzles and paradoxes. *Journal of Monetary Economics*.

Dornbusch, R. (1983). Real interest rates, home goods, and optimal external borrowing. *Journal of Political Economy*, *91*(1), 141–153.

Eggertsson, G. B. & Woodford, M. (2003). Zero bound on interest rates and optimal monetary policy. *Brookings Papers on Economic Activity*, *2003*(1), 139–233.

Eggertsson, G. B. & Woodford, M. (2004). Policy options in a liquidity trap. *American Economic Review*, *94*(2), 76–79.

Gertler, M. & Karadi, P. (2011). A model of unconventional monetary policy. *Journal of Monetary Economics*, *58*(1), 17–34.

Hall, R. E. & Reis, R. (2016). *Achieving price stability by manipulating the central bank's payment on reserves*. National Bureau of Economic Research.

Hicks, J. R. (1937). Mr. Keynes and the "classics"; A suggested interpretation. *Econometrica*, 147–159.

Krugman, P. (1998). Japan's trap. http://web.mit.edu/krugman/www/japtrap.html.

Kydland, F. E. & Prescott, E. C. (1977). Rules rather than discretion: The inconsistency of optimal plans. *Journal of Political Economy*, *85*(3), 473–491.

Piazzesi, M., Rogers, C., & Schneider, M. (2019). *Money and banking in a New Keynesian model*. Working Paper, Stanford.

Reis, R. (2016). Funding quantitative easing to target inflation. LSE Research Online, http://eprints.lse.ac.uk/67883/.

Rogoff, K. (2017). Dealing with monetary paralysis at the zero bound. *Journal of Economic Perspectives*, *31*(3), 47–66.

Summers, L. H. (2018). Secular stagnation and macroeconomic policy. *IMF Economic Review*, *66*(2), 226–250.

Sumner, S. B. (2014). Nominal GDP targeting: A simple rule to improve Fed performance. *Cato Journal. 34*, 315.

Werning, I. (2011). *Managing a liquidity trap: Monetary and fiscal policy*. National Bureau of Economic Research.

Woodford, M. (2010). Financial intermediation and macroeconomic analysis. *Journal of Economic Perspectives*, *24*(4), 21–44.

Woodford, M. (2016). *Quantitative easing and financial stability*. National Bureau of Economic Research. Working Paper 22285 http://www.nber.org/papers/w22285.

Woodford, M. (2020). Post-pandemic monetary policy and the effective lower bound.

CHAPTER 22

New developments in monetary and fiscal policy

In Chapters 19 and 20 we laid out the basics of monetary theory. Chapter 19 explored the relation between prices and money while Chapter 20 focused on the historical debate on whether monetary policy should be conducted through rules or with discretion. In Chapter 21 we discussed new challenges to monetary policy, particularly those that became clear after the Great Financial Crisis: how does the ZLB constrain the operation of monetary policy, and what is the role and scope for quantitative easing?

In this chapter we address three points that are currently being discussed. None of these are settled as of today, but we hope the presentation here will help introduce the issues.

The first topic is Alvin Hansen's secular stagnation dilemma, brought back to life by Larry Summers a few years ago. In Hansen´s (1939) own words:

> This is the essence of secular stagnation, sick recoveries which die in their infancy and depressions which feed on themselves and leave a hard and seemingly immovable form of unemployment.

While by 1939 the U.S. economy was in full recovery, the idea brewed after a decade-long recession. The idea was that depressed expectations may lead to increased savings that do not find a productive conduit, further depressing aggregate demand. This idea blends with the "savings glut" referred to in Ben Bernanke's 2005 speech pointing to the fact that the world had been awash with savings in recent years. While unemployment has been low in recent years (as opposed to the 30s), there is a sense that recoveries are slow, and policy tools are ineffective to address this. Thus, our first section in this chapter deals with models that try to formalise this pattern: excessive savings leading to depressed aggregate demand that policies cannot counteract if the interest rate has a lower bound.

The second section deals with the need to build a monetary theory in a world without money. In future years, private crypto currencies, floating and fixed, and electronic payments will make the money supply issued by central banks increasingly irrelevant. Picture a world in which payments are done through mechanisms such as QR codes, electronic transfers, while base money demand falls to zero. Imagine that the replacement of cash has gone so far that only 1 dollar of base money is left.[1] Will prices double if that one dollar becomes two? We deal with these issues by discussing the so-called "fiscal theory of the price level", a long term effort proposed by economists such as Michael Woodford, Chris Sims, and John Cochrane. The theory focuses on the budget constraint of the government. The

How to cite this book chapter:
Campante, F., Sturzenegger, F. and Velasco, A. 2021. *Advanced Macroeconomics: An Easy Guide.*
    Ch. 22. 'New developments in monetary and fiscal policy', pp. 345–362. London: LSE Press.
    DOI: https://doi.org/10.31389/lsepress.ame.v License: CC-BY-NC 4.0.

government issues debt and charges taxes, and the price level is the one that equalises the real value of debt with the present discounted value of taxes. Think of taxes as the money sucked by the government from the system. If the real value of debt is higher than this, there is an excess demand that pushes prices upwards until the equilibrium is restored. We revisit the discussion on interest rules within this framework.

While the quantitative easing policies discussed in the previous chapter initially raised eyebrows and had many skeptics and detractors who had forecasted increasing inflation and interest rates, none of those predictions bore out. Inflation rates have remained low, even when interest rates reached historical lows. In fact, low persistent interest rates have raised the issue of the possibility of an unbounded fiscal policy: if $r < g$ can the government raise debt without bound? Does that make sense? This is one of the most significant policy debates today, particularly after the debt buildup as a result of the Covid pandemic. Furthermore, if $r < g$, can assets be unbounded in their valuations or include bubbles? And if they do, what is their welfare effect? This, in turn, opens a new set of policy questions: should the monetary authorities fight bubbles? In practical terms, should the Fed worry about stock market prices? Our final section tackles this issue. It resembles somewhat the discussion on optimality that we found in the OLG section of this book. Bubbles, when they exist, improve welfare. However, bubble-driven fluctuations are not welfare-improving and monetary authorities should attempt to avoid them. This is one the hottest and most debated current topics in monetary policy.

22.1 | Secular stagnation

As we have been discussing all along, recent years have shown very low interest rates, so low that they make the zero lower bound constraint something we need to worry about. In the previous chapter we showed how monetary policy could respond to this challenge, here we provide an alternative representation that allows for financial constraints and productivity growth to play a role.

During recent years, inflation has surprised on the downside and economic recovery has been sluggish. This combination has been dubbed secular stagnation, a name taken from Hansen's 1939 depiction of the U.S. economy during the Great Depression. The story is simple: low interest rates due to abundant savings are associated with depressed demand. But this lack of demand generates lower inflation, pushing up the real interest rate and strengthening the contractionary effect. We follow Eggertsson et al. (2017) in modelling all these effects in a simple framework.

Their model is an overlapping generations framework (we will need overlapping generations if we want to produce a low interest rate). In their specification, every individual lives for three periods. In period one the individual has no income and needs to borrow in order to consume. However, it is subject to a collateral constraint D_t (this will open the door for financial effects in the model). The individual generates income in the middle period and no income in old age (this will produce the need for savings). In summary, the individual maximises

$$maxE_t \left\{ \log(C_t^y) + \frac{1}{1+\rho} \log(C_{t+1}^m) + \left(\frac{1}{1+\rho} \right)^2 \log(C_{t+2}^o) \right\}. \tag{22.1}$$

subject to

$$C_t^y = \frac{D_t}{(1+r_t)}, \tag{22.2}$$

$$C_{t+1}^m = Y_{t+1}^m - D_t + B_{t+1}^m, \tag{22.3}$$

$$C_{t+2}^o = -(1+r_{t+1})B_{t+1}^m. \tag{22.4}$$

To make things interesting, we will consider the case in which the financing constraint is binding in the first period. This implies that the only decision is how much to borrow in middle age. You should be able to do this optimisation and find out that the desired savings are

$$B_t^m = -\frac{(Y_t^m - D_{t-1})}{2 + \rho},$$

(22.5)

which is the supply of savings in the economy. Equilibrium in the bond market requires that borrowing of the young equals the savings of the middle-aged so that $N_t B_t^y = -N_{t-1} B_t^m$, and denoting as usual, n as the rate of population growth,

$$(1 + n)B_t^y = \frac{(1 + n)}{(1 + r_t)}D_t = -B_t^m = \frac{(Y_t^m - D_{t-1})}{2 + \rho},$$

(22.6)

This equation readily solves the interest rate for the economy

$$1 + r_t = (2 + \rho)(1 + n)\frac{D_t}{(Y_t^m - D_{t-1})}.$$

(22.7)

Notice that the interest rate can be lower than the growth rate, and even negative. The fact that individuals are cash constrained in the first period will also impact the interest rate: a tighter constraint today (a smaller D_t) leads to a fall in the interest rate. Notice also that a lowering of productivity growth, if it tightens the financing constraint due to lower expected future income, lowers the interest rate, as does a lower rate of population growth. These low interest rates are not transitory but correspond to the steady state of the economy.

Let's introduce monetary policy in this model. The real interest rate now is

$$(1 + r_t) = (1 + i_t)\frac{P_t}{P_{t+1}},$$

(22.8)

where the notation is self explanatory. The problem arises if we impose a zero lower bound for the nominal interest rate ($i_t \geq 0$). In a deflationary equilibrium this may not allow the desired real interest rate and will be a source of problems. In order to have output effects we will assume firms produce using labour with production function

$$Y_t = L_t^\alpha.$$

(22.9)

The critical assumption will be that a fraction γ of workers will not accept a reduction in their nominal wages, just as Keynes suggested back in the 1930s. This implies that the nominal wage of the economy will be

$$\tilde{W}_t = \gamma W_{t-1} + (1 - \gamma)W_t^{flex},$$

(22.10)

where W_t^{flex} indicates the wage that clears the labour market. In order to compute the aggregate supply curve we first look for the steady state wage when the nominal constraint is binding. Dividing (22.10) by P_t and replacing W_t^{flex} by the marginal product of labour at full employment, $\alpha \bar{L}^{\alpha-1}$ we can see that the steady state wage is

$$w = \frac{(1 - \gamma)\alpha \bar{L}^{\alpha-1}}{(1 - \frac{\gamma}{\Pi})},$$

(22.11)

where Π is gross inflation. Then, noting that firms will equate the marginal product of labour to the wage, we make the wage in (22.11) equal to the marginal product of labour $\alpha L^{\alpha-1}$. After some simplifications we get the equation

$$\frac{\gamma}{\Pi} = 1 - (1-\gamma)\frac{Y^{\frac{1-\alpha}{\alpha}}}{Y^f}, \qquad (22.12)$$

where Y^f represents full employment output. Notice that this operates as a Phillips curve, higher inflation is associated with higher output. The intuition is straightforward, as inflation increases the real wages falls and firms hire more labour. Given the rigidities of the model, this is a steady state relationship. If inflation is sufficiently high, the nominal wage rigidity does not bind and the aggregate supply becomes vertical, as drawn in Figure 22.1.

Aggregate demand follows directly from (22.7) combined with the Fisher relation (22.8) and a Taylor rule such as

$$(1+i) = (1+i^*)\left(\frac{\Pi_t}{\Pi^*}\right)^{\phi_\Pi}. \qquad (22.13)$$

Substituting both we obtain:

$$Y = D + (2+\rho)(1+n)D\frac{\Pi^{*\phi_\Pi}}{(1+i^*)}\frac{1}{\Pi^{\phi_\Pi-1}}. \qquad (22.14)$$

The upper portion of the AD curve in Figure (22.1), when inflation is high and the interest rate is unconstrained, depicts this relationship. As inflation increases, the central bank raises the nominal interest rate by more than one for one (since $\phi_\Pi > 1$), which, in turn, increases the real interest rate and reduces demand.

Figure 22.1   Shift in the AD-AS model

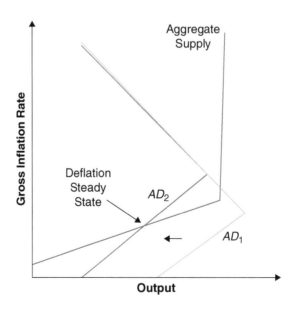

Now, in low inflation states where the interest rate hits its zero lower bound $i = 0$, this curve simplifies to

$$Y = D + (2 + \rho)(1 + n)D\Pi. \tag{22.15}$$

The key point of this equation is that it is upward sloping in Π. The reason is straightforward, as inflation decreases, the lower bound implies that the real rate increases because the interest rate cannot compensate. Therefore, in this range, a lower inflation means a higher real rate. For reasonable parameter values the AD curve is steeper than the AS curve as in Figure 22.1

With this framework, imagine a decrease in D. In (22.15) is is easy to see that this moves the aggregate demand to the left as shown in the graph. This pushes inflation and output downwards. The link between the financial crisis and a protracted stagnation process has been established.

22.2 | The fiscal theory of the price level

Let's imagine now a situation where people transact without money (in the current world of Venmo, electronic wallets, etc, this is not such a far-fetched assumption, and will become less and less far-fetched as time goes by). What pins down the price level?[2]

The fiscal theory of the price level, as its name suggests, focuses on the role of fiscal policy in determining the price level. For sure, it is the government that prints money and issues debt. It then mops up money through taxes. To build intuition, let's imagine the government issues debt that needs to be paid at the end of the period. Taxes will be used to that end and the fiscal result will be s_t. Fiscal theory postulates that

$$\frac{B_{t-1}}{P_t} = s_t. \tag{22.16}$$

The price level adjusts to equate the real value of debt to the expected surplus. Why is this the case? Imagine the price level is lower than the one that makes the real value of debt equal to the expected surplus. This means that at the end of the day the mopping up of money will be less than the value of debt. This implies that agents have an excess demand of resources to spend, which they use to push the price level up. If the price level makes the value of debt smaller than what will be mopped up, this implies that people are poorer and reduce spending. The price level comes down. In short, there is equilibrium when the real value of debt equals the expected surplus. Equation (22.16) is not the budget constraint of the government. The budget constraint is

$$B_{t-1} = s_t P_t + M_t. \tag{22.17}$$

The point is that there is no demand for M_t. This is what makes (22.16) an equilibrium condition. In the reasoning above we take s_t as exogenous, but we can also consider the case in which fiscal policy is endogenous in the sense that it adjusts in order to attain a particular P_t. When so we will say we have a passive fiscal police. We will come back to this shortly.

Of course this intuition can be extended to multiple periods. In an intertemporal setting the budget constraint becomes

$$M_{t-1} + B_{t-1} = P_t s_t + M_t + B_t E_t[\frac{1}{(1 + i_t)}], \tag{22.18}$$

but because people do not hold money in equilibrium, and using the fact that $(1 + i) = (1 + \rho)\frac{P_{t+1}}{P_t}$ we can write this as

$$B_{t-1} = P_t s_t + B_t E_t[\frac{1}{(1 + i_t)}] = P_t s_t + B_t E_t[\frac{1}{(1 + \rho)} \left(\frac{P_t}{P_{t+1}}\right)]. \qquad (22.19)$$

It is easy to solve this equation by iterating forward (and assuming a transversality condition) to obtain

$$\frac{B_{t-1}}{P_t} = E_t \sum_{j=0}^{\infty} \frac{s_{t+j}}{(1 + \rho)^j}. \qquad (22.20)$$

This equation pins down the price level as the interplay of the real value of debt and the present discounted value of expected fiscal surpluses. Again, the right-hand side is the amount of dollars to be mopped up. The left-hand side is the real value of the assets in the private sector's hands. If the former is bigger than the future surpluses, there will be an aggregate demand effect that will push prices upward.

Imagine that the government issues debt but promises to increase the surpluses required to finance it. According to this view, this will have no effect on aggregate demand, or the price level. In fact, this explains why large fiscal deficits have had no effect on the price level. According to this view, to bring inflation up you need to issue debt and commit not to collect taxes! In short, you need to promise irresponsible behaviour. In Chris Sims' (2016) words,

'Fiscal expansion can replace ineffective monetary policy at the zero lower bound, but fiscal expansion is not the same thing as deficit finance. It requires deficits aimed at, and conditioned on, generating inflation. The deficits must be seen as financed by future inflation, not future taxes or spending cuts.'

Notice that, under this light, a large increase in assets in the balance sheet of the central bank, (such as the quantitative easing exercises of last chapter), does not affect the price level. The government (the Fed) issues debt in exchange of commercial assets. If both assets and liabilities pay similar rates this does not affect future surpluses, it just adds assets and liabilities for the same amount. This result is not dissimilar to what happens when a Central Bank accumulates (foreign currency) reserves in fixed exchange rate regimes. An increase in money liabilities accompanied by an increase in backing is understood not to be inflationary. In summary in this framework the large expansions that have come with quantitative easing do not necessarily generate inflation pressures.

Finally, the FTPL shows the interplay between fiscal and monetary policy. Imagine a central bank that increases the interest rate. If the fiscal surplus does not change this would decrease the surpluses and generate inflation. The reason why typically it is not assumed that an increase rate in the interest increases inflation is due to the fact that it is assumed that an increase in the interest rate will lead automatically to an increase in the fiscal surplus in order to pay the higher interest cost. But, according to this view, this response is not necessary. It is an assumption that we make.

22.2.1 | Interest rate policy in the FTPL

What does the FTPL have to say about the stability of interest rate policies? Let's analyse this within the context of the New Keynesian model we discussed in Chapter 15. As always, the behavioural equations include the New Keynesian IS curve (NKIS):

$$\log(Y_t) = E_t \left[\log(Y_{t+1})\right] - \sigma(i_t - E_t \pi_{t+1}), \qquad (22.21)$$

and the New Keynesian Phillips Curve (NKPC):

$$\pi_t = \kappa y_t + \beta E_t \left[\pi_{t+1}\right]. \tag{22.22}$$

And an exogenous interest rule

$$i_t = \bar{i}. \tag{22.23}$$

Notice that we use the exogenous interest rate rule that delivered instability in the traditional NK framework. The key innovation now is an equation for the evolution of the debt to GDP level in the model. The dynamics of the log of the debt to GDP can be approximated by

$$d_{t+1} + s_{t+1} = d_t + (i_{t+1} - \pi_{t+1}) - g_{t+1}. \tag{22.24}$$

The debt to GDP ratio grows from its previous value with the primary deficit plus the real interest rate minus the growth rate.

The difference with the traditional NK model is that the NK model assumes that s_t adjusts to balance the budget to make debt sustainable, responding in a passive way, for example, to a change in the interest rate. This is the assumption that we lift here. Substituting the interest rate in the other equations we have a system of future variables on current variables with a coefficient matrix

$$\Omega = \begin{bmatrix} \frac{1}{\beta} & -\frac{\kappa}{\beta} & 0 \\ -\frac{\sigma}{\beta} & 1 + \frac{\kappa\sigma}{\beta} & 0 \\ -\frac{1}{\beta} & \frac{\kappa}{\beta} & 1 \end{bmatrix}. \tag{22.25}$$

The last column suggests that one of the eigenvalues is equal to one.[3] Of the other two, one can be shown to be smaller than one, and the other larger than one. Because the system has two jumpy variables (output and inflation) and one state variable (debt), the system is stable.

The above may have sounded like a bit of mathematical jargon. But here we are interested in the economics of the model. First of all, what does the above mean? And then, why does the model uniquely pin down the equilibrium here?

Remember that in the standard NK model we needed the Taylor principle, an interest rule that reacted with strength to deviations in inflation to pin down the equilibrium. The above suggests the the Taylor principle is not necessary in this context. Here the equilibrium is stable even with relatively stable interest rates. But why is this the case? The key difference here is that the interest rate change does not lead to any reaction in fiscal policy. Typically we ignore the implications of monetary policy on the government´s budget constraint, but in doing so we are assuming (perhaps inadvertently) that fiscal policy *responds automatically* to monetary policy to keep the debt stable or sustainable. This may very well be the case, particularly in stable economies where fiscal stability is not at stake or questioned, but, at any rate, it is an assumption that we make.

What happens if we explicitly assume that there is no response of fiscal policy? Well, in that case the jump in the interest rate in an economy with sticky prices increases the real interest rate, but now there is only one path of inflation and output dynamics that insures the stability of the debt dynamics. The need to generate stability in the debt dynamics is what pins down the equilibria!

The increase in the real interest rate, though transitory, reduces the present value of surpluses (alternatively you can think of it as increasing the interest cost) leading to a higher level of inflation in equilibrium! The fact that higher interest rates imply a higher rate of inflation, is not necessarily contradictory with our previous findings, it just makes evident that in the previous case we were assuming that fiscal policy responded passively to insure debt stability.

The exercise helps emphasise that it is key to understand that relationship between fiscal and monetary policy. This relationship may become critical in the aftermath of the debt buildup as the result of Covid. If, imagine, interest rates increase at some point, what will be the response of fiscal policy? It is obvious that that channel cannot be ignored.

22.3 | Rational asset bubbles

Our final topic is the role of bubbles in asset prices and their implications for the economy, both in terms of efficiency and stability.

Perhaps the right place to start is a standard asset-pricing arbitrage equation:

$$r = \frac{\dot{q}_t}{q_t} + \frac{c}{q_t},$$ (22.26)

where r is the real interest rate,[4] c the (constant) coupon payment, and q_t the price of the asset[5]. The equation states, as we have encountered multiple times, that the dividend yield plus the capital gain have to equal the opportunity cost of holding the asset.

That relationship can also be written as the differential equation

$$\dot{q}_t = rq_t - c.$$ (22.27)

You may want to review in the mathematical appendix to check out that the solution of this differential equation has the form

$$q_t = \int_0^\infty ce^{-rt}dt + Be^{rt} = \frac{c}{r} + Be^{rt},$$ (22.28)

with B an arbitrary number (the fact that we use the letter B is not a coincidence). The solution has two terms. We call $\frac{c}{r}$ the fundamental value of the asset (naturally, the present discounted value of the coupon stream). The term Be^{rt} is the bubble term, which has no intrinsic value. We sometimes refer to this term as a "rational bubble".

Unless we arbitrarily impose a terminal condition (like requiring that q does not exceed some boundary after some given time period), then every value of q that satisfies the differential equation above is a candidate solution. The set of possible solutions is shown in Figure 22.2, which graphs the dynamics of the differential equation.

If q starts to the right of $\bar{q}$, it will go to infinity; if it starts to the left of $\bar{q}$, it will go to zero. All these paths satisfy the relevant arbitrage condition and the corresponding differential equation.

Before moving on, one important point to note is that the bubble term has a very tight structure: it grows at r. This is intuitive: the asset can price above it's fundamental value only if agents expect this extra cost will also deliver the required rate of return ... forever. Thus, transitory increases in asset prices cannot be associated with bubbles.[6]

Can we rule out these bubbly paths? If $r > g$ – that is, the interest rate is larger than the growth rate – then the bubble eventually becomes so big that it is impossible for it to continue growing at the required rate (think of it becoming larger than the economy!). But if it cannot grow it cannot exist, and if it does not exist at a given moment in time by backward induction it cannot exist at anytime before. In dynamically efficient economies bubbles cannot exist.

That is the *unsustainable* element in bubbles; but there is also the *de-stabilising* element. Most borrowing contracts require collateral. Families use their homes as collateral; financial intermediaries

Figure 22.2   Solutions of the bubble paths

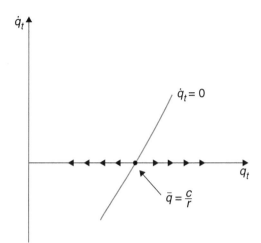

use stocks and bonds as collateral. When the prices of these assets become inflated, so does people's ability to borrow. So debt and leverage go up, which in turn may further stimulate the economy and causes asset prices to rise even more. The problem, of course, is that if and when asset prices come back to earth, it will find firms and businesses highly indebted, thus triggering a painful process of de-leveraging, recession, and bankruptcies.

So are bubbles all bad, then? Not necessarily. Imagine an overlapping generations ice cream economy in which people live for two days only. At any given time there are only two people alive: a 1-day-old person and a 2-day-old person. Each 1-day-old person gets an ice-cream cone in the evening. In this strange world, 1-day-olds do not like ice-cream, but 2-day-olds do. The problem is, anyone trying to store an ice cream cone overnight will only have a melted mess in her hands the next morning.

The 1-day-old person could kindly offer her cone to the 2-day-old person, but the 2-day-old cannot offer anything in return, because they will be dead by morning. In this economy, therefore, one possible equilibrium is that all ice-cream melts and no one gets to eat any.

Unless, that is, one enterprising 2-day-old comes up with a new idea: give the 1-day-old a piece of paper (you can call it a dollar, or a bond if you prefer) in exchange for her cone, arguing that 24 hours later the then 2-day-old will be able to give that same piece of paper to a 1-day-old in exchange for a nice, fresh and un-melted ice cream cone! If today the 1-day-old agrees to the deal, and so do all successive 1-day-olds until kingdom come, then the problem will have been solved: all ice cream cones will be consumed by 2-day-olds who really appreciate their flavour, no ice cream will melt and welfare has improved.

But notice, the piece of paper that begins to change hands is like a bubble: it has no intrinsic value, and it is held only because of the expectation that others will be also willing to hold it in the future. In the simple story we have told the value of the bubble is constant: one piece of paper is worth one ice cream cone forever.[7] But in slightly more complicated settings (with population growth, for instance, or with changing productivity in the ice cream business), the value of the piece of paper could be rising over time, or it could even be falling! People might willingly exchange one cone today for 0.9 cones tomorrow simply because the alternative is so bad: eating no ice cream at all!

You may have found a resemblance between this ice-cream story and our discussion of dynamic efficiency when analysing the overlapping generations models in Chapter 8. When the return on capital is low (in this case it is -100% because if everyone saves the ice-cream cone overnight, then there is no ice-cream to consume tomorrow), finding a way to transfer income from the young to old is welfare enhancing.

In Samuelson's (1958) contribution that introduced the overlapping generations (OLG) model Samuelson already pointed out that bubble-like schemes (he called them "the social contrivance of money") could get economies out of that dynamic inefficiency and raise welfare[8].

But again, here is the rub: those schemes are inherently fragile. Each 1-day-old accepts the piece of paper if and only if they expect all successive 1-day-olds will do the same. If not, they have no incentive to do so. The conclusion is that, in a bubbly environment, even slight shifts in expectations can trigger big changes in behaviour and asset prices, what, in modern parlance, we call financial crises.

In another very celebrated paper, Samuelson's fellow Nobelist Jean Tirole (1985) took a version of the OLG model and analysed what kinds of bubbles could arise and under what conditions. The main conclusion is what we mentioned above: rational asset bubbles only occur in low interest rate OLG economies where the rate of interest is below the rate of growth of the economy. This is how Weil (2008) explains the intuition:

> 'This result should not be a surprise: I am willing to pay for an asset more than its fundamental value (the present discounted value of future dividends) only if I can sell it later to others. A rational asset bubble, like Samuelsonian money, is a hot potato that I only hold for a while-until I find someone to catch it.'

Tirole's paper gave rise to a veritable flood of work on bubbles, rational and otherwise. Recent surveys covering this new and fast-growing literature are Miao (2014) and Martin and Ventura (2018). One result from that literature is that there is nothing special in the 2 -generation Samuelson model that generates bubbles. Overlapping generations help, but other kinds of restrictions on trade (which is, essentially, what the OLG structure involves) can deliver very similar results.

In what follows we develop a simple example of rational bubbles using the Blanchard-Yaari perpetual youth OLG model that we studied in Chapter 8. In building this model we draw on recent work by Caballero et al. (2008), Farhi and Tirole (2012) and Galí (2020).

22.3.1 | The basic model

Consider an economy made up of overlapping generations of the Blanchard type with age-independent probability of death p (which by the law of large numbers is also the death rate in the population) and birth rate $n > p$. Together they mean population grows at the rate $n - p$. As in Blanchard (1985), assume there exist insurance companies that allow agents to insure against the risk of death (and, therefore, of leaving behind unwanted bequests)[9].

Let r_t be the interest rate and ρ the subjective rate of time discounting. Starting on the day of their birth, agents receive an endowment that cannot be capitalised and that declines at the rate $\gamma > \rho$. It is this assumption that income goes down as agents get older that will create a demand for a savings vehicle in order to move purchasing power from earlier to later stages of life.

The per capita (or, if you prefer, average) endowment received by agents who are alive at time t is (see Appendix 1 for details) a constant y.

Next let h_t stand for per capita (or average) household wealth. Appendix 2 shows that h_t evolves according to

$$\dot{h}_t = \left(r_t + p + \gamma\right) h_t - y. \tag{22.29}$$

To develop some intuition for this last equation, it helps to think of h_t as the present per capita value of the income flow y the household receives. What is the relevant rate at which the household should discount those future flows? The total discount rate is $(r_t + p + \gamma)$. In addition to the standard rate of interest r_t, the household must also discount the future by p, the instantaneous probability of death, and by γ, which is the rate at which an individual's income falls over time.

The only way to save is to hold a bubble, whose per capita value is b_t. Arbitrage requires that per capita gains on the value of the bubble equal the interest rate:

$$\frac{\dot{b}_t}{b_t} = r_t - (n - p). \tag{22.30}$$

Recall that b_t is the per capita stock of the bubble, and $(n - p)$ is the rate of population growth. So this equation says that, by arbitrage, the percentage rate of growth of the (per capita) bubble must be equal to the (per capita) return on financial assets, which equals the interest rate net of population growth.

Finally, if utility is logarithmic, then (see Appendix 3) the per capita consumption function is

$$c_t = (p + \rho)\left(b_t + h_t\right), \tag{22.31}$$

so that consumption is a fixed portion of household wealth and financial wealth (the bubble). This condition mimics those we found for all Ramsey problems with log utility as we know from earlier chapters of this book. Because the economy is closed, all output must be consumed. Market-clearing requires

$$c_t = y = (p + \rho)\left(b_t + h_t\right). \tag{22.32}$$

Therefore, differentiating with respect to time we have

$$\dot{b}_t + \dot{h}_t = 0. \tag{22.33}$$

Replacing (22.29) and (22.30) in (22.33) yields

$$\left(r_t + p + \gamma\right) h_t + \left(r_t + p - n\right) b_t = y. \tag{22.34}$$

Combining this equation with the market-clearing condition (22.32) we get after some simplifications

$$r_t + \gamma - \rho = \frac{(p + \rho)(n + \gamma)b_t}{y}, \tag{22.35}$$

so that r_t is increasing in b_t: a larger bubble calls for a higher interest rate. Next we can use this equation to eliminate $r_t - n$ from the arbitrage equation (22.30) that governs the bubble:

$$\dot{b}_t = \frac{(p + \rho)(n + \gamma)b_t^2}{y} - (n - p + \gamma - \rho)b_t. \tag{22.36}$$

It follows that $\dot{b}_t = 0$ implies

$$[(p + \rho)(n + \gamma)b - (n - p + \gamma - \rho)y]b = 0. \tag{22.37}$$

This equation has solutions $b = 0$ and

$$b = \frac{(n - p + \gamma - \rho)y}{(p + \rho)(n + \gamma)} > 0. \tag{22.38}$$

Figure 22.3 describes the dynamic behaviour of the bubble. There are two steady states. The one with $b = 0$ is stable, while the one with with $b > 0$ is unstable. So bubbles can exist, but they are very fragile. Starting from the bubbly steady state, a minuscule shift in expectations is enough to cause the value of the bubble to start declining until it reaches zero.

Because this is a closed economy, per capita consumption must be equal to per capita income. But the same is not true of the consumption profiles of individual cohorts. It is easy to check that, in the bubbly steady state individual cohort consumption grows over time, while in the non-bubbly steady state, individual cohort consumption is flat. The bubble amounts to a savings vehicle that allows individuals to push consumption to later stages of life.

Put differently, in the steady state with no bubble, the interest rate is negative (you can see that the interest rate is $\rho - \gamma < 0$ by just assuming $b = 0$ in (22.35)). This is, trivially, smaller than the rate of population growth $(n - p) > 0$. So in that steady state the economy is dynamically inefficient. The existence of a bubble allows the economy to escape that inefficiency and settle on a golden rule steady state in which the interest rate is equal to the rate of population growth (to check this replace the level of b from (22.38) in (22.35) to find that $r = n - p$). But that equilibrium is fragile, as we have seen.

22.3.2 | Government debt as a bubble

Now define d_t as per capita public debt. The government budget constraint is

$$\dot{d}_t = \left(r_t - n + p\right) d_t + s, \tag{22.39}$$

where s is constant net spending per capita - the equivalent of the per capita primary deficit. Assume that all government spending is transfers to households (as opposed to government consumption), so

Figure 22.3 Bubbles in the Blanchard model

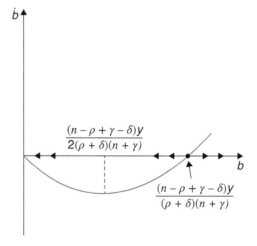

the law of motion of household wealth must be modified to read

$$\dot{h}_t = \left(r_t + p + \gamma\right) h_t - y - s. \tag{22.40}$$

The consumption function is still (22.32), and $c_t = y$ which again implies that $\dot{h}_t + \dot{d}_t = 0$. We can then repeat the steps in the previous subsection replacing b_t by d_t to get an expression for the interest rate as a function of d_t:

$$\left(r_t + \gamma - \rho\right) y = (n + \gamma)(p + \rho)d_t, \tag{22.41}$$

which is virtually identical to (22.35). As before r_t is increasing in d_t: a larger stock of government debt requires a higher interest rate. Using this last expression in the government budget (22.39) constraint to eliminate $r_t - n$ we have

$$\dot{d}_t = \left(r_t - n + p\right) d_t + s = y^{-1}(n + \gamma)(p + \rho)d_t^2 - (n - p + \gamma - \rho)d_t + s. \tag{22.42}$$

Notice $\dot{d}_t = 0$ implies

$$(n + \gamma)(p + \rho)d^2 - (n - p + \gamma - \rho)yd + sy = 0. \tag{22.43}$$

This equation has two solutions, given by

$$\frac{d}{y} = \frac{(n - p + \gamma - \rho) \pm \sqrt{(n - p + \gamma - \rho)^2 - 4(n + \gamma)(p + \rho)\frac{s}{y}}}{2(n + \gamma)(p + \gamma)}. \tag{22.44}$$

Solutions exist as long as spending does not exceed a maximum allowable limit, given by

$$s = \frac{(n - p + \gamma - \rho)^2 y}{4(n + \gamma)(p + \rho)}. \tag{22.45}$$

If s is below this maximum, we have two equilibria, both with positive levels of debt. Figure (22.4) confirms that in this case the bubble is fragile: the steady state with the larger stock of debt is unstable. A slight shift in expectations will cause the value of the bubble to start declining.

It is straightforward to show that there are also two solutions for the real interest rate, given by

$$r = \frac{(n - p) - (\gamma - \rho) \pm \sqrt{((n - p) + (\gamma - \rho))^2 - 4(n + \gamma)(p + \rho)\frac{s}{y}}}{2}. \tag{22.46}$$

If $s = 0$, then

$$r = \frac{(n - p) - (\gamma - \rho) \pm ((n - p) + (\gamma - \rho))}{2}, \tag{22.47}$$

so $r = n - p$ or $r = -(\gamma - \rho)$, just as in the case of a pure bubble.

If $s > 0$, then in both equilibria $r < n - p$, so government debt turns out to be a bubble. In either steady state, the government budget constraint is

$$(n - p - r)d = s. \tag{22.48}$$

When the steady state interest rate is higher, so is the steady state value of the debt for a given primary deficit. One steady state is bubblier, with a larger valuation for public debt and a higher interest rate. But that steady state, as we saw graphically in the phase diagram above, is fragile. It only takes a shift in expectations to drive the economy out of that resting place and toward the alternative steady state with a lower valuation for public debt.

Figure 22.4   Government debt as a bubble

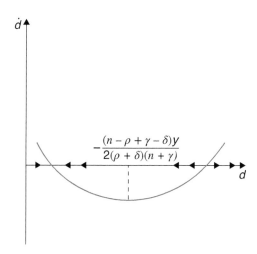

22.3.3 | Implications for fiscal, financial and monetary policy

As the discussion in the previous section should make clear, bubbles have huge implications for fiscal policy. We saw that in an economy with strong demand for liquidity, private sector agents may be willing to hold government debt even if that debt pays an interest rate that is lower than the rate of population growth, which is also the rate of growth of the economy.

This is good news for treasury officials and fiscal policymakers: the model suggests, they can run a primary deficit forever without ever having to raise taxes to retire the resulting debt. This is not just a theoretical *curiosum*. Today in most advanced economies, the real rate of interest is below the rate of economic growth (however paltry that rate of growth may be). This fact is motivating a deep rethinking about the limits of fiscal policy and the scope for a robust fiscal response not only to the Covid-19 pandemic, but also to the green infrastructure buildup that global warming would seem to require. Olivier Blanchard devoted his Presidential Lecture to the American Economic Association (2019) to argue that a situation in which $r < g$ for a prolonged period of time opens vast new possibilities for the conduct of fiscal policy[10].

But, at the same time, a bubbly world also bears bad news for those in charge of fiscal policy because, as we have seen above, bubbly equilibria are inherently fragile. Could it be that an advanced country issues a great deal of debt at very low interest rates and one day investors decide to dump it simply because of a self-fulfilling change in expectations? Hard to say, but it is not a possibility that can be entirely ignored. In fact, Blanchard (2019) acknowledges that arguments based on the possibility of multiple equilibria are "the most difficult to counter" when making the case for the increased fiscal space that low interest rates bring.

Bubbles also have vast implications for financial markets and financial regulation. The obvious concern, mentioned at the outset, is that asset bubbles typically end in tears, with overvaluation abruptly reversing itself and wrecking balance sheets. But here, also, the news is not all bad. Financial markets typically involve inefficient borrowing constraints that keep a subset of agents (especially small and medium enterprises) from undertaking positive net-present-value projects. Therefore, as Martin and Ventura (2018) emphasise, to the extent that bubbles pump up the value of collateral and relax borrowing constraints, they can promote efficiency and raise welfare as long as those bubbles do not burst [11].

Last but certainly not least, bubbles present difficult dilemmas for central banks and for monetary policy more generally. In the presence of sticky prices, if bubbles affect aggregate demand they also affect output and inflation, giving rise to bubble-driven business cycles. The implication is that standard monetary and interest rate rules need to be modified to take into account this new source of fluctuations. In some cases those modifications are relatively minor, but that is not always the case. Galí (2020) discusses the issues involved in greater detail than we can here.

22.4 | Appendix 1

Let $N_{t,\tau}$ be the size at time t of the cohort born at τ. The initial size of the cohort born at τ is nN_τ. In addition, the probability that someone born at τ is still alive at $t \geq \tau$ is $e^{-p(t-\tau)}$. It follows that

$$N_{t,\tau} = nN_\tau e^{-p(t-\tau)}. \tag{22.49}$$

Now, $N_t = N_\tau e^{(n-p)(t-\tau)}$, so

$$\frac{N_{t,\tau}}{N_t} = ne^{-p(t-\tau)}e^{-(n-p)(t-\tau)} = ne^{-n(t-\tau)}. \tag{22.50}$$

We conclude the relative size at time t of the cohort born at τ is $ne^{-n(t-\tau)}$ For any variable $x_{t,\tau}$ define the per capita (or average) x_t as

$$x_t = \int_{-\infty}^t x_{t,\tau}\left(\frac{N_{t,\tau}}{N_t}\right)d\tau, \tag{22.51}$$

$$x_t = \int_{-\infty}^t x_{t,\tau}\, ne^{-n(t-\tau)}d\tau. \tag{22.52}$$

For a person belonging to the cohort born on date τ, endowment income at time t is

$$y_{t,\tau} = \left(\frac{n+\gamma}{n}\right)ye^{-\gamma(t-\tau)}, \tag{22.53}$$

where y is a constant. Next define per capita (or average) endowment at time t as

$$y_t = \int_{-\infty}^t y_{t,\tau}\, ne^{-n(t-\tau)}d\tau, \tag{22.54}$$

$$y_t = y\left(\frac{n+\gamma}{n}\right)\int_{-\infty}^t e^{-\gamma(t-\tau)}ne^{-n(t-\tau)}d\tau, \tag{22.55}$$

$$y_t = y(n+\gamma)\int_{-\infty}^t e^{(n+\gamma)(t-t)}d\tau, \tag{22.56}$$

$$y_t = y. \tag{22.57}$$

22.5 | Appendix 2

The following derivation follows Blanchard (1985). Let the human wealth at time t of someone born on date τ be

$$h_{t,\tau} = \int_t^\infty y_{s,\tau} e^{-\int_t^s (r_v+p)dv} ds. \tag{22.58}$$

The income at time s of an individual is born on date τ is (this is the key declining income path assumption)

$$y_{s,\tau} = \left(\frac{n+\gamma}{n}\right) y e^{-\gamma(s-\tau)} = \left(\frac{n+\gamma}{n}\right) y e^{-\gamma(s-t)} e^{\gamma(t-\tau)}. \tag{22.59}$$

Therefore, the expression for $h_{t,\tau}$ can be written

$$h_{t,\tau} = e^{\gamma(\tau-t)} \int_t^\infty \left(\frac{n+\gamma}{n}\right) y e^{-\int_t^s (r_v+p+\gamma)dv} ds. \tag{22.60}$$

Next define per capita (or average) human wealth held by those still alive at t, given by

$$h_t = \int_{-\infty}^t h_{t,\tau} n e^{n(\tau-t)} d\tau. \tag{22.61}$$

Using the expression for $h_{t,\tau}$ the last equation can be written as

$$h_t = \int_{-\infty}^t e^{\gamma(\tau-t)} \left\{ \int_t^\infty \left(\frac{n+\gamma}{n}\right) y e^{-\int_t^s (r_v+p+\gamma)dv} ds \right\} n e^{n(\tau-t)} d\tau, \tag{22.62}$$

where the expression in curly brackets is the same for all agents. It follows that

$$h_t = \left\{ \int_t^\infty y e^{-\int_t^s (r_v+p+\gamma)dv} ds \right\} (n+\gamma) \int_{-\infty}^t e^{(n+\gamma)(\tau-t)} d\tau, \tag{22.63}$$

$$h_t = \int_t^\infty y e^{-\int_t^s (r_v+p+\gamma)dv} ds. \tag{22.64}$$

Finally, differentiating with respect to time t we arrive at

$$\dot{h}_t = (r_t + p + \gamma) h_t - y, \tag{22.65}$$

which is the equation of motion for human capital in the text.

22.6 | Appendix 3

One can show the individual Euler equation at time t for an agent born at date s is

$$\dot{c}_{t,\tau} = c_{t,\tau} (r_t - \rho). \tag{22.66}$$

The present-value budget constraint of this agent is

$$\int_t^\infty c_{s,\tau} e^{-\int_t^s (r_v+p)dv} ds = b_{t,\tau} + h_{t,\tau}. \tag{22.67}$$

Using the Euler equation here, we have

$$c_{t,\tau} \int_t^\infty e^{\int_t^s (r_v - \rho)dv} e^{-\int_t^s (r_v + p)dv} ds = b_{t,\tau} + h_{t,\tau}, \tag{22.68}$$

$$c_{t,\tau} \int_t^\infty e^{-(p+\rho)(s-t)} ds = b_{t,\tau} + h_{t,\tau}, \tag{22.69}$$

$$c_{t,\tau} = (p + \rho)\left(b_{t,\tau} + h_{t,\tau}\right). \tag{22.70}$$

Next derive the per capita consumption function, given by

$$c_t = \int_{-\infty}^t c_{t,\tau} ne^{-n(t-\tau)} d\tau. \tag{22.71}$$

Using (22.70) this becomes

$$c_t = (p + \rho) \int_{-\infty}^t \left(b_{t,\tau} + h_{t,\tau}\right) ne^{-n(t-\tau)} d\tau, \tag{22.72}$$

$$c_t = (p + \rho) \int_{-\infty}^t b_{t,\tau} ne^{-n(t-\tau)} d\tau + (p + \rho) \int_{-\infty}^t h_{t,\tau} ne^{-n(t-\tau)} d\tau, \tag{22.73}$$

$$c_t = (p + \rho)\left(b_t + h_t\right), \tag{22.74}$$

which is the per capita (or average) consumption function.

Notes

[1] Economists such as Ken Rogoff have been advocating the phasing out of cash, see Rogoff (2016). Recently, India implemented a drastic reduction of cash availability, which is analysed in Chodorow-Reich et al. (2020).

[2] This section follows mostly the work of John Cochrane as presented in his book Cochrane (2021), to which we refer for those interested in further exploration of this topic.

[3] If you find this statement confusing, remember that to find the characteristic equation you need to find the determinant of this matrix. Expanding by the last column means that the equation is $1 - \lambda$ times the determinant of the upper left quadrant. This quickly indicates that 1 is one of the eigenvalues.

[4] Actually, the opportunity cost of an asset with similar risk characteristics.

[5] The assumption of a constant coupon is done for simplification but in no way necessary.

[6] Another interesting point is that if the bubble bursts, its value goes to zero: there is no gradual undoing of a bubble. Thus, the pattern of the unwinding of an asset price will tell you a lot about whether the previous surge was or was not a bubble or just a change in the perception on fundamentals.

[7] In the framework of (22.28) this would be a case in which the interest rate is zero.

[8] For a crystal-clear explanation of this see Weil (2008), on which this introduction draws.

⁹ This is a slightly simplified version of the same model we presented in Chapter 8 and here follows Acemoglu (2009). Rather than having you go back to that model we have moved some computations to three appendices of this chapter for ease of reference.

¹⁰ On the same topic, see also Reis (2020).

¹¹ Caballero and Krishnamurthy (2006) explore this tension in the context of bubbly capital flows to emerging markets.

References

Acemoglu, D. (2009). *Introduction to modern economic growth*. Princeton University Press.

Blanchard, O. (2019). Public debt and low interest rates. *American Economic Review*, *109*(4), 1197–1229.

Blanchard, O. J. (1985). Debt, deficits, and finite horizons. *Journal of Political Economy*, *93*(2), 223–247.

Caballero, R. J., Farhi, E., & Gourinchas, P.-O. (2008). An equilibrium model of "global imbalances" and low interest rates. *American Economic Review*, *98*(1), 358–93.

Caballero, R. J. & Krishnamurthy, A. (2006). Bubbles and capital flow volatility: Causes and risk management. *Journal of Monetary Economics*, *53*(1), 35–53.

Chodorow-Reich, G., Gopinath, G., Mishra, P., & Narayanan, A. (2020). Cash and the economy: Evidence from India's demonetization. *The Quarterly Journal of Economics*, *135*(1), 57–103.

Cochrane, J. H. (2021). The fiscal theory of the price level. *Manuscript*. *URL* https://www.johnhcochrane.com/research-all/the-fiscal-theory-of-the-price-level-1.

Farhi, E. & Tirole, J. (2012). Bubbly liquidity. *The Review of Economic Studies*, *79*(2), 678–706.

Galí, J. (2020). *Monetary policy and bubbles in a New Keynesian model with overlapping generations*. National Bureau of Economic Research.

Martin, A. & Ventura, J. (2018). The macroeconomics of rational bubbles: A user's guide. *Annual Review of Economics*, *10*, 505–539.

Miao, J. (2014). Introduction to economic theory of bubbles. *Journal of Mathematical Economics*, *53*, 130–136.

Reis, R. (2020). The constraint on public debt when r<g but g<m.

Rogoff, K. S. (2016). *The curse of cash*. Princeton University Press.

Samuelson, P. A. (1958). An exact consumption-loan model of interest with or without the social contrivance of money. *Journal of Political Economy*, *66*(6), 467–482.

Sims, C. A. (2016). Fiscal policy, monetary policy and central bank independence. https://bit.ly/3BmMJYE.

Tirole, J. (1985). Asset bubbles and overlapping generations. *Econometrica*, 1499–1528.

Weil, P. (2008). Overlapping generations: The first jubilee. *Journal of Economic Perspectives*, *22*(4), 115–34.

Very brief mathematical appendix

Throughout this book, we make use of a few key mathematical tools that allow us to handle the dynamic problems that arise when dealing with issues of macroeconomic policy. In this appendix, we briefly go over the key solution techniques that we use as a simple user guide. Note that our focus here is not on rigor, but rather on user-friendliness, which may lead to some hair-raising moments for those more familiar with the formalism. For a more thorough (yet still economist-friendly) presentation, the reader can consult a number of textbooks, such as Acemoglu (2009) or Dixit and Pindyck (1994).

We now go over three key areas: (i) Dynamic optimisation in continuous time, (ii) Dynamic optimisation in discrete time, and (iii) Differential equations.

A.1 | Dynamic optimisation in continuous time

We have described macroeconomic policy problems in discrete and continuous time at different points, depending on convenience. In continuous time, we can solve these problems using the optimality conditions from *optimal control* theory.[1]

What kinds of problems fit the optimal control framework? The idea is that you choose a certain path for a choice variable – the *control* variable – that maximises the total value over time of a function affected by that variable. This would be relatively easy, and well within the realm of standard constrained optimisation, if whatever value you chose for the control variable at a certain moment in time had no implication for what values it may take at the next moment. What makes things trickier, and more interesting, is when it is not the case. That is to say, when what you do now affects what your options are for tomorrow – or, in continuous time, the next infinitesimal moment. That's what is captured by the *state* variable: a variable that contains the information from all the previous evolution of the dynamic system. The evolution of the state variable is described by a dynamic equation, the *equation of motion*.

The simplest way to see all of this is to look at a simple example. Consider a simplified consumer problem:[2]

$$\max_{\{c_t\}_{t=0}^{T}} \int_0^T u(c_t)e^{-\rho t}dt, \tag{A.1}$$

How to cite this book chapter:

Campante, F., Sturzenegger, F. and Velasco, A. 2021. *Advanced Macroeconomics: An Easy Guide.*
   Appendix A. 'Very brief mathematical appendix', pp. 363–370. London: LSE Press.
   DOI: https://doi.org/10.31389/lsepress.ame.w   License: CC-BY-NC 4.0.

subject to the budget constraint $c_t + \dot{a}_t = y_t + ra_t$ and to an initial level of assets a_0. In words, the consumer chooses the path for their consumption so as to maximise total utility over their lifetime, and whatever income (labour plus interest on assets) they do not consume is accumulated as assets. The control variable is c_t that is, what the consumer chooses in order to maximise utility and the state variable is a_t that is, what links one instant to the next, as described by the equation of motion:

$$\dot{a}_t = y_t + ra_t - c_t. \tag{A.2}$$

The maximum principle can be summarised as a series of steps:

Step 1 - Set up the Hamiltonian function: The Hamiltonian is simply what is in the integral – the instantaneous value, at time t, of the function you are trying to maximise over time plus, "the right-hand-side of the equation of motion" multiplied by a function called the co-state variable, which we will denote as λ_t. In our example, we can write:

$$H_t = u(c_t) + \lambda_t[y_t + ra_t - c_t]. \tag{A.3}$$

(This is the current-value version of the Hamiltonian because utility at time t is being evaluated at the current t, that is, without the time discounting represented by the term $e^{-\rho t}$. The present-value version, where we would add that discounting term and write $u(c_t)e^{-\rho t}$, works just as well, with some minor adaptation in the conditions we will lay out below. We believe the current-value Hamiltonian lends itself to a more natural economic interpretation.)

This looks a lot like the Lagrangian function from static optimisation, right? Well, the co-state variable has a natural economic interpretation that is analogous to the familiar Lagrange multiplier. It is the marginal benefit of a marginal addition to the stock of the state variable – that is, of relaxing the constraint. In economic parlance, it is the shadow value of the state variable.

The key idea behind the maximum principle is that the optimal trajectory of control, state, and co-state variables must maximise the Hamiltonian function. But what are the conditions for that?

Step 2 - Maximise the Hamiltonian with respect to the control variable(s): There is no integral in the Hamiltonian, it's just a function evaluated at a point in time. So this is just like static optimisation! The intuition is pretty clear: if you were not maximising the function at all instants considered separately, you probably could be doing better, right? For our purposes, this will boil down to taking the first-order condition with respect to the control variable(s). In our specific example, we would write

$$H_c = 0 \Rightarrow u'(c_t) = \lambda_t. \tag{A.4}$$

This has your usual FOC interpretation: the marginal utility gain of increasing consumption has to be equal to the marginal cost, which is not adding to the stock of your assets, and is thus given by the co-state variable.

Importantly, you could have more than one control variable in a problem. What do you do? Well, as in static optimisation, you take FOCs for each of them.

Step 3 - Figure out the optimal path of the co-state variable(s): The Hamiltonian is static, but the problem is dynamic. This means that, at any given instant, you must figure out that whatever you leave to the next instant (your state variable) is consistent with optimisation. This is a key insight. Intuitively, maximising an infinite-dimensional problem (i.e. what's the right value for your control variable at every instant in a continuum) can be broken down into a sequence of choices between the current instant and the (infinitesimally) next.

Fair enough, but how can we guarantee that? The maximum principle tells you: it's about satisfying the co-state equations. These are basically about optimising the Hamiltonian with respect to the state variable(s). The FOC here is a bit different from what you are used to, as you won't set derivatives equal to zero. Instead, you set them equal to $-\dot{\lambda}_t + \rho\lambda_t$.[3] In our example

$$H_a = -\dot{\lambda}_t + \rho\lambda_t \Rightarrow r\lambda_t = -\dot{\lambda}_t + \rho\lambda_t. \tag{A.5}$$

It seems like this does not have much of an economic intuition, but think again. Consider your state variable as a (financial) asset. (It is literally true in our specific example, but also more broadly.) This condition can be rewritten as

$$H_a + \dot{\lambda}_t = \rho\lambda_t. \tag{A.6}$$

The LHS is the total marginal return of holding this asset for an additional instant: the "dividend" from the flow of utility coming from it (measured by the marginal impact on the Hamiltonian, H_a) plus the "capital gain" coming from the change in its valuation in utility terms ($\dot{\lambda}_t$). The RHS is the required marginal payoff for it to make sense for you to hold the asset this additional instant; it has to compensate for your discount rate ρ. If the LHS is greater (resp. smaller) than the RHS, you should hold more (resp. less) of that asset. You can only be at an optimum if there is equality. In other words, you can think about this as an "asset pricing" condition that is necessary for dynamic optimality.

What if there were more than one state variable? Well, then you will have more than one equation of motion, and you will need to impose one such "asset pricing" dynamic optimality condition for each of them.

Equations (A.4) and (A.5), put together, yield a first-order differential equation that contains the information for the static and dynamic requirements for optimisation. As we will see in more detail later in the Appendix, a first-order differential equation allows for an infinite number of solutions, up to two constants. How do we pin down which solution is the true optimum?

Step 4 - Transversality condition: We need two conditions to pin down the constants that are left free by the differential equation. One of them is the initial condition: we know the state variable starts off at a value that is given at $t = 0$ – in our example, a_0. The second is a terminal condition: how much should we have left at the end, to guarantee that we have indeed maximised our objective function? This is what the transversality condition gives us in the example:

$$a_T \lambda_T e^{-\rho T} = 0. \tag{A.7}$$

Intuitively, as long as our state variable has any positive value in terms of generating utility (and that shadow value is given by the co-state variable, λ), you should not be left with any of it at the end. After all, you could have consumed it and generated additional utility!

These optimality conditions fully characterise the solution for any dynamic problem we will have encountered in this book.

A.2 | Dynamic optimisation in discrete time

In dynamic problems, it is sometimes just more convenient to model time as evolving in discrete intervals, as opposed to continuously. This doesn't make a difference for the economic intuition, as we will see, but does require different techniques.

These techniques come from *dynamic programming* theory.[4] The key (and truly remarkable) insight behind these techniques is to recognise the iterative (or recursive) nature of a lot of dynamic problems. Their structure essentially repeats over and over again through time. This means that – not coincidentally, echoing the lessons from optimal control theory in a different context – you can break down such problems into a sequence of smaller ones. Optimizing through time is achieved by making sure that you choose properly between today and tomorrow, while accounting for the fact that tomorrow you will face a similar choice again.

This insight is beautifully encapsulated in the *Bellman equation*. To see it in action, let's consider the discrete-time version of the consumer problem we have seen in the previous section

$$\max_{\{c_t\}_{t=0}^T} \sum_0^T \beta^t u(c_t), \tag{A.8}$$

subject to the equation of motion,

$$a_{t+1} - a_t = y_t + ra_t - c_t. \tag{A.9}$$

The information in this recursive problem can be summarised using the concept of the *value function*, $V(a_t)$: it is the value of total utility at a given point in time (as a function of the state variable), conditional on optimal decisions being made over the entire future path. In other words, we can rewrite the problem as

$$V(a_t) = max_{c_t}\{u(c_t) + \beta V(a_{t+1})\}. \tag{A.10}$$

Here is the intuition: choosing optimal consumption means maximising current utility, while also leaving the amount of the state variable that lets you make the optimal choice at $t + 1$. Picking today's consumption is a much simpler task than choosing an entire path. If you do it right, it leads you to the same solution. That's the beauty of dynamic programming.

That seems reasonable enough, but how do you solve it?

Step 1 - Maximise the value function with respect to the control variable: Well, the first thing is, naturally enough, to take the first-order condition with respect to the control variable. In our example, where the control variable is c_t, we get

$$u'(c_t) - \beta V'(a_{t+1}) = 0, \tag{A.11}$$

where the second term on the LHS is using the fact that, as per the equation of motion, a_{t+1} is a function of c_t. The intuition is the same as ever: the optimal choice between today and tomorrow equates the marginal gain of additional consumption to the marginal cost of leaving a marginal unit of assets for tomorrow. The latter is that it detracts from the future choice possibilities encapsulated in the value function.

Just as with optimal control theory, this summarises the fact that dynamic optimisation requires static optimisation – otherwise, you could have been doing better!

Step 2 - Figure out the optimal path for the state variable: Again, by analogy with the intuition from optimal control, we also need to figure out that the choice we are making today leaves the right amount of the state variable for an optimal decision tomorrow. This means figuring out the value function.

To see how that works, let's look at our example again. Since our problem has a nice, continuously differentiable value function, we can differentiate the value function with respect to the state variable:

$$V'(a_t) = (1 + r)u'(c_t). \tag{A.12}$$

It's easy enough to see why we get this marginal utility term. Consumption is a function of the state variable, as per the equation of motion. But shouldn't there be a term on $V'(a_{t+1})$ somewhere? After all, a_{t+1} is also a function of a_t. The trick is that we used an *envelope condition*.[5] Intuitively, as with any so-called envelope theorem, if you are optimising the value function, you should set the path of the state variable such that you cannot get additional utility from a marginal change, at the optimum. This means that the term on $V'(a_{t+1})$ simplifies to zero.

In short, at the optimum, the only impact of an additional marginal unit of your state variable is the additional utility brought by converting it into consumption – the impact on the future value is, at the optimum, equal to zero.

Step 3 - Putting it all together: You will have noticed that, once you know $V'(a_t)$, you also know $V'(a_{t+1})$: just stick a $t + 1$ wherever you see a t. We can put (A.11) and (A.12) together and obtain

$$u'(c_t) = \beta(1 + r)u'(c_{t+1}), \tag{A.13}$$

that is to say: our familiar Euler equation.

That will do it for our purposes here, though you should keep in mind that to nail the full path of your control variable, you still need the initial and terminal conditions. (In our specific example, it is pretty obvious that the consumer would choose to consume all of their assets in the last period of their life: a transversality condition.)

A.3 | First-order differential equations

A.3.1 | Integrating factors

Typically, the solution to a dynamic problem will be a system of differential (or difference) equations, describing the evolution of key variables of interest over time. In the main text of the book, we have introduced *phase diagrams* as a tool for analysing the behaviour of such systems.

Oftentimes, though, we were interested in finding an analytical solution for a variable whose behaviour is described by a dynamic equation. In these cases, we used a method of solution involving integrating factors, which we will elaborate on now.

As usual, this is easiest to motivate in the context of a specific example. Let's take the consumer problem discussed above, and in particular the equation of motion described by (A.2), which we rewrite here, for convenience, in slightly different form:

$$\dot{a}_t - ra_t = y_t - c_t. \tag{A.14}$$

This illustrates a kind of first-order differential equation that can generally be written as

$$\frac{dz}{dx} + Pz = Q, \tag{A.15}$$

where P, Q are functions of x only. This is the kind that can be solved using integrating factors. The integrating factor is defined as:

$$I = e^{\int P dx}. \tag{A.16}$$

The trick is to multiply both sides of A.15 by the integrating factor, which yields

$$\frac{dz}{dx}e^{\int P dx} + Pze^{\int P dx} = Qe^{\int P dx}. \tag{A.17}$$

You will notice that the LHS of this equation is what you get from differentiating $ze^{\int P dx}$ with respect to x, using the product rule of differentiation. In other words, we can integrate both sides of A.17, using the Fundamental Theorem of Calculus, and obtain

$$\int(\frac{dz}{dx}e^{\int P dx} + Pze^{\int P dx})dx = \int Qe^{\int P dx}dx \Rightarrow ze^{\int P dx} = \int Qe^{\int P dx}dx + \kappa \tag{A.18}$$

This allows us to find a general solution for z, up to the constant κ (recall that any constant term would not affect the derivative, so any solution has to be up to a constant).

Let's look at that in the context of our consumer problem in (A.14). You can see that z is a, x is t, P is $-r$, and Q is $y_t - c_t$. So the integrating factoris $e^{-\int r dt}$, which can be simplified to e^{-rt}. Multiplying both sides by that integrating factor yields

$$\dot{a}_t e^{-rt} - r_t a_t e^{-rt} = y_t e^{-rt} - c_t e^{-rt}. \tag{A.19}$$

Applying (A.18) allows us to find a general solution for a_t:

$$a_t e^{-rt} = \int_0^t (y_s e^{-rs} - c_s e^{-rs}) ds + \kappa \Rightarrow a_t = e^{rt}\left(\int_0^t (y_s e^{-rs} - c_s e^{-rs}) ds + \kappa\right) \Rightarrow a_t = \int_0^t (y_s - c_s) e^{r(t-s)} ds + \kappa e^{rt},$$
$$\tag{A.20}$$

where we are using s to denote each instant over which we are integrating, up to t. How do we pin down the constant? This equation must hold for $t = 0$, which entails that $\kappa = a_0$. In other words,

$$a_t = \int_0^t (y_s - c_s) e^{r(t-s)} ds + a_0 e^{rt} \tag{A.21}$$

This tells us that the consumer's assets, at any given point in time, equal the initial value of assets (compounded by the interest rate), plus the compound sum of their savings over time.

The differential equations we deal with can all be solved using this method, which is quite convenient. Depending on the specific problem, this solution then allows us to figure out the optimal level of consumption, or the path of the current account, or whatever else that interests us in the case at hand.

A.3.2 | Eigenvalues and dynamics

In other occasions, we do not need an analytical solution, but want to have a way of figuring out the dynamic properties of a system of differential equations. Here's where linear systems are very convenient, because we can use tools of linear algebra to come to the rescue. This helps explain why we often focus on linear approximations (around a BGP, typically). Note that this focus entails important consequences: a linear approximation is good enough when you are sufficiently close to the point around which you are doing the approximation. If a shock gets you far from the BGP, then maybe the approximation is not going to work that well as a description of your economy!

Let's talk about the tools, and especially one concept that we mention quite a bit in the book: eigenvalues.

Consider a system of differential equations that we have studied, describing the solution of the basic AK model. In its simplest version, we can write it as

$$\dot{c}_t = (A - \rho)c_t \tag{A.22}$$
$$\dot{k}_t = Ak_t - c_t \tag{A.23}$$

The nice thing is that this system is already linear in c_t, k_t, meaning that we can write it in matrix form:

$$\begin{bmatrix} \dot{c}_t \\ \dot{k}_t \end{bmatrix} = \begin{bmatrix} A - \rho & 0 \\ -1 & A \end{bmatrix} \begin{bmatrix} c_t \\ k_t \end{bmatrix} \tag{A.24}$$

Let us denote the vector $[c_t, k_t]$ as x_t; we can write this more concisely as

$$\dot{x}_t = \Gamma x_t. \tag{A.25}$$

Here's where the trick comes in: solutions to a system like (A.25) can be written as

$$x_t = \kappa_1 e^{\lambda_1 t} \eta^1 + \kappa_2 e^{\lambda_2 t} \eta^2, \qquad (A.26)$$

where λ_1 and λ_2 are the eigenvalues of the matrix Γ, η^1 and η^2 are the corresponding eigenvectors, and κ_1 and κ_2 are the standard constants, of which there are two because this is a system of two differential equations.[6]

This means that the dynamic behaviour of the system will be closely tied to the eigenvalues. Why so? Imagine that both $\lambda_1, \lambda_2 > 0$.[7] It is easy to see that the solution (A.26) will behave explosively: as t grows, x_t will grow without bound, in absolute value, for any (nonzero) κ_1, κ_2. Such a system will not converge.

What if $\lambda_1, \lambda_2 < 0$? Then, eventually, the solution will converge to zero (which means that the solution to the general differential equation will converge to the particular solution). This is a *stable* system; it will converge no matter where it starts.

Economists like stable systems that converge – but not quite so stable. After all, it seems natural to think that there is room for human choices to make a difference! Particularly since, in economic terms, there will often be the jumpy variables that we've been alluding to through the book – that is to say, those that need not follow an equation of motion.

You will have noticed, though, that there is a third case: $\lambda_1 > 0, \lambda_2 < 0$. (This is without loss of generality, of course!) In that case, the system will converge only in the case where κ_1 is exactly equal to zero. Such a system is, technically speaking, not stable – it generally will not converge. But we refer to it as saddle-path stable. These are the most interesting, from an economic perspective, as convergence depends on purposeful behaviour by the agents in the model.

How do we know if a system is saddle-path stable without having to compute the eigenvalues? It suffices to recall, from linear algebra, that the determinant of a matrix is equal to the product of its eigenvalues. It immediately follows that, if $det(\Gamma) < 0$, we are in a situation of saddle-path stability.[8] Such a system will converge only if the initial choice of the jumpy variable is the one that puts the system on the saddle path – that is to say, the one that delivers $\kappa_1 = 0$ in the notation above.

Notes

[1] These optimality conditions are synthesised in Pontryagin's maximum principle, derived in the 1950s from standard principles from the classical calculus of variations that goes back to Euler and Lagrange and others.

[2] Again, we are using subscripts to denote time, as opposed to parentheses, as more often done in continuous-time settings. We are iconoclasts!

[3] With the present-value Hamiltonian, this becomes $-\dot{\lambda}_t$. It is easy to check that they are equivalent.

[4] These techniques were developed by Richard Bellman in the 1950s.

[5] The relevant envelope theorem here is due to Benveniste and Scheinkman (1979).

[6] Recall that the eigenvalues of matrix Γ can be computed as the solution λ to the equation $det(A - \lambda I) = 0$, where I is the identity matrix. The eigenvectors are defined as vectors η such that $\Gamma \eta = \lambda \eta$.

[7] More precisely, we are referring here to the *real* part of the eigenvalues – they can be complex numbers with an imaginary part.

[8] It is easy to check that the system in (A.24) does not converge if $A > \rho$. You will recall that this is exactly our conclusion from studying the AK model in Chapter 5.

Simulating an RBC model

Chapter 14 outlined the basic building blocks of an RBC model. This appendix will take you through the steps to estimate it and then compute the empirical counterpart to the business cycle data.

The steps are quite simple. Imagine first that you were to do this by hand. Of course the starting point would be your specific model with its associated parameter values. The conditions that describe your model typically will be a combination of FOCs and budget constraints that determine the evolution of variables through time. Plugging the parameter values into the model, you could compute the steady state of the economy (pretty much as we did in Chapter 14). (We use the word "could" because this may be quite difficult.) Once you know the steady state, you could linearise the model around that steady state (pretty much as we did, for example, in Chapter 3). Now you have a linear dynamic system, that can be shocked to compute the trajectory of the variables in response. For an RBC model, you shock it over and over again to get a series for the variables, from which you can compute the correlations that you will confront with the data. This is easy to say but involves computing the saddle path in which variables converge to the equilibrium. And to be able to do this we would also need to check first that that dynamic properties are those required for convergence (also see Chapter 3 and the mathematical appendix for a discussion of this).

Well, if all that looked a bit daunting, you are lucky that most of this work will be done by the computer itself. What remains of this appendix shows you how to go about it.

First of all, you will need to have MATLAB, and we will assume you are minimally knowledgeable. MATLAB offers a free trial, so you may want to practice first using that.

Before starting you need to download Dynare[1] which is pre-programmed to run these models. Below we will write the model, and, say, we call it Model1. We will then run Dynare Model1.mod in MATLAB. It is as easy as that, but we have to do some setting up before.

In MATLAB, go to the HOME tab, and look for the Set Path button. In the new window, go to the Add Folder command and search in the Dynare download the "matlab" folder. This means going to "dynare/xxx/matlab" (where xxx means which version of MATLAB you have; in other words, you need to go to the "matlab" folder in Dynare), select that folder, and then select to add this. It typically places it first, but if it does not make sure to use the left buttons to place it first. Then save.

Now we need to open a folder to save the results (any regular folder in your computer will do). We will write the model (see below) and save it in this folder. It is important to save the model with the extension .mod. So if you call the model "Model1" you need to save it in this folder as "Model1.mod". This will indicate to Matlab that it is a Dynare file when you run "Dynare Model1.mod". Then, you

How to cite this book chapter:
Campante, F., Sturzenegger, F. and Velasco, A. 2021. *Advanced Macroeconomics: An Easy Guide.*
   Appendix B. 'Simulating an RBC model', pp. 371–380. London: LSE Press.
   DOI: https://doi.org/10.31389/lsepress.ame.x   License: CC-BY-NC 4.0.

have to specify to MATLAB that you are currently working on the desired folder. You can do this by clicking the "browse for folder" button:

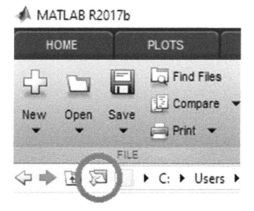

Now to the model. The specification we will work with is the same as in Chapter 14. You can find more complex structures (including open-economy versions) within the framework of Dynare. For our purposes of taking a first step in modelling, this simple specification will do.

In what follows we will take you through the steps to run this simple model. First, we need to define the variables.

---

var y c n ii lambda k z r w;

varexo u_z;

parameters BETA PHI ALPHA VARPHI DELTA;

parameters n_ss r_ss z_ss;

The "var" command sets all the variables of the model, both exogenous and endogenous. In this case, we have output (y), consumption (c), labour (n), investment (ii), the shadow price of consumption (lambda), the stock of capital (k), the nominal interest rate (r), productivity (z), and wages (w). The "varexo" command defines shocks. u_z indicates the exogenous shock that will hit the variable z. The command "parameters" is used to define the parameters of the model. Also, some steady-state values will remain free for our model to *match* certain moments of the variables.

Next we need to provide a numerical value for these parameters. For this you will typically rely on previous literature, or use the calibration exercises that we saw in the chapter.

Once you've figured out what values you want to use, setting the values in the model is straightforward, and is the next step. (You can later play around by considering the response of the model to different values of these parameters.) Here we assume, for example

---

ALPHA=1/3;

PHI=2/3;

VARPHI=0.95;

DELTA=0.1;

z_ss=1;

r_ss=0.01;

n_ss=0.32353;

With the variables defined and the parameter values established, we next have to specify the model. We use the command "model" for that. We will conclude the section with the "end" command. We also define a process for the shock, that here will be an autoregressive process.

Lagged and forward variables are indicated by a −1 or +1 respectively, between parentheses, immediately after the variable name, and can be added without any problem. Dynare will work with a log-linearised version, so we need to define our variables as the log version of the original variables. But this is no problem, it just means that where we had y we write $exp(y)$. (This change of variables can only be done with variables that always take positive values, though, so watch out!)

So the model is a series of FOCs and budget constraints. For example, our first equation below is the resource constraint, the second and third are the optimal choice of consumption and labour, the fourth is the FOC relative to capital, and the fifth is the definition of the interest rate. The last equations are the production function, the law of motion of capital, the definition of the real wage as the marginal productivity of labour, and the process for productivity.

---

model;

// Aggregate Demand

exp(y)=exp(c)+exp(ii);

// FOC for consumption

(1-PHI)/(exp(c))=exp(lambda);

// FOC for labour

PHI/(1-exp(n))=(1-ALPHA)*((exp(y)/exp(n))*exp(lambda));

// FOC for capital

exp(lambda)=BETA*exp(lambda(+1))*(ALPHA*exp(y(+1))/exp(k)+1-DELTA);

// The interest rate equation

exp(r) = exp(z)*ALPHA*(exp(k(-1)))^(ALPHA-1)*(exp(n))^(1-ALPHA);

// Production Function

$$exp(y)=exp(z)*(exp(k(-1)))\hat{}(ALPHA)*(exp(n))\hat{}(1-ALPHA);$$

// Law of movement of capital

$$exp(k)=(1-DELTA)*exp(k(-1))+exp(ii);$$

// Wage equation

$$exp(w)=(1-ALPHA)*exp(z)*exp(k(-1))\hat{}ALPHA*exp(n)\hat{}(-ALPHA);$$

// Productivity process

$$log(exp(z)/z\_ss)=VARPHI*log(exp(z(-1))/z\_ss)+u\_z;$$

end;

Now we need to compute the steady state, by hand (endogenous variables as a function of exogenous variables). Dynare needs to work with a steady state, so if you don't write it down, Dynare will try to compute it directly. However, doing so in a non-linear model (like this RBC model) generally will not work. For that reason, it is advisable to provide it manually. To do that, we have to introduce the "steady_state_model" command as shown below. This is not as difficult as it sounds, and understanding the steady state properties of the model is always useful to do. Finally, we need to establish that the initial values for the model are those for the steady state (in logs)

---

steady_state_model;

$$BETA=1/(1+r\_ss);$$

$$y\_to\_k\_ss=(1-BETA*(1-DELTA))/(BETA*ALPHA);$$

$$k\_ss=((y\_to\_k\_ss)\hat{}(1/(1-ALPHA))*(1/z\_ss)\hat{}(1/(1-ALPHA))*(1/n\_ss))\hat{}(-1);$$

$$y\_ss=y\_to\_k\_ss*k\_ss;$$

$$ii\_ss=DELTA*k\_ss;$$

$$c\_ss=y\_ss-ii\_ss;$$

$$lambda\_ss=(1-PHI)/c\_ss;$$

$$w\_ss=(1-ALPHA)*z\_ss*(k\_ss)\hat{}ALPHA*n\_ss\hat{}(-ALPHA);$$

$$z=log(z\_ss);$$

$$y=log(y\_ss);$$

$$n=log(n\_ss);$$

$$k=log(k\_ss);$$

$$c=\log(c\_ss);$$

$$ii=\log(ii\_ss);$$

$$r=\log(r\_ss);$$

$$lambda=\log(lambda\_ss);$$

$$w=\log(w\_ss);$$

$$end;$$

———————————————————————

Then we have to check if the steady state is well defined. For that we use the "steady" and "check" commands, these will compute the eigenvalues of the model around the steady state, to verify that the dynamic properties are the desired ones.

steady;
check;

Next, we have to set the shocks that we want to study. In this simplified model, we want to analyse the effect of a productivity shock. We use the "shocks" command for that. For example, a shock of 10% can be coded as

shocks;
var u_z = .1;
end;

Finally, we set the simulation to allow Dynare to show us the impulse-response functions. We use "stoch_simul" for that

stoch_simul(periods=10000, irf = 100, order = 1);

This completes the script for the model. It has to look something like this

```
%------------------------------------------------------------
% 1. Defining variables
%------------------------------------------------------------

// Endogenous variables (7)
var y c n ii lambda k z r w; //

// Exogenous variables (1)
varexo u_z;

// Parameters
parameters BETA PHI ALPHA VARPHI DELTA;
parameters n_ss r_ss z_ss;
```

```
%----------------------------------------------------------------
% 2. Calibration
%----------------------------------------------------------------

ALPHA=1/3;
PHI=2/3;
VARPHI=0.95;
DELTA=0.1;

// Targeted steady state values
z_ss=1;
r_ss=0.01;
n_ss=0.32353;


%----------------------------------------------------------------
% 3. Model
%----------------------------------------------------------------

model;
//Agreggate Demand
exp(y)=exp(c)+exp(ii);

//FOC for the consumption
(1-PHI)/(exp(c))=exp(lambda);

PHI/(1-exp(n))=(1-ALPHA)*((exp(y)/exp(n))*exp(lambda));

exp(lambda)=BETA*exp(lambda(+1))*(ALPHA*exp(y(+1))/exp(k)+1-DELTA);


//Production Function
exp(y)=exp(z)*(exp(k(-1)))^(ALPHA)*(exp(n))^(1-ALPHA);

//interest rate equation
exp(r) = exp(z)*ALPHA*(exp(k(-1)))^(ALPHA-1)*(exp(n))^(1-ALPHA);

//Law of movement of capital
exp(k)=(1-DELTA)*exp(k(-1))+exp(ii);

//Wage equation
exp(w)=(1-ALPHA)*exp(z)*exp(k(-1))^ALPHA*exp(n)^(-ALPHA);

//stochastic proccess
log(exp(z)/z_ss)=VARPHI*log(exp(z(-1))/z_ss)+u_z;
end;
```

```
%----------------------------------------------------------------
% 4. Steady State
%----------------------------------------------------------------

steady_state_model;

// Computing the steady state and calibrated parameters
BETA=1/(1+r_ss);
y_to_k_ss=(1-BETA*(1-DELTA))/(BETA*ALPHA);
k_ss=((y_to_k_ss)^(1/(1-ALPHA))*(1/z_ss)^(1/(1-ALPHA))*(1/n_ss)^(-1);
y_ss=y_to_k_ss*k_ss:
ii_ss=DELTA*k_ss;
c_ss=y_ss-ii_ss;
lambda_ss=(1-PHI)/c_ss;
w_ss=(1-ALPHA)*z_ss*(k_ss)^ALPHA*n_ss^(-ALPHA);
z=log(z_ss);
y=log(y_ss);
n=log(n_ss);
k=log(k_ss);
c=log(c_ss);
ii=log(ii_ss);
r=log(r_ss);
lambda=log(lambda_ss);
w=log(w_ss);
end;


%----------------------------------------------------------------
% 4. Computation
%----------------------------------------------------------------

steady;
check;

shocks;
var u_z = .1;
end;

stoch_simul(periods=10000, irf = 100, order = 1);
```

Now we run "Dynare Model1.mod", and voila! The output will be like this:

```
STEADY-STATE RESULTS:

y           -0.574132
c           -0.935145
n           -1.12846
ii          -1.76805
lambda      -0.163467
k           0.534531
z           0
r           -4.60517
w           0.148866


EIGENVALUES:
        Modulus           Real         Imaginary

        0.8508           0.8508              0
        0.95             0.95                0
        1.187            1.187               0
        3.419e+16        3.419e+16           0


There are 2 eigenvalue(s) larger than 1 in modulus
for 2 forward-looking variable(s)

The rank condition is verified.
```
fx

```
Command Window
    The rank condition is verified.


    MODEL SUMMARY

      Number of variables:           9
      Number of stochastic shocks:   1
      Number of state variables:     2
      Number of jumpers:             2
      Number of static variables:    5


    MATRIX OF COVARIANCE OF EXOGENOUS SHOCKS
    Variables        u_z
    u_z          0.100000

    POLICY AND TRANSITION FUNCTIONS
```

	y	c	n	ii	lambda	k
Constant	-0.574132	-0.935145	-1.128463	-1.768055	-0.163467	0.534531
k(-1)	0.198027	0.498055	-0.202960	-0.492037	-0.498055	0.850796
z(-1)	1.236740	0.600924	0.430110	2.699119	-0.600924	0.269912
u_z	1.301832	0.632551	0.452748	2.841177	-0.632551	0.284118

```
Command Window
 MOMENTS OF SIMULATED VARIABLES
 VARIABLE           MEAN      STD. DEV.      VARIANCE      SKEWNESS      KURTOSIS
 y              -0.578647      1.576789      2.486263      0.034337      0.279139
 c              -0.939969      1.384754      1.917545      0.052236      0.401153
 n              -1.128255      0.250405      0.062703     -0.097217      0.060892
 ii             -1.771862      2.198706      4.834307     -0.012844      0.088130
 lambda         -0.158644      1.384754      1.917545     -0.052236      0.401153
 k               0.528261      1.634713      2.672288      0.056699      0.444578
 z              -0.002473      0.995335      0.990692      0.019705      0.204198
 r              -4.583508      6.746014     45.508711     -0.073543      0.069825
 w               0.144143      1.439289      2.071554      0.047530      0.364309


 CORRELATION OF SIMULATED VARIABLES
 VARIABLE       y        c        n       ii    lambda        k        z        r        w
 y         1.0000   0.9771   0.6046   0.9512  -0.9771   0.9320   0.9937   0.0022   0.9904
 c         0.9771   1.0000   0.4211   0.8638  -1.0000   0.9878   0.9470  -0.2107   0.9971
 n         0.6046   0.4211   1.0000   0.8208  -0.4211   0.2747   0.6901   0.7979   0.4883
 ii        0.9512   0.8638   0.8208   1.0000  -0.8638   0.7747   0.9798   0.3106   0.8993
 lambda   -0.9771  -1.0000  -0.4211  -0.8638   1.0000  -0.9878  -0.9470   0.2107  -0.9971
 k         0.9320   0.9878   0.2747   0.7747  -0.9878   1.0000   0.8855  -0.3604   0.9732
 z         0.9937   0.9470   0.6901   0.9798  -0.9470   0.8855   1.0000   0.1144   0.9686
 r         0.0022  -0.2107   0.7979   0.3106   0.2107  -0.3604   0.1144   1.0000  -0.1364
 w         0.9904   0.9971   0.4883   0.8993  -0.9971   0.9732   0.9686  -0.1364   1.0000
fx

 AUTOCORRELATION OF SIMULATED VARIABLES
 VARIABLE       1        2        3        4        5
 y         0.9658   0.9290   0.8910   0.8523   0.8151
 c         0.9884   0.9707   0.9483   0.9222   0.8940
 n         0.8232   0.6657   0.5294   0.4110   0.3173
 ii        0.9145   0.8343   0.7609   0.6936   0.6360
 lambda    0.9884   0.9707   0.9483   0.9222   0.8940
 k         0.9954   0.9837   0.9661   0.9440   0.9185
 z         0.9492   0.8983   0.8489   0.8009   0.7571
 r         0.8434   0.7030   0.5807   0.4736   0.3878
 w         0.9820   0.9589   0.9321   0.9025   0.8717
 Total computing time : 0h00m37s
 Note: warning(s) encountered in MATLAB/Octave code
fx >> |
```

Figure 1: Orthogonalized shock to u_z

Note

[1] https://www.dynare.org/

Simulating a DSGE model

Chapter 15 outlined the basic building blocks of a New Keynesian model. How do we estimate it?

We laid out the framework in Appendix B, so you may want to check out the setup section there. At any rate, we will repeat most of it here, for convenience.

The starting point would be your specific model with its associated parameter values. Again, the conditions that describe your model will typically be a combination of FOCs and budget constraints that determine the evolution of variables through time. Plugging the parameter values in the model, you could compute the steady state of the economy (pretty much as we did in the RBC case). Once you know the steady state, you could linearise the model around that steady state (pretty much as we did for example in Chapter 3). Now you have a linear dynamic system, that can be shocked to compute the trajectory of the variables in response. This is easy to say but involves computing the saddle path in which variables converge to the equilibrium. And to be able to do this you would also need to check first that that dynamic properties are those required for convergence (also see Chapter 3 and the Mathematical Appendix for a discussion of this).

Well, if all that looked a bit daunting, you are lucky that most of this work will be done by the computer itself. What remains of this appendix shows you how to go about it.

These are all quite mechanical steps, so most of the work has already been done for us. First of all, you will need to have MATLAB, and we will assume you are minimally knowledgeable. MATLAB offers a free trial, so you may want to practice first using that.

Before doing this we will need to download Dynare[1] which is pre-programmed to run these models. Below we will write the model, say you call it Model1. We will eventually run Dynare Model1.mod in MATLAB. It is as easy as that, but we have to do some setting up before.

In MATLAB, go to the HOME tab, and look for the Set Path button. In the new window, go to the Add Folder command and search in the Dynare download for the "matlab" folder. This means going to "dynare/xxx/matlab" (you need to go to the "matlab" folder in Dynare), select that folder and select to add this. It typically places it first, but if it does not, make sure to use the left buttons to place it first. Then save.

Now we need to open a folder to save the results. Any folder will do. You can do this by clicking the "browse for folder" button

How to cite this book chapter:
Campante, F., Sturzenegger, F. and Velasco, A. 2021. *Advanced Macroeconomics: An Easy Guide.*
    Appendix C. 'Simulating a DSGE model', pp. 381–386. London: LSE Press.
    DOI: https://doi.org/10.31389/lsepress.ame.y   License: CC-BY-NC 4.0.

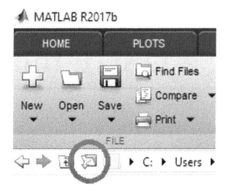

We will write the model (see below) and then we will save this model in this folder. It is important to save the model with the extension ".mod"[2]. So if you call the model Model1 you need to save it in this folder as Model1.mod. This will indicate to MATLAB it is a Dynare file when you run Dynare Model1.mod.

Now to the model. The specification we will work with here replicates the framework of Chapter 15, but you can find more complex structures (including open-economy versions) within the framework of Dynare. For our purposes of taking a first step in modelling, this simple specification will do.

In what follows we will take you through the steps to run this simple model. First, we need to define the variables. You need to start your code in the editor. Type the following

---

var pi y i v r;

varexo eps_v;

parameters beta sigma phi alpha phi_pi phi_y rho_v;

The "var" command sets all the variables of the model both exogenous and endogenous. In this case, we have inflation (pi), output (y), nominal interest rate (i), the exogenous shock (v) and the real interest rate (r). The "varexo" command defines shocks. eps_v indicates the exogenous shock that will hit the variable v. The command "parameters" is used to define the parameters of the model.

Our model will implement versions of the equations (15.62), (15.65) and (15.70). The parameters then correspond to those in those equations. We add rho_v, which will be the autoregressive parameter for the shock process (explained below).

Next we need to provide a numerical value for these parameters. For this you will typically rely on previous literature, or use the calibration exercises that we first saw in Chapter 14.

Setting the values is straightforward and is the next step. (You can later play by changing the response of the model to a different value of these parameters). Here we assume, for example

---

alpha = 3/4;

beta = 0.99;

$$sigma = 1;$$

$$phi = 1;$$

$$phi\_pi = 1.5;$$

$$phi\_y = 0.5/4;$$

$$rho\_v = 0.5;$$

With the variables defined and the parameter values established, we next have to specify the model. We use the command model for that. We will conclude the section with the end command.

The model is written in a self-explanatory fashion below, which, in this case, as said, replicates equations (15.62), (15.65) and (15.70). We also define a process for the shock, here we define it as an autoregressive process. (Lagged and forward variables are indicated by a −1 or +1 respectively and can be added without any problem.)

```
model(linear);

// Taylor-Rule
i = phi_pi*pi+phi_y*y+v;

// NKIS-Equation
y = y(+1)-1/sigma*(i-pi(+1));

// NK Phillips Curve
pi = (alpha/(1-alpha))*(1-beta*(1-alpha))*phi*y +beta*pi(+1);

// Autoregressive Error
v = rho_v*v(-1) + eps_v;

// Real rate
r=i-pi(+1);

end;
```

To check if the steady state is well defined we use the "check" command. It computes the eigenvalues of the model. Generally, the eigenvalues are only meaningful if the linearisation is done around a steady state of the model. It is a device for local analysis in the neighbourhood of this steady state.

```
check;
```

This will show something like this

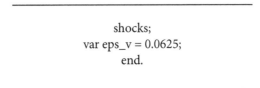

```
Command Window
  Processing outputs ...
  done
  Preprocessing completed.


  EIGENVALUES:
          Modulus                Real              Imaginary

            0.5                  0.5                    0
          1.645                1.645                    0
          2.771                2.771                    0


  There are 2 eigenvalue(s) larger than 1 in modulus
  for 2 forward-looking variable(s)

  The rank condition is verified.
```

Next, we have to set the shocks that we want to study. In this simplified model, we want to analyse the effect of an interest rate policy shock. We use the "shocks" command for that. For example, a shock of 6.25%

shocks;
var eps_v = 0.0625;
end.

Finally, we set the simulation to allow Dynare to show us the impulse-response functions. We use "stoch_simul" for that

stoch_simul(periods=1000,irf=12,order=1).

This completes the script for the model. It has to look something like this

```
//------------------------------------------
// Preamble
//------------------------------------------
// Variables
var pi y i v r;
varexo eps_v;
//
// Parameters
parameters beta sigma phi alpha phi_pi phi_y rho_v;
 alpha=3/4;
 beta = 0.99;
 sigma = 1;
 phi = 1;
 phi_pi = 1.5;
 phi_y = 0.5/4;
 rho_v = 0.5;
//------------------------------------------
// Model
//------------------------------------------
model(linear);
// Taylor-Rule
 i = phi_pi*pi+phi_y*y+v; // eq'n. (25), p. 50

// NKIS-Equation
 y = y(+1)-1/sigma*(i-pi(+1)); // y is output gap (22), equal to actual output if there are only policy shocks


// NKIS-Equation
 y = y(+1)-1/sigma*(i-pi(+1)); // y is output gap (22), equal to actual output if there are only policy shocks

// NK Phillips Curve
 pi = (alpha/(1-alpha))*(1-beta*(1-alpha))*phi*y +beta*pi(+1); // (21) listo

// Autoregressive Error
 v = rho_v*v(-1) + eps_v; // shock to i (bottom p. 50)

// Real rate
r=i-pi(+1);

end;
//
//------------------------------------------
// Steady State
//------------------------------------------
check;
//------------------------------------------
// Shocks
//------------------------------------------
shocks;
var eps_v = 0.0625;
end;


//------------------------------------------
// Computation
//------------------------------------------
//stoch_simul(irf=12, nograph);
stoch_simul(periods=10000,irf=12);
```

Now we run dynare Model1.mod. The output will be like this

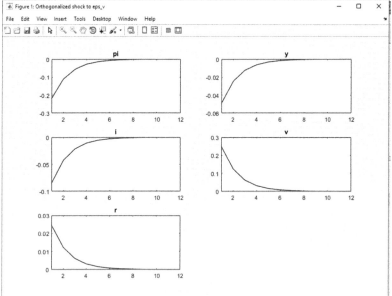

An interest rate shock reduces transitorily output and inflation.

Notes

[1] https://www.dynare.org/
[2] If you are using MAC, maybe MATLAB will be unable to save it with the .mod extension. If that were the case you could write the whole model in a .txt outside of MATLAB and then save it in the appropriate folder.

Index

differences in growth rates and income levels, 89, 91
estimated regressions, 91, 92
growth accounting, 87–89
measures of technological progress, 88
Mincerian wage regression, 89

Q

Quality ladder, 69
business stealing effect, 75
consumer surplus effect, 75
incentives to innovate, 74
innovation, 72, 75
intertemporal spillover effect, 75
labour market condition, 74
Quantitative easing, 3
Quantitative easing policies, 337, 346

R

Ramsey, Frank, 23
Ramsey–Cass–Koopmans model (Ramsey growth model), 23
assumptions, 24
consumer's problem, 24, 26, 37, 39
effects of shocks, 34
growth in per capita variables, 38
Ramsey rule, 27
resource constraint, 25
transitional dynamics, 31
Random walk hypothesis of consumption, 173
Rational asset bubbles, 352, 359
arbitrage equation governing, 355
dynamic behaviour, 356
government debt, 356, 357
per capita gains, 355
Rational expectations revolution in macroeconomics, 2
Real Business Cycle (RBC) model, 205, 211
application in macroeconomics, 215, 218
at work, 211
calibration equation, 211, 212
case of US GDP, 212, 216
consumer's problem, 206
depreciation seems to be a reasonable, 212

first-order condition (FOC), 207, 210, 211
labour endowment equation, 206
labour supply choice, 207, 210
labour-leisure choice, 207
optimal intertemporal allocation of consumption, 207
production function, 206
productivity shock process, 206, 212
reasonable rate of depreciation, 211
return on capital, 211
Real Business Cycles (RBC), 2
Real rigidities, 229
Regional income per capita, evolution, 148
Returns to scale, constant, 11
Ricardian equivalence, 263, 271, 279, 287
caveats, 265
debt vs tax financing, 264, 265
The Rise and Decline of Nations Olson, 79
Rodrik, Dani, 92
Romer, Paul M., 59, 61

S

Saddle path, 33
Samuelson, Paul, 1, 3
Samuelson-Diamond model,
cyclical behaviour in steady state, 132
decentralised competitive equilibrium, 118
decentralised competitive equilibrium of, 116
dynamic adjustments, 121
dynamic behaviour of capital stock, 118, 119
factor market equilibrium condition, 118
goods market equilibrium condition, 118
optimisation problem of individuals and firms, 117
steady state behaviour of economy, 119, 121
steady-state income per-capita, 120
substitution effects, 118
time structure of, 116
Savings
permanent income hypothesis, 164
with constant income, 165
Savings over life cycle, 168

Milton Keynes UK
Ingram Content Group UK Ltd.
UKHW051122070224
437355UK00004B/24